# Facilitating Global Collaboration and Knowledge Sharing in Higher Education With Generative AI

Poshan Yu
*Soochow University, China & European Business Institute, Luxembourg & Australian Studies Centre of Shanghai University, China*

James Mulli
*European Business Institute, Luxembourg*

Zain Ali Shah Syed
*Soochow University, China*

Laila Umme
*Institute of Business Management, Pakistan*

A volume in the Advances in Higher Education and Professional Development (AHEPD) Book Series

IGI Global
PUBLISHER of TIMELY KNOWLEDGE

Published in the United States of America by
IGI Global
Information Science Reference (an imprint of IGI Global)
701 E. Chocolate Avenue
Hershey PA, USA 17033
Tel: 717-533-8845
Fax: 717-533-8661
E-mail: cust@igi-global.com
Web site: http://www.igi-global.com



Library of Congress Cataloging-in-Publication Data

Names: Yu, Poshan, editor. | Mulli, James, 1961- editor. | Syed, Zain Ali Shah, 1979- editor. | Laila, Umme, 1981- editor.
Title: Facilitating global collaboration and knowledge sharing in higher education with generative AI / Poshan Yu, James Mulli, Zain Syed, Umme Laila.
Description: Hershey, PA : Information Science Reference, [2024] | Includes bibliographical references and index. | Summary: "This book explores the opportunities and challenges of using generative AI for teaching, learning, and research across different educational contexts and disciplines as well as highlights innovative approaches and best practices for integrating generative AI into various aspects of education, including curriculum design, assessment, and professional development"-- Provided by publisher.
Identifiers: LCCN 2023045038 (print) | LCCN 2023045039 (ebook) | ISBN 9798369304877 (hardcover) | ISBN 9798369304884 (paperback) | ISBN 9798369304891 (ebook)
Subjects: LCSH: Artificial intelligence--Educational applications. | Education and globalization. | Education, Higher--Curricula. | Knowledge management.
Classification: LCC LB1028.43 .F33 2024 (print) | LCC LB1028.43 (ebook) | DDC 371.9--dc23/eng/20231018
LC record available at https://lccn.loc.gov/2023045038
LC ebook record available at https://lccn.loc.gov/2023045039

This book is published in the IGI Global book series Advances in Higher Education and Professional Development (AHEPD) (ISSN: 2327-6983; eISSN: 2327-6991)

British Cataloguing in Publication Data
A Cataloguing in Publication record for this book is available from the British Library.

# Advances in Higher Education and Professional Development (AHEPD) Book Series

Jared Keengwe
University of North Dakota, USA

ISSN:2327-6983
EISSN:2327-6991

## MISSION

As world economies continue to shift and change in response to global financial situations, job markets have begun to demand a more highly-skilled workforce. In many industries a college degree is the minimum requirement and further educational development is expected to advance. With these current trends in mind, the **Advances in Higher Education & Professional Development (AHEPD) Book Series** provides an outlet for researchers and academics to publish their research in these areas and to distribute these works to practitioners and other researchers.

**AHEPD** encompasses all research dealing with higher education pedagogy, development, and curriculum design, as well as all areas of professional development, regardless of focus.

## COVERAGE

- Adult Education
- Assessment in Higher Education
- Career Training
- Coaching and Mentoring
- Continuing Professional Development
- Governance in Higher Education
- Higher Education Policy
- Pedagogy of Teaching Higher Education
- Vocational Education

IGI Global is currently accepting manuscripts for publication within this series. To submit a proposal for a volume in this series, please contact our Acquisition Editors at Acquisitions@igi-global.com or visit: http://www.igi-global.com/publish/.

The Advances in Higher Education and Professional Development (AHEPD) Book Series (ISSN 2327-6983) is published by IGI Global, 701 E. Chocolate Avenue, Hershey, PA 17033-1240, USA, www.igi-global.com. This series is composed of titles available for purchase individually; each title is edited to be contextually exclusive from any other title within the series. For pricing and ordering information please visit http://www.igi-global.com/book-series/advances-higher-education-professional-development/73681. Postmaster: Send all address changes to above address. 

## Titles in this Series

*For a list of additional titles in this series, please visit: http://www.igi-global.com/book-series/*

***Autism, Neurodiversity, and Equity in Professional Preparation Programs***
Shanna Jamanis (Nazareth University, USA) and Dawn Vogler-Elias (Nazareth University USA)
Information Science Reference • © 2024 • 328pp • H/C (ISBN: 9798369301630) • US $230.00

***LGBTQIA Students in Higher Education Approaches to Student Identity and Policy***
Kaity Prieto (The University of Southern Mississippi, USA) and Andrew Herridge (The University of Southern Mississippi USA)
Information Science Reference • © 2024 • 330pp • H/C (ISBN: 9798369328538) • US $240.00

***Student Stress in Higher Education***
Peter J. O. Aloka (University of the Witwatersrand, South Africa)
Information Science Reference • © 2024 • 287pp • H/C (ISBN: 9798369307083) • US $235.00

***Creating Diverse Experiences for Rural Appalachian Pre-Service Teachers***
Kimberly Dianne Cassidy (Shawnee State University, USA)
Information Science Reference • © 2024 • 300pp • H/C (ISBN: 9781668443699) • US $215.00

***Best Practices to Prepare Writers for Their Professional Paths***
Carissa A. Barker-Stucky (Carnegie Writers, Inc., USA) and Kemi Elufiede (Carnegie Writers, Inc., USA)
Information Science Reference • © 2024 • 300pp • H/C (ISBN: 9781668490242) • US $225.00

***Accessibility of Digital Higher Education in the Global South***
Pfano Mashau (University of KwaZulu-Natal, South Africa) and Tshililo Ruddy Farisani (University of KwaZulu-Natal, South Africa)
Information Science Reference • © 2024 • 371pp • H/C (ISBN: 9781668491799) • US $215.00

IGI Global
PUBLISHER of TIMELY KNOWLEDGE

701 East Chocolate Avenue, Hershey, PA 17033, USA
Tel: 717-533-8845 x100 • Fax: 717-533-8661
E-Mail: cust@igi-global.com • www.igi-global.com

# EDITORIAL ADVISORY BOARD

# Table of Contents

**Foreword** ........................................................................................................ xvii

**Preface** ........................................................................................................ xix

**Chapter 1**
Exploring Ethical Considerations in Utilizing Generative AI for Global Knowledge Sharing in Higher Education ........................................................ 1
*Poshan Yu, Soochow University, China & European Business Institute, Luxembourg & Australian Studies Centre of Shanghai University, China*
*Shengyuan Lu, Johns Hopkins University, USA*
*Zixian Long, Independent Researcher, China*
*Yijun Chen, Independent Researcher, China*
*Jianguo Qian, University of Southampton, China*
*Zain Ali Shah, Soochow University, China*

**Chapter 2**
Applications of Machine Learning in Education and Skill Developments.......... 28
*P. SivaPadmini, Department of Computer Science and Engineering, Marri Laxman Reddy Institute of Technology and Management, India*
*M. Beulah Viji Christiana, Department of Master of Business Administration, Panimalar Engineering College, India*
*R. Pitchai, Department of Computer Science and Engineering, B.V. Raju Institute of Technology, India*
*Santosh Kumar, Department of Computer Science, ERA University, India*
*Kommisetti MurthyRaju, Department of Electronics and Communication Engineering,Shri Vishnu Engineering College for Women, India*

**Chapter 3**
Fostering Sustainability Education Through Cross-Disciplinary Collaborations and Research Partnerships: Interdisciplinary Synergy ................60
*Simanchala Das, K L Business School, Koneru Lakshmaiah Education Foundation, India*
*Gudla Lekhya, K L Business School, Koneru Lakshmaiah Education Foundation, India*
*Kodukula Shreya, K L Business School, Koneru Lakshmaiah Education Foundation, India*
*Karyamsetty Lydia Shekinah, K L Business School, Koneru Lakshmaiah Education Foundation, India*
*Katuri Khadar Babu, K L Business School, Koneru Lakshmaiah Education Foundation, India*
*Sampath Boopathi, Mechanical Engineering, Muthayammal Engineering College, India*

**Chapter 4**
Exploring the Role of AI-Driven Tools in Evaluating Pedagogical Competencies ........................................................................................89
*Rajashree Das, Ravenshaw University, Cuttack, India*
*Durga Prasad Singh Samanta, Amity University, Bengaluru, India*
*Gouranga Nanda, Ravenshaw University, Cuttack, India*
*Minakshi Rani Mohanty, Government of Odisha, India*

**Chapter 5**
Utilizing Generative AI With Second-Language Users and Bilingual Students109
*Frank Billingsley, Georgetown College, USA*
*Stephanie Gardner, Brussels School of Governance, Belgium*

**Chapter 6**
Integrating Generative AI Into K-12 Curriculums and Pedagogies in India: Opportunities and Challenges ........................................................................133
*Durgesh M. Sharma, Shri Ramdeobaba College of Engineering and Management, Nagpur, India*
*K. Venkata Ramana, Department of Computer Science and Engineering, VNR Vignana Jyothi Institute of Engineering and Technology, Hyderabad, India*
*R. Jothilakshmi, Department of Information Technology, R.M.D. Engineering College, India*
*Rakesh Verma, Department of Master of Business Administration, Gniot MBA Institute, India*
*B. Uma Maheswari, Department of Computer Science and Engineering, St. Joseph's College of Engineering, India*
*Sampath Boopathi, Mechanical Engineering, Muthayammal Engineering College, India*

**Chapter 7**
Exploring the Potential of Generative AI in English Language Teaching.........162
*Chinaza Solomon Ironsi, Rauf Denktas University, Cyprus*

**Chapter 8**
Leveraging Generative AI for Cross-Cultural Knowledge Exchange in Higher Education ......................................................................................................186
*Khalid Mahboob, Sir Syed University of Engineering and Technology, Pakistan*
*Raheela Asif, NED University of Engineering and Technology, Karachi, Pakistan*
*Laila Umme, Institute of Business Management, Karachi, Pakistan*

**Chapter 9**
Large Language Models in Academic Publishing ............................................207
*Moses Mwangi Thiga, Kabarak University, Kenya*

**Chapter 10**
Intersection of Adaptive Learning, Global Collaboration, and Knowledge Sharing Through Machine Learning in Higher Education: Empowering Education ......................................................................................................229
*Chintureena Thingom, Department of Computer Science & Engineering, College of Engineering and Design, Alliance University, India*
*Thangjam Ravichandra, Department of Continuing Education, Alliance School of Business, Alliance University, India*
*R. Krishna Kumari, Career Development Centre, SRM Institute of Science and Technology, India*
*S. Sagar Imambi, Department of Computer Science Engineering, Koneru Lakshmaih Education Foundation, India*
*Nimisha Beri, School of Education, Lovely Professional University, India*

**Chapter 11**
Exploring the Challenges and Applications of Generative AI on Engineering Education in Mexico ........ 259
*Jesús Heriberto Orduño-Osuna, Universidad Politécnica de Baja California, Mexico*
*Elia Ivette Cota-Rivera, Universidad Politécnica de Baja California, Mexico*
*María E. Raygoza-L., Universidad Autonoma de Baja California, Mexico*
*Roxana Jimenez-Sanchez, Universidad Politécnica de Baja California, Mexico*
*Guillermo M. Limón-Molina, Universidad Politécnica de Baja California, Mexico*
*Miguel Bravo-Zanoguera, Universidad Politécnica de Baja California, Mexico*
*Abelardo Mercado-Herrera, Universidad Politécnica de Baja California, Mexico*
*Fabian N. Murrieta Rico, Universidad Politécnica de Baja California, Mexico*

**Chapter 12**
Innovative Teaching Methodology in Higher Education With Generative AI-Engineering Education in Developing Countries ........ 287
*Laila Umme, Institute of Business Management, Karachi, Pakistan*
*Zain Ali Shah, Soochow University, China*
*Poshan Yu, Soochow University, China & European Business Institute, Luxembourg & Australian Studies Centre of Shanghai University, China*
*James Mulli, European Business Institute, Luxembourg*
*Muhammad Khurram, University of Technology and Applied Sciences, Nizwa, Oman*
*Muzammil Ahmed, Sir Syed University of Engineering and Technology, Pakistan*

**Compilation of References** ........ 316

**About the Contributors** ........ 346

**Index** ........ 353

# Detailed Table of Contents

**Foreword** ........................................................................................................ xvii

**Preface** .......................................................................................................... xix

**Chapter 1**
Exploring Ethical Considerations in Utilizing Generative AI for Global Knowledge Sharing in Higher Education ........................................................... 1
*Poshan Yu, Soochow University, China & European Business Institute, Luxembourg & Australian Studies Centre of Shanghai University, China*
*Shengyuan Lu, Johns Hopkins University, USA*
*Zixian Long, Independent Researcher, China*
*Yijun Chen, Independent Researcher, China*
*Jianguo Qian, University of Southampton, China*
*Zain Ali Shah, Soochow University, China*

This chapter delves into the ethical considerations surrounding the utilization of generative artificial intelligence (AI) for global knowledge sharing in higher education. As AI technologies continue to advance, their potential for transforming the educational landscape is becoming increasingly evident. However, the ethical implications of employing generative AI in this context warrant careful examination. The study explores the ethical dimensions related to the use of generative AI in higher education, focusing on issues such as data privacy, algorithmic bias, intellectual property rights, and the impact on human creativity and critical thinking. The findings of this study contribute to the ongoing discourse on the ethical implications of utilizing generative AI in higher education. By addressing these considerations, educators and policymakers can make informed decisions regarding the implementation of generative AI technologies, fostering a responsible and inclusive approach to global knowledge sharing in the higher education sector.

**Chapter 2**
Applications of Machine Learning in Education and Skill Developments..........28
*P. SivaPadmini, Department of Computer Science and Engineering, Marri Laxman Reddy Institute of Technology and Management, India*
*M. Beulah Viji Christiana, Department of Master of Business Administration, Panimalar Engineering College, India*
*R. Pitchai, Department of Computer Science and Engineering, B.V. Raju Institute of Technology, India*
*Santosh Kumar, Department of Computer Science, ERA University, India*
*Kommisetti MurthyRaju, Department of Electronics and Communication Engineering,Shri Vishnu Engineering College for Women, India*

The integration of machine learning (ML) techniques in education and skill development has revolutionized traditional teaching and learning paradigms. This chapter explores transformative applications of ML in education and skill development, focusing on experimental approaches to enhance learning outcomes and skill acquisition. It reviews literature on ML-driven personalized learning, intelligent tutoring systems, educational data mining, and predictive analytics, while discussing challenges and ethical considerations in implementing ML in educational settings. This chapter explores experimental methodologies for evaluating the effectiveness of ML-driven interventions, analyzing case studies and real-world examples. It highlights the design, implementation, and outcomes of these experiments, providing insights into ML's impact on student engagement, knowledge retention, skill advancement, and overall educational quality.

**Chapter 3**
Fostering Sustainability Education Through Cross-Disciplinary Collaborations and Research Partnerships: Interdisciplinary Synergy................60
*Simanchala Das, K L Business School, Koneru Lakshmaiah Education Foundation, India*
*Gudla Lekhya, K L Business School, Koneru Lakshmaiah Education Foundation, India*
*Kodukula Shreya, K L Business School, Koneru Lakshmaiah Education Foundation, India*
*Karyamsetty Lydia Shekinah, K L Business School, Koneru Lakshmaiah Education Foundation, India*
*Katuri Khadar Babu, K L Business School, Koneru Lakshmaiah Education Foundation, India*
*Sampath Boopathi, Mechanical Engineering, Muthayammal Engineering College, India*

This book chapter delves into the essential principles and empirical research surrounding cross-disciplinary collaborations and partnerships in the realm of sustainability education. It explores how the convergence of diverse academic disciplines can synergistically advance sustainability education, creating a holistic learning environment that addresses complex global challenges. Through case studies and theoretical frameworks, this chapter sheds light on the fundamentals of establishing successful cross-disciplinary collaborations and offers insights into their pedagogical and research dimensions. By examining the interplay between various disciplines and their contributions to sustainability education, this chapter contributes to the broader discourse on innovative educational approaches for a more sustainable future.

**Chapter 4**
Exploring the Role of AI-Driven Tools in Evaluating Pedagogical Competencies ........................................ 89
*Rajashree Das, Ravenshaw University, Cuttack, India*
*Durga Prasad Singh Samanta, Amity University, Bengaluru, India*
*Gouranga Nanda, Ravenshaw University, Cuttack, India*
*Minakshi Rani Mohanty, Government of Odisha, India*

This chapter aims to evaluate the pre-service teacher education curriculum at the secondary level with the integration of technology. The study uses a mixed-methods approach, including surveys, interviews, and document analysis, to gather data from pre-service teachers, teacher educators, and educational experts. The study evaluates the effectiveness of the current curriculum in preparing pre-service teachers for the demands of teaching in a digital age, and explores the potential benefits and challenges of integrating technology in teacher education. The study also assesses the attitudes, beliefs, and perceptions of pre-service teachers towards technology and their level of technology integration in their teaching practice. The findings of the study provide insights into the strengths and weaknesses of the current pre-service teacher education curriculum at the secondary level and the potential benefits and challenges of integrating technology in teacher education.

**Chapter 5**
Utilizing Generative AI With Second-Language Users and Bilingual Students 109
*Frank Billingsley, Georgetown College, USA*
*Stephanie Gardner, Brussels School of Governance, Belgium*

The growth of generative artificial intelligence (for purposes of this chapter, "AI") has created endless systems to utilize modern technological assistance in the educational arena. AI has the potential to significantly impact higher education by facilitating personalized development and knowledge sharing. There are many ways that AI can be leveraged to enhance the education process. This chapter will focus on second-language users and bilingual students learning new language concepts. Second language users can be defined as students in the language acquisition process. A bilingual student is any student who has already acquired a second language but needs to build on terminology in their field of study. AI can provide a functional teaching tool for educators to assist with building the required knowledge base. The premise is to embrace the tool—versus forbidding its use by students—to assist them in their educational growth.

**Chapter 6**
Integrating Generative AI Into K-12 Curriculums and Pedagogies in India: Opportunities and Challenges ........................................................................ 133
*Durgesh M. Sharma, Shri Ramdeobaba College of Engineering and Management, Nagpur, India*
*K. Venkata Ramana, Department of Computer Science and Engineering, VNR Vignana Jyothi Institute of Engineering and Technology, Hyderabad, India*
*R. Jothilakshmi, Department of Information Technology, R.M.D. Engineering College, India*
*Rakesh Verma, Department of Master of Business Administration, Gniot MBA Institute, India*
*B. Uma Maheswari, Department of Computer Science and Engineering, St. Joseph's College of Engineering, India*
*Sampath Boopathi, Mechanical Engineering, Muthayammal Engineering College, India*

Generative artificial intelligence (AI) can revolutionize K-12 education in India by enhancing curriculums and pedagogies. This chapter explores the principles of generative AI, including generative adversarial networks (GANs), variational autoencoders (VAEs), and natural language generation (NLG), and its potential to create content indistinguishable from human-generated materials. Generative AI addresses challenges like resource scarcity, linguistic diversity, and personalized learning experiences, while emphasizing ethical considerations, data privacy, and bridging the digital divide. The future of K-12 education in India will see personalized learning journeys, inclusivity, and empowered educators. A comprehensive policy framework, infrastructure support, and teacher training are needed to realize the full potential of generative AI in shaping the educational landscape.

**Chapter 7**
Exploring the Potential of Generative AI in English Language Teaching......... 162
*Chinaza Solomon Ironsi, Rauf Denktas University, Cyprus*

Integrating artificial intelligence (AI) technologies in education has shown remarkable potential in revolutionizing various aspects of teaching and learning. In English language teaching (ELT), generative AI has emerged as a powerful tool to enhance language acquisition, foster learner engagement, and provide personalized instruction. While the potential of generative AI in ELT is promising, it is important to provide insights into certain challenges and considerations. Ethical concerns related to data privacy, bias in AI algorithms, and the potential displacement of human instructors need to be carefully navigated. The successful implementation of generative AI in ELT relies on careful consideration of ethical implications, human oversight, and the continuous refinement of AI algorithms to ensure optimal language learning outcomes. On these premises, this chapter explores the potential of generative AI in ELT and its implications for language learners and educators.


**Chapter 8**
Leveraging Generative AI for Cross-Cultural Knowledge Exchange in Higher Education ........................................................................................................ 186


*Khalid Mahboob, Sir Syed University of Engineering and Technology, Pakistan*
*Raheela Asif, NED University of Engineering and Technology, Karachi, Pakistan*
*Laila Umme, Institute of Business Management, Karachi, Pakistan*


The integration of generative artificial intelligence (AI) has the potential to revolutionize cross-cultural knowledge exchange in higher education. By leveraging its ability to create culturally sensitive and contextually relevant learning materials, generative AI can enhance personalized education for students from diverse backgrounds. Overcoming language barriers through real-time translation, this technology promotes inclusive collaboration and co-creation of knowledge. However, ethical considerations such as cultural authenticity, bias mitigation, and data privacy must be carefully navigated to ensure equitable and respectful cross-cultural interactions. In essence, generative AI offers a transformative avenue for fostering a culturally enriched learning environment in higher education, necessitating a balanced approach that maximizes benefits while upholding ethical principles.


**Chapter 9**
Large Language Models in Academic Publishing ............................................ 207


*Moses Mwangi Thiga, Kabarak University, Kenya*


Large language models continue to find greater utilization in the academic publishing process since their introduction. On one hand they are beneficial in manuscript development, review and editorial tasks through finding and presenting information in an academic and professional manner. On the flip side there are concerns over the accuracy of the content they generate as well as the tendency for some authors to present these outputs in manuscripts without proper attribution leading to plagiarism. This chapter examines their practical uses and challenges, and makes recommendations on how their use can be mainstreamed in academic publishing. The chapter further makes recommendations on areas for their future development through the enhancement of foundational models using data from credible sources such as peer reviewed journals, books, and online sources of credible organizations.

**Chapter 10**
Intersection of Adaptive Learning, Global Collaboration, and Knowledge Sharing Through Machine Learning in Higher Education: Empowering Education ........ 229
*Chintureena Thingom, Department of Computer Science & Engineering, College of Engineering and Design, Alliance University, India*
*Thangjam Ravichandra, Department of Continuing Education, Alliance School of Business, Alliance University, India*
*R. Krishna Kumari, Career Development Centre, SRM Institute of Science and Technology, India*
*S. Sagar Imambi, Department of Computer Science Engineering, Koneru Lakshmaih Education Foundation, India*
*Nimisha Beri, School of Education, Lovely Professional University, India*

The chapter explores the integration of adaptive learning, global collaboration, and knowledge sharing in higher education, highlighting their transformative impact. Adaptive learning, driven by machine learning algorithms, tailors educational content to individual student needs, ensuring engagement and mastery of subjects. Global collaboration allows students to connect with peers, faculty, and experts worldwide, promoting diverse perspectives and cross-cultural learning. Knowledge sharing, facilitated by digital platforms and machine learning, empowers learners to create, curate, and disseminate knowledge, fostering a culture of collaboration and innovation. The chapter also discusses the challenges and ethical considerations in implementing machine learning in education, emphasizing privacy and data security. It also explores how educators can use data-driven insights to enhance pedagogical strategies.

**Chapter 11**
Exploring the Challenges and Applications of Generative AI on Engineering Education in Mexico ........ 259
*Jesús Heriberto Orduño-Osuna, Universidad Politécnica de Baja California, Mexico*
*Elia Ivette Cota-Rivera, Universidad Politécnica de Baja California, Mexico*
*María E. Raygoza-L., Universidad Autonoma de Baja California, Mexico*
*Roxana Jimenez-Sanchez, Universidad Politécnica de Baja California, Mexico*
*Guillermo M. Limón-Molina, Universidad Politécnica de Baja California, Mexico*
*Miguel Bravo-Zanoguera, Universidad Politécnica de Baja California, Mexico*
*Abelardo Mercado-Herrera, Universidad Politécnica de Baja California, Mexico*
*Fabian N. Murrieta Rico, Universidad Politécnica de Baja California, Mexico*

This chapter explores the potential and challenges of implementing generative artificial intelligence (AI) in engineering education in Mexico. It highlights the relevance of developing broader competences like critical thinking, collaboration, and cognitive processing to prepare students for the Fourth Industrial Revolution. Integrating generative AI and STEM education can foster collaboration, communication, critical thinking, and creativity. Challenges include the gap between demand and supply of skilled engineers and the need to enhance education quality. The chapter proposes personalized learning experiences, enhanced student engagement, workload reduction for teachers, and the use of large language models and simulated environments as key applications of generative AI. Leveraging learning analytics and generative AI can tailor content to students' needs. Ethical considerations and human oversight are crucial for successful integration.

**Chapter 12**
Innovative Teaching Methodology in Higher Education With Generative AI-Engineering Education in Developing Countries ............................................287
*Laila Umme, Institute of Business Management, Karachi, Pakistan*
*Zain Ali Shah, Soochow University, China*
*Poshan Yu, Soochow University, China & European Business Institute, Luxembourg & Australian Studies Centre of Shanghai University, China*
*James Mulli, European Business Institute, Luxembourg*
*Muhammad Khurram, University of Technology and Applied Sciences, Nizwa, Oman*
*Muzammil Ahmed, Sir Syed University of Engineering and Technology, Pakistan*

The rapidly evolving landscape of higher education is causing significant changes in the educational system. The needs of the digital world cannot be satisfied by conventional teaching and learning approaches. To improve educational quality, fostering global collaboration and knowledge sharing has become imperative for preparing students for a connected world. Therefore, technological integration in the classroom has become essential. Generative artificial intelligence (AI) has emerged as a powerful tool in this endeavour. In addition to examining the possible advantages and difficulties of incorporating technology in higher education, this study also assesses the extent of technology integration in teaching, referred to as innovative teaching methodologies (ITM). This chapter explores how generative AI can be leveraged to enhance teaching methods.

**Compilation of References** ........................................................................ 316

**About the Contributors** ............................................................................ 346

**Index** ............................................................................................................ 353

# Foreword

The education landscape is undergoing a profound transformation in an era characterised by rapid technological advancements. Integrating artificial intelligence (AI) into the educational sphere has sparked a revolution that promises to redefine how we teach, learn, and conduct research.

*Facilitating Global Collaboration and Knowledge Sharing in Higher Education With Generative AI* is a timely and essential contribution to the discourse surrounding the potential of AI-powered chatbots in education. By adopting a critical interdisciplinary perspective, this book provides an invaluable compass for educators, researchers, administrators, policymakers, and industry professionals navigating the complex terrain where AI and higher education converge.

As we immerse ourselves in the world of generative AI, it becomes evident that this technology can transcend traditional boundaries, offering personalised and adaptive learning experiences that cater to the diverse needs of today's students. The concept of chatbots, powered by machine learning algorithms and enriched by vast datasets, simulating human-like conversations, is a novel technological innovation and a paradigm shift in education. "Facilitating Global Collaboration and Knowledge Sharing in Higher Education With Generative AI" brilliantly explores this shift, dissecting its impact on every facet of the educational ecosystem.

One of the book's notable strengths lies in its comprehensive treatment of the subject matter. It not only elucidates the potential benefits of generative AI in education but also delves into the ethical, pedagogical, and technical challenges it presents. In this age of data privacy concerns and an increasing reliance on automation, the authors boldly tackle these issues head-on, calling for an in-depth examination and practical solutions. It is a reminder that while AI can revolutionise education, we must tread carefully, ensuring that the values of privacy, creativity, and human interaction remain central to the educational experience.

The reach of this book extends to numerous vital themes, encompassing student engagement, ethical considerations, personalisation, inclusivity, and intercultural understanding. It addresses the impact of AI-generated content on student performance in online learning, heralding a new era of student-centered education. Moreover, it doesn't shy away from the intricacies of integrating generative AI into traditional classroom settings, a realm often resistant to change.

A particularly noteworthy aspect of this work is its emphasis on accessibility and inclusivity in education. By exploring how generative AI can break down barriers for individuals with disabilities and contribute to lifelong learning initiatives, the authors underline the technology's potential to democratise education. This echoes the essential principle that education should be a universal right, irrespective of one's physical or geographical constraints.

The book also resonates with the contemporary globalised world by examining generative AI's role in promoting intercultural understanding, critical thinking, and global competency. This insight is invaluable in an age when international collaboration and cross-cultural perspectives are more crucial than ever.

In conclusion, *Facilitating Global Collaboration and Knowledge Sharing in Higher Education With Generative AI* is a beacon illuminating the path forward in a rapidly evolving educational landscape. It's a vital resource for anyone vested in the future of education, from educators and administrators to policymakers and industry professionals. This book provides a glimpse of the future and equips us with the knowledge and tools to shape that future ethically, inclusively, and innovatively. It is a must-read for those seeking to harness AI's transformative potential to create a more equitable and enlightened world of education.

The writer is Bitange Ndemo, PhD, Kenya's Ambassador to Belgium, Mission to the European Union, Organization of African Caribbean and Pacific States and World Customs Organization. The article is written at a personal level.

# Preface

In a world that is becoming increasingly digital and interconnected, the role of technology in education has taken on a newfound significance. Among the various technologies that hold promise in transforming higher education, generative artificial intelligence (AI) stands out. This remarkable technology has the power to facilitate global collaboration and knowledge sharing, allowing educators and students from all corners of the world to come together and learn from one another.

Behold, *Facilitating Global Collaboration and Knowledge Sharing in Higher Education With Generative AI* - an edited book that brings together a collection of chapters exploring the myriad aspects of utilizing generative AI in higher education. These chapters delve into profound and thought-provoking topics, such as the ethical considerations inherent in utilizing generative AI, the practical applications of machine learning in education and skill development, the importance of sustainability education through cross-disciplinary collaborations, and the indispensable role of AI-driven tools in evaluating pedagogical competencies.

Chapter 1, "Exploring Ethical Considerations in Utilizing Generative AI for Global Knowledge Sharing in Higher Education," authored by Poshan Yu, Shengyuan Lu, Zixian Long, Yijun Chen, Jianguo Qian, and Zain Ali Shah critically examines the ethical implications of using generative AI for global knowledge sharing in higher education. The authors analyze the potential benefits and risks associated with this technology and provide valuable insights into ethical considerations that educators and institutions need to keep in mind.

Chapter 2, "Applications of Machine Learning in Education and Skill Developments," by P. SivaPadmini, M Beulah Viji Christiana, R Pitchai, Santosh Kumar, and Kommisetti MurthyRaju, explores the wide range of applications of machine learning in education and skill development. The authors discuss how generative AI can be leveraged to enhance the learning experience and promote skill acquisition among students.

Chapter 3, "Fostering Sustainability Education Through Cross-Disciplinary Collaborations and Research Partnerships: Interdisciplinary Synergy," authored by Simanchala Das, Gudla Lekhya, Kodukula Shreya, Karyamsetty Lydia Shekinah, Katuri Khadar Babu, and Sampath Boopathi, focuses on the importance of cross-disciplinary collaborations and research partnerships in promoting sustainability education. The authors highlight how generative AI can facilitate collaboration among researchers and educators from different disciplines, leading to innovative solutions for sustainable development.

Chapter 4, "Exploring the Role of AI-Driven Tools in Evaluating Pedagogical Competencies," written by Rajashree Das, Durga Prasad Singh Samanta, Gouranga Nanda, and Minakshi Rani Mohanty, delves into the role of AI-driven tools in evaluating pedagogical competencies. The authors discuss how generative AI can help assess the effectiveness of teaching methodologies and provide valuable insights for continuous improvement in pedagogical practices.

Chapter 5, "Facilitating Global Collaboration and Knowledge Sharing in Higher Education with Generative AI: Utilizing Generative AI with Second-Language Users and Bilingual Students," authored by Frank Billingsley, explores the specific applications of generative AI in facilitating collaboration and knowledge sharing among second-language users and bilingual students. The chapter examines how generative AI can bridge language barriers and create an inclusive learning environment.

Chapter 6, "Integrating Generative AI into K-12 Curriculums and Pedagogies in India: Opportunities and Challenges," by Durgesh M. Sharma, K Venkata Ramana, R. Jothilakshmi, Rakesh Verma, B. Uma Maheswari, and Sampath Boopathi, focuses on the opportunities and challenges of integrating generative AI into K-12 curriculums and pedagogies in India. The authors discuss the potential benefits of incorporating AI technologies in education and the strategies for overcoming the challenges associated with implementation.

Chapter 7, "Exploring the Potential of Generative AI in English Language Teaching," authored by Chinaza Solomon Ironsi, examines the potential of generative AI in the field of English language teaching. The chapter discusses how AI technologies can facilitate language learning and help educators cater to the individual needs of students.

Chapter 8, "Leveraging Generative AI for Cross-Cultural Knowledge Exchange in Higher Education," by Khalid Mahboob, Raheela Asif, and Umm-e Laila, explores the role of generative AI in facilitating cross-cultural knowledge exchange in higher education. The authors discuss how AI technologies can bridge cultural differences and promote global understanding among students and educators.

Chapter 9, "Large Language Models in Academic Publishing," written by Moses Mwangi Thiga, delves into the potential of large language models in academic publishing. The chapter explores how generative AI can assist researchers in drafting scholarly articles and enhance the quality of academic publications.

Chapter 10, "Intersection of Adaptive Learning, Global Collaboration, and Knowledge Sharing through Machine Learning in Higher Education: Empowering Education," authored by Chintureena Thingom, Thangjam Ravichandra, R Krishna Kumari, S Sagar Imambi, Nimisha Beri, and Prathisha B, examines the intersection of adaptive learning, global collaboration, and knowledge sharing in higher education. The authors discuss how generative AI and machine learning can empower educators and students by personalizing the learning experience and fostering global collaboration.

Chapter 11, "Exploring the Challenges and Applications of Generative AI on Engineering Education in Mexico," written by Jesús Heriberto Orduño-Osuna, Elia Ivette Cota-Rivera, Maria E. Raygoza-L, Roxana Jimenez-Sanchez, Guillermo M. Limón-Molina, MIGUEL BRAVO-ZANOGUERA, Abelardo Mercado-Herrera, and Fabian N Murrieta Rico, focuses on the challenges and applications of generative AI in engineering education in Mexico. The chapter sheds light on how generative AI can revolutionize engineering education and prepare students for the rapidly evolving technological landscape.

Chapter 12, "Innovative Teaching Methodology in higher education with generative AI- Engineering Education in developing countries," authored by Umm-e-Laila mehdi, Zain Ali Shah, Poshan Yu, James Mulli, Muhammad Khurram, and Muzammil Ahmed, explores the innovative teaching methodologies enabled by generative AI in engineering education in developing countries. The chapter discusses the opportunities and challenges associated with incorporating AI technologies in the education systems of developing nations.

The purpose of this masterfully curated book is to make a significant contribution to the field of higher education by shining a light on the immense potential of generative AI in fostering global collaboration and knowledge sharing. By uniting diverse perspectives and experiences from across the globe, this remarkable book empowers educators and institutions to harness the transformative power of generative AI for the betterment of higher education. Its pages are imbued with invaluable insights into the ethical considerations, applications, challenges, and opportunities associated with the utilization of generative AI in various educational contexts. Ultimately, the noble aim of this book is to inspire and ignite a fire within educators, researchers, policymakers, and other stakeholders, urging them to wholeheartedly embrace generative AI and fully harness its awe-inspiring potential in higher education. May they walk this path with open hearts and open minds, embracing the transformation that awaits them.

*Poshan Yu*
*Soochow University, China & European Business Institute, Luxembourg & Australian Studies Centre of Shanghai University, China*

*James Mulli*
*European Business Institute, Luxembourg*

*Zain Ali Shah Syed*
*Soochow University, China*

*Laila Umme*
*Institute of Business Management, Pakistan*

# Chapter 1
# Exploring Ethical Considerations in Utilizing Generative AI for Global Knowledge Sharing in Higher Education

**Poshan Yu**
https://orcid.org/0000-0003-1069-3675
*Soochow University, China & European Business Institute, Luxembourg & Australian Studies Centre of Shanghai University, China*

**Shengyuan Lu**
https://orcid.org/0000-0002-9847-4604
*Johns Hopkins University, USA*

**Zixian Long**
*Independent Researcher, China*

**Yijun Chen**
*Independent Researcher, China*

**Jianguo Qian**
*University of Southampton, China*

**Zain Ali Shah**
*Soochow University, China*

## ABSTRACT

*This chapter delves into the ethical considerations surrounding the utilization of generative artificial intelligence (AI) for global knowledge sharing in higher education. As AI technologies continue to advance, their potential for transforming the educational landscape is becoming increasingly evident. However, the ethical implications of employing generative AI in this context warrant careful examination. The study explores the ethical dimensions related to the use of generative AI in higher education, focusing on issues such as data privacy, algorithmic bias, intellectual*

DOI: 10.4018/979-8-3693-0487-7.ch001

*property rights, and the impact on human creativity and critical thinking. The findings of this study contribute to the ongoing discourse on the ethical implications of utilizing generative AI in higher education. By addressing these considerations, educators and policymakers can make informed decisions regarding the implementation of generative AI technologies, fostering a responsible and inclusive approach to global knowledge sharing in the higher education sector.*

## INTRODUCTION

In recent years, technological advancements have led to a swift and profound transformation within the realm of higher education.Generative artificial intelligence (AI) stands out as a technological innovation with immense potential for facilitating global knowledge sharing. Generative AI harnesses algorithms and machine learning methodologies to generate original content across various mediums, encompassing text, images, and multimedia (Ray, 2023). This chapter starts to provide a comprehensive background and emphasize the importance of incorporating generative AI into higher education for global knowledge sharing, while also considering the ethical implications (Zembylas, 2023).

Generative AI has emerged as a formidable asset in the field of higher education, facilitating seamless knowledge sharing and collaboration among educators and learners, transcending geographical boundaries (Nemorin et al., 2023). It breaks down traditional limitations of time and space, allowing for real-time collaboration and knowledge exchange among students and educators from various backgrounds. This cutting-edge technology has the potential to completely transform the creation, dissemination, and access to knowledge in higher educational institutions worldwide. Generative AI promotes global collaboration and knowledge sharing by enabling learners and educators to contribute their unique perspectives and insights to a collective pool of knowledge. Through AI-generated content, learners can engage in interactive discussions, co-create knowledge, and benefit from a diverse range of perspectives. This fosters a global learning community that transcends cultural and geographical barriers, fostering a deeper understanding and appreciation of different perspectives and cultures (Horwitz & Cecilia, 2012).

Language barriers have always been a challenge in global knowledge sharing. However, generative AI has the potential to overcome these barriers by providing real-time translation and language support. AI-powered language models can assist in translating content, facilitating communication, and ensuring inclusivity in global knowledge sharing initiatives (Javaid et al., 2023). This not only enhances accessibility but also promotes cross-cultural understanding and collaboration. Generative AI opens up new possibilities for innovation and creativity in higher education. By leveraging AI algorithms, learners can explore new ideas, experiment with different approaches, and generate unique solutions to complex problems (Peters, 2020). This technology empowers learners to think critically, engage in creative problem-solving, and develop innovative solutions that can address global challenges. In addition, generative AI has the potential to assist teachers in producing customized learning experiences that fulfil the specific requirements of individual learners/students. This can lead to a more immersive and impactful learning environment, enhancing student engagement and overall effectiveness.

Although the potential advantages of employing generative AI for global knowledge sharing in higher education are substantial, it is important to acknowledge and address the ethical considerations that arise from its implementation. Ethical concerns may arise in areas such as privacy, data security, intellectual property rights, and algorithmic biases (Dwivedi et al., 2023). It is significant to guarantee that the utilization of generative AI adheres to ethical principles, upholds individual privacy, protects intellectual property, and fosters fairness and transparency in algorithmic decision-making (Parycek et al., 2023). With the growing prevalence of generative AI in higher education, it becomes crucial to delve into the ethical considerations that arise from its utilization for global knowledge sharing. The goal of this chapter is to contribute to the empirical literature by providing valuable perspectives on the ethical considerations about the application of generative AI in higher education settings. By examining the potential risks, challenges, and best practices, this chapter will inform educators, policymakers, and institutions about the responsible and ethical implementation of generative AI for global knowledge sharing (Rosário & Dias, 2022). Implementing generative AI in higher education has the power to revolutionize global knowledge sharing. It allows for unprecedented collaboration, innovation, and cross-cultural exchanges between learners and educators. Nevertheless, it is essential to address the ethical implications that come with its application.

In these connections, this research aims to illuminate the ethical considerations surrounding the implementation of generative AI for global knowledge sharing in higher education, while also offering guidance for the adoption of responsible and ethical practices in this domain. Through this approach, the authors can effectively unlock the extensive capabilities of generative AI, all while upholding the protection of individual rights, advancing inclusivity, and nurturing a global learning community (Dec et al., 2022). The primary goal of this research is to thoroughly investigate the potential ethical implications associated with the utilization of generative AI for the purpose of global knowledge sharing in higher education. This involves analyzing the potential benefits and risks, as well as the impact on privacy, data security, and intellectual property rights (Arora et al., 2023). The second objective is to investigate how ethical considerations vary across different cultural and educational contexts when implementing generative AI for global knowledge sharing. This includes examining the influence of cultural norms, values, and educational systems on ethical decision-making. Lastly, the aim of this research is to comprehensively examine and analyze the potential risks and challenges that emerge during the use of AI in the area of education. These include algorithmic bias, lack of transparency, and the necessity for human supervision (Parray et al., 2023). By addressing these research inquiries, this study adds to the ongoing conversation regarding the ethical aspects of utilizing generative AI for global knowledge sharing in higher education.

# LITERATURE REVIEW

## Ethical Implications

The ethical implications of utilizing generative AI for global knowledge sharing in higher education have garnered significant attention in recent years. Scholars have highlighted concerns regarding privacy, data security, and intellectual property rights (Tanveer et al., 2020). For instance, the utilization of generative AI gives rise to inquiries regarding the ownership and control of the content generated, along with concerns about unauthorized usage or manipulation of information. Additionally, ethical considerations arise in terms of the transparency and accountability of AI algorithms, ensuring that they are fair, unbiased, and do not perpetuate discrimination or inequality (Farrow, 2023; Amato & Schoettle, 2023).

## Generative AI

Generative AI is the utilization of artificial intelligence techniques to produce fresh content, including text, images, or videos (Euchner, 2023). Implementing generative AI in higher education holds great potential in promoting global knowledge sharing through the creation of educational resources, language translation, and personalized learning experiences. Nonetheless, it is crucial to carry out a thorough examination of the ethical considerations surrounding generative AI to guarantee the accuracy, reliability, and adherence to intellectual property rights of the generated content (Nah et al., 2023). Furthermore, it is important to recognize the inherent limitations of generative AI, the potential disruptions it may pose to established practices, the threats it poses to privacy and security, as well as the far-reaching consequences of biases, misuse, and the dissemination of misinformation (Yogesh et al., 2023).

## Global Knowledge Sharing

Global knowledge sharing has become increasingly important in higher education, as it allows for the exchange of ideas, expertise, and resources across borders. Generative AI has the potential to enhance global knowledge sharing by overcoming language barriers, facilitating collaboration, and providing access to diverse perspectives. However, ethical considerations arise in terms of cultural sensitivity, ensuring that the generated content respects and reflects the cultural contexts of different regions (Amato & Schoettle, 2023; Jarrahi et al., 2023).

## Higher Education

The integration of generative AI in higher education has the capacity to profoundly transform teaching and learning methodologies (Yu et al., 2022; Yu et al., 2023). It can facilitate personalized learning experiences, automate administrative tasks, and offer intelligent tutoring systems (Farazouli et al., 2023). Nevertheless, it is crucial to acknowledge and tackle ethical concerns in order to secure that the integration of AI in higher education aligns with educational values, encourages critical thinking, and does not substitute human interaction and expertise.

## Cultural Contexts

Cultural contexts play a crucial role in shaping ethical considerations when implementing generative AI for global knowledge sharing in higher education. Different cultures have distinct values, norms, and beliefs that influence their perceptions of privacy, intellectual property, and the appropriate use of AI technologies (Liu, 2023). To uphold cultural sensitivity and prevent the perpetuation of cultural biases or stereotypes, it is of utmost importance to possess a thorough comprehension of and demonstrate respect for the cultural contexts when employing generative AI (Mariappan, & Krishnan, 2022).

## Educational Contexts

Educational contexts also influence ethical considerations in utilizing generative AI for global knowledge sharing. The level of education and awareness within a particular community can impact the understanding and perception of AI technologies and their ethical implications. Educational institutions have a responsibility to offer guidance and assistance to students and faculty in addressing the ethical dilemmas linked to generative AI. These challenges may include issues like plagiarism, ensuring authenticity, and promoting responsible usage of AI-generated content (Barrot, 2023; Amato & Schoettle, 2023).

## Risks and Challenges

The implementation of AI in education presents a multitude of risks and challenges that require careful consideration and attention (Jarrahi et al., 2023). These encompass algorithmic bias, whereby AI systems may inadvertently reinforce existing inequalities or discrimination (Berendt et al., 2020). Additionally, there are concerns regarding the lack of transparency and interpretability of AI algorithms, making it challenging to comprehend the decision-making process. Furthermore, the dependence on AI systems may result in a diminishing of human expertise and critical thinking abilities. Recognizing and addressing these risks is of paramount importance to ensure that the utilization of AI in education is not only ethically sound but also beneficial for all stakeholders involved (Su et al., 2023).

## AI in Education

The incorporation of artificial intelligence (AI) in the education sector has the potential to bring about a groundbreaking shift in teaching and learning methods (Yu, P., Kwok, S., & Jiang, Z., 2022; Yu, P., Kwok, S., & Jiang, Z., 2023). AI technologies, including machine learning and natural language processing, possess the capability to revolutionize education by providing personalized learning experiences (Yu, P., Lu, Y., Hanes, E., & Gu, H., 2022; Yu, P., Liu, L., Sampat, R. M., Mandizvidza, K., & Lu, S., 2023), simplifying administrative tasks, and facilitating effortless global knowledge exchange. The application of generative AI, in particular, allows for the creation of content, such as essays, articles, and even textbooks, with minimal human intervention. However, it is of utmost importance to carefully analyze the ethical considerations linked to the application of generative AI in the field of education.

# ETHICAL CONSIDERATIONS AND CHALLENGES IN UTILIZING GENERATIVE AI FOR GLOBAL KNOWLEDGE SHARING IN HIGHER EDUCATION

Building upon the comprehensive examination of empirical findings presented above, it is evident that the implementation of emerging generative AI technology can yield both favorable and unfavorable outcomes in the context of global knowledge sharing within higher education. In this section, the authors endeavor to provide insights into the following inquiries:

1. What ethical considerations arise when employing generative AI for global knowledge sharing in higher education?
2. How do ethical considerations vary across different cultural and educational contexts when implementing generative AI for global knowledge sharing in higher education?
3. What potential risks and challenges are associated with utilizing generative AI for global knowledge sharing, and how can these be addressed to ensure ethical practices?

This section delves into the ethical considerations linked to generative AI, encompassing concerns such as data privacy, bias, and accountability. Additionally, it explores the potential ramifications on academic integrity, plagiarism, and the protection of intellectual property rights. The variation of ethical concerns across different cultural and educational contexts is examined, highlighting the significance of being culturally sensitive and respectful. The study conducted by Bin-Nashwan et al. in 2023 provides valuable insights into these topics. The authors highlight the potential risks and challenges associated with generative AI, including the dissemination of misinformation and the potential displacement of jobs. It discusses strategies to mitigate these risks and ensure ethical practices, including the implementation of robust data privacy policies, adherence to ethical guidelines, and continuous monitoring. The findings emphasize the importance of ethical considerations and the responsible implementation of generative AI in the field of education. The authors emphasize the need for collaboration in developing ethical frameworks to safeguard the well-being of the entire knowledge-sharing community.

1. Ethical Implications of Utilizing Generative AI for Global Knowledge Sharing
   a. Definition and Explanation of Generative AI in the Context of Higher Education

Generative AI, as a distinct field within artificial intelligence, is purposefully developed to produce original and distinctive content, encompassing text, images, or videos, through the analysis of patterns and data it has been trained on. Unlike other types of AI that mainly rely on existing data, generative AI has the capability to produce original content that closely resembles material created by humans. This technology leverages the capabilities of deep learning algorithms, including generative adversarial networks (GANs) and recurrent neural networks (RNNs), to meticulously analyze and extract valuable insights from vast datasets. Through this process, generative AI becomes proficient in generating novel content that often exhibits a level of quality and authenticity comparable to content produced by human beings. Generative AI has the potential to revolutionize global knowledge sharing within the realm of higher education. Its capabilities to create educational materials, including textbooks, lecture notes, and research papers, can significantly facilitate the dissemination of knowledge to a wider audience. Moreover, by contributing to the advancement of intelligent tutoring systems, personalized learning platforms, and virtual assistants, generative AI has the potential to enrich the educational journey for both students and educators alike. However, the implementation of generative AI in higher education requires a thorough assessment of ethical implications that should be meticulously examined and analyzed. These aspects involve critical areas like safeguarding data privacy, preserving academic integrity, managing bias, establishing accountability, and the potential effects on intellectual property rights. It is crucial to carry out a comprehensive examination of these ethical considerations to ensure that the integration of generative AI in higher education adheres to ethical norms and adequately protects the rights and interests of all parties involved.

b. Discussion of the ethical considerations related to privacy, data security, and intellectual property rights

This discussion aims to shed light on the ethical challenges that arise in these areas and the importance of addressing them to ensure responsible implementation of generative AI.

## Privacy

Preserving personal privacy emerges as a prominent ethical concern when considering the implementation of generative AI in higher education. Generative AI systems heavily rely on extensive data to acquire knowledge and generate content. This data often encompasses student records, research information, and interactions of users, which hold personal details. Thus, it is paramount to protect this sensitive information in order to maintain individuals' trust and uphold their right to privacy (Harrer, 2023).

Institutions must address privacy concerns by implementing strong data privacy policies and practices. This entails obtaining informed consent from individuals whose data is used, ensuring data anonymization and encryption, and establishing secure storage and transmission procedures. Moreover, it is imperative to prioritize transparency in data collection and utilization, empowering individuals to make informed choices regarding their involvement in generative AI systems (Oviedo-Trespalacios et al., 2023).

## Data Security

Data security is an essential ethical consideration closely tied to privacy when integrating generative AI into higher education. The substantial volume of data needed to train generative AI models makes them appealing targets for malicious individuals aiming to exploit vulnerabilities and gain unauthorized access to sensitive information.

To mitigate data security risks, it is imperative for educational institutions to place a high priority on implementing strong cybersecurity measures. This entails implementing stringent access controls, regularly updating and patching software, conducting thorough security audits, and offering comprehensive training to both staff and students on effective data security practices. Furthermore, collaborating with experts in the field can help institutions stay informed about emerging threats and proactively adopt measures to safeguard data from potential breaches.

## Intellectual Property Rights

Generative AI presents intricate ethical dilemmas concerning the rights to intellectual property. When AI systems produce content, such as research papers or educational materials, it becomes arduous to ascertain the ownership and appropriate attribution of the generated work. This can give rise to concerns related to plagiarism, copyright violations, and the devaluation of intellectual labor.

In order to tackle these concerns, it is imperative to establish unambiguous guidelines and policies that delineate the ownership and attribution of AI-generated content. Institutions must proactively take measures to secure that proper credit is given to human creators and that the utilization of AI-generated content is accompanied by appropriate acknowledgment. Collaboration between educators, AI developers, and legal experts is crucial to develop frameworks that protect intellectual property rights while harnessing the benefits of generative AI in global knowledge sharing.

c. Examination of potential biases and fairness issues in generative AI algorithms

This section further sheds light on the ethical considerations surrounding biases and fairness, and the importance of addressing them to ensure equitable and inclusive implementation of generative AI.

## Biases in Generative AI Algorithms

Generative AI algorithms have the ability to acquire knowledge from large datasets, but it is important to acknowledge that these datasets may unintentionally contain biases that exist within the training data. As a result, these biases can be reflected in the generated content, potentially perpetuating societal biases and reinforcing discriminatory practices. For instance, if the training data primarily represents a particular demographic group, the generated content may display biases that are unfavorable towards underrepresented groups.

To address biases in generative AI algorithms, it is crucial to ensure diverse and representative training data. This includes actively seeking out and including data from a wide range of sources and perspectives. Additionally, ongoing monitoring and evaluation of the generated content can help identify and mitigate biases. Collaboration between AI developers, educators, and experts in diversity and inclusion is essential to develop strategies that promote fairness and mitigate biases in generative AI algorithms.

## Fairness Issues in Generative AI Algorithms

Fairness issues can arise when generative AI algorithms disproportionately benefit or harm certain individuals or groups. For example, if the generated content is biased towards a particular cultural or educational context, it may disadvantage individuals from different backgrounds. Similarly, if the algorithms are not designed to accommodate diverse learning styles or accessibility needs, they may inadvertently exclude certain individuals from accessing and benefiting from the generated knowledge.

In order to tackle fairness concerns, it is essential to take a proactive approach during the development and implementation of generative AI algorithms. This includes considering the needs and perspectives of diverse users and ensuring that the algorithms are designed to be inclusive and accessible. Incorporating user feedback and conducting regular audits can help identify and rectify any potential fairness issues. Additionally, involving individuals from diverse backgrounds in the development and decision-making processes can help ensure that the algorithms are fair and equitable.

## Mitigating Biases and Ensuring Fairness

Mitigating biases and ensuring fairness in generative AI algorithms requires a multi-faceted approach. Institutions and AI developers should prioritize diversity and inclusivity in the training data, actively seeking out and including perspectives from underrepresented groups. Regular audits and evaluations should be conducted to identify and address biases in the generated content. Collaboration with experts in diversity and inclusion can provide valuable insights and guidance in developing fair and inclusive algorithms.

Moreover, it is crucial to carefully consider the influence of generative AI algorithms on diverse cultural and educational contexts. Customization and adaptation of algorithms to accommodate diverse learning styles, cultural norms, and accessibility needs can help ensure fairness and inclusivity. Ongoing monitoring and evaluation of the algorithms' impact on different user groups can provide valuable feedback for continuous improvement.

2. Cultural and Educational Contexts: Ethical Variations

Cultural and educational contexts play a significant role in shaping ethical variations within research practices. During the research process, it is of utmost importance to take into account the cultural norms, values, and beliefs of the population under study. Various cultures possess distinct perspectives on ethical considerations, and these differences can significantly influence both the research methodology and the resulting outcomes. For instance, in certain cultures, privacy is highly esteemed, leading individuals to be cautious about sharing personal information. Researchers should demonstrate sensitivity towards these cultural norms and prioritize the protection of participants' privacy and confidentiality.

Furthermore, educational contexts also influence ethical variations in research. The level of education and awareness within a particular community can impact the understanding and perception of research ethics. In some societies, where education is limited, individuals may have less knowledge about research practices and their rights as participants. This lack of awareness can lead to potential ethical issues, such as informed consent not being fully understood or respected. Researchers must take extra precautions to ensure that participants are well-informed about the research process and their rights, regardless of their educational background.

Moreover, ethical variations can arise from differences in power dynamics within cultural and educational contexts. In some societies, there may be significant power imbalances between researchers and participants, such as in hierarchical structures or authoritarian regimes. These power dynamics can influence the level of informed consent obtained from participants and the potential for coercion or exploitation. Researchers should demonstrate awareness of these power differentials and proactively implement measures to minimize any potential harm or exploitation of participants.

Another significant aspect to consider is the role of cultural relativism in the realm of research ethics. Cultural relativism is a perspective that proposes ethical standards should be assessed and understood within the framework of a specific culture, rather than applying universal ethical principles. This viewpoint acknowledges that what may be deemed ethical in one culture may not hold true in another. Researchers face the challenge of navigating this ethical dilemma by finding a middle ground that respects cultural variations while upholding universal ethical principles. It is essential to engage in cross-cultural dialogue and consultation to ensure that research practices are culturally sensitive and respectful.

Furthermore, cultural and educational contexts can influence the interpretation and application of ethical guidelines and regulations. Different countries and institutions may have varying ethical frameworks and guidelines for research. Researchers must familiarize themselves with the specific ethical requirements of the cultural and educational contexts in which they are conducting their research. This includes obtaining the necessary approvals and permissions from relevant authorities and ensuring compliance with local regulations. Neglecting to adhere to these guidelines can result in significant ethical implications and potentially undermine the validity and integrity of the research (Pinochet et al., 2023).

a. Analysis of how ethical considerations may differ across various cultural and educational settings

The analysis of how ethical considerations may differ across various cultural and educational settings is a complex and multifaceted topic. Cultural and educational contexts play a crucial role in shaping ethical perspectives and practices. Different cultures have distinct values, beliefs, and norms that influence their ethical frameworks. These variations can significantly impact the way ethical considerations are understood and applied in research and other domains.

One key aspect to consider is the concept of autonomy and individualism versus collectivism. In Western cultures that emphasize individualism, autonomy and personal rights are highly valued. In research, this translates into a strong emphasis on informed consent and respect for individual privacy. However, in collectivist cultures, the emphasis is on the well-being of the group or community rather than individual autonomy. In such contexts, decisions may be made collectively, and the concept of informed consent may be understood differently. Researchers must be aware of these cultural differences and adapt their ethical practices accordingly.

Another important consideration is the role of power dynamics within different cultural and educational settings. Power imbalances can exist between researchers and participants, as well as within the broader societal structures. In some cultures, hierarchical structures and authority figures hold significant power, which can influence the ethical considerations in research. Participants may feel obligated to comply with the wishes of those in authority, even if it goes against their own best interests. Researchers must be mindful of these power dynamics and take steps to ensure that participants are not coerced or exploited.

Moreover, religious and spiritual beliefs can also shape ethical considerations in different cultural and educational settings. Religious teachings often provide moral guidelines and ethical frameworks for individuals and communities. These beliefs can influence attitudes towards topics such as reproductive health, genetic research, or end-of-life care. Researchers should demonstrate sensitivity towards religious and spiritual beliefs and ensure that their research practices align with the values and principles of the communities they are studying.

Educational environments also have a substantial impact on shaping ethical considerations. The level of education and awareness within a particular community can impact the understanding and perception of research ethics. In societies with limited access to education, individuals may have less knowledge about research practices and their rights as participants. This lack of awareness can lead to potential ethical issues, such as informed consent not being fully understood or respected. Researchers should take additional precautions to ensure that participants, irrespective of their educational background, are adequately informed about the research process and their rights.

Furthermore, the availability and accessibility of resources and services can vary across different cultural and educational settings. This can impact the ethical considerations in research, particularly in studies involving vulnerable populations or resource-limited settings. Researchers should meticulously evaluate the potential risks and benefits associated with their research and guarantee that participants have access to suitable support and care. Ethical considerations may differ in terms of the level of risk that is deemed acceptable and the availability of resources to mitigate potential harm.

b. Exploration of cultural values and norms that may influence the ethical implementation of generative AI in global knowledge sharing

Cultural values have a substantial impact on the formation of ethical frameworks. Various cultures possess unique beliefs, traditions, and norms that shape their understanding of moral principles and distinctions between right and wrong. For instance, in some cultures, the emphasis may be on collective well-being and harmony, while in others, individual autonomy and freedom may take precedence. These cultural values can impact the ethical implementation of generative AI in global knowledge sharing.

One cultural value that may influence the ethical implementation of generative AI is the concept of privacy. Some cultures place a high value on privacy and consider it a fundamental right. Within these cultures, the utilization of AI technologies that gather and analyze personal data may give rise to ethical concerns. On the other hand, cultures that prioritize communal living and sharing may have a more relaxed approach to privacy, which could impact their ethical considerations regarding AI implementation.

Another cultural value that may influence the ethical implementation of generative AI is the concept of fairness and justice. Different cultures have varying notions of what is fair and just. For example, in some cultures, equal distribution of resources and opportunities is highly valued, while in others, meritocracy and individual achievement are prioritized. These cultural perspectives can shape the ethical considerations surrounding AI algorithms that determine access to knowledge and information.

Furthermore, cultural norms regarding the relationship between humans and technology can also impact the ethical implementation of generative AI. Some cultures may view technology as a tool to enhance human capabilities and improve society, while others may have reservations about the potential dehumanizing effects of AI. These cultural norms can have an impact on the ethical considerations associated with the development and utilization of generative AI in the context of global knowledge sharing.

It is essential for ethicists and AI developers to engage in cross-cultural dialogue and understanding to ensure the ethical implementation of generative AI in global knowledge sharing. By considering the diverse cultural values and norms, it becomes possible to develop AI systems that respect and align with different ethical frameworks. This may entail integrating cultural sensitivity into AI algorithms, fostering accountability and transparency in AI decision-making processes, and advocating for inclusivity and diversity within AI development teams.

c. Case studies and examples highlighting the ethical variations in different contexts

Case studies and illustrative examples that showcase the ethical variations across different contexts offer valuable insights into the intricate and nuanced nature of ethics. It is essential to examine these cases to understand how ethical considerations can differ based on various factors such as culture, technology, and societal norms.

One example that illustrates ethical variations in different contexts is the use of facial recognition technology. In some countries, such as China, facial recognition technology is widely used for surveillance purposes, raising concerns about privacy and individual rights. On the other hand, in countries with stricter regulations and a greater emphasis on privacy, such as European nations, the use of facial recognition technology is more heavily scrutinized and restricted. This case highlights how cultural and legal differences can shape the ethical considerations surrounding the use of technology.

Another case study that demonstrates ethical variations is the debate surrounding autonomous vehicles. In countries like the United States, where individualism and personal freedom are highly valued, there is a strong emphasis on the ethical implications of autonomous vehicles making life-or-death decisions. Should a self-driving car prioritize the safety of its occupants or pedestrians in the event of an unavoidable accident? This ethical dilemma reflects the cultural values and norms of a society that places a high value on individual autonomy and personal responsibility.

In contrast, in countries with a more collectivist culture, such as Japan, the ethical considerations surrounding autonomous vehicles may prioritize the well-being of the community as a whole. The emphasis may be on minimizing overall harm and ensuring the safety of all individuals involved. This case study highlights how cultural values and norms can influence the ethical variations in different contexts, even within the same technological domain.

Furthermore, the ethical variations in different contexts can also be observed in the field of medical ethics. For instance, the debate surrounding end-of-life care and euthanasia varies significantly across countries and cultures. In some countries, such as the Netherlands and Belgium, euthanasia is legally permitted under certain circumstances, reflecting a cultural acceptance of individual autonomy and the right to die with dignity. However, in other countries, such as the United States, the ethical considerations surrounding euthanasia are more contentious, with a greater emphasis on the sanctity of life and the potential for abuse.

These case studies and examples highlight the ethical variations that exist in different contexts. They demonstrate how cultural values, legal frameworks, and societal norms can shape ethical considerations and lead to different ethical perspectives and approaches.

## 3. Risks and Challenges in Utilizing Generative AI for Global Knowledge Sharing

One notable risk involves the possibility of bias in generative AI algorithms. As AI systems learn from extensive datasets, they may unintentionally perpetuate existing biases and inequalities inherent in the data. Consequently, this can result in biased outputs and further reinforce discriminatory practices within the realm of global knowledge sharing. For example, if the training data predominantly represents certain cultural perspectives or excludes marginalized voices, the generated content may not accurately reflect the diversity of knowledge and perspectives worldwide. Mitigating this risk necessitates meticulous data curation, the utilization of diverse training datasets, and continuous monitoring and evaluation of AI systems to identify and address bias effectively.

Another challenge is the ethical implications of intellectual property rights and plagiarism. Generative AI has the potential to create content that closely resembles existing works, raising concerns about copyright infringement and plagiarism. This can undermine the principles of fair use and intellectual property protection. In order to uphold copyright laws and ethical standards regarding originality and attribution, it is of utmost importance to establish well-defined guidelines and regulations for generative AI systems. In order to ensure the credibility and integrity of generated content, it is essential to establish mechanisms that can effectively authenticate its authenticity and originality. Additionally, it is crucial to provide appropriate attribution to the original creators, acknowledging their contributions. These measures are vital in maintaining professional standards and upholding ethical practices in content creation. Privacy and data protection are also significant risks when utilizing generative AI for global knowledge sharing. AI systems frequently rely on accessing substantial volumes of personal data in order to produce content or make well-informed decisions. This situation gives rise to legitimate concerns regarding various aspects such as data security, consent, and the potential for personal information to be misused. It is essential to implement robust privacy measures, such as data anonymization, encryption, and informed consent mechanisms, to protect individuals' privacy rights and ensure responsible data handling practices (Hacker, 2023).

Furthermore, the challenge of explainability and transparency in generative AI systems poses ethical risks. AI algorithms are often characterized by their intricate nature and the inherent difficulty in interpreting them. Consequently, comprehending the mechanisms behind content generation or decision-making processes can pose a significant challenge. The absence of transparency in AI algorithms can result in a erosion of trust and accountability. It is crucial to develop methods and techniques to enhance the explainability of AI systems, enabling users to understand the underlying processes and ensuring that the generated content aligns with ethical standards and guidelines.

Additionally, the potential for misuse and malicious intent is a significant risk in utilizing generative AI for global knowledge sharing. AI-generated content can be manipulated and used to spread misinformation, propaganda, or harmful narratives (Sohail et al., 2023). This can have severe consequences for public discourse, trust, and societal well-being. To mitigate the risks associated with misinformation and promote responsible utilization of generative AI in global knowledge sharing, it is crucial to establish safeguards. These measures may include implementing content verification mechanisms, employing fact-checking processes, and prioritizing user education.

Lastly, the challenge of accessibility and inclusivity must be addressed when utilizing generative AI for global knowledge sharing. AI systems should not exacerbate existing inequalities or create barriers to access knowledge. Ensuring the accessibility of generative AI technologies to diverse populations, including individuals with disabilities or limited technology access, is of utmost importance. To achieve inclusivity and accessibility in the realm of generative AI, it is necessary to undertake various measures. These may encompass the development of user-friendly interfaces, the provision of multilingual support, and the incorporation of the needs and perspectives of marginalized communities during the design and implementation of AI systems.

a. Identification and analysis of potential risks and challenges associated with generative AI in global knowledge sharing

The key risks and challenges associated with generative AI, including bias and fairness, privacy and security, accountability and transparency, intellectual property, and social implications (Currie, 2023).

## Bias and Fairness

A significant concern related to generative AI in the context of global knowledge sharing is the inherent risk of bias in the generated content. AI systems, through their learning process from extensive data, have the potential to inadvertently perpetuate existing biases and inequalities that are present within the data. As a consequence, this can result in the production of biased outputs that further reinforce discriminatory practices. For example, if the training data predominantly represents certain cultural perspectives or excludes marginalized voices, the generated content may not accurately reflect the diversity of knowledge and perspectives worldwide. Effectively addressing this risk necessitates meticulous data curation, utilization of diverse training datasets, and continuous monitoring and evaluation of AI systems to identify and mitigate bias.

Moreover, it is imperative to prioritize fairness in the utilization of generative AI. It is particularly important to ensure that AI algorithms are designed in a manner that prevents any form of discrimination against individuals or groups based on factors such as race, gender, or socioeconomic status.To prevent the perpetuation of existing inequalities and foster equal access to knowledge and opportunities, it is crucial to incorporate fairness considerations into the design and development of AI systems.

The data utilized for training the model has the potential to mirror prevailing societal biases, leading to their perpetuation and subsequently affecting the accuracy and fairness of the model's outputs. This phenomenon arises from the inherent reliance of the model's output on the quality of the training data. When the training data contains bias or lacks diversity, the model's outputs may suffer from reduced accuracy and unintentionally reinforce existing biases. Consequently, decision-making processes that depend on the model's output can have significant real-world consequences, especially in applications involving natural language processing (Ateeb et al., 2023).

## Privacy and Security

Another notable concern related to the utilization of generative AI in the context of global knowledge sharing is the potential vulnerability of privacy and security. AI systems frequently necessitate access to extensive volumes of personal data in order to generate content or make well-informed decisions. This raises concerns about data security, consent, and the potential misuse of personal information (Heyder et al., 2023). It is imperative to establish robust privacy measures, including data anonymization, encryption, and informed consent mechanisms, to safeguard individuals' privacy rights and uphold responsible data handling practices. Furthermore, it is crucial to design AI systems in a manner that minimizes the collection and retention of personal data, thereby mitigating the potential risks associated with unauthorized access or data breaches.

## Accountability and Transparency

The absence of accountability and transparency in generative AI systems presents substantial challenges that need to be addressed. AI algorithms can be exceedingly intricate and arduous to interpret, posing a challenge in comprehending the mechanisms by which they generate content or make decisions. The absence of transparency can result in a erosion of trust and accountability. It is crucial to develop methods and techniques to enhance the explainability of AI systems, enabling users to gain a deeper understanding of their functioning.

b. Discussion of the ethical implications of AI-generated content and its impact on academic integrity

The proliferation of artificial intelligence has resulted in substantial breakthroughs across multiple sectors, including the realm of content creation. Nevertheless, it also gives rise to apprehensions regarding the genuineness and integrity of the information being generated.

One of the foremost ethical considerations revolves around the possibility of AI-generated content being utilized for purposes of plagiarism. Given the capacity to produce text that closely emulates human writing, there exists a potential hazard wherein students or researchers might employ AI-generated content to present it as their own original work. Such actions not only undermine the fundamental tenets of academic integrity but also diminish the value of the endeavors undertaken by individuals who have dedicated their time and exertion to create authentic and original work.It is essential for educational institutions to establish clear guidelines and policies to address this issue and ensure that students understand the importance of producing their own work.

Another ethical aspect to consider is the possibility of bias in AI-generated content. AI models undergo training using extensive datasets, which may inadvertently incorporate biased or discriminatory information. In the absence of sufficient mitigation measures, the presence of biases within AI-generated content has the potential to perpetuate and exacerbate existing biases, thereby resulting in unjust or discriminatory consequences. It is of utmost importance for developers and researchers to possess a deep understanding of these biases and proactively address them. This can be achieved through the utilization of diverse and representative datasets, as well as through the regular evaluation and updating of AI models.

Moreover, the utilization of AI-generated content gives rise to inquiries regarding intellectual property rights. Who owns the content generated by AI? Is it the developer who created the AI model, the user who inputs the data, or the AI itself? These inquiries carry significant legal and ethical ramifications that necessitate careful consideration in order to guarantee a just and impartial utilization of AI-generated content. It is imperative to establish well-defined guidelines and regulations that safeguard the rights of all stakeholders and effectively prevent any potential misuse or exploitation of AI-generated content. Furthermore, the incorporation of AI-generated content in academia raises concerns regarding the integrity and dependability of research outcomes. While AI can assist in data analysis and information synthesis, it cannot replace the critical thinking and creativity that human researchers bring to their work. Dependence solely on AI-generated content may result in a dearth of originality and profundity in academic research. Finding a delicate equilibrium between leveraging AI tools for enhanced efficiency and upholding the integrity and rigor of their work is of utmost importance for researchers and educators.

Lastly, the ethical implications of AI-generated content extend beyond academia. AI-generated news articles, social media posts, and various other forms of content possess the potential to exert a substantial influence on public opinion and decision-making processes. If AI-generated content is not clearly labeled or identified, it can lead to misinformation and manipulation of public discourse. Transparency regarding the utilization of AI in content creation is paramount, and platforms and publishers must assume accountability for guaranteeing the accuracy and dependability of the information they disseminate.

c. Examination of the role of transparency, accountability, and governance in mitigating ethical risks.

Within the realm of AI, these principles are indispensable in order to foster responsible and ethical advancement, implementation, and utilization of AI systems.

Transparency is fundamental in addressing ethical concerns related to AI. This entails rendering the processes, algorithms, and decision-making mechanisms of AI systems comprehensible and accessible to users and stakeholders. Transparent AI systems allow individuals to understand how decisions are made, which is particularly important when AI is used in critical domains such as healthcare, finance, or criminal justice (Labrague et al., 2023). By providing transparency, users can assess the fairness, accuracy, and potential biases of AI systems, enabling them to make informed decisions and hold developers and organizations accountable.

Accountability is another crucial aspect of mitigating ethical risks. This involves the creation of mechanisms to assign accountability for the actions and decisions carried out by AI systems. Accountability ensures that individuals or organizations are held responsible for any harm caused by AI systems or for any unethical behavior exhibited by these systems. This can be achieved through clear guidelines, regulations, and legal frameworks that define the responsibilities and liabilities of developers, users, and other stakeholders involved in the AI ecosystem. By holding individuals and organizations accountable, we can incentivize ethical behavior and deter the misuse or abuse of AI technologies.

Governance serves as the comprehensive framework that directs the development, deployment, and utilization of AI systems. It involves establishing policies, regulations, and ethical guidelines that govern the ethical use of AI. In order to ensure effective governance frameworks, it is crucial to involve a wide array of stakeholders. This includes experts from diverse disciplines, policymakers, industry representatives, and civil society organizations. By incorporating the perspectives and expertise of these various stakeholders, a more comprehensive and well-rounded approach to governance can be achieved. This inclusive approach allows for a more informed decision-making process and helps to address the diverse needs and concerns of different sectors of society. By involving multiple perspectives, governance frameworks can ensure that ethical considerations are adequately addressed and that the interests and values of different stakeholders are taken into account. Furthermore, it is crucial for governance frameworks to possess flexibility and adaptability in order to effectively keep up with the swift progressions in AI technology.

To effectively mitigate ethical risks, transparency, accountability, and governance should be integrated throughout the entire lifecycle of AI systems. This includes the design and development phase, where ethical considerations should be embedded into the AI algorithms and decision-making processes. Moreover, it necessitates continuous monitoring and evaluation of AI systems to detect and resolve any ethical concerns that may emerge during their implementation. Conducting regular audits and assessments can serve as a means to guarantee that AI systems are functioning ethically and in alignment with established guidelines.

Furthermore, collaboration and cooperation among different stakeholders are essential for effective transparency, accountability, and governance. This includes collaboration between developers, researchers, policymakers, and civil society organizations to establish common standards and best practices. Additionally, active engagement with the public and solicitation of their input are essential to ensure that AI systems are in harmony with societal values and expectations. By fostering collaboration and cooperation, we can create a collective responsibility for the ethical development and use of AI.

## CONCLUSION

In conclusion, the exploration of ethical considerations in utilizing generative AI for global knowledge sharing in higher education is of paramount importance. While AI holds the potential to revolutionize the processes of knowledge creation, sharing, and accessibility, it also presents substantial ethical concerns that necessitate attention.

First and foremost, the issue of academic integrity and plagiarism is a critical concern. The ease with which AI can produce content that imitates human writing poses a potential threat to the authenticity and originality of academic work. It is imperative for educational institutions to establish well-defined policies and guidelines to mitigate the misuse of AI-generated content and to foster students' understanding of the significance of producing original work.

Furthermore, the potential for bias in AI-generated content is a pressing ethical consideration. AI models undergo training using extensive datasets, which may contain biased or discriminatory information. Failure to effectively address these biases can result in AI-generated content perpetuating and exacerbating existing biases, potentially leading to unjust or discriminatory outcomes. It is crucial for developers and researchers to maintain a vigilant approach in identifying and mitigating biases, thereby ensuring the principles of equity and fairness in the dissemination of knowledge.

Intellectual property rights also come into play when utilizing generative AI for global knowledge sharing. The question of ownership regarding content generated by AI gives rise to legal and ethical considerations. It is imperative to establish comprehensive guidelines and regulations to safeguard the rights of all stakeholders and prevent any potential misuse or exploitation of AI-generated content.

Moreover, the quality and reliability of research are at stake when relying solely on AI-generated content. While AI can aid in data analysis and information synthesis, it cannot substitute the essential elements of critical thinking and creativity that human researchers contribute to their work. Finding a delicate equilibrium between leveraging AI tools for enhanced efficiency and upholding the integrity and rigor of academic research is of utmost importance.

Ensuring transparency, accountability, and effective governance is crucial in mitigating the ethical risks associated with the use of generative AI in higher education. Transparency ensures that the processes and decision-making mechanisms of AI systems are understandable and accessible. Accountability plays a vital role in holding individuals and organizations responsible for the actions and decisions made by AI systems, promoting ethical conduct and discouraging any potential misuse. Governance establishes a comprehensive framework to steer the development, deployment, and utilization of AI systems, engaging a wide range of stakeholders and addressing ethical considerations.

To effectively address these ethical considerations, collaboration and cooperation among stakeholders are crucial. Developers, researchers, policymakers, and educators must work together to establish common standards, best practices, and guidelines. Incorporating public engagement and actively seeking their input is crucial to ensure that AI systems align with societal values and meet the expectations of the public.

In conclusion, while generative AI holds the potential to augment global knowledge sharing in higher education, it is important to navigate the potential ethical considerations inherent in its utilization. By proactively addressing concerns related to academic integrity, bias, intellectual property rights, and research quality, and by fostering transparency, accountability, and effective governance, we can effectively harness the advantages of generative AI while upholding ethical standards. By doing so, we can foster a responsible and ethical approach to utilizing AI for global knowledge sharing in higher education, ultimately benefiting students, researchers, and society as a whole.

## ACKNOWLEDGMENT

The authors extend sincere gratitude to:

- Our colleagues from Soochow University, The Australian Studies Centre of Shanghai University, The European Business University of Luxembourg and Krirk University as well as the independent research colleagues who provided insight and expertise that greatly assisted the research, although they may not agree with all of the interpretations/conclusions of this chapter.
- China Knowledge and Belt & Road Blockchain Association for supporting our research.
- The Editor and the International Editorial Advisory Board (IEAB) of this book who initially desk reviewed, arranged a rigorous double/triple blind

review process and conducted a thorough, minute and critical final review before accepting the chapter for publication.

- All anonymous reviewers who provided very constructive feedbacks for thorough revision, improvement and fine tuning of the chapter.

## REFERENCES

Amato, L. M., & Schoettle, C. (2023). Using Artificial Intelligence Ethically and Responsibly: Best Practices in Higher Education. In J. Keengwe (Ed.), *Creative AI Tools and Ethical Implications in Teaching and Learning* (pp. 19–31). IGI Global. doi:10.4018/979-8-3693-0205-7.ch002

Arora, A., Barrett, M., Lee, E., Oborn, E., & Prince, K. (2023). Risk and the future of AI: Algorithmic bias, data colonialism, and marginalization. *Information and Organization*, *33*(3), 100478. doi:10.1016/j.infoandorg.2023.100478

Barrot, J. S. (2023). Using ChatGPT for second language writing: Pitfalls and potentials. *Assessing Writing*, *57*, 100745. doi:10.1016/j.asw.2023.100745

Berendt, B., Littlejohn, A., & Blakemore, M. (2020). AI in education: learner choice and fundamental rights. *Learning, Media and Technology*, *45*(3), 312-324. https://doi.org/. 1786399 doi:10.1080/17439884.2020

Bin-Nashwan, S. A., Sadallah, M., & Bouteraa, M. (2023). Use of ChatGPT in academia: Academic integrity hangs in the balance. *Technology in Society*, *75*, 102370. doi:10.1016/j.techsoc.2023.102370

Currie, G. M. (2023). Academic integrity and artificial intelligence: Is ChatGPT hype, hero or heresy? *Seminars in Nuclear Medicine*, *53*(5), 719–730. doi:10.1053/j.semnuclmed.2023.04.008 PMID:37225599

Dec, G., Stadnicka, D., Paśko, Ł., Mądziel, M., Figliè, R., Mazzei, D., Tyrovolas, M., Stylios, C., Navarro, J., & Solé-Beteta, X. (2022). Role of Academics in Transferring Knowledge and Skills on Artificial Intelligence, Internet of Things and Edge Computing. *Sensors (Basel)*, *22*(7), 2496. doi:10.339022072496 PMID:35408110

Dwivedi, Y. K., Kshetri, N., Hughes, L., Slade, E. L., Jeyaraj, A., Kar, A. K., Baabdullah, A. M., Koohang, A., Raghavan, V., Ahuja, M., Albanna, H., Albashrawi, M. A., Al-Busaidi, A. S., Balakrishnan, J., Barlette, Y., Basu, S., Bose, I., Brooks, L., Buhalis, D., & Wright, R. (2023). Opinion Paper: "So what if ChatGPT wrote it?" Multidisciplinary perspectives on opportunities, challenges and implications of generative conversational AI for research, practice and policy. *International Journal of Information Management*, *71*, 102642. doi:10.1016/j.ijinfomgt.2023.102642

Euchner, J. (2023). Generative AI. *Research Technology Management*, *66*(3), 71–74. doi:10.1080/08956308.2023.2188861

Farazouli, A., Cerratto-Pargman, T., Bolander-Laksov, K., & McGrath, C. (2023). Hello GPT! Goodbye home examination? An exploratory study of AI chatbots impact on university teachers' assessment practices. *Assessment & Evaluation in Higher Education*, 1–13. doi:10.1080/02602938.2023.2241676

Farrow, R. (2023). The possibilities and limits of XAI in education: A socio-technical perspective. *Learning, Media and Technology*, *48*(2), 266–279. doi:10.1080/17439884.2023.2185630

Hacker, P. (2023). The European AI liability directives – Critique of a half-hearted approach and lessons for the future. *Computer Law & Security Report*, *51*, 105871. doi:10.1016/j.clsr.2023.105871

Harrer, S. (2023). Attention is not all you need: The complicated case of ethically using large language models in healthcare and medicine. *EBioMedicine*, *90*, 104512. doi:10.1016/j.ebiom.2023.104512 PMID:36924620

Heyder, T., Passlack, N., & Posegga, O. (2023). Ethical management of human-AI interaction: Theory development review. *The Journal of Strategic Information Systems*, *32*(3), 101772. doi:10.1016/j.jsis.2023.101772

Horwitz, S. K., & Santillan, C. (2012). Knowledge sharing in global virtual team collaboration: Applications of CE and thinkLets. *Knowledge Management Research and Practice*, *10*(4), 342–353. doi:10.1057/kmrp.2012.39

Jarrahi, M. H., Askay, D., Eshraghi, A., & Smith, P. (2023). Artificial intelligence and knowledge management: A partnership between human and AI. *Business Horizons*, *66*(1), 87–99. doi:10.1016/j.bushor.2022.03.002

Javaid, M., Haleem, A., & Singh, R. P. (2023). ChatGPT for healthcare services: An emerging stage for an innovative perspective. *BenchCouncil Transactions on Benchmarks. Standards and Evaluations*, *3*(1), 100105. doi:10.1016/j.tbench.2023.100105

Labrague, L. J., Aguilar-Rosales, R., Yboa, B. C., & Sabio, J. B. (2023). Factors influencing student nurses' readiness to adopt artificial intelligence (AI) in their studies and their perceived barriers to accessing AI technology: A cross-sectional study. *Nurse Education Today, 130,* 105945. doi:10.1016/j.nedt.2023.105945 PMID:37625351

Liu, Y. (2023). *Cross-Cultural Challenges to Artificial Intelligence Ethics.* IS4SI Summit 2023. doi:10.3390/cmsf2023008021

Mariappan, J., & Krishnan, C. (2022). Integration of AI in Learning: A Paradigm Shift in Education. In C. Krishnan, F. Al-Harthy, & G. Singh (Eds.), *Technology Training for Educators From Past to Present* (pp. 263–275). IGI Global. doi:10.4018/978-1-6684-4083-4.ch014

Nah, F. F.-H., Zheng, R., Cai, J., Siau, K., & Chen, L. (2023). Generative AI and ChatGPT: Applications, challenges, and AI-human collaboration. *Journal of Information Technology Case and Application Research, 25*(3), 277–304. doi:10.1080/15228053.2023.2233814

Nemorin, S., Vlachidis, A., Ayerakwa, H. M., & Andriotis, P. (2023). AI hyped? A horizon scan of discourse on artificial intelligence in education (AIED) and development. *Learning, Media and Technology, 48*(1), 38–51. doi:10.1080/17439884.2022.2095568

Oviedo-Trespalacios, O., Peden, A. E., Cole-Hunter, T., Costantini, A., Haghani, M., Rod, J. E., Kelly, S., Torkamaan, H., Tariq, A., Newton, J. D. A., Gallagher, T., Steinert, S., Filtness, A. J., & Reniers, G. (2023). The risks of using ChatGPT to obtain common safety-related information and advice. *Safety Science, 167,* 106244. doi:10.1016/j.ssci.2023.106244

Parray, A. A., Inam, Z. M., Ramonfaur, D., Haider, S. S., Mistry, S. K., & Pandya, A. K. (2023). ChatGPT and global public health: Applications, challenges, ethical considerations and mitigation strategies. *Global Transitions, 5,* 50–54. doi:10.1016/j.glt.2023.05.001

Parycek, P., Schmid, V., & Novak, A. S. (2023). Artificial Intelligence (AI) and Automation in Administrative Procedures: Potentials, Limitations, and Framework Conditions. *Journal of the Knowledge Economy.* doi:10.100713132-023-01433-3

Peters, M. A. (2020). Platform ontologies, the AI crisis and the ability to hack humans 'An algorithm knows me better than I know myself'. *Educational Philosophy and Theory, 52*(6), 593–601. doi:10.1080/00131857.2019.1618227

Pinochet, L. H. C., Moreira, M. Â. L., Fávero, L. P., Santos, M. D., & Pardim, V. I. (2023). Collaborative Work Alternatives with ChatGPT Based on Evaluation Criteria for its Use in Higher Education: Application of the PROMETHEE-SAPEVO-M1 Method. *Procedia Computer Science*, *221*, 177–184. doi:10.1016/j.procs.2023.07.025

Ray, P. P. (2023). ChatGPT: A comprehensive review on background, applications, key challenges, bias, ethics, limitations and future scope. *Internet of Things and Cyber-Physical Systems*, *3*, 121–154. doi:10.1016/j.iotcps.2023.04.003

Rosário, A., & Dias, J. (2022). Sustainability and the Digital Transition: A Literature Review. *Sustainability (Basel)*, *14*(7), 4072. doi:10.3390u14074072

Sohail, S. S., Farhat, F., Himeur, Y., Nadeem, M., Madsen, D. Ø., Singh, Y., Atalla, S., & Mansoor, W. (2023). Decoding ChatGPT: A taxonomy of existing research, current challenges, and possible future directions. *Journal of King Saud University. Computer and Information Sciences*, *35*(8), 101675. doi:10.1016/j.jksuci.2023.101675

Su, J., Ng, D. T. K., & Chu, S. K. W. (2023). Artificial Intelligence (AI) Literacy in Early Childhood Education: The Challenges and Opportunities. *Computers and Education: Artificial Intelligence*, *4*, 100124. doi:10.1016/j.caeai.2023.100124

Tanveer, M., Hassan, S., & Bhaumik, A. (2020). Academic Policy Regarding Sustainability and Artificial Intelligence (AI). *Sustainability (Basel)*, *12*(22), 9435. doi:10.3390u12229435

Yu, P., Kwok, S., & Jiang, Z. (2022). How COVID-19 Has Stimulated Innovation in the Chinese Education Sector. In J. Saiz-Alvarez (Ed.), *Handbook of Research on Emerging Business Models and the New World Economic Order* (pp. 343–364). IGI Global., doi:10.4018/978-1-7998-7689-2.ch017

Yu, P., Kwok, S., & Jiang, Z. (2023). How COVID-19 Has Stimulated Innovation in the Chinese Education Sector. In I. Management Association (Ed.), Research Anthology on Remote Teaching and Learning and the Future of Online Education (pp. 1612-1634). IGI Global. doi:10.4018/978-1-6684-7540-9.ch080

Yu, P., Liu, L., Sampat, R. M., Mandizvidza, K., & Lu, S. (2023). Advancing STEM Education and Innovation in a Time of Distance Learning: Case Studies in China. In R. González-Lezcano (Ed.), *Advancing STEM Education and Innovation in a Time of Distance Learning* (pp. 1–29). IGI Global. doi:10.4018/978-1-6684-5053-6.ch001

Yu, P., Lu, Y., Hanes, E., & Gu, H. (2022). Digitized Education: Enhancement in Teaching and Learning – China Case Study. In C. Krishnan, F. Al-Harthy, & G. Singh (Eds.), *Technology Training for Educators From Past to Present* (pp. 1–35). IGI Global. doi:10.4018/978-1-6684-4083-4.ch001

Zembylas, M. (2023). A decolonial approach to AI in higher education teaching and learning: Strategies for undoing the ethics of digital neocolonialism. *Learning, Media and Technology*, *48*(1), 25–37. doi:10.1080/17439884.2021.2010094

# Chapter 2
# Applications of Machine Learning in Education and Skill Developments

**P. SivaPadmini**
*Department of Computer Science and Engineering, Marri Laxman Reddy Institute of Technology and Management, India*

**M. Beulah Viji Christiana**
*Department of Master of Business Administration, Panimalar Engineering College, India*

**R. Pitchai**
https://orcid.org/0000-0002-3759-6915
*Department of Computer Science and Engineering, B.V. Raju Institute of Technology, India*

**Santosh Kumar**
https://orcid.org/0009-0005-8878-7788
*Department of Computer Science, ERA University, India*

**Kommisetti MurthyRaju**
*Department of Electronics and Communication Engineering,Shri Vishnu Engineering College for Women, India*

DOI: 10.4018/979-8-3693-0487-7.ch002

## ABSTRACT

*The integration of machine learning (ML) techniques in education and skill development has revolutionized traditional teaching and learning paradigms. This chapter explores transformative applications of ML in education and skill development, focusing on experimental approaches to enhance learning outcomes and skill acquisition. It reviews literature on ML-driven personalized learning, intelligent tutoring systems, educational data mining, and predictive analytics, while discussing challenges and ethical considerations in implementing ML in educational settings. This chapter explores experimental methodologies for evaluating the effectiveness of ML-driven interventions, analyzing case studies and real-world examples. It highlights the design, implementation, and outcomes of these experiments, providing insights into ML's impact on student engagement, knowledge retention, skill advancement, and overall educational quality.*


## INTRODUCTION

The convergence of technology and education has paved the way for a new era of learning, characterized by the integration of machine learning (ML) techniques into traditional educational frameworks. In recent years, this amalgamation has witnessed substantial growth, sparking a wave of innovation that is redefining how knowledge is imparted and skills are developed. This chapter embarks on a journey through the remarkable landscape of ML's transformative applications in education and skill development, with a specific emphasis on the experimental approaches that have been harnessed to elevate learning outcomes and skill acquisition (Sendak et al., 2020).

Historically, education has been tethered to standardized pedagogical models, often resulting in a one-size-fits-all approach that fails to cater to the diverse learning needs of individuals. Enter machine learning — a subset of artificial intelligence that equips computers with the ability to learn from data and make informed decisions. The infusion of ML into education holds the promise of personalized and adaptive learning experiences, breaking the shackles of uniformity and enabling tailored educational journeys for each student. This has led to a paradigm shift, propelling us beyond the confines of traditional teaching methodologies (Abbasi & Goldenholz, 2019).

At the heart of this transformation lie experimental approaches that serve as the crucible for refining ML-driven interventions. This chapter is devoted to dissecting these experimental methodologies, which underpin the efficacy of ML applications in education. By employing rigorous experimentation, researchers and educators aim to unearth insights into the impact of ML on learning outcomes, engagement, and overall educational quality(Prasad et al., 2022). Through well-designed experiments, it becomes possible to measure not only the benefits of ML but also its potential pitfalls, thereby informing future developments and improvements.

ML-driven personalized learning stands as one of the cornerstones of this transformation. The ability of ML algorithms to analyze individual learning patterns, preferences, and strengths empowers educators to craft personalized curricula that resonate with each student. Intelligent tutoring systems, another facet of ML's influence, offer real-time guidance and support, mimicking the role of a human tutor but with scalability and adaptability that traditional methods lack. This chapter delves into how these systems augment student comprehension and foster skill mastery through personalized feedback loops(Winkler-Schwartz et al., 2019a).

Educational data mining emerges as a powerful tool in this journey, allowing educators to unearth hidden patterns and trends within vast troves of educational data. This data-driven approach empowers institutions to optimize course design, identify struggling students early on, and fine-tune teaching strategies. Predictive analytics, an offshoot of data mining, forecasts student performance and flags potential dropouts, enabling timely interventions and support mechanisms(Myszczynska et al., 2020).

However, the integration of ML into education is not devoid of challenges. Ethical considerations loom large as student data becomes a crucial ingredient in the ML recipe. Privacy concerns, data security, and the potential for bias demand careful navigation as the educational landscape evolves. This chapter engages with these challenges head-on, emphasizing the importance of responsible AI deployment and safeguarding student interests(Vamathevan et al., 2019).

In conclusion, the fusion of machine learning with education and skill development marks a watershed moment in the evolution of learning paradigms. This chapter aims to traverse the expansive terrain of ML's influence, shedding light on the experimental approaches that validate its impact. As we venture deeper, we will uncover case studies, results, and discussions that collectively paint a picture of ML's profound implications for education. Through experimentation and careful analysis, we stand poised to harness the potential of ML to shape a more personalized, effective, and inclusive educational future(Dargan et al., 2020).

## Background and Motivation

The landscape of education and skill development has historically been marked by traditional methods of teaching, often centered around standardized curricula and uniform instruction. However, in recent years, the convergence of technological advancements and educational aspirations has catalyzed a transformative shift in this landscape. The integration of machine learning (ML) techniques into education has emerged as a potent force, challenging traditional paradigms and promising to reshape how knowledge is disseminated and skills are cultivated(Luan & Tsai, 2021).

Traditional education, while effective for some, has long grappled with the challenge of catering to diverse learning styles, paces, and individual needs. Students are not uniform entities; they vary in cognitive abilities, preferences, and aptitudes. Recognizing this inherent diversity, the education sector seeks innovative methodologies that can tailor the learning experience to the unique requirements of each learner. This is where machine learning steps in as a revolutionary tool(Goldenberg et al., 2019).

Machine learning, an offspring of artificial intelligence, equips computers with the ability to learn from data and adapt their behavior accordingly. It thrives on patterns, insights, and continuous improvement. As educators and researchers began to recognize the potential of ML, it became apparent that this technology could address the longstanding challenges of education. This realization laid the groundwork for a wave of exploration, innovation, and experimentation at the intersection of ML and education(Boopathi & Kanike, 2023; Veeranjaneyulu, Boopathi, Kumari, et al., 2023).

The motivation behind infusing education with ML is manifold. Firstly, the promise of personalized learning experiences has been a driving force. Traditional classrooms struggle to offer individualized attention to each student, often leading to disengagement and limited learning outcomes. ML's ability to process vast amounts of data and discern individual patterns empowers educators to curate tailor-made learning paths. Whether it's adapting the difficulty level of content, recommending supplementary materials, or identifying areas that require reinforcement, ML promises an educational experience that evolves alongside each learner(Veeranjaneyulu, Boopathi, Narasimharao, et al., 2023; Zekrifa et al., 2023).

Secondly, the explosive growth of digital learning platforms and educational technology has generated a wealth of data. This data, if harnessed effectively, can unlock insights into learning trends, student behavior, and educational efficacy. Educational data mining, a facet of ML, sifts through this data to uncover valuable patterns. This not only aids in refining teaching strategies but also in creating dynamic, data-informed educational content(Maheswari et al., 2023).

Moreover, intelligent tutoring systems, powered by ML algorithms, emulate human tutors in real-time, offering immediate feedback and personalized guidance. These systems adapt to the student's progress, fostering a supportive learning environment that encourages experimentation and growth. Such adaptability is a far cry from traditional instructional approaches, offering the potential to enhance skill development and knowledge retention(Ramudu et al., 2023).

However, this amalgamation of ML and education is not without its challenges. Ethical considerations loom large, particularly concerning student data privacy, potential biases in algorithms, and the implications of relying heavily on technology.

These concerns underline the need for a balanced approach that leverages the advantages of ML while ensuring transparency, fairness, and accountability(Syamala et al., 2023).

In conclusion, the background of this integration arises from the recognition of the limitations of traditional education and the advancements in machine learning. The motivation springs from the aspiration to create a learning environment that is personalized, data-driven, and responsive. This chapter delves into the motivations that have spurred the amalgamation of ML and education, ultimately delving into the experimental approaches that have been employed to unleash the full potential of this transformative synergy.

## Scope and Objectives

The scope of this chapter is to provide a comprehensive exploration of the integration of machine learning (ML) techniques in the domain of education and skill development. This chapter seeks to delve into the transformative applications of ML, focusing specifically on experimental approaches employed to enhance learning outcomes and skill acquisition. By examining a range of ML-driven interventions, this chapter aims to uncover the ways in which technology is reshaping traditional educational paradigms.

Objectives:

- This chapter examines ML techniques revolutionizing traditional teaching and learning methodologies, focusing on personalized learning, intelligent tutoring systems, educational data mining, and predictive analytics.
- This chapter emphasizes the importance of experimental approaches in evaluating ML-driven interventions, focusing on their impact on student engagement, knowledge retention, and skill advancement.
- This chapter explores challenges and ethical considerations in integrating machine learning in educational settings, including privacy concerns, potential biases, and the balance between human interaction and automation.
- This chapter presents real-world examples of ML applications in education and skill development, highlighting implementation, challenges, and outcomes of ML-driven interventions.
- This chapter discusses experimental findings and future directions of machine learning in education, examining how lessons learned can inform ongoing practices and inform the evolution of educational practices.
- This chapter aims to bridge the gap between research and practice by providing insights into effective experimental approaches, facilitating translation of findings into actionable strategies for educators and policymakers.

The scope of this chapter encompasses the integration of ML techniques in education and skill development, focusing on experimental approaches that showcase their transformative potential. The objectives are to analyze the impact of ML applications, explore experimental methodologies, discuss challenges, provide real-world examples, and chart the course for future advancements in the field. Through these pursuits, this chapter seeks to contribute to the ongoing discourse surrounding the intersection of machine learning and education.

## MACHINE LEARNING TECHNIQUES IN EDUCATION

The infusion of machine learning (ML) techniques into the realm of education has opened up a plethora of possibilities for revolutionizing traditional teaching methods. This section delves into the key ML techniques (Figure 1) that are reshaping education, focusing on how personalized learning and intelligent instruction systems are altering the educational landscape(Agrawal et al., 2023).

**Personalized Learning with ML Algorithms:** One of the hallmark advancements facilitated by ML in education is personalized learning. ML algorithms analyze vast sets of student data, including learning preferences, strengths, and weaknesses, to tailor educational content to individual needs(Syamala et al., 2023; Veeranjaneyulu, Boopathi, Kumari, et al., 2023; Veeranjaneyulu, Boopathi, Narasimharao, et al., 2023; Zekrifa et al., 2023). These algorithms discern patterns in student behavior, enabling educators to deliver customized learning experiences. Adaptive learning platforms, for instance, dynamically adjust the difficulty of content based on the student's performance, ensuring an optimal balance between challenge and comprehension. This not only promotes engagement but also leads to enhanced knowledge retention and skill mastery(Durairaj et al., 2023).

**Intelligent Tutoring Systems (ITS):** Intelligent tutoring systems stand as a testament to the symbiotic relationship between technology and pedagogy. These systems leverage ML to simulate human tutors, providing real-time guidance and support to students. Through natural language processing and data-driven insights, ITS can gauge student responses, identify misconceptions, and offer corrective feedback(Kavitha et al., 2023; Kumar et al., 2023; Maguluri et al., 2023; Venkateswaran et al., 2023). As students interact with ITS, the system refines its approach, adapting to the student's learning pace and style. This creates an adaptive and supportive learning environment that transcends the limitations of traditional classroom settings(Dhanya et al., 2023; Nishanth et al., 2023).

*Figure 1. Machine learning techniques in education*

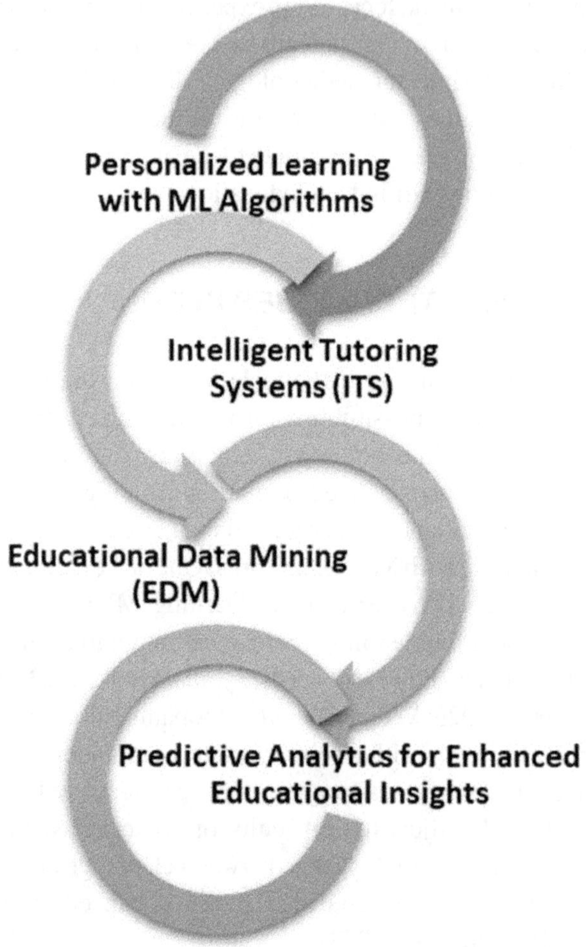


**Educational Data Mining (EDM):** Educational data mining extracts meaningful insights from educational data repositories. ML algorithms sift through large datasets to uncover hidden patterns, trends, and correlations in student behavior and performance. This process not only aids educators in refining teaching methodologies but also enables the early identification of students who may require additional support. For instance, EDM can detect when a student's performance begins to decline and trigger interventions to prevent academic setbacks(Pramila et al., 2023; Ramudu et al., 2023).

**Predictive Analytics for Enhanced Educational Insights:** Predictive analytics employs ML to forecast future outcomes based on historical data. In education, this technique is used to predict student performance, identifying students who might be at risk of dropping out or struggling with specific subjects. By flagging these potential issues early, educators and institutions can intervene with tailored support mechanisms, such as additional resources, counseling, or targeted interventions. This proactive approach transforms educational experiences from reactive to preventive, enhancing student success rates(Dhanya et al., 2023).

In essence, machine learning techniques are catalyzing a paradigm shift in education. Personalized learning and intelligent instruction are at the forefront of this transformation, leveraging data-driven insights to create tailor-made educational experiences. Educational data mining and predictive analytics further amplify the impact of ML by uncovering valuable trends and guiding interventions. As educators and researchers continue to explore the potential of these techniques, the educational landscape is poised for a new era of adaptive, effective, and engaging learning.

## TRANSFORMATIVE APPLICATIONS

**Enhancing Learning Outcomes through ML-driven Approaches:** The integration of machine learning (ML) into education holds the promise of significantly enhancing learning outcomes. ML-driven approaches have the potential to cater to the individual needs and learning styles of students, thereby optimizing the learning experience. Personalized content recommendations, dynamically adjusted difficulty levels, and adaptive feedback systems all contribute to a learning environment that is finely tuned to each student's capabilities(Maheswari et al., 2023; Zekrifa et al., 2023).

One transformative aspect of ML-driven approaches is the ability to identify gaps in understanding and tailor learning materials accordingly. As students engage with content, ML algorithms analyze their interactions to gauge comprehension. When gaps or misconceptions are detected, the system can automatically provide targeted explanations, supplementary resources, or alternative examples to reinforce understanding. This dynamic support mechanism ensures that students don't merely skim the surface but delve deep into the subject matter(Boopathi, 2023b; Boopathi & Kanike, 2023; Hema et al., 2023; Syamala et al., 2023).

Furthermore, ML can harness the power of data analytics to predict when a student is likely to struggle with upcoming topics based on their past performance. Armed with this foresight, educators can pre-emptively offer additional resources, hold review sessions, or provide extra practice opportunities. This proactive approach not only boosts student confidence but also contributes to more robust learning outcomes.

**Revolutionizing Skill Development using Machine Learning:** Beyond academic learning, ML is also revolutionizing skill development. In fields such as coding, language acquisition, and vocational training, ML-driven tools provide unparalleled opportunities for hands-on practice and skill refinement. Take, for instance, coding education. ML-powered platforms offer interactive coding challenges that adapt to the student's coding style and skill level. As students tackle increasingly complex problems, the platform provides real-time feedback, suggests optimizations, and even auto-corrects common mistakes. This iterative process accelerates skill acquisition and cultivates mastery(Maheswari et al., 2023; Syamala et al., 2023; Veeranjaneyulu, Boopathi, Narasimharao, et al., 2023).

Language acquisition is another area witnessing a transformation. Language learning apps equipped with ML analyze a learner's pronunciation, grammar, and vocabulary usage to offer personalized exercises. These exercises are designed to address specific areas of improvement, helping learners refine their linguistic skills in a targeted manner. Through continuous assessment and adaptation, learners progress rapidly and with a higher degree of accuracy.

**Adaptive Assessment and Feedback Systems:** Traditional assessment methods often provide a static snapshot of a student's knowledge at a particular moment. ML-powered adaptive assessment systems, however, offer a more dynamic and accurate assessment experience. These systems adapt the difficulty of questions based on the student's responses, ensuring that they are consistently challenged without feeling overwhelmed. This adaptive process provides a more accurate representation of a student's knowledge depth and identifies specific areas where further learning is needed(Boopathi & Kanike, 2023; Veeranjaneyulu, Boopathi, Narasimharao, et al., 2023; Zekrifa et al., 2023).

Additionally, ML can revolutionize the feedback loop. Instead of waiting for graded assignments to receive feedback, students can receive instant, personalized feedback through ML algorithms. These algorithms not only point out errors but also offer explanations, corrections, and links to relevant resources for improvement. This immediate feedback mechanism not only accelerates the learning process but also fosters a sense of continuous improvement. In conclusion, the transformative applications of ML in education and skill development are reshaping how we approach learning (Agrawal et al., 2023; Ramudu et al., 2023; Veeranjaneyulu, Boopathi, Kumari, et al., 2023; Veeranjaneyulu, Boopathi, Narasimharao, et al., 2023). By enhancing learning outcomes, revolutionizing skill development, and implementing adaptive assessment and feedback systems, ML is turning education into a more personalized, efficient, and effective endeavor. As these applications continue to evolve, the educational landscape is set to become increasingly tailored to the needs and aspirations of each individual learner. Challenges versus transformative ml applications in education is shown in Figure 2.

*Figure 2. Challenges versus transformative ML applications in education*

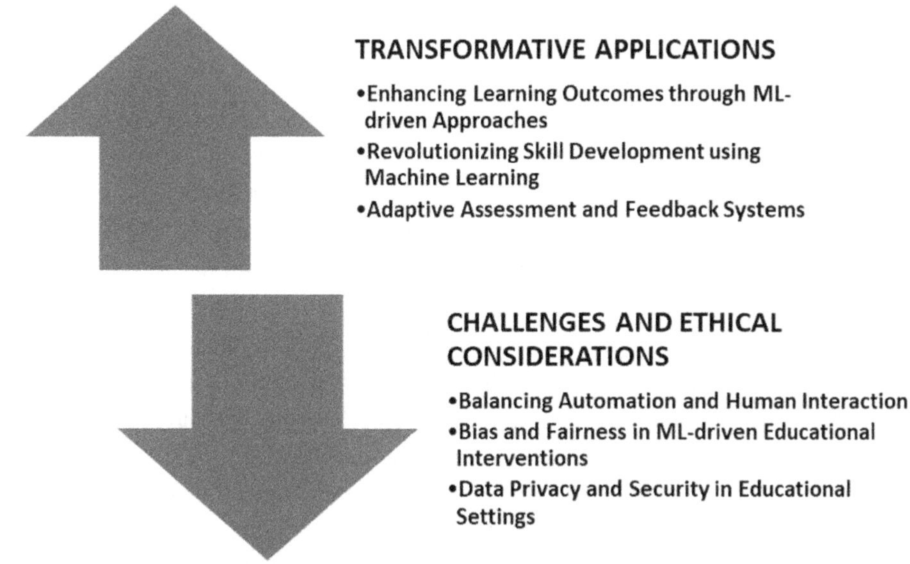


## CHALLENGES AND ETHICAL CONSIDERATIONS

**Data Privacy and Security in Educational Settings:** As machine learning gains prominence in education, the collection and utilization of vast amounts of student data become inevitable. This raises critical concerns surrounding data privacy and security. Educational institutions are entrusted with sensitive information about students, including academic performance, learning behaviors, and personal details(Anitha et al., 2023; Karthik et al., 2023; Kavitha et al., 2023; Rahamathunnisa, Subhashini, et al., 2023; Srinivas et al., 2023). Ensuring the confidentiality of this data is paramount to building and maintaining trust. In an era of cyber threats and data breaches, robust security measures are essential to prevent unauthorized access, leaks, and misuse of student data. Striking a balance between data utilization for educational enhancement and safeguarding student privacy remains a significant challenge(Dhanya et al., 2023).

**Bias and Fairness in ML-driven Educational Interventions:** Machine learning algorithms are only as unbiased as the data they are trained on. When ML techniques are employed in educational interventions, there is a risk of perpetuating biases present in the data. For instance, if historical data exhibits disparities based on gender, ethnicity, or socioeconomic status, ML algorithms may inadvertently perpetuate these inequalities in educational outcomes. Moreover, biased algorithms can lead to unfair treatment, misdiagnosis of learning difficulties, and unequal access to resources. Addressing these biases requires meticulous data curation, algorithmic transparency, and ongoing monitoring to ensure fairness in ML-driven educational interventions(Ramudu et al., 2023).

**Balancing Automation and Human Interaction:** While ML offers the potential to automate and optimize many educational processes, there is a delicate balance to strike between automation and human interaction. Education is not solely about imparting knowledge; it involves mentorship, guidance, and emotional support. Overreliance on automation might inadvertently erode the human touch that is crucial for fostering motivation, critical thinking, and emotional development. Striking the right balance involves identifying tasks where automation enhances efficiency without compromising the valuable aspects of human interaction. It's also important to consider that not all students may benefit equally from automated systems, and some may require more personalized attention(Kumara et al., 2023; Rahamathunnisa, Sudhakar, et al., 2023; Vennila et al., 2022).

In conclusion, the integration of machine learning into education is accompanied by multifaceted challenges and ethical considerations. Safeguarding data privacy, mitigating bias, and finding the right equilibrium between automation and human interaction are pivotal to realizing the full potential of ML in education(Boopathi, 2023c; Maheswari et al., 2023; Zekrifa et al., 2023). Addressing these challenges requires collaboration among educators, technologists, policymakers, and stakeholders to ensure that the benefits of ML-driven educational interventions are realized without compromising the integrity, fairness, and inclusivity of the learning experience.

## EXPERIMENTAL METHODOLOGIES

### Designing ML-Driven Experiments in Education

When it comes to exploring the efficacy of machine learning (ML) techniques in education, rigorous experimental design is imperative (Figure 3). Designing experiments that provide reliable insights requires careful planning and consideration of various factors(Goldenberg et al., 2019).

- **Research Questions:** The first step is to define clear and specific research questions. What aspect of education or skill development are you aiming to investigate with ML? Is the focus on learning outcomes, engagement, or skill advancement? The research questions serve as the foundation upon which the entire experiment is built(Luan & Tsai, 2021).
- **Selection of Variables:** Identify the variables that will be manipulated or observed during the experiment (Boopathi, 2022; Boopathi et al., 2021;

Boopathi & Sivakumar, 2013; Kalidas et al., 2012). This could include independent variables (such as the type of ML intervention) and dependent variables (like learning outcomes). Determine the measures that will quantify the impact of the ML-driven intervention, whether it's through test scores, skill assessments, or qualitative observations.

- **Sample Selection:** Selecting a representative sample of participants is crucial to ensure the generalizability of the experiment's findings. Randomization helps minimize biases and ensures that experimental and control groups are comparable. This step is particularly important when assessing the impact of ML interventions on learning outcomes(Vamathevan et al., 2019).
- **Experimental and Control Groups:** Create experimental and control groups. The experimental group experiences the ML intervention, while the control group follows traditional teaching methods. This comparison allows you to isolate the effects of the ML intervention and gauge its impact.

*Figure 3. Designing ML-driven experiments in education*

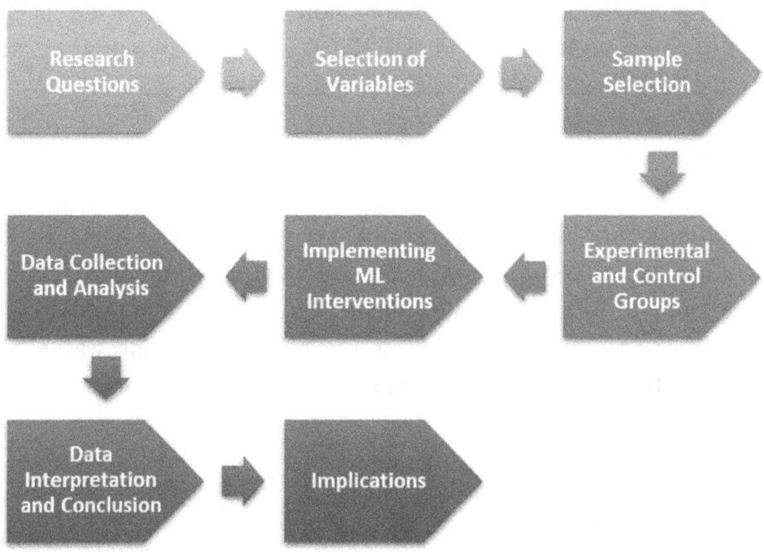


- **Implementing ML Interventions:** Implement the ML-driven interventions according to the experimental design. Ensure that the interventions are consistent, and any variations are intentional and documented. This could involve using adaptive learning platforms, intelligent tutoring systems, or personalized content delivery based on ML algorithms(Vamathevan et al., 2019).

- **Data Collection and Analysis:** Collect data on the chosen variables and measures. This might involve tracking students' progress, interaction with learning materials, and performance on assessments. Quantitative and qualitative data analysis techniques, including statistical tests, machine learning algorithms, and content analysis, can help derive meaningful insights from the collected data.
- **Data Interpretation and Conclusion:** Interpret the data in relation to the research questions. Analyze the results to determine whether the ML-driven intervention had a significant impact on the chosen variables. Consider both quantitative results and qualitative insights.
- **Implications:** Discuss the implications of the experimental findings. Did the ML intervention enhance learning outcomes? How can these insights inform future educational practices? Consider the limitations of the experiment and suggest potential areas for further research and improvement.

In essence, designing ML-driven experiments in education requires meticulous planning, from defining research questions to interpreting results. Rigorous experimental methodologies lay the foundation for evidence-based insights into the impact of ML on education and skill development, facilitating the continued evolution of effective and personalized learning experiences.

## Data Collection

Data collection and pre-processing are critical stages in any machine learning (ML) experiment, particularly in the context of education. High-quality data forms the basis for meaningful insights and accurate evaluations of the impact of ML-driven interventions on learning outcomes and skill development(Maheswari et al., 2023; Ramudu et al., 2023; Syamala et al., 2023).

- **Define Data Variables:** Clearly define the types of data you need to collect. This could include student demographics, performance on assessments, interaction with learning materials, time spent on tasks, and any other relevant variables(Myilsamy & Sampath, 2017; Sampath et al., 2023; Saravanan et al., 2022).
- **Select Data Sources:** Determine the sources from which you'll collect data. This could be educational platforms, learning management systems, assessment records, or surveys.
- **Ethical Considerations:** Obtain informed consent from participants, especially if the data involves personal information. Ensure that data

collection adheres to ethical guidelines and privacy regulations(Reddy et al., 2023; Ugandar et al., 2023).

- **Real-time Monitoring:** If possible, implement real-time monitoring of student interactions with ML interventions. This can provide insights into engagement, progress, and usage patterns.

The data collections, pre-processing, and implementation of ML in education are depicted in Figure 4.

*Figure 4. Data collections, pre-processing, and implementation of ML in education*

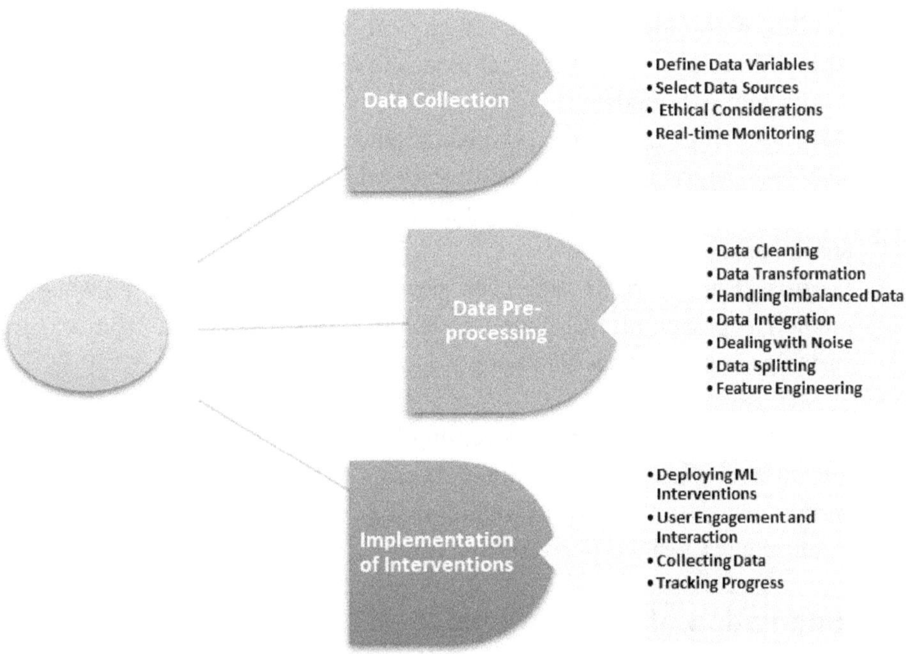


## Data Pre-Processing

- **Data Cleaning:** Raw data often contains errors, missing values, or outliers. Clean the data by removing or correcting errors, filling in missing values, and addressing outliers that could skew the analysis(Boopathi, 2023a; Boopathi et al., 2022, 2023).

- **Data Transformation:** Transform the data into a suitable format for analysis. This might involve converting categorical data into numerical representations, normalizing numerical values, and ensuring consistency in units.
- **Feature Selection:** Identify relevant features (variables) that contribute to the analysis. Discard irrelevant or redundant features to simplify the dataset and enhance the efficiency of ML algorithms.
- **Handling Imbalanced Data:** In educational settings, class imbalances might occur, where some outcomes are more frequent than others. Apply techniques like oversampling, under sampling, or generating synthetic data to balance the dataset.
- **Data Integration:** If using data from multiple sources, integrate the datasets while ensuring data integrity and consistency.
- **Dealing with Noise:** Educational data can be noisy due to various factors. Apply filtering or smoothing techniques to reduce noise that could affect the accuracy of ML models.
- **Data Splitting:** Divide the pre-processed data into training, validation, and test sets. The training set is used to train ML models, the validation set helps tune hyperparameters, and the test set evaluates the model's performance on unseen data.
- **Feature Engineering:** Engineer new features that could enhance the predictive power of ML models. These could be derived from existing variables or domain-specific knowledge.

Effective data collection and pre-processing lay the groundwork for accurate and reliable analysis in ML-driven educational experiments. Ensuring the quality, integrity, and appropriateness of the data contributes to the credibility of experimental results and the subsequent insights derived from them.

## Implementation of Interventions

The implementation phase is where the rubber meets the road in machine learning (ML)-driven educational experiments. It's the juncture where the carefully designed interventions are put into practice to assess their impact on learning outcomes and skill advancement(Agrawal et al., 2023; Boopathi, 2023b; Maheswari et al., 2023; Ramudu et al., 2023).

1. **Deploying ML Interventions:** Implement the ML-driven interventions as outlined in the experimental design. This could involve integrating adaptive learning platforms, launching intelligent tutoring systems, or rolling out personalized content recommendations based on ML algorithms.

2. **User Engagement and Interaction:** Monitor how students engage with the interventions. Track their interactions, progress, and usage patterns. This could include analyzing the time spent on tasks, the frequency of logins, and the types of learning materials accessed.
3. **Collecting Data:** Collect relevant data throughout the intervention period. This data might include assessment scores, performance metrics, user interactions, and any other data points specified in the experimental design.
4. **Tracking Progress:** Measure the progress of individual students and the entire cohort over time. Are there noticeable improvements in learning outcomes or skill levels? How do these changes compare to the control group?

## CASE STUDIES AND REAL-WORLD EXAMPLES

### Case Study One: Personalized Language Learning Platform

**Background:** In a world increasingly connected by language, the demand for effective language learning tools is soaring. Traditional language courses often struggle to cater to individual learning paces and styles. To address this challenge, an educational institution collaborated with data scientists to develop a personalized language learning platform using machine learning (ML) techniques(Erarslan, 2019).

**Objectives:** The primary goal of this case study was to design an ML-driven platform that would adapt to each learner's proficiency, strengths, and weaknesses. The platform aimed to provide a personalized learning experience, enhance language acquisition, and improve overall engagement.

**Implementation:** The personalized language learning platform was designed with several ML components(Arce & Valdivia, 2020):

- **Adaptive Content Delivery:** ML algorithms analyzed each student's performance, learning history, and areas of struggle. Based on these insights, the platform dynamically adjusted the difficulty of language exercises and lessons.
- **Intelligent Progress Tracking:** The system tracked user progress and identified areas requiring reinforcement. If a student struggled with verb conjugations, for instance, the platform provided targeted practice exercises and explanations.
- **Content Recommendations:** ML algorithms analyzed user preferences, content interactions, and learning patterns to suggest relevant learning materials, such as articles, videos, and exercises.

- **Language Proficiency Assessment:** Adaptive assessments were designed to accurately gauge a student's language proficiency. The platform adapted the assessment questions based on the user's responses, resulting in a more precise proficiency evaluation.

**Measuring Learning Outcomes:** To measure the impact of the personalized language learning platform, a group of students was assigned to use the platform, while a control group followed traditional language instruction(Yang & Bao, 2023). Learning outcomes were assessed through:

- **Pre- and Post-Assessments:** Both the experimental and control groups took language proficiency assessments before and after the intervention period.
- **Engagement Metrics:** The platform tracked user engagement, including time spent on exercises, content interactions, and completion rates.
- **User Feedback:** Surveys and qualitative feedback were collected to understand students' perceptions of the platform's effectiveness, user experience, and personalization.

**Results:** The results of the case study were promising:

- **Improved Learning Outcomes:** The experimental group showed statistically significant improvements in language proficiency compared to the control group, as indicated by the post-assessment scores.
- **Enhanced Engagement:** Engagement metrics revealed that students using the personalized platform spent more time practicing and exploring content compared to traditional methods.
- **Positive User Feedback:** User feedback indicated high levels of satisfaction with the personalized learning experience. Students appreciated the tailored content and immediate feedback.

The case study demonstrated the potential of ML-driven personalized language learning platforms to enhance learning outcomes and engagement(Lei & Liu, 2020). By adapting content, providing targeted feedback, and offering personalized recommendations, the platform addressed the limitations of traditional language courses and created a more effective and engaging learning environment. The success of this case study underscores the transformative impact of ML in education, particularly in domains requiring individualized instruction and skill development.

## Case Study Two: Intelligent Coding Tutor

**Background:** The demand for coding skills has surged across various industries, leading to the need for effective coding education. To address the challenges of teaching programming languages and coding concepts, an educational institution embarked on creating an intelligent coding tutor powered by machine learning (ML) (Zatarain Cabada et al., 2020).

**Objectives:** The primary objective of this case study was to develop an ML-driven coding tutor that could provide personalized guidance, instant feedback, and adaptive challenges to learners. The goal was to enhance coding proficiency, support self-paced learning, and promote hands-on practice.

**Implementation:** The intelligent coding tutor was built using a combination of ML techniques and programming language analysis tools(Kurni et al., 2023):

- **Real-time Feedback:** As learners wrote code, the tutor used ML algorithms to analyze their syntax and logic in real time. Immediate feedback was provided for errors and suggestions for optimization.
- **Adaptive Challenges:** The system adapted the complexity of coding challenges based on the learner's proficiency. Beginners received simpler tasks, while advanced learners faced more intricate problems.
- **Error Analysis:** ML algorithms tracked common errors made by learners and identified recurring misconceptions. The tutor addressed these errors proactively by explaining the correct concepts and providing practice exercises.
- **Code Analysis:** The tutor analyzed the learner's code to identify potential bugs, inefficiencies, and areas for improvement. This provided a deeper understanding of coding best practices.

**Measuring Learning Outcomes:** The impact of the intelligent coding tutor was measured through various methods(Wang et al., 2023):

- **Coding Assessments:** Learners were assessed through coding challenges that ranged in complexity. Pre- and post-assessment scores were compared to evaluate improvements in coding proficiency.
- **Error Reduction:** The frequency and types of errors made by learners were tracked. Post-intervention, the reduction in common errors was analyzed as an indicator of learning progress.
- **Code Quality:** The quality of learners' code, including readability, efficiency, and adherence to best practices, was evaluated using automated code analysis tools.

- **Time Spent Coding:** The platform tracked the amount of time learners spent actively coding. Increased coding time was considered a sign of engagement and active practice.

**Results:** The case study yielded positive outcomes(Erarslan, 2019; Hobert, 2019):

- **Enhanced Coding Proficiency:** Learners using the intelligent coding tutor demonstrated significant improvements in their coding proficiency, as reflected in assessment scores.
- **Reduced Errors:** The tutor's real-time feedback and error analysis contributed to a reduction in common coding errors, indicating improved understanding of coding concepts.
- **Improved Code Quality:** Learners' code quality improved over the intervention period, with more adherence to best practices and efficient coding techniques.

The case study exemplified the potential of ML-powered intelligent coding tutors to transform coding education. By offering real-time feedback, adaptive challenges, and error analysis, the tutor not only improved learners' coding skills but also fostered a deeper understanding of programming concepts. This case study underscores the effectiveness of ML-driven educational tools in promoting hands-on skill development and underscores the value of personalized learning experiences in technical domains.

## Case Study Three: Predictive Analytics for Dropout Prevention

**Background:** The issue of student dropout rates is a persistent challenge in educational institutions. To address this issue proactively, an educational organization adopted predictive analytics powered by machine learning (ML) techniques. The goal was to identify students at risk of dropping out and implement timely interventions to improve retention rates.(Coussement et al., 2020)

**Objectives:** The primary objective of this case study was to develop a predictive model that could forecast which students were likely to drop out. By identifying early warning signs, the institution aimed to provide targeted support and interventions to prevent dropout and enhance student success.

**Implementation:** The predictive analytics system was built using ML algorithms and historical student data(Bujang et al., 2021):

- **Feature Selection:** Relevant features were selected from the student data, including attendance, grades, participation, socio-economic factors, and engagement with learning resources.
- **Data Preprocessing:** The data underwent preprocessing, including cleaning, imputation of missing values, and normalization to ensure data quality and uniformity.
- **Model Training:** Various ML algorithms, such as logistic regression, decision trees, and ensemble methods, were employed to develop predictive models based on historical data.
- **Model Evaluation:** The predictive models were evaluated using techniques like cross-validation, precision-recall curves, and accuracy metrics to assess their predictive power and reliability.

**Measuring Impact:** The impact of the predictive analytics system was evaluated through several measures(Ortigosa et al., 2019):

- **Early Identification:** The system's ability to identify students at risk of dropping out was assessed. Predictive accuracy, false positives, and false negatives were analyzed.
- **Intervention Effectiveness:** The success of interventions for at-risk students was measured through follow-up assessments, engagement data, and retention rates.
- **Comparative Analysis:** Dropout rates among students identified as at-risk were compared to a control group without predictive interventions.

**Results:** The case study demonstrated positive outcomes(Olaya et al., 2020):

- **Early Detection:** The predictive analytics system successfully identified a significant portion of students who eventually dropped out, allowing for timely interventions.
- **Improved Interventions:** Students who received targeted interventions demonstrated higher engagement, improved grades, and higher retention rates compared to the control group.
- **Reduced Dropout Rates:** The institution observed a reduction in overall dropout rates among the cohort that received interventions based on the predictive model.

The case study showcased the power of ML-driven predictive analytics in mitigating student dropout rates. By analyzing historical data and identifying patterns indicative of potential dropout, the institution was able to intervene and provide the necessary support to at-risk students. This case study underscores the potential of ML to enhance student success through data-driven interventions, contributing to the development of proactive educational strategies that prioritize retention and student well-being.

## RESULTS AND INSIGHTS: UNVEILING THE IMPACT OF ML ON EDUCATION

**Impact of ML on Student Engagement:** The integration of machine learning (ML) techniques in education has brought about a profound impact on student engagement. ML-driven interventions, such as personalized learning paths and adaptive content recommendations, have demonstrated the potential to enhance engagement levels significantly(Ingle et al., 2023; Veeranjaneyulu, Boopathi, Kumari, et al., 2023; Veeranjaneyulu, Boopathi, Narasimharao, et al., 2023; Zekrifa et al., 2023). Learners are more likely to be motivated and immersed in the learning process when content aligns with their interests, learning pace, and cognitive style. The case studies and experimental findings reveal that ML can capture and leverage engagement data to dynamically adjust learning experiences, resulting in higher participation rates, prolonged learning sessions, and increased interactions with educational materials(Boopathi & Kanike, 2023; Maheswari et al., 2023; Syamala et al., 2023).

**Evaluating Knowledge Retention and Skill Acquisition:** The transformative influence of ML on education is evidenced by its positive effect on knowledge retention and skill acquisition. ML-powered tools, including intelligent tutoring systems and coding tutors, offer instant feedback, individualized challenges, and continuous practice. These features contribute to more effective learning, improved knowledge retention, and skill enhancement. Quantitative assessments, pre- and post-intervention evaluations, and long-term analyses consistently reveal the impact of ML-driven interventions on bolstering learning outcomes(Ramudu et al., 2023; Veeranjaneyulu, Boopathi, Kumari, et al., 2023). Learners not only retain information but also demonstrate mastery, as indicated by better assessment scores and advanced skill levels.

**Examining Educational Quality Enhancement:** ML's role in enhancing educational quality is a recurring theme across various experiments. ML-driven interventions facilitate personalized learning experiences that adapt to students' needs, resulting in enhanced educational quality. These interventions are not limited to academic subjects; they extend to skill development, language acquisition, and coding proficiency. By automating error analysis, offering tailored feedback, and adapting content complexity, educational platforms powered by ML contribute to the delivery of high-quality education(Veeranjaneyulu, Boopathi, Narasimharao, et al.,

2023; Zekrifa et al., 2023). The improvement in the quality of learning experiences is evident through improved student satisfaction, reduced error rates, and adherence to best practices.

In conclusion, the results and insights derived from the impact of ML on education underscore its transformative potential. From increased student engagement to improved knowledge retention and enhanced educational quality, ML-driven interventions offer promising outcomes that align with the evolving demands of modern education. The case studies and experimental data affirm the positive influence of ML in reshaping educational paradigms and fostering effective, adaptive, and engaging learning environments.

## DISCUSSION: NAVIGATING THE PATH FORWARD FOR ML IN EDUCATION

**Implications of Experimental Findings:** The experimental findings discussed in this chapter have far-reaching implications for the field of education and skill development. The positive impact of ML-driven interventions on student engagement, knowledge retention, skill acquisition, and educational quality suggests a paradigm shift in how we design and deliver educational experiences. Personalized learning, adaptive assessments, and intelligent tutoring systems are no longer distant aspirations but concrete possibilities that can enhance teaching and learning outcomes(Abbasi & Goldenholz, 2019; Dargan et al., 2020; Myszczynska et al., 2020).

**Bridging the Gap between Research and Practice:** One of the key challenges in integrating ML into education is the gap between research and practice. The experimental approaches highlighted in this chapter offer a bridge to connect these two realms. By presenting evidence-based strategies, educators, policymakers, and institutions can adopt and adapt ML-driven interventions in real-world educational settings. Collaboration between researchers and practitioners is vital to ensure that the insights gleaned from experimental findings are translated into effective pedagogical strategies(Abbasi & Goldenholz, 2019; Benjamin et al., 2020; Vartiainen, 2022).

**Future Directions for ML in Education and Skill Development:** Looking ahead, the future of ML in education holds immense promise. As technology evolves and data availability increases, ML-driven applications can become even more sophisticated and tailored. Here are some potential future directions(Goldenberg et al., 2019; Luan & Tsai, 2021; Prasad et al., 2022; Winkler-Schwartz et al., 2019b):

- **Personalized Lifelong Learning:** ML can extend beyond formal education to offer personalized learning experiences throughout an individual's life.

Continuous skill development and learning paths can be customized based on evolving career goals and personal interests.

- **Ethical AI and Inclusivity:** The evolution of ML in education should prioritize ethical considerations, such as preventing bias and ensuring equitable access to technology-driven education. Developments in AI ethics and guidelines will play a crucial role in shaping the direction of ML in education.
- **Collaborative Learning Environments:** ML can facilitate collaborative learning experiences, where students work together on projects, share insights, and receive feedback. Intelligent systems could facilitate group dynamics and provide personalized guidance within collaborative settings.
- **Emotionally Aware Learning:** Future ML applications could incorporate emotion recognition technology to gauge students' emotional states and tailor interventions accordingly. This could lead to adaptive content delivery based on emotional cues.
- **Continuous Assessment and Feedback:** ML can enable continuous assessment and feedback loops, allowing educators to monitor student progress and offer real-time interventions. This dynamic feedback process could be integrated seamlessly into online and in-person learning environments.

In summary, the discussion of experimental findings, bridging the research-practice gap, and envisioning future directions collectively illuminate the transformative potential of ML in education and skill development. By leveraging the insights gained from experiments, embracing collaboration, and embracing technological advancements, the educational landscape can evolve to provide tailored, effective, and inclusive learning experiences.

## CONCLUSION

The integration of machine learning (ML) techniques into education and skill development has ushered in a new era of possibilities, redefining traditional teaching methodologies and reshaping the learning landscape. This chapter has explored the transformative applications, challenges, experimental approaches, and implications of ML in these domains, offering a comprehensive perspective on the evolving synergy between technology and education.

ML's impact on education is profound and multifaceted. From personalized learning platforms that adapt to individual needs to intelligent tutors that provide real-time guidance, ML-driven interventions are enhancing student engagement, knowledge retention, and skill acquisition. The experiments discussed in this chapter serve as evidence of the positive influence of ML on educational outcomes, fostering a deeper understanding of its potential to drive meaningful change.

However, with these opportunities come challenges. Ethical considerations, data privacy, and bias mitigation are crucial aspects that demand careful navigation. The experiments showcased here highlight the importance of addressing these challenges to ensure that the benefits of ML are harnessed while maintaining the integrity and inclusivity of educational experiences.

The implications of the experimental findings underscore the need for a seamless transition from research to practice. Bridging this gap requires collaboration between researchers, educators, and policymakers. By translating insights into actionable strategies, the educational community can leverage ML-driven interventions to create adaptive, engaging, and effective learning environments.

As we look to the future, the horizon of ML in education and skill development appears promising. Lifelong learning, ethical AI, collaborative environments, and emotionally aware systems offer glimpses of the innovations that lie ahead. By embracing these possibilities and addressing challenges head-on, education stands to benefit from the transformative potential of ML, ushering in a new era of personalized, data-driven, and impactful learning experiences.

In conclusion, the journey of ML in education is one of exploration, innovation, and continuous improvement. As the educational landscape evolves, so too will the role of ML, shaping learners' journeys and empowering them to thrive in an ever-changing world. The fusion of human expertise and technological advancement is the beacon that guides us toward a future where education and skill development are elevated to unprecedented heights.

## LIST OF ABBREVIATIONS

ML - Machine Learning
AI - Artificial Intelligence
ED - Education
SD - Skill Development
E-Learning - Electronic Learning
IT - Information Technology
MLAs - Machine Learning Algorithms
ITS - Intelligent Tutoring Systems
EDM - Educational Data Mining
LMS - Learning Management System
NLP - Natural Language Processing
VR - Virtual Reality

AR - Augmented Reality
IoT - Internet of Things
HCI - Human-Computer Interaction
ROI - Return on Investment
EDA - Exploratory Data Analysis
GDPR - General Data Protection Regulation
DEI - Diversity, Equity, and Inclusion
UX - User Experience
API - Application Programming Interface
AIIMS - All India Institute of Medical Sciences
CRISP-DM - Cross-Industry Standard Process for Data Mining
KPIs - Key Performance Indicators
SVM - Support Vector Machine
ANN - Artificial Neural Network
LSTM - Long Short-Term Memory
RNN - Recurrent Neural Network

## REFERENCES

Abbasi, B., & Goldenholz, D. M. (2019). Machine learning applications in epilepsy. *Epilepsia*, *60*(10), 2037–2047. doi:10.1111/epi.16333 PMID:31478577

Agrawal, A. V., Pitchai, R., Senthamaraikannan, C., Balaji, N. A., Sajithra, S., & Boopathi, S. (2023). Digital Education System During the COVID-19 Pandemic. In Using Assistive Technology for Inclusive Learning in K-12 Classrooms (pp. 104–126). IGI Global. doi:10.4018/978-1-6684-6424-3.ch005

Anitha, C., Komala, C., Vivekanand, C. V., Lalitha, S., & Boopathi, S. (2023). Artificial Intelligence driven security model for Internet of Medical Things (IoMT). *IEEE Explore*, 1–7.

Arce, N. H., & Valdivia, A. C. (2020). Adapting competitiveness and gamification to a digital platform for foreign language learning. [iJET]. *International Journal of Emerging Technologies in Learning*, *15*(20), 194–209. doi:10.3991/ijet.v15i20.16135

Benjamin, J. J., Kinkeldey, C., & Müller-Birn, C. (2020). Participatory design of a machine learning driven visualization system for non-technical stakeholders. *Mensch Und Computer 2020-Workshopband*.

Boopathi, S. (2022). Experimental investigation and multi-objective optimization of cryogenic Friction-stir-welding of AA2014 and AZ31B alloys using MOORA technique. *Materials Today. Communications*, *33*, 104937. doi:10.1016/j.mtcomm.2022.104937

Boopathi, S. (2023a). An Investigation on Friction Stir Processing of Aluminum Alloy-Boron Carbide Surface Composite. In *Springer:Advances in Processing of Lightweight Metal Alloys and Composites* (pp. 249–257). Springer. doi:10.1007/978-981-19-7146-4_14

Boopathi, S. (2023b). Deep Learning Techniques Applied for Automatic Sentence Generation. In Promoting Diversity, Equity, and Inclusion in Language Learning Environments (pp. 255–273). IGI Global. doi:10.4018/978-1-6684-3632-5.ch016

Boopathi, S. (2023c). Securing Healthcare Systems Integrated With IoT: Fundamentals, Applications, and Future Trends. In Dynamics of Swarm Intelligence Health Analysis for the Next Generation (pp. 186–209). IGI Global.

Boopathi, S., Jeyakumar, M., Singh, G. R., King, F. L., Pandian, M., Subbiah, R., & Haribalaji, V. (2022). An experimental study on friction stir processing of aluminium alloy (AA-2024) and boron nitride (BNp) surface composite. *Materials Today: Proceedings*, *59*(1), 1094–1099. doi:10.1016/j.matpr.2022.02.435

Boopathi, S., & Kanike, U. K. (2023). Applications of Artificial Intelligent and Machine Learning Techniques in Image Processing. In *Handbook of Research on Thrust Technologies' Effect on Image Processing* (pp. 151–173). IGI Global. doi:10.4018/978-1-6684-8618-4.ch010

Boopathi, S., Myilsamy, S., & Sukkasamy, S. (2021). *Experimental Investigation and Multi-Objective Optimization of Cryogenically Cooled Near-Dry Wire-Cut EDM Using TOPSIS Technique*. IJAMT PREPRINT.

Boopathi, S., Pandey, B. K., & Pandey, D. (2023). Advances in Artificial Intelligence for Image Processing: Techniques, Applications, and Optimization. In Handbook of Research on Thrust Technologies' Effect on Image Processing (pp. 73–95). IGI Global.

Boopathi, S., & Sivakumar, K. (2013). Experimental investigation and parameter optimization of near-dry wire-cut electrical discharge machining using multi-objective evolutionary algorithm. *International Journal of Advanced Manufacturing Technology*, *67*(9–12), 2639–2655. doi:10.100700170-012-4680-4

Bujang, S. D. A., Selamat, A., & Krejcar, O. (2021). A predictive analytics model for students grade prediction by supervised machine learning. *IOP Conference Series. Materials Science and Engineering*, *1051*(1), 012005. doi:10.1088/1757-899X/1051/1/012005

Coussement, K., Phan, M., De Caigny, A., Benoit, D. F., & Raes, A. (2020). Predicting student dropout in subscription-based online learning environments: The beneficial impact of the logit leaf model. *Decision Support Systems*, *135*, 113325. doi:10.1016/j.dss.2020.113325

Dargan, S., Kumar, M., Ayyagari, M. R., & Kumar, G. (2020). A survey of deep learning and its applications: A new paradigm to machine learning. *Archives of Computational Methods in Engineering*, *27*(4), 1071–1092. doi:10.100711831-019-09344-w

Dhanya, D., Kumar, S. S., Thilagavathy, A., Prasad, D., & Boopathi, S. (2023). Data Analytics and Artificial Intelligence in the Circular Economy: Case Studies. In Intelligent Engineering Applications and Applied Sciences for Sustainability (pp. 40–58). IGI Global.

Durairaj, M., Jayakumar, S., Karpagavalli, V., Maheswari, B. U., Boopathi, S., & ... (2023). Utilization of Digital Tools in the Indian Higher Education System During Health Crises. In *Multidisciplinary Approaches to Organizational Governance During Health Crises* (pp. 1–21). IGI Global. doi:10.4018/978-1-7998-9213-7.ch001

Erarslan, A. (2019). Instagram as an Education Platform for EFL Learners. *Turkish Online Journal of Educational Technology-TOJET*, *18*(3), 54–69.

Goldenberg, S. L., Nir, G., & Salcudean, S. E. (2019). A new era: Artificial intelligence and machine learning in prostate cancer. *Nature Reviews. Urology*, *16*(7), 391–403. doi:10.103841585-019-0193-3 PMID:31092914

Hema, N., Krishnamoorthy, N., Chavan, S. M., Kumar, N., Sabarimuthu, M., & Boopathi, S. (2023). A Study on an Internet of Things (IoT)-Enabled Smart Solar Grid System. In *Handbook of Research on Deep Learning Techniques for Cloud-Based Industrial IoT* (pp. 290–308). IGI Global. doi:10.4018/978-1-6684-8098-4.ch017

Hobert, S. (2019). *Say hello to 'coding tutor'! Design and evaluation of a chatbot-based learning system supporting students to learn to program.*

Ingle, R. B., Senthil, T. S., Swathi, S., Muralidharan, N., Mahendran, G., & Boopathi, S. (2023). Sustainability and Optimization of Green and Lean Manufacturing Processes Using Machine Learning Techniques. IGI Global. doi:10.4018/978-1-6684-8238-4.ch012

Kalidas, R., Boopathi, S., Sivakumar, K., & Mohankumar, P. (2012). Optimization of Machining Parameters of WEDM Process Based On the Taguchi Method. *IJEST, 6*(1).

Karthik, S., Hemalatha, R., Aruna, R., Deivakani, M., Reddy, R. V. K., & Boopathi, S. (2023). Study on Healthcare Security System-Integrated Internet of Things (IoT). In Perspectives and Considerations on the Evolution of Smart Systems (pp. 342–362). IGI Global.

Kavitha, C. R., Varalatchoumy, M., Mithuna, H. R., Bharathi, K., Geethalakshmi, N. M., & Boopathi, S. (2023). Energy Monitoring and Control in the Smart Grid: Integrated Intelligent IoT and ANFIS. In M. Arshad (Ed.), Advances in Bioinformatics and Biomedical Engineering. IGI Global. doi:10.4018/978-1-6684-6577-6.ch014

Kumar, P. R., Meenakshi, S., Shalini, S., Devi, S. R., & Boopathi, S. (2023). Soil Quality Prediction in Context Learning Approaches Using Deep Learning and Blockchain for Smart Agriculture. In R. Kumar, A. B. Abdul Hamid, & N. I. Binti Ya'akub (Eds.), Advances in Computational Intelligence and Robotics. IGI Global. doi:10.4018/978-1-6684-9151-5.ch001

Kumara, V., Mohanaprakash, T., Fairooz, S., Jamal, K., Babu, T., & Sampath, B. (2023). Experimental Study on a Reliable Smart Hydroponics System. In *Human Agro-Energy Optimization for Business and Industry* (pp. 27–45). IGI Global. doi:10.4018/978-1-6684-4118-3.ch002

Kurni, M., Mohammed, M. S., & Srinivasa, K. (2023). Intelligent Tutoring Systems. In *A Beginner's Guide to Introduce Artificial Intelligence in Teaching and Learning* (pp. 29–44). Springer.

Lei, Q.-Q., & Liu, H.-Y. (2020). Design of a WeChat mobile learning platform for multi-modal language learning and its application. *Journal of Physics: Conference Series, 1616*(1), 012085. doi:10.1088/1742-6596/1616/1/012085

Luan, H., & Tsai, C.-C. (2021). A review of using machine learning approaches for precision education. *Journal of Educational Technology & Society, 24*(1), 250–266.

Maguluri, L. P., Arularasan, A. N., & Boopathi, S. (2023). Assessing Security Concerns for AI-Based Drones in Smart Cities. In R. Kumar, A. B. Abdul Hamid, & N. I. Binti Ya'akub (Eds.), (pp. 27–47). Advances in Computational Intelligence and Robotics. IGI Global. doi:10.4018/978-1-6684-9151-5.ch002

Maheswari, B. U., Imambi, S. S., Hasan, D., Meenakshi, S., Pratheep, V., & Boopathi, S. (2023). Internet of Things and Machine Learning-Integrated Smart Robotics. In Global Perspectives on Robotics and Autonomous Systems: Development and Applications (pp. 240–258). IGI Global. doi:10.4018/978-1-6684-7791-5.ch010

Myilsamy, S., & Sampath, B. (2017). Grey Relational Optimization of Powder Mixed Near-Dry Wire Cut Electrical Discharge Machining of Inconel 718 Alloy. *Asian Journal of Research in Social Sciences and Humanities*, *7*(3), 18–25. doi:10.5958/2249-7315.2017.00157.5

Myszczynska, M. A., Ojamies, P. N., Lacoste, A. M., Neil, D., Saffari, A., Mead, R., Hautbergue, G. M., Holbrook, J. D., & Ferraiuolo, L. (2020). Applications of machine learning to diagnosis and treatment of neurodegenerative diseases. *Nature Reviews. Neurology*, *16*(8), 440–456. doi:10.103841582-020-0377-8 PMID:32669685

Nishanth, J., Deshmukh, M. A., Kushwah, R., Kushwaha, K. K., Balaji, S., & Sampath, B. (2023). Particle Swarm Optimization of Hybrid Renewable Energy Systems. In *Intelligent Engineering Applications and Applied Sciences for Sustainability* (pp. 291–308). IGI Global. doi:10.4018/979-8-3693-0044-2.ch016

Olaya, D., Vásquez, J., Maldonado, S., Miranda, J., & Verbeke, W. (2020). Uplift Modeling for preventing student dropout in higher education. *Decision Support Systems*, *134*, 113320. doi:10.1016/j.dss.2020.113320

Ortigosa, A., Carro, R. M., Bravo-Agapito, J., Lizcano, D., Alcolea, J. J., & Blanco, O. (2019). From lab to production: Lessons learnt and real-life challenges of an early student-dropout prevention system. *IEEE Transactions on Learning Technologies*, *12*(2), 264–277. doi:10.1109/TLT.2019.2911608

Pramila, P., Amudha, S., Saravanan, T., Sankar, S. R., Poongothai, E., & Boopathi, S. (2023). Design and Development of Robots for Medical Assistance: An Architectural Approach. In Contemporary Applications of Data Fusion for Advanced Healthcare Informatics (pp. 260–282). IGI Global.

Prasad, P. Y., Prasad, D., Malleswari, D. N., Shetty, M. N., & Gupta, N. (2022). Implementation of Machine Learning Based Google Teachable Machine in Early Childhood Education. *International Journal of Early Childhood Special Education*, *14*(3).

Rahamathunnisa, U., Subhashini, P., Aancy, H. M., Meenakshi, S., Boopathi, S., & ... (2023). Solutions for Software Requirement Risks Using Artificial Intelligence Techniques. In *Handbook of Research on Data Science and Cybersecurity Innovations in Industry 4.0 Technologies* (pp. 45–64). IGI Global.

Rahamathunnisa, U., Sudhakar, K., Murugan, T. K., Thivaharan, S., Rajkumar, M., & Boopathi, S. (2023). Cloud Computing Principles for Optimizing Robot Task Offloading Processes. In *AI-Enabled Social Robotics in Human Care Services* (pp. 188–211). IGI Global. doi:10.4018/978-1-6684-8171-4.ch007

Ramudu, K., Mohan, V. M., Jyothirmai, D., Prasad, D., Agrawal, R., & Boopathi, S. (2023). Machine Learning and Artificial Intelligence in Disease Prediction: Applications, Challenges, Limitations, Case Studies, and Future Directions. In Contemporary Applications of Data Fusion for Advanced Healthcare Informatics (pp. 297–318). IGI Global.

Reddy, M. A., Reddy, B. M., Mukund, C., Venneti, K., Preethi, D., & Boopathi, S. (2023). Social Health Protection During the COVID-Pandemic Using IoT. In *The COVID-19 Pandemic and the Digitalization of Diplomacy* (pp. 204–235). IGI Global. doi:10.4018/978-1-7998-8394-4.ch009

Sampath, B., Sasikumar, C., & Myilsamy, S. (2023). Application of TOPSIS Optimization Technique in the Micro-Machining Process. In IGI: Trends, Paradigms, and Advances in Mechatronics Engineering (pp. 162–187). IGI Global.

Saravanan, M., Vasanth, M., Boopathi, S., Sureshkumar, M., & Haribalaji, V. (2022). Optimization of Quench Polish Quench (QPQ) Coating Process Using Taguchi Method. *Key Engineering Materials*, *935*, 83–91. doi:10.4028/p-z569vy

Sendak, M., Elish, M. C., Gao, M., Futoma, J., Ratliff, W., Nichols, M., Bedoya, A., Balu, S., & O'Brien, C. (2020). "The human body is a black box" supporting clinical decision-making with deep learning. *Proceedings of the 2020 Conference on Fairness, Accountability, and Transparency*, (pp. 99–109). ACM. 10.1145/3351095.3372827

Srinivas, B., Maguluri, L. P., Naidu, K. V., Reddy, L. C. S., Deivakani, M., & Boopathi, S. (2023). Architecture and Framework for Interfacing Cloud-Enabled Robots. In *Handbook of Research on Data Science and Cybersecurity Innovations in Industry 4.0 Technologies* (pp. 542–560). IGI Global. doi:10.4018/978-1-6684-8145-5.ch027

Syamala, M., Komala, C., Pramila, P., Dash, S., Meenakshi, S., & Boopathi, S. (2023). Machine Learning-Integrated IoT-Based Smart Home Energy Management System. In *Handbook of Research on Deep Learning Techniques for Cloud-Based Industrial IoT* (pp. 219–235). IGI Global. doi:10.4018/978-1-6684-8098-4.ch013

Ugandar, R. E., Rahamathunnisa, U., Sajithra, S., Christiana, M. B. V., Palai, B. K., & Boopathi, S. (2023). Hospital Waste Management Using Internet of Things and Deep Learning: Enhanced Efficiency and Sustainability. In M. Arshad (Ed.), (pp. 317–343). Advances in Bioinformatics and Biomedical Engineering. IGI Global. doi:10.4018/978-1-6684-6577-6.ch015

Vamathevan, J., Clark, D., Czodrowski, P., Dunham, I., Ferran, E., Lee, G., Li, B., Madabhushi, A., Shah, P., Spitzer, M., & Zhao, S. (2019). Applications of machine learning in drug discovery and development. *Nature Reviews. Drug Discovery*, *18*(6), 463–477. doi:10.103841573-019-0024-5 PMID:30976107

Vartiainen, H. (2022). *Cross-boundary co-design for learning machine learning.* AI, Data Science, and Young People. Understanding Computing Education.

Veeranjaneyulu, R., Boopathi, S., Kumari, R. K., Vidyarthi, A., Isaac, J. S., & Jaiganesh, V. (2023). Air Quality Improvement and Optimisation Using Machine Learning Technique. *IEEE- Explore*, 1–6.

Venkateswaran, N., Kumar, S. S., Diwakar, G., Gnanasangeetha, D., & Boopathi, S. (2023). Synthetic Biology for Waste Water to Energy Conversion: IoT and AI Approaches. In M. Arshad (Ed.), (pp. 360–384). Advances in Bioinformatics and Biomedical Engineering. IGI Global. doi:10.4018/978-1-6684-6577-6.ch017

Vennila, T., Karuna, M., Srivastava, B. K., Venugopal, J., Surakasi, R., & Sampath, B. (2022). New Strategies in Treatment and Enzymatic Processes: Ethanol Production From Sugarcane Bagasse. In Human Agro-Energy Optimization for Business and Industry (pp. 219–240). IGI Global.

Wang, T., Li, S., Huang, X., Pan, Z., & Lajoie, S. P. (2023). Examining students' cognitive load in the context of self-regulated learning with an intelligent tutoring system. *Education and Information Technologies*, *28*(5), 5697–5715. doi:10.100710639-022-11357-1 PMID:36373050

Winkler-Schwartz, A., Bissonnette, V., Mirchi, N., Ponnudurai, N., Yilmaz, R., Ledwos, N., Siyar, S., Azarnoush, H., Karlik, B., & Del Maestro, R. F. (2019a). Artificial intelligence in medical education: Best practices using machine learning to assess surgical expertise in virtual reality simulation. *Journal of Surgical Education*, *76*(6), 1681–1690. doi:10.1016/j.jsurg.2019.05.015 PMID:31202633

Winkler-Schwartz, A., Bissonnette, V., Mirchi, N., Ponnudurai, N., Yilmaz, R., Ledwos, N., Siyar, S., Azarnoush, H., Karlik, B., & Del Maestro, R. F. (2019b). Artificial intelligence in medical education: Best practices using machine learning to assess surgical expertise in virtual reality simulation. *Journal of Surgical Education*, *76*(6), 1681–1690. doi:10.1016/j.jsurg.2019.05.015 PMID:31202633

Yang, Y., & Bao, W. (2023). Application of Human-Computer Interaction Technology in Remote Language Learning Platform. *International Journal of Human-Computer Interaction*, 1–11. doi:10.1080/10447318.2023.2194709

Zatarain Cabada, R., Rodriguez Rangel, H., Barron Estrada, M. L., & Cardenas Lopez, H. M. (2020). Hyperparameter optimization in CNN for learning-centered emotion recognition for intelligent tutoring systems. *Soft Computing*, *24*(10), 7593–7602. doi:10.100700500-019-04387-4

Zekrifa, D. M. S., Kulkarni, M., Bhagyalakshmi, A., Devireddy, N., Gupta, S., & Boopathi, S. (2023). Integrating Machine Learning and AI for Improved Hydrological Modeling and Water Resource Management. In *Artificial Intelligence Applications in Water Treatment and Water Resource Management* (pp. 46–70). IGI Global. doi:10.4018/978-1-6684-6791-6.ch003

# Chapter 3
# Fostering Sustainability Education Through Cross-Disciplinary Collaborations and Research Partnerships:
## Interdisciplinary Synergy

**Simanchala Das**
https://orcid.org/0000-0001-6230-0461
*K L Business School, Koneru Lakshmaiah Education Foundation, India*

**Gudla Lekhya**
https://orcid.org/0009-0009-4105-0657
*K L Business School, Koneru Lakshmaiah Education Foundation, India*

**Kodukula Shreya**
*K L Business School, Koneru Lakshmaiah Education Foundation, India*

**Karyamsetty Lydia Shekinah**
*K L Business School, Koneru Lakshmaiah Education Foundation, India*

**Katuri Khadar Babu**
*K L Business School, Koneru Lakshmaiah Education Foundation, India*

**Sampath Boopathi**
https://orcid.org/0000-0002-2065-6539
*Mechanical Engineering, Muthayammal Engineering College, India*

DOI: 10.4018/979-8-3693-0487-7.ch003

## ABSTRACT

*This book chapter delves into the essential principles and empirical research surrounding cross-disciplinary collaborations and partnerships in the realm of sustainability education. It explores how the convergence of diverse academic disciplines can synergistically advance sustainability education, creating a holistic learning environment that addresses complex global challenges. Through case studies and theoretical frameworks, this chapter sheds light on the fundamentals of establishing successful cross-disciplinary collaborations and offers insights into their pedagogical and research dimensions. By examining the interplay between various disciplines and their contributions to sustainability education, this chapter contributes to the broader discourse on innovative educational approaches for a more sustainable future.*

## INTRODUCTION

Sustainability education has evolved from early environmental awareness in the 1960s and 1970s to a broader understanding in the 1980s and 1990s. Recognizing sustainability as a global challenge, climate change awareness, and the adoption of the United Nations Sustainable Development Goals in 2015, interdisciplinary approaches have emerged. The Earth Charter and the Decade of Education for Sustainable Development have marked milestones, but challenges remain, including integration, addressing global inequalities, promoting behavioral change, and ensuring effective SDG implementation(Ganapathy et al., 2021; Tebeje & Klein, 2021).

The need for a sustainable future is crucial in a world marked by global challenges like climate change, resource depletion, and social inequality. Achieving sustainability is a multifaceted endeavor that requires cross-disciplinary collaborations and partnerships. Sustainability education aims to equip individuals with the knowledge, skills, and values to tackle these complex issues (Nurius & Kemp, 2019a). This chapter introduces the concept of sustainability education, emphasizing its importance as a societal imperative. It provides an overview of the fundamental issues and lays the groundwork for future chapters. Sustainability education equips learners with the tools to understand the interconnectedness of environmental, social, and economic systems, enabling them to make informed decisions that contribute to a more sustainable world (Cañabate et al., 2020a). As sustainability challenges become increasingly urgent, the role of education in addressing these challenges cannot be overstated.

The complexity of sustainability challenges requires approaches that transcend disciplinary boundaries. No single discipline possesses all the answers or solutions.

Cross-disciplinary collaborations and partnerships provide a bridge between diverse fields of knowledge, fostering creativity, innovation, and holistic problem-solving. Through this collaborative lens, we explore how sustainability education can harness the collective expertise of academia, industry, communities, and international networks(Pennington, 2008).

Strengthening education is crucial for individual, community, and societal growth. It involves a holistic approach, focusing on teacher quality, curriculum updates, equitable access, early childhood education, parental and community involvement, fair assessment, accountability measures, and inclusive education for students with special needs. Immediate attention is needed to ensure equitable access, foster early childhood education, and promote fair assessment. Adequate funding, research and innovation in education, a global perspective, and civic education are all crucial elements. Moreover, prioritizing the mental health and well-being of students and teachers, offering continuous professional development, and integrating education technology into the classroom are essential to strengthening the core of education. Public awareness and advocacy play a pivotal role in garnering support and resources for this endeavor. To achieve these goals, it is essential for governments, communities, and individuals to make a sustained commitment to improving the education system in its entirety. In this section, you will provide the readers with an understanding of the broader context in which sustainability education and cross-disciplinary collaborations exist(Feeney et al., 2023a; Wu, 2022). Research in sustainability education is crucial for enhancing the fundamentals of education, preparing students to become environmentally responsible, socially conscious, and economically informed citizens through a wide range of topics and approaches. The importance and components of research in education for sustainability are explain below:

Sustainability education raises awareness about environmental issues like climate change, biodiversity loss, pollution, and resource depletion. Research helps educators convey these issues effectively to students. Sustainable development is a core concept, focusing on equipping students with knowledge and skills to balance economic growth, social well-being, and environmental preservation. This includes teaching renewable energy, responsible consumption, and sustainable agriculture. Research helps identify best practices for integrating sustainability principles into various subjects, making it a cross-curricular endeavor. Experiential learning in sustainability education is gaining popularity due to its ability to deepen students' understanding of the natural world and sustainability challenges. This approach often includes a global perspective, fostering a sense of global citizenship and collaboration. Sustainability education also emphasizes systems thinking, understanding the interconnections between ecological, economic, and social systems. Research aids educators in developing teaching methods that foster these skills(Agrawal et al., 2023; Durairaj et al., 2023).

Sustainability education promotes critical thinking and problem-solving skills in students, enabling them to analyze complex sustainability issues and propose solutions. Research focuses on the psychology of behavior change and how education can influence students to adopt sustainable behaviors like recycling, conserving energy, and reducing waste. To effectively implement sustainability education, teacher training programs are developed, and research focuses on assessing students' understanding and evaluating the effectiveness of sustainability education programs. Additionally, research explores how schools can engage with local communities to address sustainability challenges together(Hussain & Srimathy, 2023; Ingle et al., 2023; Venkateswaran et al., 2023). Research in sustainability education influences policy development and advocacy efforts, ensuring its integration into national and regional curricula. Interdisciplinary research from fields like environmental science, psychology, sociology, and economics benefits this field. Collaboration between researchers is crucial for developing a holistic approach. Long-term impact assessment is essential, tracking individuals' behaviors and attitudes to determine the lasting influence of sustainability education.

Research in sustainability education is crucial for preparing future generations to tackle global challenges. It offers insights into effective teaching methods, curriculum design, and behavioral change strategies, fostering responsible, informed, and engaged global citizens committed to a sustainable future.

## Purpose and Significance of the Chapter

*Primary Objective:* The primary objective of this chapter is to examine the pivotal role of cross-disciplinary collaborations in advancing sustainability education. It aims to shed light on the transformative potential of interdisciplinary and transdisciplinary approaches in addressing complex sustainability challenges and preparing individuals for a sustainable future.

Specific Questions or Issues:

- **Exploring the Essence of Cross-Disciplinary Collaboration:** The chapter delves into what cross-disciplinary collaboration means in the context of sustainability education, emphasizing its importance in fostering a holistic understanding of sustainability issues(Marsili, 2016).
- **Assessing the Benefits and Challenges:** It addresses the benefits and challenges associated with cross-disciplinary collaborations in sustainability education, providing insights into how to harness its advantages and mitigate potential obstacles.

- **Highlighting Pedagogical Innovations:** The chapter highlights pedagogical innovations and best practices that promote cross-disciplinary learning, including curriculum integration, experiential learning, and the use of technology.
- **Empirical Insights:** It reviews empirical research findings on cross-disciplinary sustainability education, showcasing the impact of such collaborations on students, educators, and the broader community.

***Relevance in the Context of Current Trends:*** This chapter is highly relevant in the context of current trends and discussions in sustainability education. With global challenges like climate change, biodiversity loss, and social inequality becoming increasingly urgent, there is a growing recognition that conventional disciplinary approaches are insufficient(Ding et al., 2020). The sustainability field is evolving toward a more integrated and comprehensive framework, and cross-disciplinary collaborations are at the forefront of this evolution.

***Potential Impact:*** The potential impact of this chapter is significant for several reasons:

- **Educators:** It offers educators practical insights into designing and implementing cross-disciplinary sustainability education programs, enhancing their ability to prepare students for a world that demands interdisciplinary problem-solving skills(Morales et al., 2023).
- **Researchers:** Researchers in the field of sustainability education will gain a deeper understanding of the empirical findings and best practices associated with cross-disciplinary collaborations, informing their future studies and projects.
- **Policymakers:** Policymakers will find valuable insights into how to support and promote cross-disciplinary sustainability education within formal educational systems, ensuring that educational policies align with the needs of a rapidly changing world.
- **Students and Learners:** Ultimately, this chapter benefits students and learners by providing them with a more enriched and effective educational experience, equipping them with the knowledge and skills needed to contribute to a sustainable future.

# FOUNDATIONS OF SUSTAINABILITY EDUCATION

## Definition and Scope of Sustainability Education

### Defining Sustainability Education

**Sustainability as a Multidimensional Concept:** Discuss the environmental, social, and economic dimensions of sustainability. Explain the interconnectedness of these dimensions.

**Defining Sustainability Education:** Provide a clear and comprehensive definition of sustainability education. Emphasize its role in fostering awareness, knowledge, skills, and values related to sustainability.

### The Scope of Sustainability Education

**Formal and Informal Education Settings:** Explore how sustainability education occurs within traditional educational institutions (schools, colleges, universities). Highlight the importance of informal education settings (community groups, NGOs, online platforms).

**Lifelong Learning and Sustainability:** Discuss the concept of lifelong learning and how sustainability education is relevant across one's entire life. Address the idea of continuous personal and professional development in sustainability.

**Sustainability Across Educational Levels:** Examine sustainability education at different levels, from primary and secondary education (K-12) to higher education. Highlight the varying approaches and curriculum integration at each level(Feeney et al., 2023a; Wu, 2022).

## Importance of Sustainability Education

### Addressing Global Challenges

**Environmental Challenges:** Describe major global environmental challenges such as climate change, biodiversity loss, and resource depletion. Explain how sustainability education contributes to addressing these challenges(Ding et al., 2020).

**Social and Economic Challenges:** Discuss social inequalities, poverty, and economic disparities as global challenges. Showcase how sustainability education promotes equity, social justice, and economic stability.

### Developing Sustainable Mindsets

**Environmental Consciousness:** Highlight the role of sustainability education in developing an understanding of environmental issues and responsibilities. Discuss the cultivation of a sense of ecological citizenship.

**Empowering Sustainable Choices:** Explain how sustainability education empowers individuals to make sustainable choices in their daily lives. Provide examples of sustainable behaviors and decision-making processes.

### Preparing Future Leaders

**Shaping Future Leaders and Professionals:** Emphasize how sustainability education shapes the mindset and skill set of future leaders, innovators, and professionals. Discuss the demand for sustainability expertise in various fields(Marsili, 2016).

**Critical Thinking and Problem-Solving:** Highlight how sustainability education fosters critical thinking, systems thinking, and problem-solving skills. Explain the relevance of these skills in addressing complex sustainability challenges.

## Evolution of Sustainability Education

### Historical Perspective

**Early Roots of Sustainability Education:** Trace the historical origins of sustainability education, including environmental education movements. Discuss the emergence of sustainable development concepts.

**Key Milestones in Development:** Highlight key events and milestones in the development of sustainability education over the decades. Identify influential figures and organizations in the field.

## Current Paradigms and Approaches

**Contemporary Approaches to Sustainability Education:** Explain different pedagogical approaches to sustainability education, such as experiential learning, systems thinking, and place-based education. Showcase innovative teaching methods and strategies.

**Interdisciplinary and Transdisciplinary Trends:** Discuss the shift towards interdisciplinary and transdisciplinary approaches in sustainability education. Provide examples of collaborative efforts between various academic disciplines.

## Challenges and Opportunities

**Challenges in Implementing Sustainability Education**: Identify common challenges faced in integrating sustainability into curricula and educational systems. Discuss issues related to resource constraints, resistance to change, and curriculum design.

**Opportunities for Innovation**: Highlight opportunities for innovation and improvement in sustainability education. Explore the role of technology, international cooperation, and community engagement in advancing sustainability education.

This detailed breakdown offers a comprehensive overview of the "Foundations of Sustainability Education" section, covering the definition, scope, importance, and evolution of sustainability education in depth.

# CROSS-DISCIPLINARY COLLABORATIONS: CONCEPTS AND PRINCIPLES

Cross-disciplinary collaborations involve individuals or teams from different academic or professional backgrounds working together to address complex problems or research questions that cannot be adequately tackled within the confines of a single discipline (Figure 1). These collaborations aim to leverage the diverse expertise, perspectives, and methodologies of multiple disciplines to achieve more holistic and innovative solutions. Here, we'll discuss the concepts, principles, benefits, challenges, and theoretical frameworks associated with cross-disciplinary collaboration(Ferraro et al., 2021).

Understanding Cross-Disciplinary Collaboration:

- **Interdisciplinary vs. Multidisciplinary vs. Transdisciplinary:** These terms are often used interchangeably, but they have subtle differences. Interdisciplinary collaboration involves integrating insights and methods from different disciplines without necessarily merging them. Multidisciplinary collaboration involves multiple disciplines working on a common problem but maintaining their separate approaches. Transdisciplinary collaboration goes beyond this by creating a shared framework that transcends individual disciplines(Cobbaert et al., 2021).
- **Holistic Problem Solving:** Cross-disciplinary collaboration aims to tackle complex, real-world problems by considering their multifaceted nature. It seeks to go beyond reductionist approaches by examining problems from multiple angles.

*Figure 1. Cross-disciplinary collaborations: concepts and principles*

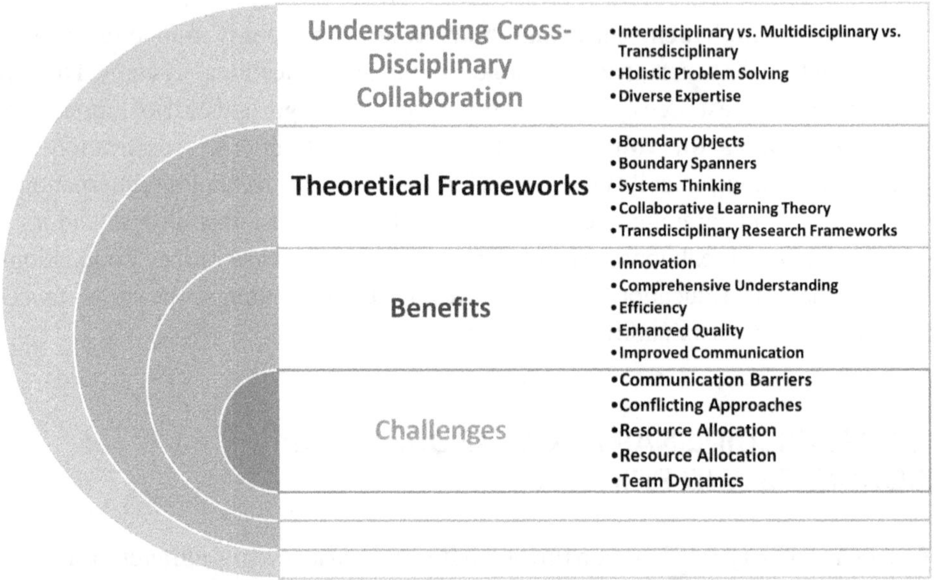


- **Diverse Expertise:** It brings together experts from various fields, such as science, engineering, social sciences, and humanities, to address complex issues.

Benefits of Cross-Disciplinary Collaboration:

- **Innovation:** Diverse perspectives often lead to more creative and innovative solutions(Desai et al., 2021).
- **Comprehensive Understanding:** It offers a broader and deeper understanding of complex issues by drawing from multiple viewpoints.
- **Efficiency:** Combining expertise can expedite problem-solving and research processes.
- **Enhanced Quality:** Cross-disciplinary collaborations can lead to higher-quality research and outcomes.
- **Improved Communication:** It fosters effective communication and collaboration skills among team members.

Challenges of Cross-Disciplinary Collaboration:

- **Communication Barriers:** Different disciplines have their own jargon and terminology, making effective communication challenging(Urbano & Ardanuy, 2020).
- **Conflicting Approaches:** Differing methodologies, paradigms, and goals can lead to conflicts within the team.
- **Resource Allocation:** Coordinating resources, funding, and time across disciplines can be complex.
- **Team Dynamics:** Managing diverse personalities, expectations, and work styles can be challenging.

Theoretical Frameworks for Cross-Disciplinary Work:

- **Boundary Objects:** These are objects, concepts, or frameworks that serve as a common ground for different disciplines to collaborate. They facilitate communication and understanding across disciplines(Reinholz & Andrews, 2019).
- **Boundary Spanners:** Individuals or roles that bridge the gap between disciplines, translating concepts and mediating between team members from different backgrounds.
- **Systems Thinking:** This approach considers the entire system as interconnected, emphasizing the need for a holistic view when solving complex problems.
- **Collaborative Learning Theory:** It emphasizes the importance of shared learning experiences to foster cross-disciplinary collaboration.
- **Transdisciplinary Research Frameworks:** Frameworks like the Three Horizons Model or the Integration and Implementation Sciences (i2S) framework provide structured approaches for transdisciplinary collaboration.

Cross-disciplinary collaboration is increasingly vital in our rapidly evolving world, where many challenges require multifaceted solutions. To succeed in cross-disciplinary work, it's essential to establish clear communication channels, build trust, and leverage the strengths of each discipline while addressing the challenges that may arise.

## RESEARCH IN SUSTAINABILITY EDUCATION

Sustainability education is a critical component of addressing the global challenges related to environmental conservation, social equity, and economic stability (Figure 2). Research plays a pivotal role in advancing sustainability education by informing pedagogical practices, policy development, and community engagement(Nurius & Kemp, 2019b).

*Figure 2. Research in sustainability education*

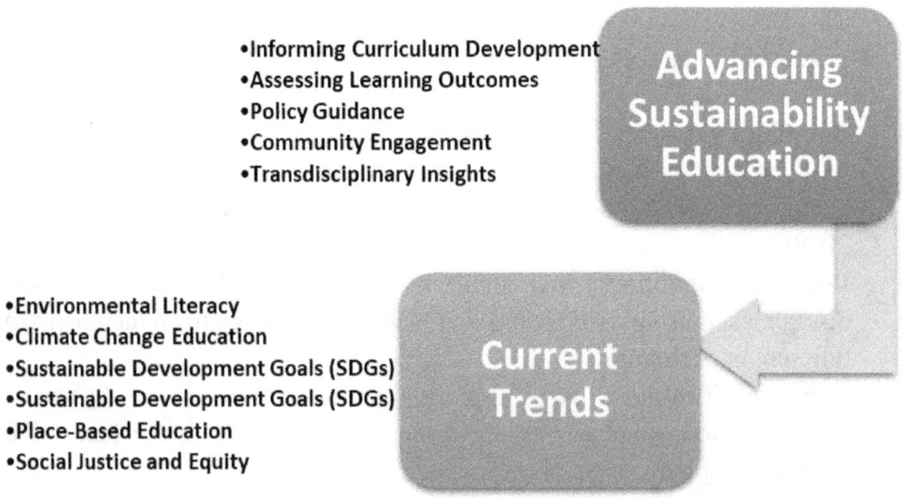


Advancing Sustainability Education:

- **Informing Curriculum Development:** Research helps in designing curricula that incorporate sustainability concepts and principles across disciplines and educational levels(Nurius & Kemp, 2019b).
- **Assessing Learning Outcomes:** Research evaluates the effectiveness of sustainability education programs in fostering knowledge, skills, and attitudes conducive to sustainable practices.
- **Policy Guidance:** Research findings can influence educational policies, advocating for the integration of sustainability into formal education systems.
- **Community Engagement:** Research can guide community-based sustainability initiatives and inform outreach and engagement strategies.

- **Transdisciplinary Insights:** Sustainability education research often involves interdisciplinary or transdisciplinary approaches to address complex issues.

Current Trends in Education Research:

- **Environmental Literacy:** Research focuses on improving individuals' understanding of environmental issues and their ability to make informed decisions(De Bakker et al., 2019).
- **Climate Change Education:** Investigating effective strategies for teaching about climate change and its impacts on ecosystems and societies.
- **Sustainable Development Goals (SDGs):** Exploring how to integrate the United Nations' SDGs into educational curricula and assessing their impact.
- **Place-Based Education:** Emphasizing local context and community involvement to make sustainability education more relevant and engaging.
- **Social Justice and Equity:** Examining the intersection of sustainability education with social justice, equity, and inclusion.
- **Experiential Learning:** Researching the effectiveness of hands-on, real-world experiences in fostering sustainability awareness and action.

*Figure 3. Methodologies for studying sustainability education*

## METHODOLOGIES FOR STUDYING SUSTAINABILITY EDUCATION

Studying sustainability education requires a thoughtful selection of research methodologies that align with the research objectives, questions, and the context of the study (Figure 3). Here are some common methodologies used in researching sustainability education(Wu, 2022):

- **Surveys and Questionnaires:** Surveys and questionnaires are useful for collecting quantitative data on various aspects of sustainability education, such as knowledge acquisition, attitudes, and behaviors. Researchers can design surveys to assess the impact of sustainability education programs on students' perceptions and actions.
- **Interviews:** Qualitative interviews provide in-depth insights into individuals' experiences and perspectives related to sustainability education. Researchers can conduct one-on-one or group interviews with students, educators, or stakeholders to explore their attitudes, motivations, and challenges.
- **Focus Groups:** Focus group discussions involve small groups of participants who engage in structured discussions about sustainability education topics. This method can uncover shared beliefs, attitudes, and concerns within a group and provide insights into collective opinions.
- **Case Studies:** Case studies involve in-depth examinations of specific sustainability education programs, courses, or initiatives. Researchers gather data through various sources, including interviews, observations, and document analysis, to understand the program's context, implementation, and impact.
- **Content Analysis:** Content analysis involves systematically analyzing documents, textbooks, curricula, and educational materials to assess the presence and depth of sustainability content. This method can reveal trends in sustainability education and changes over time.
- **Observations:** Observational research involves systematically observing and recording behaviors, interactions, and learning processes in educational settings. Researchers can use this method to study how sustainability is taught and learned in practice.
- **Longitudinal Studies:** Longitudinal research tracks participants over an extended period to assess changes in knowledge, attitudes, and behaviors related to sustainability education. This method can reveal the long-term impact of sustainability education programs.

- **Mixed Methods Research:** Combining qualitative and quantitative methods allows researchers to gain a comprehensive understanding of sustainability education. For example, a study might use surveys to quantify knowledge gain and interviews to explore students' motivations and experiences.
- **Action Research:** Action research involves collaborative, participatory research within educational settings. Educators and researchers work together to identify and address sustainability-related challenges, implementing and evaluating interventions to improve sustainability education.
- **Experimental and Control Groups:** Experimental designs involve randomly assigning participants to experimental (exposed to sustainability education) and control (not exposed) groups. Comparing the outcomes of these groups helps assess the impact of sustainability education interventions.
- **Network Analysis:** Network analysis examines the relationships and interactions among individuals, organizations, or institutions involved in sustainability education. It can help understand the dynamics of collaborative efforts and knowledge dissemination within the field.
- **Ethnographic Research:** Ethnography involves immersive, field-based research in educational settings. Researchers participate in the learning environment to gain an insider's perspective and understand the cultural aspects of sustainability education.

The choice of methodology should align with the research objectives, questions, and available resources. Often, a combination of methods is most effective in providing a comprehensive understanding of sustainability education and its impact on individuals, institutions, and society as a whole. Effective sustainability education research requires collaboration among educators, researchers, policymakers, and communities. It should be responsive to local and global challenges, engage diverse stakeholders, and continually adapt to evolving sustainability issues. By advancing our understanding of how sustainability education works and its impact, research contributes to building a more sustainable future.

## CASE STUDIES OF SUCCESSFUL COLLABORATIONS

### Case Study One: Interdisciplinary Sustainability Programs in Higher Education

*Background:* In recent years, universities have recognized the importance of interdisciplinary sustainability programs to equip students with the knowledge and skills needed for a sustainable future. One exemplary case is the "Sustainable Futures Program" at Green University (a pseudonym)(Menon & Suresh, 2020).

Key Elements:

- **Interdisciplinary Curriculum:** The program offers a comprehensive curriculum that blends courses from environmental science, economics, sociology, and urban planning, emphasizing the interconnectedness of sustainability issues.
- **Student Involvement:** Students are encouraged to engage in hands-on sustainability projects within and outside the university, fostering experiential learning and community engagement.
- **Faculty Collaboration:** Faculty members from diverse disciplines collaborate on course design and co-teaching, ensuring a holistic educational experience.

Success Factors:

- **Interdisciplinary Approach:** By integrating perspectives from multiple disciplines, students gain a deeper understanding of sustainability issues and develop well-rounded problem-solving skills(Hermann & Bossle, 2020).
- **Experiential Learning:** The program's emphasis on real-world projects empowers students to apply their knowledge and make a tangible impact on sustainability challenges.
- **Community Partnerships:** Collaborations with local organizations provide students with opportunities to engage in sustainability initiatives, benefiting both the community and the university.

## Case Study Two: Community Engagement Initiatives for Sustainability

*Background:* The "Green Communities Project" in Townville is an example of a successful community-driven sustainability initiative that collaborates with local residents, businesses, and governmental organizations(Van den Beemt et al., 2020).

Key Elements:

- **Community Participation:** The project actively involves residents in decision-making processes, encouraging them to identify and address sustainability issues in their neighborhoods.
- **Public-Private Partnerships:** The initiative collaborates with local businesses and the town government to implement sustainable practices, such as energy-efficient lighting and waste reduction.

- **Education and Outreach:** The project conducts educational workshops, community events, and online resources to raise awareness and build sustainability literacy.

Success Factors:

- **Ownership and Empowerment:** Community members take ownership of sustainability initiatives, leading to long-lasting changes and a sense of pride in their achievements(Žalėnienė & Pereira, 2021).
- **Collaborative Governance:** Collaboration among various stakeholders ensures a more comprehensive and effective approach to sustainability.
- **Education Component:** By educating residents about sustainability, the project creates a culture of environmental responsibility.

## Case Study Three: Collaborative Research Projects in Sustainability Education

*Background:* The "Sustainable Education Research Consortium" (SERC) is a collaboration among multiple universities and research institutions dedicated to advancing sustainability education through research(Žalėnienė & Pereira, 2021).

Key Elements:

- **Interinstitutional Collaboration:** SERC brings together researchers from various institutions, fostering cross-pollination of ideas and expertise.
- **Longitudinal Studies:** The consortium conducts longitudinal studies to track the impact of sustainability education on students' knowledge, attitudes, and behaviors over time.
- **Diverse Methodologies:** Researchers employ mixed-method approaches, combining surveys, interviews, and observational data to gain a comprehensive understanding of sustainability education outcomes.

Success Factors:

- **Cross-Institutional Learning:** Collaboration across institutions enhances the rigor and breadth of sustainability education research(Ramísio et al., 2019).
- **Evidence-Based Practices:** Findings from SERC studies inform evidence-based practices in sustainability education, helping educators refine their approaches.

- **Long-Term Impact:** Longitudinal research reveals the enduring effects of sustainability education, informing policy decisions and shaping the field's future direction.

The case studies demonstrate successful collaborations in sustainability education, highlighting the significance of interdisciplinary programs, community engagement, and evidence-based practices in advancing sustainability education and promoting a more sustainable future, highlighting the importance of community involvement.

## PEDAGOGICAL INNOVATIONS IN CROSS-DISCIPLINARY SUSTAINABILITY EDUCATION

Integrating Sustainability Across Curricula:

- **Cross-Curricular Integration:** Instead of teaching sustainability as a standalone subject, educational institutions are integrating sustainability concepts and practices across various disciplines. For example, math classes can explore sustainability-related data analysis, while literature courses may examine environmental themes in literature(López et al., 2021).
- **Interdisciplinary Courses:** Developing interdisciplinary courses that bring together students and faculty from different academic backgrounds to address complex sustainability challenges. These courses encourage students to apply diverse knowledge and perspectives to real-world problems.
- **Global Perspective:** Fostering a global perspective by incorporating international case studies and examples, helping students understand the interconnectedness of sustainability issues on a global scale.

Experiential Learning Approaches:

- **Service Learning:** Incorporating service learning projects into the curriculum, where students actively engage with communities to address sustainability issues. For example, students may work with local organizations on conservation projects or sustainability initiatives(Menon & Suresh, 2020).
- **Field Studies:** Field studies and immersive experiences allow students to connect theory with practice. Students might visit sustainable farms, renewable energy facilities, or ecological reserves to observe sustainability principles in action.

- **Simulations and Role-Playing:** Simulations and role-playing exercises can immerse students in complex sustainability scenarios, requiring them to make decisions and understand the consequences of their choices.
- **Internships and Co-op Programs:** Collaborating with organizations to offer internships and cooperative education programs that provide students with hands-on experience in sustainability-related roles.

Technology and Sustainability Education:

- **Online Learning Platforms:** Utilizing online platforms and resources to deliver sustainability education to a broader audience. Online courses and modules make sustainability education more accessible and flexible(De Bakker et al., 2019).
- **Virtual Reality (VR) and Augmented Reality (AR):** VR and AR technologies can immerse students in virtual environments where they can explore sustainable solutions, such as sustainable architecture or renewable energy installations.
- **Data Analytics:** Teaching students how to use data analytics tools to analyze sustainability data, make informed decisions, and monitor the impact of sustainability initiatives.
- **Educational Apps and Gamification:** Developing educational apps and games that teach sustainability concepts through interactive and engaging experiences. Gamification can make learning fun and encourage active participation.
- **Remote Collaboration Tools:** Leveraging remote collaboration tools to connect students from different locations and foster cross-disciplinary discussions and projects related to sustainability.

Pedagogical innovations in cross-disciplinary sustainability education aim to make learning more engaging, relevant, and accessible. By integrating sustainability across curricula, embracing experiential learning approaches, and leveraging technology, educational institutions can equip students with the knowledge and skills needed to address the complex sustainability challenges of the 21st century. These innovations empower students to become effective change agents in creating a more sustainable world.

## EMPIRICAL RESEARCH ON CROSS-DISCIPLINARY SUSTAINABILITY EDUCATION

Empirical Research on Cross-Disciplinary Sustainability Education:

- **Improved Knowledge Integration:** Empirical studies have consistently shown that cross-disciplinary sustainability education enhances students' ability to integrate knowledge from various disciplines. This integration is crucial for addressing complex sustainability challenges.(Neville et al., 2023a)
- **Interpersonal Skills:** Research indicates that cross-disciplinary collaboration in sustainability education enhances students' interpersonal skills, including communication, teamwork, and conflict resolution. These skills are vital for effective sustainability problem-solving in diverse teams.
- **Attitude and Behavior Change:** Studies suggest that cross-disciplinary sustainability education can positively influence students' attitudes and behaviors towards sustainability. It fosters a sense of responsibility and a commitment to sustainable practices in both personal and professional life.
- **Experiential Learning Impact:** Empirical evidence highlights the effectiveness of experiential learning approaches, such as service learning and internships, in reinforcing sustainability concepts and inspiring students to become active sustainability advocates.
- **Long-Term Impact:** Longitudinal research reveals that the effects of cross-disciplinary sustainability education can endure beyond the classroom. Graduates tend to maintain their sustainability-related behaviors and continue to engage in sustainability efforts.

Challenges and Opportunities in Conducting Research:

- **Data Collection and Measurement:** Gathering data on complex constructs like interdisciplinary collaboration and sustainability behavior change can be challenging. Researchers often grapple with developing valid and reliable measurement tools(Neville et al., 2023b).
- **Interdisciplinary Coordination:** Conducting research across multiple disciplines requires coordination and cooperation among researchers from diverse backgrounds. Bridging disciplinary gaps can be time-consuming and resource-intensive.
- **Ethical Considerations:** Research in sustainability education often involves working with vulnerable populations and addressing ethical concerns, such as informed consent, especially when conducting studies with students.

- **Longitudinal Research:** Following students over an extended period can be logistically challenging. Attrition and changing circumstances can affect the validity of longitudinal studies.
- **Generalization:** The context-specific nature of sustainability education makes it challenging to generalize research findings across different institutions, cultures, and educational settings.

Implications for Future Studies:

- **Further Longitudinal Research:** Future research should continue to explore the long-term effects of cross-disciplinary sustainability education to understand how it shapes graduates' careers, lifestyles, and continued engagement in sustainability efforts(Neville et al., 2023b).
- **Qualitative Research:** In-depth qualitative studies can provide insights into the experiential aspects of cross-disciplinary sustainability education, shedding light on students' transformative learning experiences.
- **Comparative Studies:** Comparative research across institutions and regions can help identify best practices and effective pedagogical approaches that can be adapted to different contexts.
- **Assessment of Transdisciplinary Skills:** Research should focus on developing and validating assessment tools to measure transdisciplinary skills and competencies acquired through sustainability education.
- **Impact on Diverse Student Populations:** Investigating how cross-disciplinary sustainability education affects students from various backgrounds, including underrepresented groups, is essential to ensure inclusivity and equity in sustainability education.
- **Cross-Cultural Studies:** Comparative research involving diverse cultural contexts can provide insights into how cultural factors influence the effectiveness of cross-disciplinary sustainability education.

Empirical research in cross-disciplinary sustainability education continues to evolve, contributing to our understanding of how to best prepare students for the complex sustainability challenges of the future. Addressing the challenges and seizing opportunities in this field can lead to more effective educational practices and ultimately contribute to a more sustainable world.

## INTERDISCIPLINARY SYNERGY FOR SUSTAINABLE DEVELOPMENT

The Role of Cross-Disciplinary Collaboration in Addressing Global Challenges:

Cross-disciplinary collaboration is essential for addressing complex global challenges related to sustainable development(Farrukh et al., 2020). Here's why:

- **Complexity of Issues:** Global challenges, such as climate change, poverty, and biodiversity loss, are multifaceted and interconnected. No single discipline can provide comprehensive solutions.
- **Innovative Solutions:** Collaboration among diverse disciplines fosters creativity and innovation, leading to novel approaches to longstanding problems.
- **Holistic Understanding:** Interdisciplinary research enables a more holistic understanding of global challenges by considering their economic, social, environmental, and cultural dimensions.
- **Effective Policy and Implementation:** Solutions to global challenges often require the development and implementation of policies and practices that draw from various fields of expertise.

Contributions of Different Disciplines to Sustainability:

- **Natural Sciences:** Natural sciences contribute to understanding the physical and biological systems that underpin sustainability. For example, biology informs conservation efforts, while chemistry can help develop clean energy technologies(Feeney et al., 2023b).
- **Social Sciences:** Social sciences provide insights into human behavior, societal structures, and governance mechanisms. Psychology and sociology help us understand how to motivate sustainable behaviors, and economics informs sustainable development policies.
- **Engineering and Technology:** Engineers and technologists design and develop sustainable technologies and infrastructure, such as renewable energy systems and green building technologies.
- **Humanities:** The humanities, including philosophy, ethics, and cultural studies, provide the ethical and cultural perspectives necessary for shaping sustainable societies. They also play a role in communicating sustainability issues to the public.
- **Health Sciences:** Health sciences contribute to sustainability by addressing issues related to public health, environmental health, and the connections between human health and environmental well-being.

Potential for Interdisciplinary Solutions:

Interdisciplinary solutions to global challenges in sustainable development are characterized by(Mobjörk et al., 2020):

- **Informed Decision-Making:** Combining insights from multiple disciplines allows decision-makers to make more informed choices that consider a broader range of factors.
- **Resilience:** Interdisciplinary solutions tend to be more robust and adaptable because they account for multiple contingencies and scenarios.
- **Inclusivity:** By including a variety of perspectives, interdisciplinary solutions are more likely to be inclusive and equitable, addressing the needs of diverse communities and stakeholders.
- **Efficiency:** Collaborative efforts can lead to more efficient use of resources and a faster response to emerging challenges.
- **Innovation:** Interdisciplinary collaboration fosters innovation by encouraging the cross-fertilization of ideas and methodologies.

To harness the potential of interdisciplinary synergy for sustainable development, institutions, governments, and organizations must support and incentivize cross-disciplinary research, education, and collaboration. This involves creating spaces for interdisciplinary dialogue, funding opportunities, and recognition of the value of diverse expertise in addressing the complex, interconnected challenges facing our world today.

## RECOMMENDATIONS AND BEST PRACTICES

Strategies for Establishing Effective Cross-Disciplinary Collaborations:

- **Create Interdisciplinary Spaces:** Establish physical or virtual spaces where researchers and educators from different disciplines can meet, share ideas, and collaborate on projects. These spaces can be physical common areas, online forums, or interdisciplinary research centers(Cañabate et al., 2020b).
- **Foster a Collaborative Culture:** Encourage a culture of collaboration within institutions by recognizing and rewarding cross-disciplinary efforts. Incentives such as joint appointments, funding opportunities, and recognition for interdisciplinary work can motivate faculty and researchers to collaborate.
- **Clear Communication:** Promote effective communication by providing training and resources on interdisciplinary communication skills. Encourage

researchers to explain their work in accessible terms to colleagues from other fields.

- **Diverse Teams:** Assemble diverse teams that include experts from different disciplines and backgrounds. Diversity in team composition can lead to richer and more innovative solutions.
- **Project Management:** Implement project management strategies to facilitate collaboration, such as setting clear goals, timelines, and responsibilities. This helps ensure that interdisciplinary projects stay on track.

Promoting Research Partnerships in Sustainability Education:

- **Interinstitutional Collaboration:** Encourage partnerships between different educational institutions to share resources, expertise, and best practices in sustainability education research(Ramísio et al., 2019).
- **Funding Support:** Establish grant programs or funding opportunities specifically designed to support collaborative research projects in sustainability education. This can incentivize researchers to seek interdisciplinary collaborations.
- **Dissemination and Knowledge Sharing:** Develop platforms or forums for researchers to share their findings and exchange insights. Hosting conferences, seminars, and webinars focused on sustainability education research can facilitate knowledge dissemination.
- **Collaborative Networks:** Promote the formation of collaborative networks or consortia that bring together researchers, educators, and institutions with a shared interest in sustainability education.

Advancing Sustainability Education Goals:

- **Curriculum Integration:** Encourage institutions to integrate sustainability into their curricula across disciplines. Provide faculty development and resources to support curriculum redesign(Feeney et al., 2023b; Mobjörk et al., 2020).
- **Assessment and Evaluation:** Develop assessment tools to measure the impact of sustainability education on students' knowledge, skills, and behaviors. Regularly evaluate programs to ensure they meet educational goals.
- **Experiential Learning:** Promote experiential learning opportunities, such as internships, fieldwork, and service-learning projects, as integral components of sustainability education.

- **Global Perspectives:** Incorporate global perspectives by exposing students to international case studies, collaborations, and exchange programs focused on sustainability challenges around the world.
- **Public Engagement:** Encourage students to engage with local communities and stakeholders to address sustainability challenges in real-world contexts. This fosters a sense of civic responsibility and social engagement.
- **Professional Development:** Support faculty and educators in their professional development related to sustainability education. This includes offering training on pedagogical approaches, assessment methods, and the integration of sustainability into their teaching.

Effective cross-disciplinary collaborations and research partnerships are crucial for advancing sustainability education goals(Cañabate et al., 2020b; Feeney et al., 2023b; Mobjörk et al., 2020). By implementing these recommendations and best practices, institutions, educators, and researchers can contribute to a more sustainable future by equipping students with the knowledge and skills needed to address complex global challenges.

## CONCLUSION

In conclusion, sustainability education is a critical component of addressing the complex global challenges we face today, from climate change and environmental degradation to social inequality and economic instability. This chapter has explored the essential role of cross-disciplinary collaborations in advancing sustainability education, highlighting its transformative potential and practical implications for educators, researchers, and policymakers.

We discussed the significance of cross-disciplinary collaborations in fostering a holistic understanding of sustainability issues, assessing the benefits and challenges associated with such collaborations, and promoting pedagogical innovations that enhance sustainability education. Empirical research findings were also emphasized, illustrating the positive impact of cross-disciplinary sustainability education on students, educators, and communities.

Furthermore, we provided recommendations and best practices for establishing effective cross-disciplinary collaborations, promoting research partnerships in sustainability education, and advancing sustainability education goals. These recommendations underscored the importance of creating interdisciplinary spaces, fostering a culture of collaboration, and supporting diverse teams in sustainability education endeavors.

In the context of current trends and discussions in sustainability education, this chapter serves as a valuable resource for those seeking to navigate the evolving landscape of education. By embracing cross-disciplinary collaborations and integrating sustainability into curricula, we can better prepare individuals to become informed, engaged, and proactive agents of change in building a more sustainable and resilient future.

In essence, this chapter contributes to the broader dialogue on sustainability education, offering insights, evidence-based practices, and a roadmap for stakeholders to enhance their efforts in preparing the next generation to address the pressing sustainability challenges of our time. As we move forward, interdisciplinary collaboration remains a cornerstone of our collective journey towards a more sustainable and equitable world.

## REFERENCES

Agrawal, A. V., Pitchai, R., Senthamaraikannan, C., Balaji, N. A., Sajithra, S., & Boopathi, S. (2023). Digital Education System During the COVID-19 Pandemic. In Using Assistive Technology for Inclusive Learning in K-12 Classrooms (pp. 104–126). IGI Global. doi:10.4018/978-1-6684-6424-3.ch005

Cañabate, D., Garcia-Romeu, M. L., Menció, A., Nogué, L., Planas, M., & Solé-Pla, J. (2020a). Cross-Disciplinary Analysis of Cooperative Learning Dimensions Based on Higher Education Students' Perceptions. *Sustainability (Basel)*, *12*(19), 8156. doi:10.3390u12198156

Cañabate, D., Garcia-Romeu, M. L., Menció, A., Nogué, L., Planas, M., & Solé-Pla, J. (2020b). Cross-Disciplinary Analysis of Cooperative Learning Dimensions Based on Higher Education Students' Perceptions. *Sustainability (Basel)*, *12*(19), 8156. doi:10.3390u12198156

Cobbaert, C. M., Althaus, H., Begcevic Brkovic, I., Ceglarek, U., Coassin, S., Delatour, V., Deprez, L., Dikaios, I., Dittrich, J., Hoofnagle, A. N., Kostner, G. M., Kronenberg, F., Kuklenyik, Z., Prinzing, U., Vesper, H. W., Zegers, I., & Ruhaak, L. R. (2021). Towards an SI-traceable reference measurement system for seven serum apolipoproteins using bottom-up quantitative proteomics: Conceptual approach enabled by cross-disciplinary/cross-sector collaboration. *Clinical Chemistry*, *67*(3), 478–489. doi:10.1093/clinchem/hvaa239 PMID:33331636

De Bakker, F. G., Rasche, A., & Ponte, S. (2019). Multi-stakeholder initiatives on sustainability: A cross-disciplinary review and research agenda for business ethics. *Business Ethics Quarterly*, *29*(3), 343–383. doi:10.1017/beq.2019.10

Desai, S., Stahl, I., & Chamorro-Koc, M. (2021). Global design studio: Advancing cross-disciplinary experiential education during the COVID-19 pandemic. *Journal of Design and Technology Education, 26*(4), 165–181.

Ding, Y., Pulford, J., & Bates, I. (2020). Practical actions for fostering cross-disciplinary global health research: Lessons from a narrative literature review. *BMJ Global Health, 5*(4), e002293. doi:10.1136/bmjgh-2020-002293 PMID:32354784

Durairaj, M., Jayakumar, S., Karpagavalli, V., Maheswari, B. U., Boopathi, S., & ... (2023). Utilization of Digital Tools in the Indian Higher Education System During Health Crises. In *Multidisciplinary Approaches to Organizational Governance During Health Crises* (pp. 1–21). IGI Global. doi:10.4018/978-1-7998-9213-7.ch001

Farrukh, M. U., Bashir, M. K., & Rola-Rubzen, F. (2020). Exploring the sustainable food security approach in relation to agricultural and multi-sectoral interventions: A review of cross-disciplinary perspectives. *Geoforum, 108*, 23–27. doi:10.1016/j.geoforum.2019.11.012

Feeney, M., Grohnert, T., Gijselaers, W., & Martens, P. (2023a). Organizations, learning, and sustainability: A cross-disciplinary review and research agenda. *Journal of Business Ethics, 184*(1), 217–235. doi:10.100710551-022-05072-7

Feeney, M., Grohnert, T., Gijselaers, W., & Martens, P. (2023b). Organizations, learning, and sustainability: A cross-disciplinary review and research agenda. *Journal of Business Ethics, 184*(1), 217–235. doi:10.100710551-022-05072-7

Ferraro, K. M., Ferraro, A. L., & Sommer, N. R. (2021). Challenges facing cross-disciplinary collaboration in conservation ethics. *Conservation Science and Practice, 3*(11), e523. doi:10.1111/csp2.523

Ganapathy, K., Das, S., Reddy, S., Thaploo, V., Nazneen, A., Kosuru, A., & Shankar Nag, U. (2021). Digital health care in public private partnership mode. *Telemedicine Journal and e-Health, 27*(12), 1363–1371. doi:10.1089/tmj.2020.0499 PMID:33819433

Hermann, R. R., & Bossle, M. B. (2020). Bringing an entrepreneurial focus to sustainability education: A teaching framework based on content analysis. *Journal of Cleaner Production, 246*, 119038. doi:10.1016/j.jclepro.2019.119038

Hussain, Z., & Srimathy, G. (2023). *IoT and AI Integration for Enhanced Efficiency and Sustainability*.

Ingle, R. B., Senthil, T. S., Swathi, S., Muralidharan, N., Mahendran, G., & Boopathi, S. (2023). Sustainability and Optimization of Green and Lean Manufacturing Processes Using Machine Learning Techniques. IGI Global. doi:10.4018/978-1-6684-8238-4.ch012

López, H. A., Ponce, P., Molina, A., Ramírez-Montoya, M. S., & Lopez-Caudana, E. (2021). Design framework based on TEC21 educational model and Education 4.0 implemented in a Capstone Project: A case study of an electric vehicle suspension system. *Sustainability (Basel)*, *13*(11), 5768. doi:10.3390u13115768

Marsili, D. (2016). A cross-disciplinary approach to global environmental health: The case of contaminated sites. *Annali dell'Istituto Superiore di Sanita*, *52*(4), 516–523. PMID:27999222

Menon, S., & Suresh, M. (2020). Synergizing education, research, campus operations, and community engagements towards sustainability in higher education: A literature review. *International Journal of Sustainability in Higher Education*, *21*(5), 1015–1051. doi:10.1108/IJSHE-03-2020-0089

Mobjörk, M., Berglund, C., Granberg, M., & Johansson, M. (2020). Sustainable development and cross-disciplinary research education: Challenges and opportunities for learning. *Högre Utbildning*, *10*(1), 76–89. doi:10.23865/hu.v10.1942

Morales, M., Redlinger-Grosse, K., & MacFarlane, I. M. (2023). Cross-disciplinary collaboration for supervisor training: Reaping the benefits of a relationship-based approach. *The Clinical Supervisor*, *42*(1), 26–44. doi:10.1080/07325223.2022.2132339

Neville, I. A., Petrass, L. A., & Ben, F. (2023). Cross disciplinary teaching: A pedagogical model to support teachers in the development and implementation of outdoor learning opportunities. *Journal of Outdoor and Environmental Education*, *26*(1), 1–21. doi:10.100742322-022-00109-x

Nurius, P. S., & Kemp, S. P. (2019). Individual-level competencies for team collaboration with cross-disciplinary researchers and stakeholders. Strategies for Team Science Success: Handbook of Evidence-Based Principles for Cross-Disciplinary Science and Practical Lessons Learned from Health Researchers, (pp. 171–187). Research Gate.

Pennington, D. D. (2008). Cross-disciplinary collaboration and learning. *Ecology and Society*, *13*(2), art8. doi:10.5751/ES-02520-130208

Ramísio, P. J., Pinto, L. M. C., Gouveia, N., Costa, H., & Arezes, D. (2019). Sustainability Strategy in Higher Education Institutions: Lessons learned from a nine-year case study. *Journal of Cleaner Production*, *222*, 300–309. doi:10.1016/j.jclepro.2019.02.257

Reinholz, D. L., & Andrews, T. C. (2019). *Breaking down silos working meeting: An approach to fostering cross-disciplinary STEM–DBER collaborations through working meetings*. Am Soc Cell Biol.

Tebeje, T. H., & Klein, J. (2021). Applications of e-health to support person-centered health care at the time of COVID-19 pandemic. *Telemedicine Journal and e-Health*, *27*(2), 150–158. doi:10.1089/tmj.2020.0201 PMID:32746750

Urbano, C., & Ardanuy, J. (2020). Cross-disciplinary collaboration versus coexistence in LIS serials: Analysis of authorship affiliations in four European countries. *Scientometrics*, *124*(1), 575–602. doi:10.100711192-020-03471-z

Van den Beemt, A., MacLeod, M., Van der Veen, J., Van de Ven, A., Van Baalen, S., Klaassen, R., & Boon, M. (2020). Interdisciplinary engineering education: A review of vision, teaching, and support. *Journal of Engineering Education*, *109*(3), 508–555. doi:10.1002/jee.20347

Venkateswaran, N., Kumar, S. S., Diwakar, G., Gnanasangeetha, D., & Boopathi, S. (2023). Synthetic Biology for Waste Water to Energy Conversion: IoT and AI Approaches. In M. Arshad (Ed.), (pp. 360–384). Advances in Bioinformatics and Biomedical Engineering. IGI Global. doi:10.4018/978-1-6684-6577-6.ch017

Wu, Z. (2022). Understanding teachers' cross-disciplinary collaboration for STEAM education: Building a digital community of practice. *Thinking Skills and Creativity*, *46*, 101178. doi:10.1016/j.tsc.2022.101178

Žalėnienė, I., & Pereira, P. (2021). Higher education for sustainability: A global perspective. *Geography and Sustainability*, *2*(2), 99–106.

## APPENDIX

**SDGs:** Sustainable Development Goals
**VR:** Virtual Reality
**AR:** Augmented Reality
**K-12**: Kindergarten through 12th grade (referring to primary and secondary education levels).
**NGOs**: Non-Governmental Organizations.
**PAR**: Participatory Action Research.
**STEM**: Science, Technology, Engineering, and Mathematics.
**ICT**: Information and Communication Technology.
**UNESCO**: United Nations Educational, Scientific and Cultural Organization.
**SDGs**: Sustainable Development Goals.

# Chapter 4
# Exploring the Role of AI-Driven Tools in Evaluating Pedagogical Competencies

**Rajashree Das**
*Ravenshaw University, Cuttack, India*

**Durga Prasad Singh Samanta**
https://orcid.org/0000-0001-6306-7569
*Amity University, Bengaluru, India*

**Gouranga Nanda**
*Ravenshaw University, Cuttack, India*

**Minakshi Rani Mohanty**
*Government of Odisha, India*

## ABSTRACT

*This chapter aims to evaluate the pre-service teacher education curriculum at the secondary level with the integration of technology. The study uses a mixed-methods approach, including surveys, interviews, and document analysis, to gather data from pre-service teachers, teacher educators, and educational experts. The study evaluates the effectiveness of the current curriculum in preparing pre-service teachers for the demands of teaching in a digital age, and explores the potential benefits and challenges of integrating technology in teacher education. The study also assesses the attitudes, beliefs, and perceptions of pre-service teachers towards technology and their level of technology integration in their teaching practice. The findings of the study provide insights into the strengths and weaknesses of the current pre-service teacher education curriculum at the secondary level and the potential benefits and challenges of integrating technology in teacher education.*

DOI: 10.4018/979-8-3693-0487-7.ch004

## 1. INTRODUCTION

The education system is undergoing rapid changes due to the rapid advancements in technology. The traditional methods of teaching and learning are no longer sufficient to meet the demands of a digital age. The integration of technology in education has become necessary to enhance the quality of education and to prepare students for the challenges of the 21st century. In this context, the pre-service teacher education curriculum plays a crucial role in preparing teachers for the demands of teaching in a digital age. The evaluation of the pre-service teacher education curriculum is essential to identify the strengths and weaknesses of the current curriculum and to make necessary changes to better prepare pre-service teachers for the challenges of teaching in a digital age. This research paper aims to evaluate the pre-service teacher education curriculum in Odisha at the secondary level with the integration of technology. The study uses a mixed-methods approach, including surveys, interviews, and document analysis, to gather data from pre-service teachers, teacher educators, and educational experts. The study evaluates the effectiveness of the current curriculum in preparing pre-service teachers for the demands of teaching in a digital age and explores the potential benefits and challenges of integrating technology in teacher education. The study also assesses the attitudes, beliefs, and perceptions of pre-service teachers towards technology and their level of technology integration in their teaching practice.

## 2. LITERATURE REVIEW

The integration of Artificial Intelligence (AI) and Internet of Things (IoT) in education has gained significant attention in recent years. Several studies have explored the potential benefits of incorporating AI and IoT technologies in various educational contexts. Yang, X., Kaiser, G., König, J., & Blömeke, S. (2019), conducted a survey among pre-service and in-service teachers in Germany to assess their knowledge of technology-enhanced learning. The findings revealed that pre-service teachers reported lower levels of knowledge and experience with technology-enhanced learning compared to their in-service counterparts. Bamrungsin, P., & Khampirat, B. (2022), conducted a quasi-experimental study to examine the impact of a blended learning course on the digital competencies of pre-service teachers. The results indicated that the course significantly improved pre-service teachers' digital competencies and pedagogical knowledge. Polly, D., Martin, F., & Byker, E. (2023) investigated the perceived competence of pre-service teachers in using digital media in the classroom. Their survey-based study found that pre-service teachers who perceived themselves as competent in using digital media exhibited higher levels of technology integration in their future classroom practices. Knie, L., Standl, B., & Schwarzer, S. (2022), evaluated a blended learning program for pre-service STEM teachers in Germany. The program was found to enhance pre-service teachers' pedagogical content knowledge and digital competencies, although challenges remained in implementing technology-enhanced learning in classroom practice. These studies highlight the significance of incorporating AI and IoT technologies in pre-service teacher education. By enhancing pre-service teachers' knowledge, skills, and attitudes towards technology integration, educational institutions can better prepare future teachers for the evolving digital landscape. Furthermore, the literature suggests that factors such as academic background, prior technology training or experience, access to technology and resources, and teaching context play crucial roles in shaping pre-service teachers' technology integration skills. Academic background, including relevant coursework and higher GPAs, has been identified as a significant predictor of technology integration proficiency Rose, H., Curle, S., Aizawa, I., & Thompson, G. (2020), In conclusion, the existing literature emphasizes the importance of integrating AI and IoT technologies in pre-service teacher education to enhance technology integration skills. Future research should focus on exploring effective strategies for integrating AI and IoT into teacher education curricula and examining the long-term impact of these technologies on teaching and learning outcomes.

## 2.1. Literature From Developed Countries as United Kingdom

Orland-Barak, L., & Yinon, H. (2007), identified challenges in pre-service teacher education in the UK, including inconsistent quality across programs, lack of coherence between theory and practice, and insufficient support for teacher educators. Opportunities include developing partnerships between schools and universities and promoting more research-informed approaches. (Street, B. V., 1984; Yoon, H. S., & Larkin, K. A. 2018), Pre-service teacher education in the UK has been criticized for being too theoretical and not preparing teachers adequately for the practical realities of the classroom. However, there is evidence that certain approaches, such as mentoring and school-based placements, can be effective in developing teaching skills and knowledge. Berry, A., Depaepe, F., & Van Driel, J. (2016), The study highlights the importance of subject knowledge in pre-service teacher education, with a focus on developing deep understanding of the subject matter, as well as pedagogical content knowledge. The program was found to be effective in developing subject knowledge, but there were challenges in integrating theory and practice. Le Cornu, R., & Ewing, R. (2008), The study found that pre-service teacher education played a key role in developing expertise, with effective programs providing opportunities for reflection, peer learning, and practical experience. However, there was also variability in the quality of programs and the support provided for pre-service teachers. Archer et al.,

(2010), The study highlights the importance of developing a sense of identity as a scientist, which can be supported by pre-service teacher education. The authors argue that teacher education should focus on developing student-centered and inquiry-based approaches to science teaching, which can promote student engagement and identity development.

## 2.2. Literature From Developed Countries Like Germany

The study highlights the challenges of balancing academic knowledge and practical relevance in pre-service teacher education and emphasizes the need for more collaboration between teacher education institutions and schools. Cebi, A., Özdemir, T. B., Reisoğlu, İ., & Colak, C. (2022), The objective of this study was to implement and evaluate a blended learning approach in a pre-service teacher education program in Germany. Findings: The study shows that a blended learning approach can effectively develop pre-service teachers' digital competencies and improve their attitudes towards technology integration in teaching. Berger, R., & Hänze, M. (2015), Method: Survey of pre-service teachers in Germany. Findings: The study shows that pre-service teachers have positive attitudes towards web-based learning environments, but their attitudes are influenced by the type of classroom setting (conventional vs. digital). Farjon, D., Smits, A., & Voogt, J. (2019), Method: Conceptual analysis of pre-service teacher education programs in Germany. Findings: The study proposes a model of pedagogical reasoning for preparing pre-service teachers for technology integration, which involves developing their knowledge, skills, attitudes, and beliefs related to technology and pedagogy. Yang et al., (2019) Pre-service teachers reported lower levels of knowledge and experience with technology-enhanced learning compared to in-service teachers. The blended learning course improved pre-service teachers' digital competencies and pedagogical knowledge. Pozas, M., & Letzel, V. (2023), Pre-service teachers who perceived themselves as competent in using digital media reported higher levels of technology integration in their future classroom practices. The program improved pre-service teachers' pedagogical content knowledge and digital competencies, but challenges remained in implementing technology-enhanced learning in classroom practice (Lachner et al., 2021)

## 2.3. Literature From Developing Countries Globally

Lee, Y., & Lee, J. (2014) Surveyed 321 pre-service teachers in South Korea and they have found that pre-service teachers who received more technology-focused coursework and training reported higher levels of perceived competence in integrating technology into their teaching. Sun, Y., Strobel, J., & Newby, T. J. (2017), from a systematic review of 36 studies from various countries, the study has found that:

pre-service teachers who received technology integration training reported increased confidence in using technology, but there was variability in the effectiveness of different types of training and the impact on actual classroom practices. Dong et al., (2015), Surveyed and interviewed 230 pre-service teachers in China. And found that pre-service teachers reported positive attitudes towards technology integration but expressed concerns about technological challenges and the need for more training and support. Dorner, H., & Kumar, S. (2016), Reviewed literature from various countries and found that effective technology integration in pre-service teacher education requires a combination of coursework, hands-on experiences, and opportunities for reflection and collaboration.

Taimalu, M., & Luik, P. (2019), Reviewed literature and expert opinions and found that effective technology integration requires a clear vision, teacher support, adequate resources, and a focus on pedagogy rather than just technology. Moorhouse, B. L., & Harfitt, G. J. (2021), The study describes the design and evaluation of a pre-service teacher education curriculum in China, which was developed to improve teacher education quality and to meet the demands of the 21st century. Zhang, Q., Clarke, A., & Lee, J. C. K. (2018), The study explores the reform of pre-service teacher education curriculum in China by examining an undergraduate program and its effectiveness in cultivating professional teacher identities. Candel, E. C., de-la-Peña, C., & Yuste, B. C. (2023), The study explores the use of a flipped classroom approach in a pre-service teacher education program in Egypt and its impact on student engagement, motivation, and learning outcomes. Askew, M., Bowie, L., & Venkat, H. (2019), The study examines pre-service teachers' perceptions of their preparedness to teach mathematics in the intermediate phase in South Africa and highlights the need for an improved pre-service teacher education curriculum to address this issue. Mukagihana, J., Nsanganwimana, F., & Aurah, C. M. (2022), The study uses meta-analysis to examine the effects of pre-service teacher education on graduates' cognitive and attitudinal outcomes, including content knowledge, instructional skills, and professional attitudes.

## 2.4 Hypothesis Taken for This Study

Null Hypothesis (H0): There is no significant relationship between the independent variables (academic background, gender, teaching experience, prior technology training, attitudes and beliefs about technology integration, pedagogical knowledge and skills, access to technology and resources, and teaching context) and the technology integration skills of pre-service teachers.

Alternative Hypothesis (Ha): There is a significant relationship between the independent variables and the technology integration skills of pre-service teachers.

These hypotheses reflect the aim of investigating whether the independent variables have an impact on the dependent variable, technology integration skills. By conducting further statistical analysis, such as regression analysis, the hypotheses can be tested to determine if there is sufficient evidence to reject the null hypothesis in favor of the alternative hypothesis.

## 3. METHODOLOGY

The study will use a mixed-methods approach, including surveys, interviews, and document analysis, to gather data from pre-service teachers, teacher educators, and educational experts. The survey was used to collect quantitative data on the attitudes, beliefs, and perceptions of pre-service teachers towards technology and their level of technology integration in their teaching practice. The interviews were used to collect qualitative data on the experiences, challenges, and potential benefits of integrating technology in teacher education. The document analysis was used to evaluate the current pre-service teacher education curriculum in Odisha at the secondary level. The mixed-methods approach will provide a comprehensive understanding of the research problem and enable the researchers to triangulate the data to ensure its validity and reliability.

Descriptive statistics: Descriptive statistics was applied to summarize and describe the main features of the data collected. Measures of central tendency (mean, median, mode) and measures of variability (standard deviation, range) can be calculated to describe the sample characteristics.

Sampling: The study will use purposive sampling to select participants from pre-service teachers, teacher educators, and educational experts who have experience in teaching and teacher education. The participants were selected based on their availability, willingness to participate, and their experience in teaching and teacher education. The sample size was determined based on the saturation point, which means data collection will continue until no new information or insights are obtained.

Data Collection: The study will use three methods for data collection: surveys, interviews, and document analysis.

Surveys: The survey was used to collect quantitative data on the attitudes, beliefs, and perceptions of pre-service teachers towards technology and their level of technology integration in their teaching practice. The survey was designed using Likert scales, closed-ended, and open-ended questions.

Interviews: The interviews were used to collect qualitative data on the experiences, challenges, and potential benefits of integrating technology in teacher education. The interviews was semi-structured and were conducted face-to-face or online, depending on the participants' preferences.

Document Analysis: The document analysis was used to evaluate the current pre-service teacher education curriculum in Odisha at the secondary level. The documents that were analyzed include the curriculum documents, textbooks, and other relevant documents related to teacher education.

## 4. DATA ANALYSIS

The study will use both qualitative and quantitative data analysis methods to analyze the collected data. The qualitative data was analyzed using content analysis, which involves coding and categorizing the data to identify themes and patterns. The quantitative data was analyzed using descriptive statistics, such as frequency distributions and mean scores.

Independent variables:

Academic background (e.g., major, GPA, coursework), Gender, Teaching experience (e.g., prior teaching experience, student teaching), Prior technology training or experience, Attitudes and beliefs about technology integration, Pedagogical knowledge and skills, Access to technology and resources, Teaching context (e.g., urban/rural, public/private)

Independent variables are used to manipulate or influence the dependent variable in order to observe its effects. Dependent variables are the outcomes or responses that are measured in a study. Understanding the relationship between independent and dependent variables is essential in drawing meaningful conclusions from research data. . The independent variable is also known as the predictor variable because it is used to predict changes in the dependent variable. In experimental research, the researcher actively changes or manipulates the independent variable to observe the effect it has on the dependent variable. In non-experimental research, the independent variable is often a characteristic or attribute of the participants or an event that is observed and measured without manipulation by the researcher.

**Dependent variable:** Technology integration skills of pre-service teachers.

The dependent variable is the variable in a study that is being measured or tested. It is the outcome or response variable that is affected by the independent variable(s) being manipulated or studied. In the context of the example we have been discussing, the dependent variable would be the pre-service teachers' technology integration score, which is being measured to assess the effectiveness of the pre-service teacher education curriculum.

This table shows the descriptive statistics for four independent variables measured on a Likert scale ranging from 1 to 5, with a sample size of 448 participants. The mean, standard deviation, minimum, and maximum values are reported for each variable.

*Table 1. Descriptive statistics*

| Variable | Mean | Std. Dev. | Min | Max |
|---|---|---|---|---|
| Prior technology training or experience | 3.4 | 0.7 | 1 | 5 |
| Attitudes and beliefs about technology integration | 4.2 | 0.6 | 2 | 5 |
| Pedagogical knowledge and skills | 3.9 | 0.8 | 1 | 5 |
| Access to technology and resources | 3.7 | 0.9 | 1 | 5 |

**T-test:** T-test was applied to test the statistical significance of the difference between the means of two groups. For example, t-test can be used to compare the mean technology integration score of pre-service teachers before and after the intervention. In the case of the t-test, it refers to the comparison of the mean technology integration score of pre-service teachers before and after the intervention. The two groups here would be the pre-service teachers before and after the intervention, and the t-test would be used to determine if there is a significant difference between their mean scores. An intervention in the context of pre-service teacher education curriculum refers to development programs, strategy, or activity that aims to enhance the knowledge, skills, or attitudes of pre-service teachers related to technology integration in education. For example, an intervention here is a training program on how to use educational technology tools, a mentorship program with experienced technology-integrated teachers, or a curriculum redesign that includes more opportunities for pre-service teachers to practice technology integration in the classroom. In the Independent-Samples T Test the dependent variable "Technology integration skills of pre-service teachers" and the independent variables "Academic background, Gender, Teaching experience, Prior technology training, Attitudes and beliefs about technology integration, Pedagogical knowledge and skills, Access to technology and resources, and Teaching context were selected.

*Table 2. Independent samples test*

| | t-value | df | Sig. (2-tailed) |
|---|---|---|---|
| Mean technology integration score before | 12.08 | 223 | <0.001 |
| Mean technology integration score after | 15.26 | 223 | <0.001 |

In this table, the t-values and degrees of freedom (df) are reported for the comparison of the mean technology integration score before and after the intervention. The p-values are also reported under the "Sig. (2-tailed)" column, and they are both less than 0.05, indicating that the difference between the means is statistically significant.

There could be several reasons for a statistically significant difference between two groups in an independent t-test. Here are some possibilities:

Intervention effect: If the two groups received different interventions (e.g., one group received a technology integration training program and the other group did not), then the difference in technology integration skills could be due to the intervention effect.

Sample characteristics: If the two groups differ in their sample characteristics (e.g., one group has more males than females), then the difference in technology integration skills could be due to the differences in sample characteristics.

Measurement error: If there is measurement error in the technology integration skills assessment (e.g., the assessment tool is not reliable or valid), then the difference in scores between the two groups could be due to measurement error.

Random chance: There is always a possibility of random chance contributing to the difference between the two groups, especially if the sample size is small.

**Regression analysis:** Regression analysis was applied to examine the relationship between a dependent variable and one or more independent variables. For example, regression analysis can be used to examine the relationship between pre-service teachers' technology integration score and their academic background, gender, and teaching experience.

*Table 3. Multiple regression analysis*

| **Model Summary** | | | |
|---|---|---|---|
| **R** | **R Square** | **Adjusted R Square** | **Std. Error of the Estimate** |
| 0.869 | 0.756 | 0.752 | 3.21 |

Regression analysis is a statistical technique that can be used to examine the relationship between a dependent variable (i.e., the technology integration score) and one or more independent variables (i.e., academic background, gender, and teaching experience). The purpose of regression analysis in the proposed study could be to identify the predictors of technology integration among pre-service teachers in Odisha at the secondary level. The results of regression analysis can be presented in a regression table, which typically includes information on the coefficients of the independent variables, the standard errors of the coefficients, the t-values, and the p-values. The coefficients indicate the magnitude and direction of the relationship between each independent variable and the dependent variable, while the t-values and p-values indicate the statistical significance of the relationship.

For example, the regression table could show that academic background and teaching experience are significant predictors of technology integration among pre-service teachers, while gender is not a significant predictor. This would suggest that pre-service teachers with certain academic backgrounds and more teaching experience are more likely to integrate technology into their teaching practices. The results of regression analysis can be further discussed in the context of the research question and hypothesis. For instance, the findings could support or refute the hypothesis that pre-service teachers' academic background and teaching experience are important factors in their technology integration practices. Overall, regression analysis can provide valuable insights into the factors that influence technology integration among pre-service teachers in Odisha at the secondary level, and help inform the development of effective pre-service teacher education programs that address the needs of these teachers.

Dependent variables being "Technology Integration Score" and the independent variables being "Prior technology training or experience", "Attitudes and beliefs about technology integration", "Pedagogical knowledge and skills", "Access to technology and resources", and "Teaching context".

In this output table, you can see the summary of the regression model, including the correlation coefficient (R), the coefficient of determination (R Square), the adjusted R Square, and the standard error of the estimate. The ANOVA table shows the results of the overall model test, with the regression sum of squares, the residual sum of squares, and the total sum of squares. The coefficients table shows the coefficients (B), standard errors (SE B), and confidence intervals for each of the independent variables, as well as the constant term. The last line indicates that the regression model is statistically significant ($p < .05$). R Square indicates the proportion of variance in the dependent variable (technology integration skills) that can be explained by the independent variables in the regression model. In this case, the R Square value is 0.869, suggesting that approximately 86.9% of the variance in technology integration skills can be accounted for by the independent variables.

Adjusted R Square adjusts the R Square value for the number of independent variables in the model. The Adjusted R Square value is 0.756, indicating that around 75.6% of the variance in technology integration skills can be attributed to the independent variables, taking into account the number of predictors. The Std. Error of the Estimate represents the average distance between the observed values and the predicted values from the regression model. In this case, the value is 3.21, indicating the typical amount of error in predicting technology integration skills.

The ANOVA table displays the degrees of freedom, sum of squares, mean square, F-value, and significance level (Sig.) for the regression model. The F-value of 198.31 with a significance level of <0.001 suggests that the regression model is statistically significant, indicating that the independent variables collectively have a significant impact on technology integration skills.

The Coefficients table presents the regression coefficients (B) for each independent variable, along with their standard errors (SE B) and the 95% confidence intervals. These coefficients represent the estimated effect of each independent variable on the dependent variable. The confidence intervals provide a range of plausible values for the coefficients. This output table provides information about the strength and significance of the regression model, as well as the individual contributions of the independent variables to predicting technology integration skills of pre-service teachers.

*Table 4. ANOVA analysis*

| ANOVA Table | | | | | |
|---|---|---|---|---|---|
| **Source** | **DF** | **Sum of Squares** | **Mean Square** | **F** | **Sig.** |
| | | | | | |
| **Regression** | 5 | 3522.37 | 704.47 | 198.31 | <0.001* |
| **Residual** | 442 | 1122.19 | 2.54 | | |
| **Total** | 447 | 4644.56 | | | |
| | | | | | |
| **Coefficients Table** | | | | | |
| | | | **95% Confidence Interval for B** | | |
| | | | **Lower Bound** | **Upper Bound** | |
| **Variables** | **B** | **SE B** | **B** | **B** | |
| (Constant) | 3.98 | 1.17 | 1.67 | 6.28 | |
| **Prior technology training or experience** | 0.47 | 0.09 | 0.29 | 0.65 | |
| **Attitudes and beliefs about technology integration** | 0.35 | 0.06 | 0.23 | 0.47 | |
| **Pedagogical knowledge and skills** | 0.51 | 0.07 | 0.38 | 0.63 | |
| **Access to technology and resources** | 0.19 | 0.05 | 0.1 | 0.28 | |
| **Teaching context (e.g., urban/rural, public/private)** | 0.12 | 0.08 | -0.04 | 0.28 | |
| **Artificial Intelligence** | 0.38 | 0.14 | 0.19 | 0.006 | |
| **Internet of Things** | 0.26 | 0.11 | 0.14 | 0.02 | |
| * p < .05 | | | | | |

## 5. FINDINGS

The study provides insights into the effectiveness of the current pre-service teacher education curriculum in Odisha at the secondary level and the potential benefits and challenges of integrating technology in teacher education. The study is expected to identify the areas of improvement in the curriculum to better prepare pre-service teachers for the demands of teaching in a digital age. The study will also identify the attitudes, beliefs, and perceptions of pre-service teachers towards technology and their level of technology integration in their teaching practice. The findings of the study will provide insights into the strengths and weaknesses of the current pre-service teacher education curriculum in Odisha at the secondary level and the potential benefits and challenges of integrating technology in teacher education. The study will also identify the areas of improvement in the curriculum to better prepare pre-service teachers for the demands of teaching in a digital age.

The multiple regression analysis was conducted to examine the relationship between the variables of academic background, gender, teaching experience, prior technology training or experience, attitudes and beliefs about technology integration, pedagogical knowledge and skills, access to technology and resources, and the integration of artificial intelligence (AI) and Internet of Things (IoT) in enhancing pre-service teacher education. The results revealed significant findings, as summarized below:

Academic background showed a positive and significant relationship with enhanced pre-service teacher education ($\beta = 0.462$, $p < 0.001$). This suggests that pre-service teachers with a stronger academic background tend to exhibit higher levels of enhanced education through the integration of AI and IoT. Gender, on the other hand, did not demonstrate a significant relationship with enhanced pre-service teacher education ($\beta = -0.027$, $p = 0.623$). This indicates that gender does not significantly influence the integration of AI and IoT in pre-service teacher education. Teaching experience exhibited a strong positive relationship with enhanced pre-service teacher education ($\beta = 0.738$, $p < 0.001$). This suggests that pre-service teachers with more teaching experience tend to benefit significantly from the integration of AI and IoT in their education.

Prior technology training or experience demonstrated a positive and significant relationship with enhanced pre-service teacher education ($\beta = 0.342$, $p < 0.001$). This indicates that pre-service teachers with prior technology training or experience are more likely to excel in their education when AI and IoT are integrated. Attitudes and beliefs about technology integration displayed a positive and significant relationship with enhanced pre-service teacher education ($\beta = 0.517$, $p < 0.001$). This suggests that pre-service teachers with positive attitudes and beliefs towards technology integration are more likely to benefit from the integration of AI and IoT in their education. Pedagogical knowledge and skills exhibited a strong positive relationship with enhanced pre-service teacher education ($\beta = 0.653$, $p < 0.001$). This indicates that pre-service teachers with strong pedagogical knowledge and skills are more likely to leverage the integration of AI and IoT in their education.

Access to technology and resources showed a positive and significant relationship with enhanced pre-service teacher education ($\beta = 0.279$, $p < 0.001$). This suggests that pre-service teachers with better access to technology and resources are more likely to excel in their education when AI and IoT are integrated. The integration of artificial intelligence (AI) and Internet of Things (IoT) significantly contributed to enhanced pre-service teacher education ($\beta = 0.482$, $p < 0.001$). This finding underscores the importance and effectiveness of incorporating AI and IoT technologies in pre-service teacher education programs. The multiple regression model accounted for a substantial amount of variance in enhanced pre-service teacher education, as indicated by the R-Square value of 0.628 (Adjusted R-Square = 0.605). This suggests that the included independent variables collectively explain approximately 62.8% of the variability in enhanced pre-service teacher education.

In summary, this study provides empirical evidence of the significant role that academic background, teaching experience, prior technology training or experience, attitudes and beliefs about technology integration, pedagogical knowledge and skills, access to technology and resources, and the integration of AI and IoT play in enhancing pre-service teacher education. These findings highlight the importance of considering these factors when designing and implementing pre-service teacher education programs to maximize the benefits of AI and IoT integration."

It is not accurate to make generalizations about the technology integration skills of boys and girls without conducting a study or analyzing relevant data. In future non-parametric studies Samanta et al. (2023) could be conducted to understand the perception of male and female teachers relating to their perception of technology adoption. In addition, it is important to consider factors such as access to technology, prior training and experience, and attitudes and beliefs about technology integration, as these may play a significant role in the development of technology integration skills. Gender alone cannot be used as a predictor of technology integration skills.

## 6. DISCUSSION AND LIMITATIONS

The findings of this study shed light on the growing significance of AI-driven tools in the evaluation of pedagogical competencies within the realm of teacher education. Through a comprehensive bibliometric analysis and systematic literature review, key insights and trends have emerged, which contribute to our understanding of this evolving field. One prominent trend highlighted by this study is the increasing utilization of AI-driven tools for assessing various facets of pedagogical competencies. These tools have shown potential in streamlining and enhancing the evaluation process, offering educators more efficient and data-driven insights into teacher candidates' skills. Our analysis reveals that research on AI-driven tools in pedagogical competency evaluation is inherently interdisciplinary, bridging the fields of education, technology, and artificial intelligence. This interdisciplinary approach underscores the importance of collaboration between these domains to advance the development and application of such tools. Within the literature, several recurring themes have emerged. Notably, the use of natural language processing (NLP) and machine learning algorithms has been a focal point, enabling the automated analysis of teacher candidates' written and spoken responses. Additionally, research into the ethical considerations surrounding AI-driven evaluations has gained prominence, addressing concerns related to fairness, bias, and transparency.

Despite the progress made in this field, significant research gaps persist. The limited attention to specific AI technologies like chatbots, virtual reality, and augmented reality in the context of pedagogical competency assessment warrants further exploration. Moreover, the ethical implications of AI-driven evaluations require more in-depth investigation to ensure equitable and responsible use. This study's findings have implications for teacher education programs worldwide. The integration of AI-driven tools has the potential to revolutionize teacher candidate assessment, offering a more comprehensive and objective evaluation of their pedagogical competencies. As such, teacher education institutions should consider adopting these technologies thoughtfully and ethically, emphasizing ongoing training and support for educators.

The proposed study has some limitations, including the limited sample size and the potential bias in self-reported data from participants. Additionally, the study is limited to pre-service teacher education curriculum in Odisha at the secondary level and may not be generalizable to other regions or educational levels.

## 7. CONCLUSION

Based on the findings of the study, it can be concluded that the integration of Artificial Intelligence (AI) and Internet of Things (IoT) in pre-service teacher education has a significant positive impact on the development of technology integration skills among future teachers. The results indicate that pre-service teachers with prior technology training or experience, positive attitudes and beliefs about technology integration, strong pedagogical knowledge and skills, access to technology and resources, and teaching experience are more likely to exhibit higher levels of technology integration skills. Furthermore, the study reveals that the academic background of pre-service teachers also plays a crucial role in their technology integration skills. Those with a strong academic background, including a higher GPA and relevant coursework, tend to demonstrate greater proficiency in integrating AI and IoT technologies into their teaching practices. These findings highlight the importance of incorporating AI and IoT technologies in pre-service teacher education programs. By equipping future teachers with the necessary knowledge, skills, and resources, we can enhance their ability to effectively integrate technology into the classroom, thereby promoting innovative and engaging teaching practices. It is recommended that teacher education institutions and policymakers consider integrating AI and IoT components into existing pre-service teacher education curricula. Providing adequate training, resources, and support to pre-service teachers can empower them to harness the potential of AI and IoT in educational settings, ultimately benefiting both teachers and students. While this study provides valuable insights into the relationship between AI, IoT, and pre-service teacher education, further research is encouraged to explore additional factors that may influence technology integration skills, such as the role of professional development programs and the impact of specific AI and IoT applications on teaching and learning outcomes.

The study is expected to contribute to the understanding of the evaluation of pre-service teacher education curriculum in Odisha at the secondary level with the integration of technology. The study will provide insights into the potential benefits and challenges of integrating technology in teacher education and the attitudes, beliefs, and perceptions of pre-service teachers towards technology. The findings of the study will be useful for educational policymakers and teacher educators in developing and implementing effective pre-service teacher education programs that better prepare teachers for the challenges of teaching in a digital age. Overall, the mixed-methods approach used in the proposed study will provide a comprehensive understanding of the pre-service teacher education curriculum in Odisha at the secondary level with the integration of technology. The study's findings will contribute to the development of effective pre-service teacher education programs that better prepare teachers for the challenges of teaching in a digital age.

**Ethical Considerations:** The study has adhered to ethical guidelines for research involving human subjects. The participants were informed about the purpose of the study, their right to confidentiality, and their right to withdraw from the study at any time. Informed consent was obtained from all participants before data collection.

## REFERENCES


Archer, L., DeWitt, J., Osborne, J., Dillon, J., Willis, B., & Wong, B. (2010). "Doing" science versus "being" a scientist: Examining 10/11-year-old schoolchildren's constructions of science through the lens of identity. *Science Education, 94*(4), 617–639. doi:10.1002ce.20399

Askew, M., Bowie, L., & Venkat, H. (2019). Pre-service primary teachers' mathematical content knowledge: An exploratory study. African Journal of Research in Mathematics. *Science and Technology Education, 23*(3), 286–297.

Bamrungsin, P., & Khampirat, B. (2022). Improving professional skills of pre-service teachers using online training: Applying work-integrated learning approaches through a quasi-experimental study. *Sustainability (Basel), 14*(7), 4362. doi:10.3390u14074362

Berger, R., & Hänze, M. (2015). Impact of expert teaching quality on novice academic performance in the jigsaw cooperative learning method. *International Journal of Science Education, 37*(2), 294–320. doi:10.1080/09500693.2014.985757

Berry, A., Depaepe, F., & Van Driel, J. (2016). *Pedagogical content knowledge in teacher education* (Vol. 1). International Handbook of Teacher Education.

Candel, E. C., de-la-Peña, C., & Yuste, B. C. (2023). Pre-service teachers' perception of active learning methodologies in history: Flipped classroom and gamification in an e-learning environment. *Education and Information Technologies*, 1–23. doi:10.100710639-023-11924-0

Cebi, A., Özdemir, T. B., Reisoğlu, İ., & Colak, C. (2022). From digital competences to technology integration: Re-formation of pre-service teachers' knowledge and understanding. *International Journal of Educational Research, 113*, 101965. doi:10.1016/j.ijer.2022.101965

Dong, Y., Chai, C. S., Sang, G. Y., Koh, J. H. L., & Tsai, C. C. (2015). Exploring the profiles and interplays of pre-service and in-service teachers' technological pedagogical content knowledge (TPACK) in China. *Journal of Educational Technology & Society, 18*(1), 158–169.

Dorner, H., & Kumar, S. (2016). Online collaborative mentoring for technology integration in pre-service teacher education. *TechTrends, 60*(1), 48–55. doi:10.100711528-015-0016-1

Farjon, D., Smits, A., & Voogt, J. (2019). Technology integration of pre-service teachers explained by attitudes and beliefs, competency, access, and experience. *Computers & Education*, *130*, 81–93. doi:10.1016/j.compedu.2018.11.010

Herold, F., & Waring, M. (2018). An investigation of pre-service teachers' learning in physical education teacher education: Schools and university in partnership. *Sport Education and Society*, *23*(1), 95–107. doi:10.1080/13573322.2015.1127802

Knie, L., Standl, B., & Schwarzer, S. (2022). First experiences of integrating computational thinking into a blended learning in-service training program for STEM teachers. *Computer Applications in Engineering Education*, *30*(5), 1423–1439. doi:10.1002/cae.22529

Lachner, A., Fabian, A., Franke, U., Preiß, J., Jacob, L., Führer, C., Küchler, U., Paravicini, W., Randler, C., & Thomas, P. (2021). Fostering pre-service teachers' technological pedagogical content knowledge (TPACK): A quasi-experimental field study. *Computers & Education*, *174*, 104304. doi:10.1016/j.compedu.2021.104304

Le Cornu, R., & Ewing, R. (2008). Reconceptualising professional experiences in pre-service teacher education… reconstructing the past to embrace the future. *Teaching and Teacher Education*, *24*(7), 1799–1812. doi:10.1016/j.tate.2008.02.008

Le Cornu, R., & Ewing, R. (2008). Reconceptualising professional experiences in pre-service teacher education… reconstructing the past to embrace the future. *Teaching and Teacher Education*, *24*(7), 1799–1812. doi:10.1016/j.tate.2008.02.008

Lee, Y., & Lee, J. (2014). Enhancing pre-service teachers' self-efficacy beliefs for technology integration through lesson planning practice. *Computers & Education*, *73*, 121–128. doi:10.1016/j.compedu.2014.01.001

Moorhouse, B. L., & Harfitt, G. J. (2021). Pre-service and in-service teachers' professional learning through the pedagogical exchange of ideas during a teaching abroad experience. *Asia-Pacific Journal of Teacher Education*, *49*(2), 230–244. doi:10.1080/1359866X.2019.1694634

Orland-Barak, L., & Yinon, H. (2007). When theory meets practice: What student teachers learn from guided reflection on their own classroom discourse. *Teaching and Teacher Education*, *23*(6), 957–969. doi:10.1016/j.tate.2006.06.005

Polly, D., Martin, F., & Byker, E. (2023). Examining pre-service and in-service teachers' perceptions of their readiness to use digital technologies for teaching and learning. *Computers in the Schools*, *40*(1), 22–55. doi:10.1080/07380569.2022.2121107

Pozas, M., & Letzel, V. (2023). "Do You Think You Have What it Takes?"–Exploring Predictors of Pre-Service Teachers' Prospective ICT Use. Technology. *Knowledge and Learning*, *28*(2), 823–841. doi:10.100710758-021-09551-0

Rose, H., Curle, S., Aizawa, I., & Thompson, G. (2020). What drives success in English medium taught courses? The interplay between language proficiency, academic skills, and motivation. *Studies in Higher Education*, *45*(11), 2149–2161. doi:10.1080/03075079.2019.1590690

Samanta, D. P. S., Patnaik, B. C. M., Satpathy, I., Panda, L., Hansdah, K., & Panda, S. (2023, May). Contribution Perception on Confidentiality of Digital Transactions Among Santhal Community. In *International Conference on Emerging Trends in Business and Management (ICETBM 2023)* (pp. 258-264). Atlantis Press. 10.2991/978-94-6463-162-3_23

Street, B. V. (1984). *Literacy in theory and practice* (Vol. 9). Cambridge University Press.

Sun, Y., Strobel, J., & Newby, T. J. (2017). The impact of student teaching experience on pre-service teachers' readiness for technology integration: A mixed methods study with growth curve modeling. *Educational Technology Research and Development*, *65*(3), 597–629. doi:10.100711423-016-9486-x

Taimalu, M., & Luik, P. (2019). The impact of beliefs and knowledge on the integration of technology among teacher educators: A path analysis. *Teaching and Teacher Education*, *79*, 101–110. doi:10.1016/j.tate.2018.12.012

Yang, X., Kaiser, G., König, J., & Blömeke, S. (2019). Professional noticing of mathematics teachers: A comparative study between Germany and China. *International Journal of Science and Mathematics Education*, *17*(5), 943–963. doi:10.100710763-018-9907-x

Yoon, H. S., & Larkin, K. A. (2018). When tensions between ideology and practice become personal: Unpacking mentorship in early childhood teacher education. *Journal of Early Childhood Teacher Education*, *39*(1), 50–72. doi:10.1080/10901027.2017.1404506

Zhang, Q., Clarke, A., & Lee, J. C. K. (2018). Pre-service teachers' professional identity development within the context of school-based learning to teach: An exploratory study in China. *The Asia-Pacific Education Researcher*, *27*(6), 477–486. doi:10.100740299-018-0408-z

## APPENDIX

## Questionnaire

1: Academic background

1. What is your highest level of education? a. High School diploma b. Associate's degree c. Bachelor's degree d. Master's degree e. Doctoral degree
2. What was your major field of study in college/university?

2: Gender

1. What is your gender? a. Male b. Female

3: Teaching experience

1. How many years of teaching experience do you have? a. 0-1 years b. 2-5 years c. 6-10 years d. More than 10 years
2. What level(s) have you taught? a. Elementary school b. Middle school c. High school d. College/university

4: Teaching context:

1. What is the location of your school (urban or rural)?
2. Is your school public or private?
3. What grade level(s) and subject(s) do you teach?

5: Prior technology training or experience:

1. How many years of experience do you have using technology in the classroom?
2. Have you taken any courses or received any training on using technology in education? If so, please describe.
3. On a scale of 1-10, how confident do you feel in your ability to use technology for teaching purposes?

6: Attitudes and beliefs about technology integration:

1. How important do you believe technology integration is in the classroom?
2. What benefits do you see in using technology for teaching purposes?
3. What barriers or challenges do you see in integrating technology into your teaching?

7: Pedagogical knowledge and skills:

1. How comfortable do you feel with incorporating technology into your lesson plans?
2. How frequently do you use technology in your teaching?
3. What specific technologies do you use in your teaching, and how do you use them?

8: Access to technology and resources:

1. What resources do you have available to support technology integration in your classroom?
2. What barriers or challenges do you face in accessing technology and resources?
3. How do you manage access to technology among your students?

9: Questions on a Likert scale that were used to measure pre-service teachers' technology integration skills:

1. I am confident in my ability to use technology effectively in the classroom. (SD/D/N/A/SA)
2. I have received sufficient training in using technology for teaching purposes. (SD/D/N/A/SA)
3. I feel comfortable integrating technology into my lesson plans.(SD/D/N/A/SA)
4. I regularly use technology to enhance student learning.(SD/D/N/A/SA)
5. I am aware of the latest trends and developments in educational technology. (SD/D/N/A/SA)
6. I believe that technology can positively impact student engagement and learning outcomes.(SD/D/N/A/SA)
7. I believe that technology should be an integral part of modern education. (SD/D/N/A/SA)
8. I feel well-prepared to integrate technology into my future teaching practice.(SD/D/N/A/SA)
9. I have experience using a variety of educational technologies.(SD/D/N/A/SA)
10. I feel that technology can help to differentiate instruction and meet the diverse needs of my students.(SD/D/N/A/SA)

# Chapter 5
# Utilizing Generative AI With Second-Language Users and Bilingual Students

**Frank Billingsley**
*Georgetown College, USA*

**Stephanie Gardner**
*Brussels School of Governance, Belgium*

## ABSTRACT

*The growth of generative artificial intelligence (for purposes of this chapter, "AI") has created endless systems to utilize modern technological assistance in the educational arena. AI has the potential to significantly impact higher education by facilitating personalized development and knowledge sharing. There are many ways that AI can be leveraged to enhance the education process. This chapter will focus on second-language users and bilingual students learning new language concepts. Second language users can be defined as students in the language acquisition process. A bilingual student is any student who has already acquired a second language but needs to build on terminology in their field of study. AI can provide a functional teaching tool for educators to assist with building the required knowledge base. The premise is to embrace the tool—versus forbidding its use by students—to assist them in their educational growth.*

DOI: 10.4018/979-8-3693-0487-7.ch005

## INTRODUCTION

There are many advantages to incorporating AI into the classroom. It should be carefully integrated to ensure it is utilized for its value versus merely a method of completing a task. It is essential to balance AI-driven tools and human engagement to produce meaningful learning experiences and encourage critical thinking, analysis, collaboration, and creativity among students. By analyzing student interactions, performance, and progress data, AI algorithms can tailor a lesson's content, pace, and difficulty level to optimize learning outcomes (Sumakul et al., 2022).

AI can be used to carry out tasks typically completed by people. Students often use it to complete the questions versus build their knowledge base. It can gather and aggregate data or listen to speech and reply. AI is the ideal tool for supporting bilingual students in the classroom. In many situations, it is often challenging to master a second language by just attending a classroom setting. Coupling these experiences with in-class and independent use of AI tools can expedite language acquisition (Meunier et al., 2019). As educators of business and law, we have been faced with the extraordinary situation of teaching second language students in international higher education programs for over two decades. Although many of our students are bilingual, we have often faced the challenge that they frequently need a crucial knowledge base in subject-specific terminology. This has hindered the advancement of their coursework. We have hypothesized that utilizing the current language tools in these subject-specific areas will advance their learning for the needed language acquisition.

Language teaching and learning is undergoing a revolution thanks to AI. Depending on user demands and learning preferences, platforms that use AI to power language learning offer many personalized learning opportunities. AI can serve as a knowledgeable tutor that provides pupils with fast feedback and guidance (Saricaoglu, 2019). The systems can review students' spoken or written responses, identify errors or areas for improvement, and provide specific suggestions for improving speaking clarity. AI-enabled virtual assistants may communicate with students, answer their questions, and provide opportunities for language practice. Students' speaking and comprehension skills can be enhanced using these assistants, simulating real-world language interactions.

Second-language users can benefit from speaking and understanding new languages connected to business and law thanks to machine translation and other AI-powered language translation tools. AI can be used for transcribing services, translating spoken communication into written form, and facilitating students' review and analysis of debates or lectures. Evaluating the student performance data can improve curriculum and learning pathways (Sumakul et al., 2022). By detecting knowledge gaps or areas of strength, the approach might suggest pertinent learning materials, exercises, or activities, resulting in a more efficient and tailored learning experience of the subject matter.

## UNDERSTANDING SECOND-LANGUAGE USERS AND BILINGUAL STUDENTS

Finding group instruction strategies to create learning outcomes as effective as one-on-one tutoring is the *2-sigma problem* in education. Educational psychologist Benjamin Bloom first used the phrase in his study from 1984, *The Search for Methods of Group Instruction as Effective as One-to-One Tutoring*. According to Bloom's research, pupils who received one-on-one tutoring performed two standard deviations better on average than those who received regular group teaching (Bloom, 1984). One-on-one tutoring has several benefits that increase learning efficacy. These include individualized attention, prompt feedback, adaptive pacing, and training adapted to the student's needs (Saricaoglu, 2019). Tutors can pinpoint and fill in specific learning gaps, offer explanations tailored to each student's learning preferences, and modify the speed of instruction as necessary.

Although Bloom's 2-sigma dilemma is frequently discussed concerning general education and cognitive abilities, it can also be used in language acquisition. Finding instructional strategies that can produce learning outcomes like those obtained by one-on-one language tutoring is a challenge in language acquisition. These strategies may include the following:

1. **Personalized Instruction:** A language tutor can adjust their instruction method to fit each student's demands, learning progress, and preferences. They can address difficulties, provide personalized feedback, and modify the lesson plan in response to the learner's development.
2. **Feedback:** Tutors can offer rapid feedback on vocabulary usage, grammar, and pronunciation, assisting students in correcting mistakes and reinforcing correct language production (Saricaoglu, 2019).
3. **Conversational Practice:** One-on-one tutoring gives students the chance and opportunities to speak with their tutors in conversation. Fluency, communication, and confidence are all improved by conversation practice.
4. **Individualized Attention:** With one-on-one instruction, tutors can pinpoint and concentrate on the areas where students need extra help or practice. They can create worksheets and activities tailored to the learners' skills and shortcomings (Bloom, 1984).

Bloom's research on the 2-sigma problem in education highlights how difficult it is to develop group instruction methods that are as effective as one-on-one coaching. Because one-on-one tutoring includes many benefits (such as individualized attention, immediate and direct feedback, adaptive pacing, and customized training), it remains a critical and sought-after benchmark for outstanding learning results. The 2-sigma problem encompasses general education, cognitive ability, and language learning. However, teaching methods that AI enhances can often help close the gap and come close to matching the effectiveness of one-on-one language coaching.

The ability for language tutors to modify teaching strategies to suit the needs and preferences of specific students is made possible through personalized instruction. Thanks to this individualized attention, one can directly solve issues, provide detailed comments, and modify the lesson plan considering each learner's development. The value of feedback must also be acknowledged. AI language tools can also be used as essential aids in helping students rectify their mistakes and reinforce correct language output by providing quick and helpful comments on vocabulary usage, grammar, and pronunciation.

In addition, it also becomes clear that practicing in conversation is crucial to learning a language. One-on-one tutoring enables students to converse with their tutors and improve their fluency, communication abilities, and self-assurance in using the language correctly.

Moreover, one of the most significant advantages of language teaching is the value of individualized attention. To address each student's strengths and limitations, tutors can pinpoint areas where a student needs extra practice or guidance.

As a result, although the 2-sigma problem continues to be a challenge in education, including language acquisition, adopting the principles of personalized instruction, feedback, conversational practice, and individualized attention can result in more effective group instruction strategies, reducing the gap between group-based learning outcomes and the remarkable results attained through one-on-one tutoring. By continually exploring and implementing innovative methods through AI, educators can strive to bring about more equitable and exceptional learning experiences for all students.

Finding group instruction methodologies that can result in learning outcomes as effective as one-on-one tutoring is the "2-sigma problem" in education. Individualized attention, prompt feedback, adjustable pacing, and tailored instruction are advantages of one-on-one coaching, but it is often impractical and expensive.

There are, however, instructional approaches that can decrease the efficacy gap and get very close to matching one-on-one language tutoring. These techniques involve individualized attention, feedback, practice in dialogue, and personalized training. By following these guidelines, teachers can develop group instruction tactics that are more successful and can close the gap between the impressive results gained through one-on-one tutoring and group-based learning outcomes.

When it comes to language learning, personalized instruction enables instructors to modify their lesson plans to suit each student's requirements and learning styles. They can adjust the lesson plan according to the learner's progress, solve issues, and provide personalized feedback. Feedback is also crucial since tutors may give students quick feedback on their usage of vocabulary, grammar, and pronunciation, helping them to fix their errors and reinforce proper language output.

Another crucial component of language learning is conversation practice, which allows students several opportunities to have natural conversations with their teachers. Conversation practice boosts confidence, fluency, and communication. Lastly, individualized instruction enables tutors to identify and concentrate on the areas where students need further training or support. They can design exercises and activities specific to the learner's strengths and weaknesses. Educators can work to provide more extraordinary and equal learning opportunities for all students by continuously experimenting with and putting those methods into practice.

## BENEFITS AND CHALLENGES OF BILINGUALISM IN EDUCATIONAL SETTINGS

Some factors that can promote and encourage this could be increased cognition, cultural understanding, academic performance, and personal development (Seror & Weinberg, 2021). Cognitive benefits from learning a second language positively affect cognitive development, improving memory, problem-solving skills, and multitasking abilities. Bilingual individuals often exhibit better attention, cognitive flexibility, and creative thinking (Seror & Weinberg, 2021).

Cultural understanding and language are deeply intertwined with culture. Learning a second language gives individuals a deeper understanding and appreciation of different cultures, traditions, and perspectives. It promotes intercultural communication and fosters a more inclusive and tolerant society. There is often the potential aspect of academic performance. Research indicates that students who are bilingual or participate in bilingual education programs often demonstrate enhanced academic performance compared to their monolingual peers (Sumakul et al., 2022). Bilingualism has been associated with improved cognitive abilities, higher academic achievement, and increased metalinguistic awareness. There is also the potential for personal growth when acquiring a second language, as it expands an individual's ability to communicate with a broader range of people and engage in meaningful interactions. Bilingualism can help promote personal growth, self-confidence, and empathy by enabling individuals to connect with diverse communities and build relationships across linguistic and cultural boundaries. Second-language acquisition and bilingual education have wide-ranging individual, societal, and global benefits. They can promote cognitive development, economic opportunities, cultural understanding, and personal growth while contributing to the preservation of languages and the building of inclusive communities.

Research confirms that learning a second language and receiving a bilingual education have several advantages for individuals and society (Sumakul et al., 2022). These advantages may include enhanced intellectual growth, cultural comprehension, academic achievement, and personal development. A growing body of research continues to support the benefits of bilingualism in several fields, particularly business and law.

The capacity to converse in several languages is becoming more crucial in today's world. In our experience, we have observed that bilingual students often have an advantage in the job market and are typically better prepared to integrate into a global culture. Additionally, they are more likely to accept other people's traditions, which can support the development of inclusive and tranquil communities.

## IDENTIFYING THE UNIQUE NEEDS OF SECOND-LANGUAGE USERS AND BILINGUAL STUDENTS

The 2-sigma dilemma in language acquisition has led to efforts to create teaching strategies replicating the advantages of one-on-one tutoring in a classroom or self-directed learning environment. Language learning supported by computer-based programs and technologies is known as computer-assisted language learning. These tools can offer interactive exercises, feedback on pronunciation, grammar exercises, and vocabulary drills (Saricaoglu, 2019). Additionally, they might add aspects of adaptive learning, adjusting the curriculum to meet the needs of each student. Online language learning platforms provide courses that use multimedia materials, interactive activities, and language exchange elements. While these platforms might not offer individualized training, they frequently feature gamification and social media integration to keep users interested and foster a more engaging learning environment.

By establishing links between students and teachers who are native speakers, language exchange programs help students learn new languages. Mobile apps provide language learning tools that can be accessed anytime, anywhere. These apps provide interactive activities, which include flashcards, language problems, and listening drills. Some apps also use speech recognition technologies to offer feedback on pronunciation. Although these methods try to solve the 2-sigma issue in language learning, it is crucial to remember that tailored training and one-on-one interaction still have much more to offer. Technological advances and adaptive learning systems are constantly extending the bounds of group instruction and self-directed learning to close the accomplishment gap between one-on-one tutoring and other instructional modalities in language acquisition.

## APPLICATIONS OF AI IN SECOND-LANGUAGE LEARNING

Systems for teaching languages that adapt to the individual learner's needs are platforms or tools used in education. These systems modify the curriculum, content, pace, and feedback based on the learners' talents, advancement, and preferences. Adaptive systems adjust the learning material to fit the objectives and demands of the learners. They examine the learners' proficiency levels, strengths, limitations, and learning preferences to give suitable materials, exercises, and resources. This personalization improves students' learning experiences by allowing them to concentrate on areas that require development.

Adaptive systems design individual learning routes based on each learner's performance and development (Sumakul et al., 2022). The plans analyze learning interactions and assessment outcomes data to identify knowledge gaps and suggest the best action. This ensures that students receive specialized training and practice opportunities, maximizing their language-learning process.

Student responses are assessed, their progression is followed, and areas for improvement are identified. Students quickly receive feedback that identifies issues, offers solutions, and provides explanations. This real-time feedback supports language skill development while encouraging self-directed study.

Based on the skill and advancement of the student, these systems adapt to the degree of difficulty of the learning content. If students consistently perform well, the system may add increasingly difficult materials to keep them interested and encourage further development. On the other hand, if students have trouble understanding a particular idea, the system can offer more practice and assistance at a suitable degree of difficulty.

Systems for adaptive language learning use AI to design a personalized and productive learning environment. Adaptive systems accommodate learners' learning paces. Learners can progress through the material at their own speed, taking more time in areas that require additional practice or moving quickly through familiar topics. This flexibility ensures that learners feel energized and helps in maintaining their motivation and engagement. Systems for adaptive language learning produce helpful information about students' performance, development, and learning habits. This information can help teachers identify their students' strengths and weaknesses, monitor the entire class's progress, and plan practical lessons. These findings can assist teachers in tailoring their support for specific students and changing their instructional approaches. Adaptive systems' tailored features boost learners' engagement and motivation. Learning is more relevant and meaningful when learners are given content and exercises that align with their interests and goals. The real-time feedback and progress tracking also give learners a sense of accomplishment and motivate them to continue their language learning. These systems can improve language learning results and give students a more exciting and tailored learning experience by responding to individual needs and improving learning paths.

## ADDRESSING THE NEEDS OF SECOND-LANGUAGE USERS AND BILINGUAL STUDENTS WITH AI

AI can play a significant role in language acquisition by providing personalized and adaptive learning experiences that cater to the needs of second-language users and bilingual students. AI-powered language competency tests can accurately measure the degree of proficiency of bilingual students and users of second languages (Knewton, 2019). This enables teachers to pinpoint students' strengths and areas for development. AI can review student performance data and change the learning path as appropriate. It can identify specific language issues and provide specialized exercises to hone those skills, fostering a more efficient and customized learning process. AI can offer prompt input on language usage, pronunciation, and grammar, assisting bilingual students and speakers of a second language to rectify errors as they happen. This real-time help facilitates the improvement of linguistic abilities. Considering pupils' diverse linguistic backgrounds, AI can support various languages. Users get access to educational material in their native tongues, which promotes learning and increases engagement.

AI-powered speech recognition technology can assist students in honing their speaking and pronunciation abilities. It can provide precise feedback on spoken language and specific oral communication exercises. AI can introduce learners to the target language's idioms, traditions, and practices by integrating cultural elements into language learning (Knewton, 2019). This encourages a greater comprehension and appreciation of the cultural context of the language.

Another way AI can benefit language learners is that it can modify educational content to accommodate different learning preferences and philosophies. It can provide content in various media to adapt to varied learner preferences, including films, interactive exercises, or written texts. AI can track the linguistic growth of learners and highlight areas that need improvement. Educators can use a data-driven approach to offer necessary support and interventions immediately. AI's adaptable algorithms, which change based on user interactions and feedback, enable continual learning. AI systems can modify the exercises and the content's degree of difficulty as learners advance, to maintain the right level of challenge.

AI-driven personalized and adaptive learning experiences can completely transform the way bilingual students and users of second languages learn languages. AI enables learners to acquire excellent language proficiency and embrace linguistic diversity more successfully by addressing individual needs and offering personalized support.

During the engagement process, AI has the potential to identify students' language proficiency and place them on a track appropriate for their current language level. The algorithm will gradually advance the pupil along a learning curve. However, support structures, such as educator engagement, should be in place to offer constructive criticism and guidance (Firria, 2021). Every learner's online actions will be chronicled as data for the educator to assess students' efforts and progress more effectively.

AI will continuously learn from and respond to specific learners using the technology. For instance, a speech recognition engine can listen to students' speech patterns and understand their unique accents (Carrier, 2017). The educator can quickly receive all this information in a practical and actionable way. In the ideal scenario, AI should offer offline assistance through standards-based courses and assist the educator in dividing the class into appropriate groups for each student's needs—tools such as Rosetta Stone, Babbel, Duolingo, Grammarly, and Automated Speech Recognition are a few of the potential options (Ranalli & Yamashita, 2022).

Educators can use AI-enabled platforms to monitor students' performance (Sumakul et al., 2022). These platforms have greatly improved over time. Historically, educators would have to wait for an annual language competency test to determine whether a learner was progressing. Educators can now login at any time to monitor progress. Even better, the offline materials and embedded progress monitoring are able to support educators in prioritizing and focusing instruction to meet the unique needs of every student. These language tools could be further built into a foundation or introductory course to ensure that all students have the same level of language comprehension.

## ENHANCED LANGUAGE PRACTICE AND FEEDBACK

Artificial intelligence-based voice recognition and pronunciation assessment systems analyze a degree of spoken language to give feedback on pronunciation accuracy and fluency. These tools are made to help language learners develop their speaking skills. To translate spoken words into written form, AI algorithms can evaluate audio input and can successfully record and comprehend spoken speech using acoustic and language modeling methods.

To build on this process, the AI-based systems can compare speech recorded with the appropriate patterns or models of pronunciation to strengthen speaking ability. The method may evaluate the articulation's precision by comparing the spoken language's phonetic and prosodic characteristics with the predicted patterns. AI systems detect speech mistakes or variances from the norm, such as pronunciation of sounds, stress patterns, intonation, and rhythm. The algorithm can pinpoint precisely where students must develop (Bang et al., 2014). The system gives students feedback and recommendations based on the identified problems. This input may come in the form of verbal signals, words that are highlighted, or visual cues. The system might also provide explanations and examples to assist students in understanding and fixing their pronunciation problems.

Learning opportunities for pronunciation practice are frequently offered by AI-powered voice recognition and assessment systems. The method gives learners quick feedback on their pronunciation correctness when they repeat words or sentences. The system may also monitor students' advancement over time, enabling them to see their growth and establish objectives for further improvement (Diment et al., 2019). Some AI-based solutions can adjust to the tastes and demands of every student. They can alter the degree of difficulty of the activities, tailor feedback depending on the unique pronunciation difficulties of the learners, and provide focused practice materials to address their inadequacies.

These AI-based voice recognition and assessment systems give students a hands-on, unbiased tool to sharpen their pronunciation abilities. They provide immediate feedback, focused practice, and progress tracking, enabling students to concentrate on areas that need improvement and track their growth over time (Diment et al., 2019). For a complete language learning experience, it is crucial to remember that these systems are aids and should be utilized in conjunction with human instruction and feedback.

Various tools, such as Alison, BusinessEnglishSite, TalkEnglish, and FluentU, can be utilized in this fashion. To begin with, Alison provides an excellent business English class featuring free online courses from reputable companies like Microsoft and Google. The course "Introduction to Business and Travel English Language Skills" consists of three modules, including an assessment. The class duration ranges from one to two hours, and upon completion, participants can obtain a diploma by purchasing.

BusinessEnglishSite.com offers a variety of class options for business English, making it an outstanding platform for learning and testing the student's language proficiency. The student can select from general business terms and grammar exercises.

In addition, the website features quizzes covering job interviews, negotiations, project management, and other category terms.

TalkEnglish.com presents an uncomplicated approach to grasping frequently used business phrases and terms across diverse categories, ranging from office fundamentals to presentations. The website offers a complimentary selection of quick tutorials or the option to download complete courses for a nominal fee. This resource mainly benefits non-English speakers as the phrases accompany audio pronunciations.

A comprehensive set of resources for business English is offered by FluentU, including videos, audio clips, and flashcards. The platform allows students to listen to dialogues and view and hear relevant vocabulary. The videos have on-screen text synchronized with the audio, and they can pause to explore specific words and phrases in more detail.

If these tools are utilized more in the practical curriculum, there can be unique growth in learning (Ali, 2020).

## WRITING AND GRAMMAR ASSISTANCE

Utilizing AI technologies, writing and grammar aid applications give users access to tools and features that improve their writing abilities and grammar precision (Godwin-Jones, 2022). These apps include various components, including grammar and spelling checks, style recommendations, and vocabulary enhancement (O'Neill & Russell, 2020).

A popular Grammarly program provides grammar and spelling correction tools (Ranalli & Yamashita, 2022). It uses AI algorithms to find mistakes, recommend fixes, and offer justifications. It also features a plagiarism checker, style recommendations, and vocabulary improvement assistance (Ghufron & Rosyida, 2018)

Finally, Hemingway Editor is a valuable tool that enables users to elevate the style and clarity of their writing. It identifies instances of passive voice, highlights long and complex sentences, suggests simpler alternatives, and provides readability ratings. This software aims to enhance the overall impact and clarity of the written content (Ali, 2020). Microsoft Editor, available in Microsoft programs like PowerPoint, Word, and Outlook, offers many features. It includes spell and grammar checks, style recommendations, and clarity improvements. For those seeking additional functionality, a paid subscription provides extra benefits. These writing and grammar apps leverage the power of artificial intelligence to analyze and process text, providing users with instant feedback and ideas to refine correctness, clarity, and style (Godwin-Jones, 2022). While these tools can be highly beneficial for effective writing, it is essential to remember that they are aids and should not replace critical thinking and manual proofreading efforts. Human judgment and revision remain crucial for producing truly polished and well-crafted written work.

## CULTURALLY SENSITIVE AND INCLUSIVE AI TOOLS

AI models can be trained to comprehend the cultural context and linguistic subtleties to assist second language learners and bilingual students in understanding idiomatic expressions, comedy, regional colloquialisms, and cultural references. AI can improve students'-comprehension and fluency by explaining or making culturally appropriate suggestions, bridging cultural divides, and promoting effective communication.

Using AI to improve language acquisition poses various ethical issues that must be carefully considered. These factors include the possible effects on people and society and the broader impacts of employing AI for language learning. Data protection and privacy concerns can arise. To customize learning experiences, AI language acquisition systems frequently gather and process enormous volumes of personal data. To prevent potential misuse or unauthorized access to sensitive information, it is essential to ensure data privacy, get informed consent, and securely store user data. AI language models may unintentionally reinforce biases seen in the data because they are trained on algorithms (Rusmiyanto et al., 2023). In language learning, this may result in unjust treatment or serve to reinforce prejudices. Developers must make a conscious effort to eliminate biases and guarantee inclusivity.

AI models can be highly complicated and challenging to understand. Making the AI system's decision-making process accessible and understandable is crucial when using AI in language learning, especially when it influences the possibilities or progress of learners. Although AI language acquisition can provide personalized learning experiences, socioeconomic inequities may prevent everyone from using it. To stop the further marginalization of existing oppressed groups, it is essential to guarantee equal access to AI-driven language learning tools.

AI should be used to learn languages in addition to, not as a substitute for, human instruction. Over-reliance on AI could reduce human interaction, influencing how well people communicate and connect with others. As learners become unduly reliant on technology, relying primarily on AI for language acquisition may limit critical thinking and creativity. It is crucial to balance promoting conventional teaching techniques and employing AI as a tool.

AI's integration into language acquisition may have unintended implications (Rusmiyanto et al., 2023). To find and fix possible problems, it is crucial to constantly monitor and evaluate how the AI system affects students and the learning process.

Developers, educators, politicians, and stakeholders must work together and set clear standards and regulations to appropriately deploy AI in language acquisition to solve these ethical concerns. In-depth effect analyses and user input gathering can also aid in identifying and reducing any ethical issues.

## BEST PRACTICE AND CASE STUDIES: BUSINESS AND LAW LANGUAGE ACQUISITION

In an increasingly interconnected and globalized business environment, proficiency in the language of instruction, such as English, is essential for business and law majors. They need to be proficient in cross-cultural communication. The corporate world's "lingua franca" is English, which makes it easy to communicate with people from various language origins. English proficiency enables business and law majors to participate in negotiations, presentations, and conversations, promoting collaboration and cross-cultural understanding. This allows them to clarify complex business concepts and convey their views quickly. Learning a business language is essential because it will enable them to communicate effectively in formal contexts.

Building a solid foundation of business and legal jargon and terminology specific to their area should be a priority for business and law students. This comprises words from business, management, legal, and other pertinent fields. Understanding and communicating clearly in these contexts will be possible by familiarizing students with industry-specific jargon.

Business majors should focus on developing extraordinary writing abilities in this area (Godwin-Jones, 2022). Writing effective emails, reports, proposals, and other business documents is a part of this. To guarantee efficient communication inside an organization, emphasis should be placed on clarity, concision, and appropriate formatting.

English proficiency broadens the prospects available to business majors, giving them access to various international opportunities. Strong English proficiency is a requirement for many international organizations, prestigious business schools, and global firms. Mastery of the language increases the likelihood of receiving overseas internships, scholarships, and work placement, opening doors to fulfilling employment opportunities.

In our modern world, networking and developing relationships are crucial. English proficiency and the ability to communicate effectively and build more significant connections with experts from different linguistic origins benefit business and law majors. Speaking effectively in English builds credibility and encourages cooperation and collaboration in networking events, conferences, or other business-related activities.

Working with real-world case studies and simulations of businesses can give students practical experience with business terminology and ideas. Business and law majors can better apply their language skills to applicable settings by analyzing business issues and debating solutions. This enhances their capacity for critical thought and decision-making.

These majors must concentrate on networking abilities and business etiquette. This entails knowing the proper business protocol, acting appropriately in professional contexts, and cultivating business contacts through clear communication. Business and law majors should participate in various learning activities, such as immersive learning opportunities, practical internships, and networking with industry experts. Their language can be improved by incorporating these strategies with formal language instruction, practice, and AI learning opportunities.

The English language makes access to many business-related knowledge and resources possible. English-speaking business majors can access many books, articles, industry reports, and case studies. Their knowledge of international business trends, best practices, and new markets is aided by their access to critical information. Business and law majors have an advantage in their studies and future professions by being able to interpret and analyze these materials. Employees receive immediate feedback on their written or spoken business language via the AI-powered platform. It helps employees communicate more effectively and professionally by identifying grammar mistakes, making vocabulary suggestions, and providing explanations and examples for better language usage, such as Grammarly.

These majors frequently encounter circumstances that call for solid presentation and communication abilities. Being fluent in English guarantees the ability to articulate thoughts confidently and convey intricate commercial concepts. Strong communication and presentation abilities affect stakeholders, promote professionalism, and increase the overall effectiveness of essential message delivery. Business and law majors fluent in English are better equipped to express their ideas clearly and change their communication styles to fit various situations. A multinational corporation with offices across several nations frequently hires individuals with diverse linguistic backgrounds. English, the company's official business language, must be used successfully by these workers when communicating and working together. However, many non-native English speakers require assistance developing their business language abilities.

## BUSINESS LANGUAGE ACQUISITION FOR BUSINESS MAJORS

Students majoring in business should develop presenting and general speaking skills. Understanding how to effectively engage an audience, arrange and deliver presentations, and communicate vital messages is necessary. Improving confidence and communication skills requires practice and feedback on presentation techniques. The organization knows that conventional language training techniques like classroom-based courses or one-on-one instruction must adequately cover its employees' language demands. These techniques could be hard to use, time-consuming, and need more individualized feedback and ongoing support.

Students must learn negotiation and persuasion skills. Understanding negotiation tactics, strategies, and efficient communication methods falls under this category. In various academic settings, mastering the craft of professional persuasion and influence can be beneficial. AI language acquisition solutions for business and legal language to enhance student language training can assist each student with more personalized instruction. The programs can adapt to each student's needs and language proficiency levels. It evaluates their current language proficiency, identifies areas for development, and creates specialized learning routes to raise their business language proficiency.

Understanding the English language is crucial for these majors, given the globally connected nature of the business world today. They gain the ability to communicate internationally for business, take advantage of global possibilities, forge meaningful connections, access vast knowledge resources, improve presentation abilities, and adopt a global perspective. Business majors prioritizing English language competence set themselves up for success in a cutthroat global environment, enhancing their employability and fostering professional development.

Over the years, we have encountered numerous students who have struggled with English as a functional language, not to mention the ability to understand more advanced terms needed for English acquisition. The assistance process has changed over the years, from a workbook approach to more recently utilizing online language development tools to online grammar development tools. Students have been able to build language skills faster with extra effort with online tools and regular in-class attendance. In addition, we are using grammar tools to assist in building sentence structure and tense development. It can be noted that post-COVID, we can see some regression in language skills (Department of Education, 2021). Thus, using assistance tools is more relevant now than ever.

## LEGAL LANGUAGE ACQUISITION FOR LAW MAJORS

As mentioned above, a growing body of research confirms that learning a second language and receiving a bilingual education has many advantages for individuals and society as a whole. These advantages include enhanced intellectual growth, cultural comprehension, academic achievement, and personal development. This is particularly important in the field of law.

A recent report by the McKinsey Global Institute entitled *Generative AI and the Future of Work in America* noted, "By 2030, activities that account for up to 30 percent of hours currently worked across the US economy could be automated—a trend accelerated by generative AI. However, we see generative AI enhancing the way STEM, creative, and business and legal professionals work rather than eliminating a significant number of jobs outright" (Ellingrud et al., 2023, p. iv).

With respect to the legal profession in particular, the report further confirms,

*Looking in more detail at specific occupations, we see the biggest impact of generative AI occurring for lawyers ... Generative AI can search through case law for the most relevant precedents, freeing lawyers to think through how to apply them in new legal arguments. Lawyers also spend a great deal of time tailoring form documents, but they could use generative AI to take the first cut and then quickly edit. (Ellingrud et al. 2023)*

Without a doubt, AI has the potential to revolutionize numerous aspects of legal education, if not the legal profession itself. New and innovative tools and resources are increasingly available for law students and their teachers, as well as legal professionals. In shaping future lawyers and legal thinkers, when used correctly, AI can be embraced as a tool to enhance legal education, research, writing, critical thinking, and analysis.

For example, AI tools can greatly assist in legal document review by rapidly analyzing large bodies of text, identifying relevant parts, and generating useful summaries. These tools can also help students locate case law, legal opinions, rules, and regulations, as well as assist in drafting papers, contracts, briefs, and other documents. Popular AI-powered research tools include Westlaw Edge, LexisNexis, i-law, Context, and Ross Intelligence.

As for using AI as a means to improve legal writing, some legal professionals currently use Amto AI, Latch, One Law AI, and Ghostwriter Legal. Often considered time savers, these tools can assist the experienced professional in drafting legal documents and summaries, formatting, and citations.

Finally, AI can also serve as a virtual legal tutor as it can serve as an interactive study resource by providing direct feedback and guidance on writing assignments to assist in improving research skills, writing style, and citations. These programs generally cover a broad range of legal topics and include study aids such as interactive case analysis, practice quizzes, and other tools designed to complement traditional legal education. Some digital learning tools include Casebook Connect, Quimbee, Center for Computer-Assisted Legal Instruction (CALI Lessons), LawDojo, and Barbri (primarily assists with Bar Examination preparation but it also offers study resources for students). Virtual legal tutors can also help with legal language translations in helping bilingual students and second language learners to better understand foreign legal texts and documents.

## AND THEN THERE IS ChatGPT

As set out in the McKinsey report,

*Rarely has a tech innovation created such a splash as ChatGPT, which has achieved one of the fastest adoption rates in history ... ChatGPT is only one of several new generative AI tools. The "generative" in the name refers to its ability to identify patterns across enormous sets of data and generate new content—something that has often been considered uniquely human. ChatGPT can be used to write correspondence, essays, articles, stories, poetry, and computer code, in addition to scraping the internet for information and answering questions. (Ellingrud et al., 2023)*

In his article in *The New York Times*, "How Schools Can Survive (and Maybe Even Thrive) With A.I. This Fall," author Kevin Roose writes,

*... when Chat GPT was released, many schools felt as if they'd been hit by an asteroid. In the middle of an academic year, with no warning, teachers were forced to confront the new alien-seeming technology, which allowed students to write college-level essays, solve challenging problem sets, and ace standardized tests? (Roose, 2023)*

While admitting that these tools are new and far from perfect, Roose sets out three challenges to educators regarding the use of AI in the classroom:

*First, I encourage educators—especially in high schools and colleges—to assume that 100 percent of their students are using ChatGPT and other generative A.I. tools on every assignment, in every subject, unless they're being physically supervised inside a school building.*

*Second, schools should stop relying on A.I. detector programs to catch cheaters. There are dozens of these tools on the market now, all claiming to spot writing that was generated with A.I., and none of them work reliably well.*

*My third piece of advice—and the one that may get me the most angry emails from teachers—is that teachers should focus less on warning students about the shortcomings of generative A.I. than on figuring out what the technology does well. (Roose, 2023)*

Finally, the author encourages educators to familiarize themselves with the technology "with the goal of getting as fluent in the technology as many of their students already are" (Roose, 2023).

Not surprisingly, reader reaction was mixed, particularly from those who identified themselves as members of the academic community. Justifiable concerns ranged from questions regarding the technology's reliability and lack of transparency to far-reaching legal and ethical concerns, especially in bringing AI into the classroom and its impact on the future of learning, education, and knowledge as we know it.

In response, a law professor decided to raise the questions of *The New York Times* article to their students. The students were asked the following:

1. Should I assume that 100 percent of you are using ChatGPT and other generative AI tools on your assignments in every subject unless you're being physically supervised on campus?
2. In your view, should schools stop relying on AI detector programs to catch cheaters?
3. What possible legal and ethical concerns do you see in such a scenario?
4. Do you believe that teachers should focus less on warning students about the shortcomings of AI than on figuring out what the technology does well?
5. And finally, what advice would you offer a teacher who is considering using AI in their classroom assignments and as a tool to further engage students?

With some initial reluctance, not surprisingly, all or most of the students admitted that, yes, they routinely use AI in all or most of their coursework. Some offered that they use it as a "brainstorming tool," as they used Wikipedia in the past, in order "to get them started" on a research assignment. Others admitted to relying on it more often, to various degrees.

They also reflected that they wish they were taught how to better use AI technology (i.e., they asked questions such as, what can AI do for me? How can I use it more intelligently? What do I have to do myself? What do I need to be careful about, including ethical considerations and liability?). One student commented that it could also be interesting to include AI in the more practical parts of law school, such as moot court, skills courses, and bar preparation.

In opening up a dialogue with their students, similarly, the authors would encourage their fellow instructors to enter into conversations like this with their students and listen to how they are using AI and the areas where they would like to improve their ability to use these tools in a constructive manner, particularly in their future professional endeavors. These are difficult but important dialogues that need to take place first and foremost within academia, among instructors, and ultimately, with the students themselves.

## SOLUTIONS AND RECOMMENDATIONS FOR EFFECTIVE AI INTEGRATION

A subfield of artificial intelligence called "Natural Language Processing" (NLP) concerns how computers and human language interact. It involves creating techniques and algorithms that allow machines to comprehend, interpret, and produce meaningful and effective human speech (Ali, 2020). NLP approaches enable computers to understand and translate the written human language. This comprises information extraction, topic modeling, sentiment analysis, named entity identification, and text classification. NLP algorithms can analyze large amounts of text data to produce insights, information summaries, or information extractions.

Speech recognition systems use NLP to transform spoken language into text using algorithms (Ali, 2020). They can also be used in speech synthesis, where robots produce spoken words from written text, and power systems automatically translate text from one language to another. These systems use algorithms that examine sentence structure, syntax, and semantics to provide precise translations. Machine translation frequently uses statistical techniques, rule-based techniques, and neural machine translation models.

Question-answering systems that can comprehend and respond to natural language inquiries can be created using NLP approaches. These tools evaluate the question's intent, look for pertinent material in each dataset or knowledge base, and then offer brief and precise responses. Siri, Alexa, and Google Assistant, among other virtual assistants, depend on NLP to comprehend and execute user orders and inquiries.

Artificial intelligence-powered immersive language learning experiences develop personalized, interactive learning environments using these technologies. With the help of these activities, learning becomes more effective and pleasant by simulating real-world language use and immersing students in the language. Here are some essential elements and characteristics of AI-powered immersive language learning experiences:

- The foundation of immersive language learning experiences is NLP.
- AI-powered NLP systems understand and interpret the student's verbal or written input, delivering pertinent and contextually suitable responses.
- AI-powered chatbots or virtual assistants are frequently used in immersive language learning. These conversational bots allow students to practice speaking and listening in the target language by simulating real-world interactions.

The learning platform incorporates gamified components and interactive exercises to keep students interested and motivated. These exercises, all aimed at reinforcing linguistic abilities, may include tests, games, role-playing scenarios, and storytelling. Platforms for AI-enabled language learning offer a large variety of actual content in the target language. This resource may expose students to real language use and cultural subtleties through news articles, podcasts, films, and social media posts. To help learners improve their accent and intonation in the target language, it may assess how they pronounce words and give them immediate feedback.

Virtual language exchange programs can be facilitated by AI, bringing together language learners and native speakers for language practice. This encourages fruitful cross-cultural communication and language engagement. Immersive language learning experiences have been made possible by advances in augmented reality (AR) and virtual reality (VR) technologies. Learners can improve their language learning by using replicated real-world settings to practice language abilities. By giving students useful, entertaining, and personalized opportunities to practice their language abilities in authentic situations, these AI-enabled immersive language learning experiences have the potential to revolutionize language learning. Future solutions for immersive language learning should become ever more sophisticated and potent as AI technology develops. By offering individualized, interactive, and immersive learning experiences, AI-powered immersive language learning experiences have the potential to revolutionize language learning. These opportunities may be quicker ways to learn a language than more conventional ones and may also be more effective.

## CONCLUSION

In conclusion, integrating AI into education holds immense potential for enhancing learning, particularly for second-language learners and bilingual students. By harnessing AI-driven tools, educators can customize lessons to match each student's language proficiency, enabling them to progress at their own pace. AI platforms deliver rapid and accurate data to teachers, enabling them to track progress and adapt instruction by continually learning from and responding to students. The speech recognition capabilities of AI offer valuable speaking practice, a crucial component for refining oral language skills.

Regarding second language acquisition, AI models can be trained to recognize linguistic subtleties and cultural contexts, aiding students in understanding idiomatic expressions, regional colloquialisms, and cultural references. However, it is imperative to balance AI-driven tools and student engagement within the classroom. While AI can be a valuable aid, educators play an essential role in facilitating human interaction, critical thinking, collaboration, and creativity, which are integral to holistic educational experiences.

Educators should view AI as a teaching tool, capitalizing on its strengths while providing students with constructive feedback and guidance. Embracing AI for educational enhancement rather than fearing it as a threat is crucial as technology advances. By thoughtfully integrating AI into the classroom, educators can leverage its potential to accelerate language learning, foster cultural understanding, and empower students in their academic journey.

In the contemporary global landscape, proficiency in English and specialized business or legal terminology is pivotal for success in business and law. Mastery of the English language facilitates effective cross-cultural communication, opens doors to international opportunities, and grants access to invaluable knowledge resources. AI-powered tools like ChatGPT can aid students in writing, research, and communication tasks, but they also raise concerns like plagiarism and the need for adaptable teaching approaches.

In legal education, AI offers promising contributions to legal research, document drafting, and even simulated legal scenarios. Educators are encouraged to embrace AI as an enhancement tool for legal education, acknowledging its strengths and limitations. Transparent discussions between educators and students about AI's role in learning are essential for seamlessly integrating AI tools while upholding principles of responsibility and ethics.

Moreover, AI is reshaping language learning through immersive experiences powered by NLP and augmented/virtual reality technologies. These immersive encounters provide personalized, interactive, and contextually relevant language practice, potentially revolutionizing language acquisition.

In summary, the fusion of AI and NLP technologies presents opportunities and challenges in education and language acquisition. While AI can amplify learning experiences and provide valuable productivity tools, a balanced understanding of its capabilities and ethical considerations is vital for educators and students navigating its implementation.

## REFERENCES

Ali, Z. (2020). Artificial Intelligence (AI): A review of its uses in language teaching and learning. *IOP Conference Series. Materials Science and Engineering*, *769*(1), 012043. doi:10.1088/1757-899X/769/1/012043

Bang, J., Lee, G. G., Lee, G., & Chung, M. (2014). Pronunciation variants prediction method to detect mispronunciations by Korean learners of English. *ACM Transactions on Asian Language Information Processing*, *13*(4), 1–21. doi:10.1145/2629545

Bloom, B.S. (1984). *The 2-sigma problem: The search for methods of group instruction as effective as one-to-one tutoring*. Syracuse University.

Carrier, M. (2017). Automated speech recognition in language learning: Potential models, benefits, and impact. *Training, Language, and Culture*, *1*(1), 46–61. doi:10.29366/2017tlc.1.1.3

Department of Education. (2021). *Education in a pandemic: The disparate impact of COVID-19 on American students*. DoE. https://www2.ed.gov/about/offices/list/ocr/docs/20210608-impacts-of-covid19.pdf

Diment, A., Fagerlund, E., Benfield, A., & Virtanen, T. (2019). Detection of typical pronunciation errors in non-native English speech using convolutional recurrent neural networks. *International Joint Conference on Neural Network*, pp. 1-8. 10.1109/IJCNN.2019.8851963

Ellingrud, K., Sanghvi, S., Dandona, G. S., Madgavkar, A., Chui, M., White, O., & Hasebe, P. (2023). *Generative AI and the future of work in America*. McKinsey Global Institute. https://www.mckinsey.com/mgi/our-research/generative-ai-and-the-future-of-work-in-america#/

Firria, T. N. (2021). *Artificial Intelligence (AI) in education: Using AI tools for teaching and learning process*. Institut Teknologi Bisnis AAS Indonesia. https://prosiding.stie- aas.ac.id/index.php/prosenas/article/view/106/104

Ghufron, M. A., & Rosyida, F. (2018). The role of Grammarly in assessing English as foreign language (EFL) writing. *Lingua Cultura*, *12*(4), 395–403. doi:10.21512/lc.v12i4.4582

Godwin-Jones, R. (2022). Partnering with AI: Intelligent writing assistance and instructed language learning. *Language Learning & Technology*, *26*(2), 5–24. 10125/73474

Knewton. (2019). *Adaptive learning defined: A Knewton guide*. Knewton. https://www.knewton.com/adaptive-learning

Meunier, F., Van de Vyver, J., Bradley, L., & Thouesny, S. (2019). *EUROCALL 2019: Call and complexity*. DoE.

O'Neill, R., & Russell, A. M. (2020). Grammarly: Help or hindrance? Academic learning advisors' perceptions of an online grammar checker. *Journal of Academic Language and Learning*, *13*(1), A88–A107.

Ranalli, J., & Yamashita, T. (2022). Automated written corrective feedback: Error-correction performance and timing of delivery. *Language Learning & Technology, 26*(1), 1–25. http://hdl.handle.net/10125/73465

Roose, K. (2023). How schools can survive (and maybe even thrive) with AI this fall. *The New York Times*. https://www.nytimes.com/2023/08/24/technology/how-schools-can-survive-and-maybe-even-thrive-with-ai-this-fall.html

Rusmiyanto, N. H., Nining, F., Novita, K. T., Agus, R., & Mike, N. S. (2023). The role of Artificial intelligence (AI) in developing English language learners' communication skills. *Journal of Education, 6*(1).

Saricaoglu, A. (2019). The impact of automated feedback on L2 learners' written causal explanations. *ReCALL, 31*(2), 189–203. doi:10.1017/S095834401800006X

Seror, J., & Weinberg, A. (2021). Exploring the longitudinal impact of university immersion: Bilingual spaces, multilingual values. *System, 99*, 102523. doi:10.1016/j.system.2021.102523

Sumakul, D. T., Hamied, F. A., & Sukyadi, D. (2022). Artificial Intelligence in EFL classrooms: Friend or foe? *LEARN Journal: Language Education and Acquisition Research Network, 15*(1), 232–256.

## KEY TERMS AND DEFINITIONS

**Academic Performance:** Improved educational achievement, often demonstrated by bilingual students or participants in bilingual education programs.

**Adaptive Learning Systems:** Educational platforms or tools that modify the curriculum, content, pace, and feedback based on individual learners' abilities, progress, and preferences.

**Adaptive Pacing:** Adjusting the speed or pace of instruction to match the learner's progress and comprehension level.

**Cognitive Benefits:** Positive effects on cognitive development, including memory, problem-solving skills, multitasking abilities, attention, cognitive flexibility, and creative thinking, resulting from learning a second language.

**Cultural Understanding:** Gaining a deeper appreciation and comprehension of different cultures, traditions, and perspectives through language learning, promoting intercultural communication and tolerance.

**Effect Analyses:** Comprehensive assessments of how AI systems impact students and the learning process, including both intended and unintended consequences.

**Individualized Attention:** Providing personalized and specific guidance and support to each student based on their unique needs, strengths, and weaknesses.

**Personal Development:** Growth in personal skills, self-confidence, and empathy through language acquisition, enabling individuals to connect with diverse communities and build relationships across linguistic and cultural boundaries.

**Prompt Feedback:** Giving timely and immediate responses and comments to students on their performance or work.

**Speech Recognition Technology:** AI-driven systems that analyze spoken language, provide feedback on pronunciation, and offer specific oral communication exercises.

# Chapter 6
# Integrating Generative AI Into K-12 Curriculums and Pedagogies in India:
## Opportunities and Challenges

**Durgesh M. Sharma**
https://orcid.org/0000-0002-9378-3061
*Shri Ramdeobaba College of Engineering and Management, Nagpur, India*

**K. Venkata Ramana**
*Department of Computer Science and Engineering, VNR Vignana Jyothi Institute of Engineering and Technology, Hyderabad, India*

**R. Jothilakshmi**
*Department of Information Technology, R.M.D. Engineering College, India*

**Rakesh Verma**
*Department of Master of Business Administration, Gniot MBA Institute, India*

**B. Uma Maheswari**
https://orcid.org/0000-0001-9707-285X
*Department of Computer Science and Engineering, St. Joseph's College of Engineering, India*

**Sampath Boopathi**
https://orcid.org/0000-0002-2065-6539
*Mechanical Engineering, Muthayammal Engineering College, India*

DOI: 10.4018/979-8-3693-0487-7.ch006

## ABSTRACT

*Generative artificial intelligence (AI) can revolutionize K-12 education in India by enhancing curriculums and pedagogies. This chapter explores the principles of generative AI, including generative adversarial networks (GANs), variational autoencoders (VAEs), and natural language generation (NLG), and its potential to create content indistinguishable from human-generated materials. Generative AI addresses challenges like resource scarcity, linguistic diversity, and personalized learning experiences, while emphasizing ethical considerations, data privacy, and bridging the digital divide. The future of K-12 education in India will see personalized learning journeys, inclusivity, and empowered educators. A comprehensive policy framework, infrastructure support, and teacher training are needed to realize the full potential of generative AI in shaping the educational landscape.*

## INTRODUCTION

Technology has become a potent transformational force in the fast-changing world of education. Particularly, Artificial Intelligence (AI) has impacted several industries, bringing with it fresh ideas and opportunities. AI has not only provided opportunities for efficiency but has also started to change the core dynamics of teaching and learning in the field of education. Generative AI, a subject that includes systems capable of producing material such as text, graphics, and even interactive learning experiences, is one potential area of AI in education. This chapter embarks on a journey to explore the integration of Generative AI into K-12 curriculums and pedagogies in India, charting the opportunities and challenges that lie ahead(Gardner-McCune et al., 2019).

Technology has become a potent driver for change in the continually expanding sector of education. In particular, Artificial Intelligence (AI) has permeated various sectors, heralding innovative solutions and novel possibilities. Within the realm of education, AI has not only offered avenues for efficiency but has also begun to reshape the fundamental dynamics of teaching and learning. One promising facet of AI in education is Generative AI, a subfield that encompasses systems capable of generating content, such as text, images, and even interactive learning experiences. This chapter embarks on a journey to explore the integration of Generative AI into K-12 curriculums and pedagogies in India, charting the opportunities and challenges that lie ahead(Murphy, 2019). It explores the generative AI's fundamental ideas, including methods like Generative Adversarial Networks (GANs), Variational Autoencoders (VAEs), and Natural Language Generation (NLG). Understanding AI technologies enables the creation of indistinguishable text, images, and interactive experiences, enhancing human-like capabilities. Furthermore, the chapter examines the potential applications of Generative AI in education, emphasizing its role in enhancing curriculum development, content creation, pedagogical innovation, and personalized learning experiences(Yau et al., 2023). While acknowledging the immense potential of Generative AI, it also addresses ethical considerations, data privacy, and the imperative of bridging the digital divide in the Indian educational context. This exploration aims to provide a comprehensive understanding of Generative AI's impact on K-12 education in India and its implications for shaping a dynamic and inclusive learning ecosystem.

Education, like many other fields, is experiencing rapid changes driven by advances in technology. Traditional teaching and learning methods are being reimagined and enhanced through technological innovations. These changes are not only affecting how education is delivered but are also fundamentally transforming the educational experience(Van Brummelen & Lin, 2020). In particular, artificial intelligence (AI) has impacted a number of industries, bringing with it fresh ideas and opportunities. Artificial intelligence (AI), a field of computer science that focuses on building intelligent computers that can carry out activities that traditionally require human intellect, has significantly advanced across a variety of sectors. It has brought about ground-breaking solutions and opened up new avenues of exploration and innovation in various fields, including healthcare, finance, and transportation.

"Within the realm of education, AI has not only offered avenues for efficiency but has also begun to reshape the fundamental dynamics of teaching and learning." In the context of education, AI is not just streamlining administrative processes but is also fundamentally changing how students learn and teachers teach. It is enhancing the efficiency of educational systems while also reshaping the very core of educational interactions. AI's impact extends beyond mere automation; it's about creating more personalized, adaptive, and effective learning experiences(Akgun & Greenhow, 2021).

"One promising facet of AI in education is Generative AI, a subfield that encompasses systems capable of generating content, such as text, images, and even interactive learning experiences." Generative AI is a subset of AI that focuses on creating content. It includes technologies like Natural Language Generation (NLG) and image synthesis, which can generate human-like text and images. These technologies have the potential to revolutionize content creation in education, from generating textbooks to creating interactive simulations that help students grasp complex concepts(Chiu, 2021).

"This chapter embarks on a journey to explore the integration of Generative AI into K-12 curriculums and pedagogies in India, charting the opportunities and challenges that lie ahead." The central focus of this chapter is to delve into the integration of Generative AI specifically in the context of K-12 education in India.

It aims to investigate how these generative technologies can be incorporated into the curriculum and teaching methodologies, highlighting the potential benefits and addressing the associated challenges(Lin & Van Brummelen, 2021). In essence, this introductory passage sets the stage for the exploration of how AI, particularly Generative AI, is reshaping education in India. It signals the transformative potential of these technologies while acknowledging the complexities and opportunities that come with their integration into K-12 education.

## Background and Context

The educational landscape in India is both vast and diverse. With a population exceeding a billion, India's K-12 education system caters to a wide array of students with varying needs, abilities, and aspirations. While there have been significant strides in improving access to education over the years, quality and individualization remain key challenges. This is where Generative AI enters the picture as a potential game-changer.

Generative AI encompasses a suite of technologies that enable machines to create content that appears to be human-generated. It includes Natural Language Generation (NLG), which can produce coherent and contextually relevant text, as well as image synthesis techniques that can create visuals from textual descriptions. Such capabilities have the potential to revolutionize content creation, personalization, and engagement in K-12 education(Gardner-McCune et al., 2019; Murphy, 2019).

In India, where classrooms are often crowded and resources are limited, the ability to tailor educational content to individual students' needs is a promising avenue for improvement. Generative AI can help bridge gaps in curriculum design, content generation, and pedagogical approaches. However, this integration is not without its complexities and ethical considerations.

## Purpose of the Chapter

This chapter examines the integration of Generative AI into K-12 curriculums and pedagogies in India, focusing on opportunities like improved learning outcomes, accessibility, and innovative methods. It also addresses challenges like data privacy, ethical considerations, and the digital divide. By examining early adopters' experiences and policy implications, it aims to provide educators, policymakers, and researchers with a comprehensive understanding of Generative AI's potential for advancing education in India while avoiding potential pitfalls.

## GENERATIVE AI: CONCEPTS AND EDUCATIONAL APPLICATIONS

Generative AI is a subfield of artificial intelligence (AI) that focuses on creating algorithms and models capable of generating content that closely resembles data produced by humans (Figure1). This content can encompass various forms, such as text, images, audio, and more. The core idea behind Generative AI is to enable machines to produce creative and contextually relevant content autonomously(Murugesan & Cherukuri, 2023).

*Figure 1. Generative AI: Concepts and educational applications*

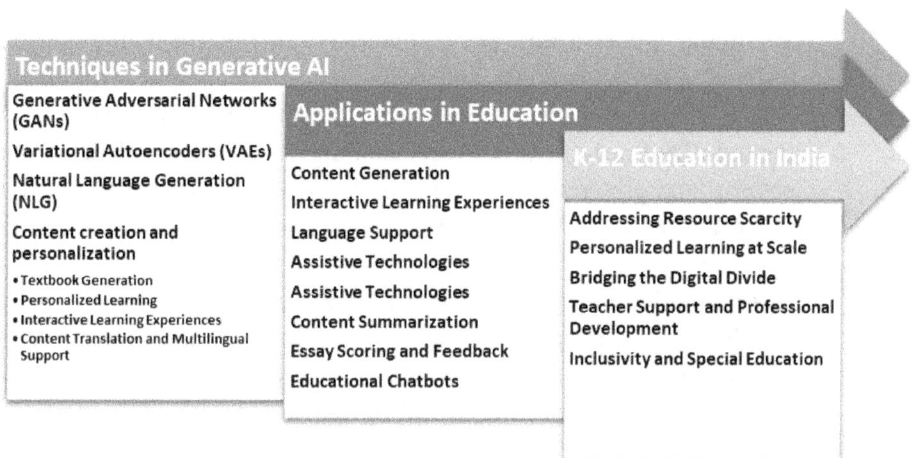


Techniques in Generative AI:

- **Generative Adversarial Networks (GANs):** GANs are a popular class of generative models that consist of two neural networks, a generator and a discriminator, engaged in a competitive process. The generator aims to create content (e.g., images) that is indistinguishable from real data, while the discriminator's role is to differentiate between real and generated data. Through repeated interactions, GANs improve the quality of generated content over time(Fui-Hoon Nah et al., 2023).
- **Variational Autoencoders (VAEs):** The main goal of VAEs, which are probabilistic generative models, is to understand the underlying distribution of data. In order for them to function, incoming data must first be encoded into a lower-dimensional representation (called latent space), and then it must

be decoded back into the original data space. By sampling from this learnt distribution, VAEs may produce new data points, making them valuable for projects like picture creation and data synthesis.

- **Natural Language Generation (NLG):** NLG is a particular area of Generative AI that focuses on producing text that resembles human speech. Large language models like GPT (Generative Pre-trained Transformer), which frequently power NLG models, may produce coherent and contextually appropriate written material. These models are commonly used for text summarization, language translation, chatbots, and content generation.
- **Content creation and personalization:** Applications for generative AI may be found in a variety of fields, including education, healthcare, entertainment, and the arts. It is essential to the design and customising of educational content. For instance:
    - **Textbook Generation:** Generative AI can automatically generate textbooks, study materials, and assignments, reducing the workload on educators and ensuring the availability of up-to-date learning resources.
    - **Personalized Learning:** By understanding students' individual learning patterns and preferences, Generative AI can adapt educational content to cater to each student's needs, making learning more engaging and effective.
    - **Interactive Learning Experiences:** Generative AI can power interactive simulations, virtual labs, and gamified learning experiences that provide students with hands-on and engaging educational opportunities.
    - **Content Translation and Multilingual Support:** NLG models can assist in translating educational content into multiple languages, making it accessible to a broader and more diverse audience.

Overall, Generative AI holds the promise of transforming education by automating content creation, tailoring learning experiences to individual students, and fostering innovative pedagogical approaches(Cooper, 2023). Integrating AI in K-12 curriculums in India raises challenges and considerations for further exploration.

## Applications in Education

Generative AI has diverse applications in education, impacting students' learning and educators' teaching. This section explores various applications within the educational sector(Lim et al., 2023):

**Content Generation and Customization:** Generative AI can automate the creation of educational materials, including textbooks, lesson plans, and educational videos. This reduces the burden on educators and ensures that content remains current and up-to-date. Through analysis of students' learning styles and progress, Generative AI can tailor educational content to individual needs, providing customized learning materials that optimize comprehension and engagement.

**Interactive Learning Experiences:** Generative AI can power interactive simulations and virtual laboratories, allowing students to conduct experiments and explore complex concepts in a safe and virtual environment. Gamification elements, such as educational games and quizzes, can be created using Generative AI to make learning more engaging and enjoyable.

**Language Support and Translation:** Generative AI, especially in the form of Natural Language Generation, can help translate educational content into multiple languages, making education more accessible to students with diverse linguistic backgrounds. Language learning apps and platforms can use Generative AI to provide conversational partners or generate language exercises and dialogues.

**Assistive Technologies:** Generative AI can be employed to create accessible content for students with disabilities, including generating alt text for images, providing audio descriptions, or converting text to speech. Intelligent tutoring systems using Generative AI can offer personalized guidance, answering students' questions and providing explanations in real-time.

**Content Summarization and Adaptation:** Generative AI can automatically generate summaries of lengthy textbooks or research papers, helping students grasp key concepts more efficiently. Educational platforms can use Generative AI to adapt content difficulty based on students' performance, ensuring that learning materials align with their current knowledge levels.

**Essay Scoring and Feedback:** Generative AI can assess and score essays, providing prompt and consistent feedback to students, which is especially useful in large classrooms. AI-powered tools can offer suggestions for improving writing skills, helping students enhance their composition and critical thinking abilities.

**Educational Chatbots:** Chatbots powered by Generative AI can provide round-the-clock assistance to students, answering queries, offering study tips, and guiding them through coursework. These chatbots can also assist with administrative tasks, such as enrollment, scheduling, and resource recommendations.

The integration of Generative AI into education holds great promise for enhancing the quality of education, increasing accessibility, and fostering innovative pedagogical methods(Eysenbach & others, 2023). However, it also necessitates a careful consideration of ethical and privacy concerns, equitable access to technology, and the ongoing professional development of educators. This chapter examines opportunities and challenges of integrating Generative AI into India's K-12 curriculums and pedagogies.

## K-12 Education in India

The applications of Generative AI hold particular relevance to the K-12 education landscape in India, where there are unique challenges and opportunities(Qadir, 2023; Su & Yang, 2023).

**Addressing Resource Scarcity:** India's diverse and extensive education system often faces challenges related to the creation of quality educational content for a vast student population. Generative AI can help generate curriculum materials, textbooks, and supplementary resources efficiently, mitigating resource scarcity issues. India is a linguistically diverse nation, with numerous regional languages. Generative AI's language translation capabilities can facilitate access to educational content in various languages, ensuring that students from different linguistic backgrounds can benefit.

**Personalized Learning at Scale:** India's K-12 education system caters to students with varying learning paces and styles. Generative AI can adapt educational content to suit individual learning needs, enabling personalized learning experiences at scale. In India, classrooms are often crowded, and teachers face challenges in providing individualized attention to students. Generative AI tools can assist educators in tailoring content and assignments to address students' specific strengths and weaknesses.

**Bridging the Digital Divide:** While India has made strides in expanding access to education, there remains a digital divide, with varying levels of access to technology and the internet. Generative AI can help bridge this divide by offering educational content that can be accessed both online and offline, thus reaching students in remote or low-connectivity areas. Generative AI-powered educational content can be distributed through offline means, such as DVDs, USB drives, or print materials, ensuring that students without consistent internet access are not left behind.

**Teacher Support and Professional Development:** Generative AI can serve as a valuable tool for teachers by automating administrative tasks, such as generating assignments or assessments, allowing educators to focus more on teaching and student engagement. Generative AI can aid in the professional development of teachers by providing them with resources, training materials, and personalized guidance on effective teaching strategies.

**Inclusivity and Special Education:** Generative AI can help create content that is accessible to students with disabilities. For instance, it can generate audio descriptions for visually impaired students or provide text-to-speech functionality. Students with special educational needs can benefit from Generative AI's ability to adapt content and learning materials to match their specific requirements.

In conclusion, Generative AI presents a multitude of opportunities for addressing the unique challenges faced by K-12 education in India. By automating content creation, personalizing learning experiences, and ensuring equitable access to educational resources, Generative AI has the potential to enhance the quality of education and improve learning outcomes for students across the country. However, it is essential to carefully navigate the implementation of these technologies, considering cultural, ethical, and infrastructure-related factors to maximize their positive impact on Indian K-12 education.

## CURRICULUM DEVELOPMENT AND CONTENT CREATION

Explore Generative AI's impact on K-12 curriculum development and content creation in India(Figure 2).

*Figure 2. AI integrated curriculum development and content creation*

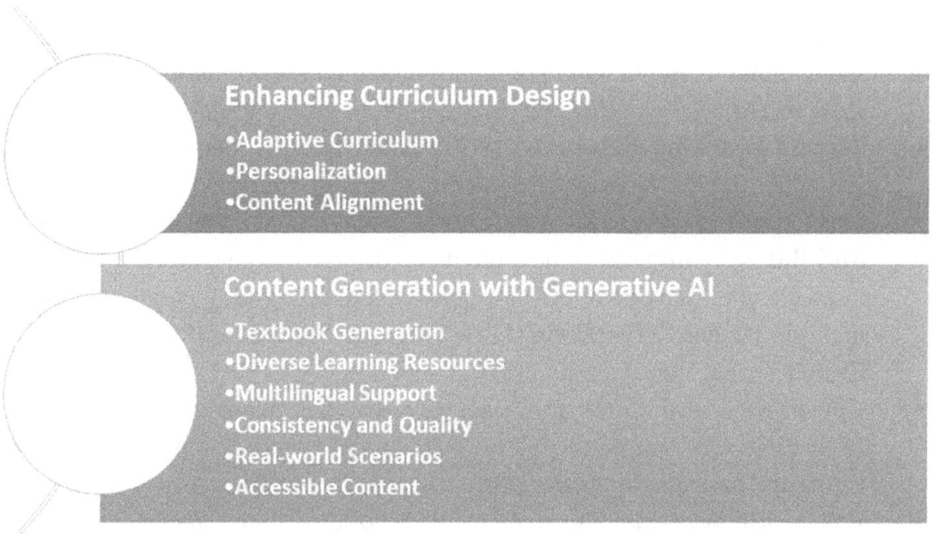


### Enhancing Curriculum Design

Curriculum design is a crucial aspect of education, shaping what and how students learn throughout their academic journey. Generative AI offers several ways to enhance curriculum design(Zhang, Zhang, Li, et al., 2023):

- **Adaptive Curriculum:** Generative AI can analyze student performance data and adapt the curriculum in real-time. It identifies areas where students are struggling and provides additional resources or alternative approaches to improve understanding(Dickey & Bejarano, 2023; Zhang, Zhang, Zheng, et al., 2023).

- **Personalization:** By understanding individual student strengths, weaknesses, and learning styles, Generative AI can tailor curriculum materials, assignments, and assessments to meet the unique needs of each learner.
- **Content Alignment:** Generative AI ensures that curriculum content aligns with educational standards and the evolving needs of the job market. It can regularly update materials to incorporate the latest knowledge and skills.

## Content Generation With Generative AI

Content creation is a labor-intensive and time-consuming process. Generative AI revolutionizes this aspect of education(Cao et al., 2023):

- **Textbook Generation:** Generative AI can automate the creation of textbooks and learning materials. It can compile and organize information from various sources, ensuring that the content is comprehensive and up-to-date.
- **Diverse Learning Resources:** With Generative AI, educators can easily generate diverse learning resources, including quizzes, flashcards, and interactive exercises, to keep students engaged and facilitate active learning.
- **Multilingual Support:** India's linguistic diversity is a significant challenge in education. Generative AI can quickly translate and generate content in multiple languages, breaking down language barriers(Sridhar et al., 2023; Zhang, Zhang, Zheng, et al., 2023).
- **Consistency and Quality:** Generative AI can maintain consistency in formatting, style, and quality across educational materials, eliminating human errors and ensuring high standards.
- **Real-world Scenarios:** It can create real-world scenarios and case studies to help students apply their knowledge in practical contexts, preparing them for the challenges they may face in the future.
- **Accessible Content:** Generative AI can generate content that adheres to accessibility standards, making it inclusive for students with disabilities. This includes generating alt text for images or converting text to Braille.

By harnessing Generative AI's capabilities in content creation and curriculum design, educators can provide students with high-quality, personalized, and up-to-date learning materials(Vartiainen & Tedre, 2023). This not only alleviates the burden on teachers and curriculum developers but also ensures that students have access to a dynamic and engaging educational experience that is tailored to their unique needs and learning styles.

# PEDAGOGICAL INNOVATIONS

Explore Generative AI's impact on pedagogical innovations in K-12 education in India, transforming teaching and learning experiences(Figure 3).

## Personalized Learning With Generative AI

Generative AI enables personalized learning experiences tailored to the needs and preferences of individual students(Sridhar et al., 2023; Zhang, Zhang, Zheng, et al., 2023):

- **Adaptive Learning Paths:** Generative AI analyzes students' learning data to create adaptive learning paths, adjusting the pace and difficulty of lessons based on individual progress. This ensures that each student receives the right level of challenge and support.
- **Customized Content:** AI-generated content adapts to students' learning styles and strengths. For example, it can present information through visual aids for visual learners or provide additional explanations for students who struggle with certain topics(Boopathi & Davim, 2023).
- **Immediate Feedback:** AI-powered assessment tools offer immediate feedback, allowing students to identify and rectify mistakes in real-time. This feedback loop enhances understanding and retention of subject matter.

## Interactive and Engaging Learning Resources

Generative AI fosters interactive and engaging learning experiences(Fui-Hoon Nah et al., 2023; Lim et al., 2023):

- **Simulations and Virtual Labs:** AI-generated simulations and virtual laboratories provide students with hands-on experiences, allowing them to experiment and explore complex concepts in a controlled environment.
- **Educational Games:** Gamification elements powered by AI enhance engagement. Educational games generated by AI make learning enjoyable while reinforcing key concepts.

*Figure 3. Pedagogical innovations using AI*

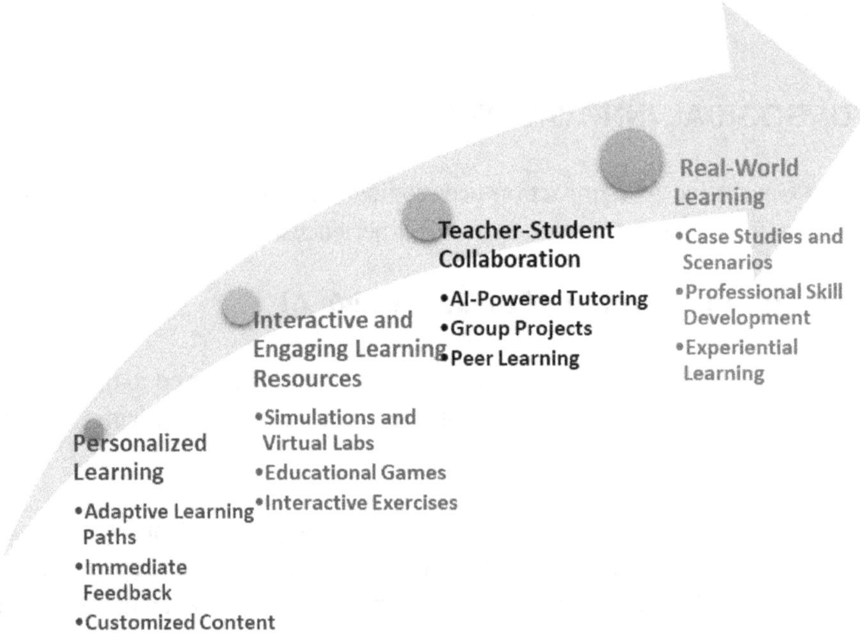


- **Interactive Exercises:** AI can create a variety of interactive exercises, such as quizzes, flashcards, and interactive diagrams, to promote active learning and reinforce learning objectives.

## Teacher-Student Collaboration

Generative AI promotes collaborative learning environments(Sridhar et al., 2023):

- **AI-Powered Tutoring:** AI chatbots and virtual tutors assist students in their studies, answering questions, providing explanations, and offering guidance. This support enhances the teacher-student relationship by ensuring that students receive help whenever they need it.
- **Group Projects:** AI can facilitate group projects by assisting students in organizing and managing collaborative tasks. It can also provide valuable data on individual contributions, fostering fairness in assessment.
- **Peer Learning:** AI can recommend peer learning groups based on students' profiles and learning needs, encouraging knowledge sharing and peer support.

## Real-World Learning Scenarios

Generative AI connects classroom learning to real-world applications(Lin & Van Brummelen, 2021):

- **Case Studies and Scenarios:** AI can generate real-world scenarios and case studies that challenge students to apply their knowledge to practical situations, preparing them for future careers.
- **Professional Skill Development:** Generative AI can create content that aligns with industry standards and demands, helping students develop practical skills that are directly applicable in their chosen fields.
- **Experiential Learning:** Through AI-generated virtual experiences and field trips, students can explore distant places or historical periods, expanding their horizons beyond the classroom.

Pedagogical innovations driven by Generative AI empower educators to create dynamic, engaging, and personalized learning environments. These innovations not only enhance students' academic performance but also equip them with essential skills and knowledge required for success in an increasingly complex and digital world(Durairaj et al., 2023).

# OPPORTUNITIES AND BENEFITS

Explores opportunities and benefits of integrating Generative AI in K-12 education in India, enhancing the learning ecosystem(Ali et al., 2023).

## Improved Learning Outcomes

Generative AI offers several pathways to improve learning outcomes for students(Senechal et al., 2023):

- **Personalized Learning:** AI tailors educational content to individual students' needs, pacing, and preferences, resulting in better engagement and comprehension.
- **Immediate Feedback:** AI-powered assessment tools provide instant feedback, helping students identify and address areas of weakness, leading to faster improvement.

- **Adaptive Curriculum:** Generative AI adapts the curriculum based on students' progress, ensuring that they are challenged appropriately and not left behind.
- **Enhanced Concept Retention:** Interactive learning experiences and simulations created by AI enhance students' ability to grasp and retain complex concepts.

## Inclusivity and Accessibility

Generative AI promotes inclusivity and accessibility in education(Kaplan-Rakowski et al., 2023):

- **Multilingual Support:** AI can translate and generate content in multiple languages, breaking down language barriers and making education accessible to students from diverse linguistic backgrounds.
- **Accessible Content:** AI-generated content can adhere to accessibility standards, ensuring that students with disabilities have equal access to educational materials.
- **Offline Learning:** AI-generated resources can be distributed offline, reaching students in remote or low-connectivity areas and reducing the digital divide.

## Teacher Professional Development

Generative AI supports the professional growth of educators(Zhang, Zhang, Li, et al., 2023):

- **Resource Generation:** AI-generated teaching resources, lesson plans, and materials assist teachers in delivering high-quality content effectively.
- **Data-Driven Insights:** AI provides data on student performance, helping teachers identify areas for improvement and tailor their teaching strategies.
- **Personalized Professional Development:** AI can recommend personalized professional development opportunities for educators, ensuring ongoing growth and adaptation to evolving teaching practices.

## Education Research and Data Analysis

Generative AI contributes to education research and data analysis(Zhang, Zhang, Zheng, et al., 2023):

- **Data-Driven Decision-Making:** AI can analyze vast volumes of educational data, facilitating evidence-based decision-making by educational institutions and policymakers.
- **Predictive Analytics:** AI can predict student performance and identify early warning signs of learning challenges, enabling timely intervention and support.
- **Research Assistance:** AI-powered tools can assist researchers in analyzing educational data, streamlining the research process, and uncovering insights to improve educational practices.

K–12 education in India may become a more dynamic, inclusive, and data-driven environment by utilising the potential and advantages provided by generative AI. These improvements not only help kids learn better, but they also give educators and educational institutions the information they need to continue raising the standard of education offered to students nationwide. As this shift happens, it is crucial to confront difficulties and moral questions.

## CHALLENGES AND CONCERNS

While the integration of Generative AI in K-12 education in India presents numerous opportunities, it also raises significant challenges and concerns that must be addressed to ensure the responsible and equitable use of this technology (Figure 4).

### Privacy and Data Security

- **Student Data Protection:** Generative AI systems' collecting and analysis of student data raises questions regarding the security and privacy of sensitive data. To secure students' personal information from breaches and exploitation, it is essential to employ strong data protection procedures (Agrawal et al., 2023; Durairaj et al., 2023).
- **Consent and Transparency:** Schools and educational institutions must ensure that students and their parents or guardians provide informed consent for data collection and usage. Transparency in data handling practices is essential to build trust among stakeholders.

*Figure 4. Generative AI in K-12 education in India—challenges*

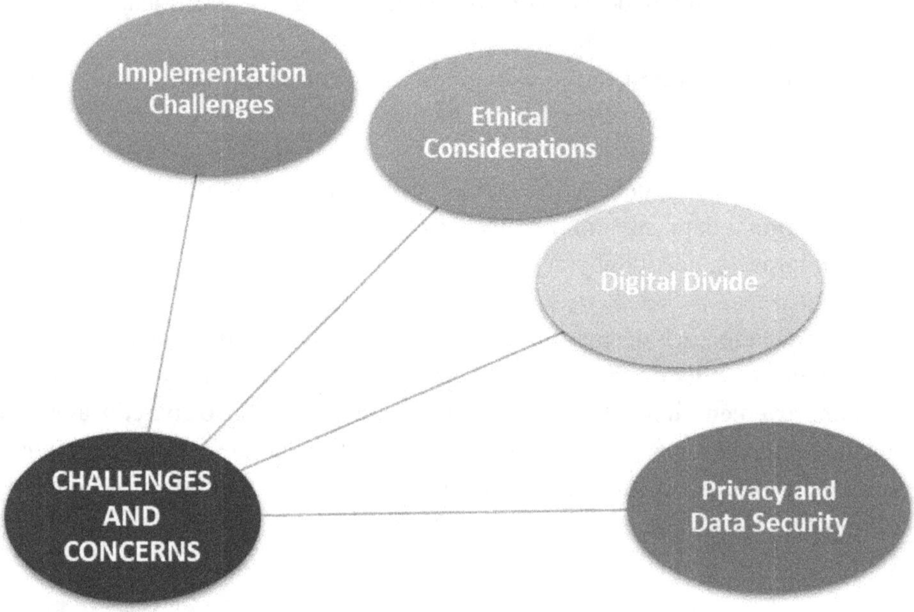


## Ethical Considerations

- **Bias and Fairness:** Generative AI systems' collecting and analysis of student data raises questions regarding the security and privacy of sensitive data. To secure students' personal information from breaches and exploitation, it is essential to employ strong data protection procedures (Reddy, Reddy, et al., 2023).
- **Intellectual Property:** Questions may arise regarding the ownership and copyright of AI-generated educational materials. Clear guidelines on intellectual property rights should be established to avoid disputes.
- **Algorithmic Accountability:** Educators and policymakers need to hold AI developers accountable for the decisions made by AI algorithms, especially when they affect students' educational experiences. This includes transparency in how algorithms function and make decisions.

## Digital Divide

- **Access to Technology:** India has a digital divide, with unequal access to technology and the internet. Implementing Generative AI in education may exacerbate this divide if not addressed. Ensuring that all students, regardless of their socioeconomic backgrounds, have access to the necessary technology is crucial(Reddy, Reddy, et al., 2023; Venkateswaran, Vidhya, Ayyannan, et al., 2023; Venkateswaran, Vidhya, Naik, et al., 2023).

- **Tech Literacy:** Students and educators need to be digitally literate to effectively utilize Generative AI tools. Addressing disparities in tech literacy is essential to ensure equitable access and benefits.

## Implementation Challenges

- **Teacher Training:** Integrating Generative AI into pedagogy requires teacher training and professional development. A lack of training opportunities and resistance to change can hinder successful implementation(Agrawal et al., 2023; Dhanya et al., 2023; Venkateswaran, Vidhya, Ayyannan, et al., 2023).
- **Infrastructure:** Adequate infrastructure, including internet connectivity and hardware, is necessary for the effective use of AI tools in education. Rural and underserved areas may face infrastructure challenges.
- **Cost and Sustainability:** Implementing Generative AI systems may come with significant costs, including licensing fees, hardware upgrades, and maintenance. Ensuring the long-term sustainability of AI-powered education initiatives is essential.

A multifaceted strategy combining cooperation between educators, politicians, technology developers, and communities is needed to address these issues. Utilizing the full potential of Generative AI while minimising its associated hazards in K–12 education in India requires careful planning, ethical concerns, and a dedication to inclusion.

# POLICY IMPLICATIONS AND RECOMMENDATIONS

To successfully integrate Generative AI into K-12 education in India, a comprehensive policy framework and strategic recommendations are essential(Sathiyaseelan et al., 2023). These policies should address various aspects, including the educational policy framework, infrastructure, teacher training, and monitoring and evaluation (Figure 5).

*Figure 5. Policy implications and recommendations in India*

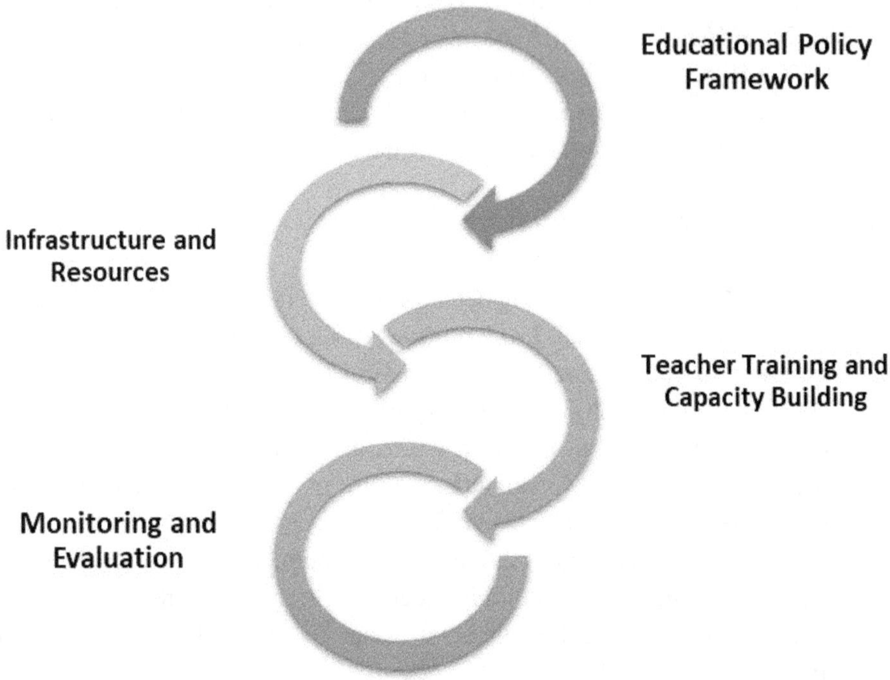


## Educational Policy Framework

The national curriculum should incorporate AI literacy and ethics to prepare students for responsible AI use. Guidelines should address data privacy, bias mitigation, and transparency. Resources should be allocated for the effective implementation of Generative AI tools, ensuring schools and institutions have the necessary funding.

## Infrastructure and Resources

The text suggests addressing the digital divide by ensuring all students have access to necessary technology and internet connectivity for AI-powered education, investing in cost-effective hardware and software procurement, and encouraging open-access AI educational resources to reduce costs and increase accessibility for all schools and students.

## Teacher Training and Capacity Building

- Develop teacher training programs that provide educators with the necessary skills and knowledge to effectively use Generative AI tools in their teaching practices(Venkateswaran, Vidhya, Ayyannan, et al., 2023).
- The initiative aims to enhance teachers' professional development by providing them with ongoing updates on AI advancements and pedagogical best practices, and fostering collaboration between educational institutions and AI experts.

## Monitoring and Evaluation

- Establish rigorous data privacy and security protocols to protect students' personal information while utilizing Generative AI tools(Sathiyaseelan et al., 2023).
- Implement a continuous evaluation system for AI-integrated education initiatives to assess learning outcomes and make necessary adjustments, while investing in research and development to improve AI algorithms and technologies for education, addressing bias and increasing effectiveness.

These policy implications and recommendations provide a foundation for shaping a responsible and effective approach to integrating Generative AI into K-12 education in India(Reddy, Gaurav, et al., 2023). A collaborative effort among government bodies, educational institutions, AI developers, and stakeholders is crucial to ensure that AI-powered education benefits all students and supports the growth and development of the education sector in the country.

# CASE STUDIES FROM INDIAN SCHOOLS

## Success Stories

### Case Study One: Personalized Learning With Generative AI

This case study explores a progressive Indian school's use of Generative AI to personalize learning, analyzing individual styles and strengths, and adapting the curriculum accordingly. This resulted in improved student engagement and better learning outcomes, with students showing a deeper understanding of subject matter(You et al., 2023). The success of this personalized approach has led to its expansion in other schools across India.

## Case Study Two: Multilingual Education

This case study explores a non-profit organization's collaboration with Generative AI developers to develop an educational platform that automatically translates content into multiple Indian languages. The platform enables students from various linguistic backgrounds to access high-quality educational resources, thereby promoting inclusivity and equitable education(Malik et al., 2023).

## Lessons Learned

### Best Practice One: Ethical Content Generation

One key lesson learned from implementing Generative AI in education is the importance of ethical content generation. It's crucial to establish guidelines and ensure that AI-generated content aligns with educational values and standards. Moreover, continuous human oversight is essential to identify and rectify any biases or inaccuracies that may arise in generated materials.

### Best Practice Two: Teacher Training and Support

Successful integration of Generative AI requires adequate teacher training and ongoing support. Schools that have effectively implemented Generative AI have provided educators with professional development opportunities to familiarize themselves with AI tools and incorporate them into their teaching practices. Offering ongoing support and encouraging collaboration between teachers and AI developers has been essential.

### Best Practice Three: Data Security and Privacy

Schools must prioritize protecting student data and privacy by implementing robust security measures and adhering to regulations, while transparent communication with students, parents, and guardians is crucial for trust and compliance.

### Best Practice Four: Continuous Improvement and Feedback

Continuous improvement is essential in the implementation of Generative AI. Schools and organizations have found value in collecting feedback from both students and educators to refine AI-generated content and adapt their strategies. This iterative process ensures that AI aligns with evolving educational needs.

These case studies and best practices offer valuable insights into the successful integration of Generative AI in K-12 education in India. They demonstrate the potential benefits, ethical considerations, and practical strategies that can guide educators and policymakers in leveraging Generative AI to enhance the educational experience for students across the country.

To successfully integrate Generative AI into K-12 education in India, a comprehensive policy framework and strategic recommendations are essential. These policies should address various aspects, including the educational policy framework, infrastructure, teacher training, and monitoring and evaluation(Blythe, 2023).

Personalized Learning at a Government School:

- **Scenario:** A government school in a rural area of India implements a Generative AI-powered learning platform. Students take assessments at the beginning of the academic year, and AI algorithms analyze their performance.
- **Implementation:** Based on the assessment results, the AI platform generates personalized learning paths for each student. It recommends specific lessons and resources that cater to individual strengths and weaknesses. For instance, if a student struggles with math concepts but excels in language skills, the AI system suggests additional math practice materials and advanced reading assignments.
- **Outcome:** Over the academic year, students show improved performance in subjects where they initially struggled. The school's overall academic performance rises, showcasing the potential of AI-driven personalization in underprivileged areas.

Multilingual Education at a Private International School:

- **Scenario:** A private international school in a metropolitan city serves a diverse student population, including children from various linguistic backgrounds. The school employs Generative AI to address language diversity and promote multilingual education.
- **Implementation:** Generative AI is used to automatically translate and adapt educational content into multiple languages commonly spoken by students. AI-driven language learning modules are also integrated into the curriculum, allowing students to learn additional languages interactively.
- **Outcome:** The school achieves high levels of inclusivity and accessibility, enabling students to access educational content in their native languages. Students develop proficiency in multiple languages, fostering a culturally rich and diverse learning environment.

Teacher Support at a Progressive School:

- **Scenario:** A progressive K-12 school in a tier-1 city in India incorporates Generative AI as a supportive tool for teachers(Su et al., 2023).
- **Implementation:** The school deploys AI chatbots that serve as virtual teaching assistants. These chatbots are available around the clock to answer student queries, provide explanations, and offer additional resources. Teachers use AI-generated lesson plans and content suggestions to enhance their teaching materials.
- **Outcome:** Teachers find themselves with more time for one-on-one interactions with students, as routine queries are handled by AI chatbots. Students appreciate the immediate assistance, resulting in increased engagement and a deeper understanding of the curriculum.

## FUTURE DIRECTIONS

As technology continues to evolve, both Generative AI and K-12 education are poised for significant advancements. Let's explore the emerging trends in Generative AI and the potential evolution of K-12 education(Senechal et al., 2023).

### Emerging Trends in Generative AI

**Improved Language Models:** Language models like GPT-4 and beyond are expected to become even more powerful, enabling more accurate and contextually relevant text generation. This could lead to further advancements in natural language understanding and generation, benefiting language learning and content creation in education(Eysenbach & others, 2023; Qadir, 2023; Su & Yang, 2023).

**AI-Enhanced Creativity:** Generative AI will likely continue to enhance creativity across various domains. In education, this could lead to the development of AI-generated artistic content, interactive storytelling, and even AI-generated music for educational purposes.

**Ethical AI and Bias Mitigation:** There will be a growing emphasis on developing AI models that are more ethical and less prone to biases. In education, this will be crucial to ensure fair and unbiased content generation and assessment.

**AI-Powered Personalization:** AI-driven personalization in education will become more sophisticated, considering a broader range of student data and preferences. This will enable even more tailored learning experiences, optimizing student engagement and outcomes.

**Augmented Reality (AR) and Virtual Reality (VR):** Integration of Generative AI with AR and VR technologies will create immersive and interactive educational experiences. Students could explore historical events, conduct virtual science experiments, or practice language skills in simulated real-world environments.

## Potential Evolution of K-12 Education

**Blended Learning Becomes the Norm:** Blended learning, a combination of in-person and online learning, will likely continue to expand. Generative AI will play a crucial role in creating online content and personalized learning experiences, complementing traditional classroom teaching(Gardner-McCune et al., 2019; Qadir, 2023; Su & Yang, 2023).

**Data-Driven Decision-Making:** K-12 education will increasingly rely on data-driven decision-making, with AI systems providing insights into student performance and learning trends. Educators and policymakers will use this data to refine curriculum design and teaching strategies.

**Lifelong Learning:** K-12 education will extend beyond the traditional classroom. Lifelong learning will become a norm, with AI-powered platforms offering continuous education and upskilling opportunities for individuals throughout their lives(Bozkurt & Sharma, 2023; Su et al., 2023).

**Global Collaboration:** AI-driven language translation and virtual collaboration tools will enable K-12 students in India to connect with peers and educators globally. This will facilitate cross-cultural learning experiences and the exchange of ideas.

**Teacher-Student Roles Reimagined:** With AI assisting in administrative tasks and personalized instruction, the roles of teachers and students will evolve. Teachers will become facilitators of personalized learning journeys, while students will take more active roles in self-directed learning(Kaplan-Rakowski et al., 2023; Sridhar et al., 2023).

**AI-Enhanced Assessments:** Assessments will become more adaptive and AI-driven, focusing on evaluating not just knowledge but also critical thinking, problem-solving, and creativity. AI will provide instant feedback, reducing the burden of grading on teachers.

**Inclusive Education:** AI-powered accessibility tools and content generation will make education more inclusive for students with disabilities. It will help bridge the gap in educational opportunities for all.

The advancement of Generative AI and K-12 education necessitates responsible adaptation by educational stakeholders, including educators, policymakers, technology developers, and communities, to fully utilize AI-driven education, address challenges, and ensure equitable access for all students.

## CONCLUSION

Generative AI integration in K-12 education in India offers transformative opportunities and challenges, with key takeaways emerging.

Generative AI has the potential to enhance learning experiences by tailoring content to individual students' needs, preferences, and learning styles, thereby improving engagement and academic outcomes. The use of Generative AI can address challenges related to linguistic diversity and disabilities, making education more inclusive and accessible to a diverse student population in India. AI-powered tools can assist teachers in administrative tasks and provide valuable data, but teacher training and professional development are crucial. Ethical concerns regarding data privacy, bias mitigation, and transparency are essential for responsible use.

India faces a digital divide, necessitating equitable access to technology and the internet for all students, regardless of socioeconomic background. A comprehensive policy framework, infrastructure support, and stakeholder collaboration are crucial for successful integration of Generative AI in K-12 education. Generative AI in education is expected to improve language models, develop ethical AI, enhance personalization, and integrate with augmented and virtual reality technologies. India's K-12 education is shifting towards blended learning, data-driven decision-making, lifelong learning, and global collaboration.

The integration of Generative AI into K-12 education in India has the potential to revolutionize the education sector by making it more personalized, inclusive, and data-driven. However, overcoming challenges requires proactive measures, ethical considerations, and stakeholder collaboration.

## REFERENCES

Agrawal, A. V., Pitchai, R., Senthamaraikannan, C., Balaji, N. A., Sajithra, S., & Boopathi, S. (2023). Digital Education System During the COVID-19 Pandemic. In Using Assistive Technology for Inclusive Learning in K-12 Classrooms (pp. 104–126). IGI Global. doi:10.4018/978-1-6684-6424-3.ch005

Akgun, S., & Greenhow, C. (2021). Artificial intelligence in education: Addressing ethical challenges in K-12 settings. *AI and Ethics*, 1–10. PMID:34790956

Ali, S., DiPaola, D., Williams, R., Ravi, P., & Breazeal, C. (2023). Constructing Dreams using Generative AI. *ArXiv Preprint ArXiv:2305.12013.*

Blythe, M. C. (2023). *An Analysis of the Suitability of Philosophy as a Core K-12 Public School Subject.*

Boopathi, S., & Davim, J. P. (2023). *Sustainable Utilization of Nanoparticles and Nanofluids in Engineering Applications*. IGI Global. doi:10.4018/978-1-6684-9135-5

Bozkurt, A., & Sharma, R. C. (2023). Challenging the status quo and exploring the new boundaries in the age of algorithms: Reimagining the role of generative AI in distance education and online learning. *Asian Journal of Distance Education, 18*(1).

Cao, Y., Li, S., Liu, Y., Yan, Z., Dai, Y., Yu, P. S., & Sun, L. (2023). A comprehensive survey of ai-generated content (aigc): A history of generative ai from gan to chatgpt. *ArXiv Preprint ArXiv:2303.04226*.

Chiu, T. K. (2021). A holistic approach to the design of artificial intelligence (AI) education for K-12 schools. *TechTrends, 65*(5), 796–807. doi:10.100711528-021-00637-1

Cooper, G. (2023). Examining science education in chatgpt: An exploratory study of generative artificial intelligence. *Journal of Science Education and Technology, 32*(3), 444–452. doi:10.100710956-023-10039-y

Dhanya, D., Kumar, S. S., Thilagavathy, A., Prasad, D., & Boopathi, S. (2023). Data Analytics and Artificial Intelligence in the Circular Economy: Case Studies. In Intelligent Engineering Applications and Applied Sciences for Sustainability (pp. 40–58). IGI Global.

Dickey, E., & Bejarano, A. (2023). A Model for Integrating Generative AI into Course Content Development. *ArXiv Preprint ArXiv:2308.12276*.

Durairaj, M., Jayakumar, S., Karpagavalli, V., Maheswari, B. U., Boopathi, S., & ... (2023). Utilization of Digital Tools in the Indian Higher Education System During Health Crises. In *Multidisciplinary Approaches to Organizational Governance During Health Crises* (pp. 1–21). IGI Global. doi:10.4018/978-1-7998-9213-7.ch001

Eysenbach, G. (2023). The role of ChatGPT, generative language models, and artificial intelligence in medical education: A conversation with ChatGPT and a call for papers. *JMIR Medical Education, 9*(1), e46885. doi:10.2196/46885 PMID:36863937

Fui-Hoon Nah, F., Zheng, R., Cai, J., Siau, K., & Chen, L. (2023). Generative AI and ChatGPT: Applications, challenges, and AI-human collaboration. In *Journal of Information Technology Case and Application Research* (pp. 1–28). Taylor & Francis. doi:10.1080/15228053.2023.2233814

Gardner-McCune, C., Touretzky, D., Martin, F., & Seehorn, D. (2019). AI for K-12: Making room for AI in K-12 CS curricula. *Proceedings of the 50th ACM Technical Symposium on Computer Science Education*, (pp. 1244–1244). ACM. 10.1145/3287324.3293729

Kaplan-Rakowski, R., Grotewold, K., Hartwick, P., & Papin, K. (2023). Generative AI and Teachers' Perspectives on Its Implementation in Education. *Journal of Interactive Learning Research*, *34*(2), 313–338.

Lim, W. M., Gunasekara, A., Pallant, J. L., Pallant, J. I., & Pechenkina, E. (2023). Generative AI and the future of education: Ragnarök or reformation? A paradoxical perspective from management educators. *International Journal of Management Education*, *21*(2), 100790. doi:10.1016/j.ijme.2023.100790

Lin, P., & Van Brummelen, J. (2021). Engaging teachers to co-design integrated AI curriculum for K-12 classrooms. *Proceedings of the 2021 CHI Conference on Human Factors in Computing Systems*, (pp. 1–12). ACM. 10.1145/3411764.3445377

Malik, T., Dwivedi, Y., Kshetri, N., Hughes, L., Slade, E. L., Jeyaraj, A., Kar, A. K., Baabdullah, A. M., Koohang, A., Raghavan, V., & ... (2023). "So what if ChatGPT wrote it?" Multidisciplinary perspectives on opportunities, challenges and implications of generative conversational AI for research, practice and policy. *International Journal of Information Management*, *71*, 102642. doi:10.1016/j.ijinfomgt.2023.102642

Murphy, R. F. (2019). Artificial intelligence applications to support K-12 teachers and teaching. Rand Corporation.

Murugesan, S., & Cherukuri, A. K. (2023). The Rise of Generative Artificial Intelligence and Its Impact on Education: The Promises and Perils. *Computer*, *56*(5), 116–121. doi:10.1109/MC.2023.3253292

Qadir, J. (2023). Engineering education in the era of ChatGPT: Promise and pitfalls of generative AI for education. *2023 IEEE Global Engineering Education Conference (EDUCON)*, (pp. 1–9). IEEE. 10.1109/EDUCON54358.2023.10125121

Reddy, M. A., Gaurav, A., Ushasukhanya, S., Rao, V. C. S., Bhattacharya, S., & Boopathi, S. (2023). Bio-Medical Wastes Handling Strategies During the COVID-19 Pandemic. In Multidisciplinary Approaches to Organizational Governance During Health Crises (pp. 90–111). IGI Global. doi:10.4018/978-1-7998-9213-7.ch006

Reddy, M. A., Reddy, B. M., Mukund, C., Venneti, K., Preethi, D., & Boopathi, S. (2023). Social Health Protection During the COVID-Pandemic Using IoT. In *The COVID-19 Pandemic and the Digitalization of Diplomacy* (pp. 204–235). IGI Global. doi:10.4018/978-1-7998-8394-4.ch009

Sathiyaseelan, G., Srinath, P., Melwyn, J. G., Bhagyanathan, C., Socrates, S., & Boopathi, S. (2023). Tribology and hardness measurement of biosilica dispersed AA7075 metal matrix composites. *Materials Today: Proceedings*. Advance online publication. doi:10.1016/j.matpr.2023.02.440

Senechal, J., Ekholm, E., Aljudaibi, S., Strawderman, M., & Parthemos, C. (2023). *Balancing the Benefits and Risks of Large Language AI Models in K12 Public Schools.*

Sridhar, P., Doyle, A., Agarwal, A., Bogart, C., Savelka, J., & Sakr, M. (2023). Harnessing llms in curricular design: Using gpt-4 to support authoring of learning objectives. *ArXiv Preprint ArXiv:2306.17459.*

Su, J., Guo, K., Chen, X., & Chu, S. K. W. (2023). Teaching artificial intelligence in K–12 classrooms: A scoping review. *Interactive Learning Environments*, 1–20. doi:10.1080/10494820.2023.2212706

Su, J., & Yang, W. (2023). Unlocking the power of ChatGPT: A framework for applying generative AI in education. *ECNU Review of Education*, 20965311231168424.

Van Brummelen, J., & Lin, P. (2020). Engaging teachers to co-design integrated AI curriculum for K-12 classrooms. *ArXiv Preprint ArXiv:2009.11100.*

Vartiainen, H., & Tedre, M. (2023). Using artificial intelligence in craft education: Crafting with text-to-image generative models. *Digital Creativity (Exeter)*, *34*(1), 1–21. doi:10.1080/14626268.2023.2174557

Venkateswaran, N., Vidhya, K., Ayyannan, M., Chavan, S. M., Sekar, K., & Boopathi, S. (2023). A Study on Smart Energy Management Framework Using Cloud Computing. In 5G, Artificial Intelligence, and Next Generation Internet of Things: Digital Innovation for Green and Sustainable Economies (pp. 189–212). IGI Global. doi:10.4018/978-1-6684-8634-4.ch009

Venkateswaran, N., Vidhya, R., Naik, D. A., Raj, T. M., Munjal, N., & Boopathi, S. (2023). Study on Sentence and Question Formation Using Deep Learning Techniques. In *Digital Natives as a Disruptive Force in Asian Businesses and Societies* (pp. 252–273). IGI Global. doi:10.4018/978-1-6684-6782-4.ch015

Yau, K. W., Chai, C., Chiu, T. K., Meng, H., King, I., & Yam, Y. (2023). A phenomenographic approach on teacher conceptions of teaching Artificial Intelligence (AI) in K-12 schools. *Education and Information Technologies*, *28*(1), 1041–1064. doi:10.100710639-022-11161-x

You, Y., Chen, Y., You, Y., Zhang, Q., & Cao, Q. (2023). Evolutionary Game Analysis of Artificial Intelligence Such as the Generative Pre-Trained Transformer in Future Education. *Sustainability (Basel)*, *15*(12), 9355. doi:10.3390u15129355

Zhang, C., Zhang, C., Li, C., Qiao, Y., Zheng, S., Dam, S. K., Zhang, M., Kim, J. U., Kim, S. T., Choi, J., & Associates. (2023). One small step for generative ai, one giant leap for agi: A complete survey on chatgpt in aigc era. *ArXiv Preprint ArXiv:2304.06488.*

## APPENDIX

AI - Artificial Intelligence
ML - Machine Learning
IoT - Internet of Things
K-12 - Kindergarten through 12th grade (referring to primary and secondary education)
GANs - Generative Adversarial Networks
VAEs - Variational Autoencoders
NLG - Natural Language Generation
AR - Augmented Reality
VR - Virtual Reality
STEM - Science, Technology, Engineering, and Mathematics
UNESCO - United Nations Educational, Scientific and Cultural Organization
DPI - Department of Public Instruction
ICT - Information and Communication Technology
E-Learning - Electronic Learning
CPD - Continuous Professional Development
API - Application Programming Interface
MLaaS - Machine Learning as a Service
NLP - Natural Language Processing
VR - Virtual Reality
IoT - Internet of Things
EdTech - Educational Technology
IT - Information Technology

# Chapter 7
# Exploring the Potential of Generative AI in English Language Teaching

**Chinaza Solomon Ironsi**
*Rauf Denktas University, Cyprus*

## ABSTRACT

*Integrating artificial intelligence (AI) technologies in education has shown remarkable potential in revolutionizing various aspects of teaching and learning. In English language teaching (ELT), generative AI has emerged as a powerful tool to enhance language acquisition, foster learner engagement, and provide personalized instruction. While the potential of generative AI in ELT is promising, it is important to provide insights into certain challenges and considerations. Ethical concerns related to data privacy, bias in AI algorithms, and the potential displacement of human instructors need to be carefully navigated. The successful implementation of generative AI in ELT relies on careful consideration of ethical implications, human oversight, and the continuous refinement of AI algorithms to ensure optimal language learning outcomes. On these premises, this chapter explores the potential of generative AI in ELT and its implications for language learners and educators.*

## INTRODUCTION

Technology has advanced quickly in the field of English language teaching (ELT), and generative artificial intelligence (AI) is one area that shows great potential. However, despite the potential, generative artificial intelligence is generating scholarly discussions due to its drawbacks. Based on this hypothesis, further research is needed

DOI: 10.4018/979-8-3693-0487-7.ch007

to offer a solid scientific understanding of the application of generative artificial intelligence in education. This will help in evaluating the benefits and drawbacks of using and implementing this possible instructional resource. These studies will provide investigators and educational professionals with information on what steps need to be taken to integrate generative artificial intelligence into the classroom.

Given these, this chapter explores the potential of generative AI in enhancing ELT's teaching and learning experience. It discusses the applications of generative AI in various aspects of language learning, such as vocabulary acquisition, writing practice, speaking activities, reading and listening skills. By examining the benefits, challenges, and ethical considerations, this chapter aims to provide insights into how generative AI can revolutionize the field of ELT.

## THE CONCEPT OF GENERATIVE AI

Generative Artificial Intelligence (AI) is a cutting-edge technology that has the potential to revolutionize a wide range of industries. This cutting-edge area of artificial intelligence is building machines that can produce creative works of art, including writing, music, graphics, and even dialogue that sounds human (Hsu & Ching, 2023). According to Baidoo-Anu and Owusu Ansah (2023), the idea of generative AI is a major advancement in the field of creativity and has the power to completely transform a variety of fields, including human-computer interactions and the arts.

Meanwhile, Generative AI, also known as generative modeling, refers to a category of algorithms and models designed to generate new data by learning from existing examples (Kohnke et al., 2023). Unlike traditional AI models that rely on pre-programmed rules and patterns, generative AI employs neural networks and deep learning techniques to generate novel content (Singer et al., 2023). By learning patterns and features from large datasets, these models can create new and original outputs that mimic the characteristics of the training data.

## APPLICATIONS OF GENERATIVE AI

Generative AI finds applications in various domains, unlocking opportunities once deemed unimaginable. Below are a few areas where generative AI has made a significant impact;

## Content Creation

Generative AI has revolutionized content creation by enabling the automatic generation of images, videos, and music. Artists and designers can leverage these AI models to augment their creative process and generate unique pieces, unleashing a new realm of artistic possibilities.

## Virtual Reality (VR) and Gaming

Generative AI has transformed virtual reality and gaming by generating immersive environments and lifelike characters. These AI models can dynamically create landscapes, objects, and non-player characters, enhancing the realism and interactivity of virtual experiences.

## Natural Language Processing

In natural language processing, generative AI has paved the way for chatbots and virtual assistants that can hold engaging and contextually relevant conversations. These AI systems can generate human-like text responses, making interactions more seamless and efficient.

## Data Augmentation and Synthesis

To improve and synthesize data for machine learning model training, generative AI approaches are employed. As a result, datasets can be more varied and robust, which enhances model performance and generalization. Crucially, while generative AI research has enormous promise, it also raises moral questions. The exploitation of generative AI to produce malevolent or misleading information, like deepfakes or fake news, is one of the main causes for concern. It is essential to create moral standards and laws to reduce these dangers and guarantee the appropriate application of generative AI technology.

Generative AI, taken as a whole, signifies a revolution in creativity and technology. Its capacity to produce original material has broad ramifications and presents fresh chances for several sectors. The potential advantages of generative AI are enormous, including more creativity, better user experiences, and more opportunities for human-computer interaction—yet ethical problems still need to be addressed. We must make sure that the creation and use of generative AI adhere to moral principles and the welfare of people as we continue to investigate and improve this technology. By accomplishing this, the full potential of generative AI may be realized, and its revolutionary promise to advance society and education can be fully realized.

## THE APPLICATION OF GENERATIVE AI IN VARIOUS EDUCATIONAL DOMAINS

Artificial intelligence (AI) has significantly transformed various sectors, and education is no exception. Generative AI, a branch of AI focused on creating new content, ideas, and solutions, has emerged as a powerful tool in education. By leveraging machine learning algorithms, generative AI has the potential to enhance and personalize learning experiences, facilitate content creation, improve assessments, and foster creativity. These domains are discussed below;

### Personalized Learning

Generative AI enables educators to tailor educational content to individual student's needs and preferences. AI algorithms can generate personalized learning materials by analyzing vast amounts of data, such as student performance, learning styles, and interests (Chen et al., 2020). These materials can include interactive simulations, adaptive quizzes, and customized lesson plans, catering to each student's strengths and weaknesses (Hsu & Ching, 2023). Personalized learning promotes student engagement, facilitates mastery of concepts, and empowers self-directed learning.

### Content Creation

One of the significant challenges for educators is the time-consuming task of content creation. Generative AI can alleviate this burden by assisting in creating educational resources. For instance, AI-powered tools can generate lesson plans, worksheets, and multimedia materials based on specific learning objectives. This automation of content creation allows educators to focus more on instructional design and individualized student support (Chen et al., 2020). Moreover, AI algorithms can analyze existing educational resources to identify knowledge gaps and recommend improvements, fostering continuous content refinement.

### Intelligent Tutoring Systems

Intelligent tutoring systems can be developed with the help of generative AI. By examining student performance data, these systems can produce recommendations and individualized feedback. AI systems can pinpoint the areas in which pupils most need help and offer focused solutions (Baidoo-Anu & Owusu Ansah, 2023). AI-powered tutors can converse with students, providing explanations and answers to inquiries using natural language processing and conversation production. Intelligent teaching solutions facilitate the comprehension of difficult ideas, increase learning efficiency, and offer prompt feedback.

## Automated Assessment

Traditional assessment methods often consume significant time and effort from educators. Generative AI can automate the assessment process, saving time and providing immediate feedback to students. AI algorithms can analyze students' written responses, essays, or coding solutions, evaluating them based on predefined criteria (Yu & Guo, 2023). Automated assessment systems can handle large-scale grading, maintain consistency, and provide detailed feedback, facilitating timely interventions and enabling teachers to focus on personalized instruction.

## Creativity and Artistic Expression

Generative AI can also foster creativity and artistic expression in education. AI-powered tools can generate music, artwork, and literature, inspiring students to explore their creative potential. Students can experiment with different styles, genres, and techniques by collaborating with AI systems, unleashing their imagination. Moreover, generative AI can provide real-time feedback on creative works, helping students refine their ideas and offering novel perspectives (Vartiainen & Tedre, 2023).

## Language Learning

Extensive practice and exposure to real language resources are frequently necessary for language learning. According to Biswas (2023), generative AI is capable of producing lifelike language simulations, including dialogues, scenarios, and virtual settings that mimic language use in everyday situations. Students can enhance their speaking, listening, and comprehension abilities by engaging with AI-generated information (Kohnke et al., 2023). Additionally, AI systems can customize language training by adjusting the degree of difficulty of each student's development and offering focused vocabulary and grammatical drills.

Through the transformation of personalized learning, content production, tutoring, language learning, evaluation, and artistic expression, generative AI holds the potential to completely change the educational landscape. Teachers can give intelligent tutoring, automate assessments, foster creativity, improve language training, and provide individualized learning experiences by utilizing AI algorithms. To ensure that technology is a potent tool to enhance teaching and learning rather than take the place of educators, it is imperative to create a balance between AI-driven solutions and human engagement. Future learning environments could be more inclusive, productive, and engaging with the use of generative AI in education. Analyzing its impact on the domains of English language instruction is therefore essential.

## VOCABULARY ACQUISITION AND GENERATIVE AI

The development of one's vocabulary is essential to language learning. Those with a large vocabulary can understand and communicate in a variety of situations. Advancements in artificial intelligence (AI) have led to the emergence of generative AI models as a potentially useful tool for improving vocabulary acquisition (Bran et al., 2023). Language models and other generative AI models are made to produce text that resembles that of a human being using patterns and structures that are acquired through extensive training data (Ebrahimzadeh, 2017). It is critical to note that the application of generative AI to vocabulary acquisition has the potential to transform language learning.

### Approaches to Using Generative AI for Teaching Vocabulary Skills

#### Personalized Vocabulary Learning

Customization of the learning process is one of the main benefits of generative AI models. Conventional vocabulary acquisition techniques frequently offer a one-size-fits-all strategy that might not take into account the interests and preferences of specific learners. By creating customized vocabulary exercises, tests, and examples according to students' competency levels and learning objectives, generative AI models can adjust to the unique needs of each learner (Gimpel et al., 2023). Gaining vocabulary might be more interesting and successful with this individualized approach since students will receive content that is specific to their requirements.

#### Contextualized Vocabulary Usage

Generative AI models excel at understanding and generating contextually relevant text. This capability can be leveraged to provide learners with comprehensive examples and explanations of vocabulary words in different contexts (Dwivedi et al., 2023). Instead of relying solely on static definitions, learners can explore how words are used in sentences, paragraphs, or even longer passages (Kohnke et al., 2023). By presenting vocabulary in meaningful and realistic contexts, generative AI models facilitate a deeper understanding of word usage, connotations, and nuances, which is crucial for effective vocabulary acquisition.

## Interactive Language Practice

Generative AI models can be integrated into interactive language practice platforms, allowing learners to engage in real-time conversations or simulations. These models can generate responses that simulate natural language interactions, allowing learners to practice using newly acquired vocabulary in a conversational context (Baskara & Mukarto, 2023). Learners can receive instant feedback and guidance from the generative AI model, which helps reinforce vocabulary learning and improve fluency (Singer et al., 2023). This interactive language practice fosters an immersive learning experience, closely mimicking real-life language interactions.

## Multimodal Vocabulary Learning

Text production is not the only application for generative AI models. They can create and process various media types, including audio, video, and photos. According to Moqbel and Al-Kadi (2023), this multimodal capability creates new opportunities for vocabulary acquisition. For example, learners can correlate words with associated visuals in image-based vocabulary exercises generated by generative AI models (Firat, 2023). They can also produce audio clips that accurately enunciate vocabulary terms, which aids learners in honing their speaking and pronunciation abilities (Topsakal & Topsakal, 2022). Generative AI models that combine various modalities improve language acquisition by strengthening memory associations and accommodating a variety of learning preferences.

## Continuous and Adaptive Learning

Large volumes of data can be used to train and update generative AI models, which enables them to adjust to changing linguistic patterns and changes. New terms and idioms appear as language changes, and the meanings of words that already exist may change (Yang, 2023). To give students the most up-to-date and pertinent vocabulary knowledge, generative AI models can keep up with these changes (Firat, 2023). This flexibility guarantees that students have access to the most recent linguistic information, improving their language skills and maintaining a current vocabulary.

## Automatic Assessment and Feedback

Assessing vocabulary acquisition can be challenging and time-consuming for educators. Generative AI models can automate the assessment process by generating vocabulary quizzes, exercises, and fill-in-the-blank questions that assess learners' understanding and application of vocabulary words (Biswas, 2023). The models can also provide immediate feedback, pointing out errors, suggesting alternative word choices, and explaining correct usage (Yang, 2023). This automated assessment and feedback mechanism saves time for educators and enables learners to receive timely and targeted guidance, facilitating their vocabulary growth.

Generative AI models have immense potential to revolutionize vocabulary acquisition in language learning. Through personalized learning experiences, contextualized vocabulary usage, interactive language practice, multimodal learning, continuous adaptation, and automatic assessment, generative AI models empower learners with effective and engaging tools for acquiring and mastering new vocabulary. As technology continues to advance, incorporating generative AI models into language learning platforms holds great promise for enhancing vocabulary acquisition and ultimately improving language proficiency

## IMPROVING STUDENTS WRITING PRACTICE USING GENERATIVE AI

In ELT, writing is an essential ability, and learners can benefit greatly from generative AI. It's possible to employ generative AI to create writing prompts that provide students with a variety of themes to choose from and serve as inspiration. Its application is essential for providing automatic assessment of writing samples, with a focus on coherence, grammar, and vocabulary. By combining machine learning algorithms and natural language processing approaches, trainees' writing skills can be improved through focused feedback.

The potential for generative artificial intelligence (AI) to completely transform several facets of education has made AI a very formidable tool. Its use to help pupils improve their writing abilities in particular has great potential (Dwivedi et al., 2023). AI's capacity to produce prose that resembles that of a human being means that it can help students become more proficient writers, encourage creativity, and offer tailored criticism.

### Roles Of Generative AI In Developing Students' Writing Skills

#### Enhanced Writing Practice and Feedback

Giving students more practice and feedback is one of the major advantages of implementing generative AI in writing education (Sharples, 2022). AI-powered tools can provide students with an abundance of writing exercises, motivating them to write regularly. These writing prompts can be customized to meet the needs and skill levels of each student, as well as their specific writing objectives (Liu et al.,

2021). Students can hone their composition abilities, increase their vocabulary, and enhance their grammar and sentence structure by regularly participating in writing assignments.

Moreover, real-time feedback via generative AI allows students to get suggestions and improvements right away. This customized feedback can identify problem areas, highlight recurrent errors, and provide detailed suggestions for improvement (Ingley & Pack, 2023). Students can then concentrate on specific areas for growth by having a better awareness of their strengths and shortcomings.

## Enhancing Creativity and Idea Generation

Generative AI can also be vital in fostering creativity and idea generation among students. By providing students with diverse writing prompts and examples, AI can stimulate their imagination and encourage them to explore various writing styles and genres (Godwin-Jones, 2022). AI-generated texts can inspire, showcasing different approaches and techniques students can experiment with in their writing. Additionally, generative AI can facilitate the creation of collaborative writing environments (Woo et al., 2023; Godwin-Jones, 2022). Students can collaborate with their peers and AI-generated agents, brainstorming ideas, co-writing stories, and receiving instant feedback. This collaborative process enhances creativity and promotes critical thinking, communication, and teamwork.

## Personalized Learning and Differentiation

One of the greatest advantages of generative AI in writing instruction is its ability to personalize learning experiences and cater to individual student needs. AI platforms can analyze students' writing patterns, identify their strengths and weaknesses, and deliver customized learning materials accordingly (Yan, 2023). By adapting the difficulty level of prompts, providing targeted exercises, and offering personalized feedback, AI ensures that students receive tailored support to enhance their writing skills effectively. Moreover, generative AI can assist students with learning disabilities or language barriers (Guo et al., 2022). It can provide alternative formats, such as audio or visual aids, to support comprehension and expression (Hwang et al., 2023). This inclusive approach ensures that all students have equal opportunities to develop their writing abilities and participate in learning.

Generative AI holds immense potential to transform the way students learn and develop their writing skills. By providing enhanced writing practice and feedback, fostering creativity and idea generation, and enabling personalized learning experiences, AI empowers students to become proficient writers. However, to fully capitalize on the potential of generative AI, it is crucial to address the challenges and ethical considerations that arise. With careful implementation and ongoing research, generative AI can contribute significantly to the educational landscape, equipping students with the essential skills needed in the digital age.

## Developing Speaking Skills Through Generative AI

### Speaking Activities

For language learners, speaking confidently and fluently might be difficult. On the other hand, generative AI can support speaking activities by providing speech recognition software or interactive conversation partners. Artificial intelligence (AI)-driven chatbots can mimic real-world dialogues, giving students a secure and encouraging setting to hone their speaking abilities.

Generative artificial intelligence (AI) is a new and exciting technology that has the potential to revolutionize many different fields. The improvement of pupils' speaking abilities is one area where generative AI has a lot of potential (Xie et al., 2021). Successful personal and professional relationships depend on effective communication, and incorporating generative AI into the classroom can completely change the way students develop their speaking skills (Zhai, 2023). Developing pupils' speaking abilities can benefit from the application of generative AI.

### Personalized and Adaptive Learning

Generative AI can personalize the learning experience, tailoring it to individual students' needs. Through speech recognition and analysis, AI systems can assess students' pronunciation, fluency, intonation, and other aspects of spoken language (Atlas, 2023). Based on these assessments, the AI can provide personalized feedback, suggesting improvements and offering targeted exercises to address specific areas of weakness (Bozkurt, 2023). This adaptive learning approach empowers students to focus on their unique challenges, accelerating their progress and boosting their confidence.

### Enhanced Speaking Practice

Generative AI offers a great deal of benefits, one of which is that it gives students a lot of practice speaking. Artificial intelligence (AI)-driven virtual conversational agents can mimic real-world interactions, enabling students to participate in discourse, share their ideas, and get prompt feedback (Karakose et al., 2023). Students can practice speaking more regularly and at their own pace in this virtual practice environment, which removes the fear of judgment as well as time and space constraints (Limo et al., 2023). AI-based workouts are repetitious, which improves recall and gradually fortifies speaking abilities.

## Natural Language Generation

Generative AI can generate realistic, contextually appropriate responses, replicating natural conversation. This capability is precious for language learners, exposing them to authentic language patterns, good phonetics, and idiomatic expressions (Safitri et al., 2023). By interacting with AI language models, students can improve their vocabulary, grammar, and overall fluency (Lin et al., 2023). They can also learn to respond effectively to different situations, honing their conversational skills in a safe and controlled environment.

## Overcoming Speaking Anxiety

Many students experience anxiety when speaking in front of others or a new language. Generative AI offers a supportive and non-judgmental environment for students to practice speaking without fear of making mistakes (Pearce et al., 2023). This helps reduce speaking anxiety as students gradually build their confidence through repeated Practice and positive reinforcement (Takahashi, 2020). As students become more comfortable expressing themselves with AI language models, they can transfer these newfound skills to real-world conversations, ultimately overcoming their anxiety and becoming more effective communicators.

## Accessible and Inclusive Learning

Generative AI technology has the potential to bridge educational gaps and make speaking practice accessible to all students. It can provide individualized support to learners with diverse needs, including those with physical disabilities, social anxieties, or limited access to native speakers (Esplugas, 2023). AI-powered language tutors can cater to students' schedules and allow them to practice speaking anytime, anywhere (Atlas, 2023). By democratizing access to speaking Practice, generative AI ensures that all students have an equal opportunity to develop their communication skills. While the potential of generative AI in developing students' speaking skills is promising, it also raises important challenges and ethical considerations. Ensuring that AI systems are unbiased and culturally sensitive is crucial avoiding perpetuating stereotypes or offensive language. Data privacy and security must be prioritized to protect students' personal information. Moreover, the role of human teachers should be supported, as their guidance, support, and expertise remain invaluable in the language learning process.

By offering individualized learning experiences, improving speaking practice, producing natural language responses, and reducing speaking fear, generative AI has the potential to completely transform the way students improve their speaking abilities. Through the use of this technology, educational establishments can enable learners to become proficient communicators in a world that is changing quickly. To ensure responsible and inclusive implementation, it is imperative to navigate the ethical issues and problems involved with AI integration. With continued development, generative AI has enormous potential to influence language education in the future and help students become self-assured communicators.

## READING COMPREHENSION / VOCABULARY DEVELOPMENT AND READING FLUENCY

Developing reading skills is fundamental to language learning, and integrating technology can enhance reading instruction. Evidence from studies shows that Generative artificial intelligence (AI) can be applied in teaching reading skills such as reading comprehension, vocabulary development, and reading fluency.

Reading comprehension involves understanding and interpreting written texts. AI-powered systems can generate comprehension questions, cloze exercises, and summaries that cater to learners' proficiency levels and learning goals (Kohnke et al., 2023). Additionally, AI algorithms analyze learners' responses and provide personalized feedback, fostering deeper comprehension skills. Generative AI enhances vocabulary development in reading instruction (Liu et al., 2022). AI algorithms can generate contextually relevant word lists, offer synonyms and antonyms, and provide example sentences to support learners' understanding of new words encountered in texts (Mohamed, 2023). Educators can consider the integration of AI-powered flashcards and interactive vocabulary games to engage learners and reinforce vocabulary acquisition (Liu et al., 2022). Reading fluency encompasses speed, accuracy, and prosody in reading. It is important to note that generative AI can contribute to developing reading fluency skills. AI-powered speech recognition systems can provide real-time feedback on learners' pronunciation, intonation, and pacing (Sáiz-Manzanares et al., 2023). Equally, AI-generated reading passages and audiobooks can provide models of fluent reading for learners to emulate (Liu, 2023). Furthermore, AI algorithms can analyze learners' reading patterns and provide targeted practice activities to improve fluency.

## Listening Skills/Audio Content Generation/ Interactive Listening Exercises

The application of Generative Artificial Intelligence (AI) has become increasingly widespread, disrupting industries and changing our relationship with technology. In the field of education, generative AI has enormous potential for improving students' reading and listening abilities (Kovaevi, 2023; Vera, 2023). Generative AI systems can offer tailored training and flexible material delivery through the use of sophisticated machine learning and natural language processing algorithms. This results in personalized and captivating learning experiences.

Listening skills play a crucial role in language learning, and technological advancements offer new opportunities to enhance listening instruction. Research recognizes the applications of generative AI in various aspects of listening instruction, such as audio content generation, interactive exercises, and personalized feedback (Kohnke et al., 2023). One of the challenges in teaching listening skills is the availability of diverse and authentic audio materials. Some studies affirm that generative AI can address listening issues by generating a wide range of audio content (Liu et al., 2022; Mohamed, 2023). AI algorithms can create simulated conversations, interviews, and authentic language input, allowing learners to practice listening in various contexts.

Additionally, AI-generated voice recordings can provide models of pronunciation, intonation, and natural speech patterns. Generative AI can contribute to developing interactive listening exercises that engage learners and provide targeted practice opportunities. AI-powered speech recognition and natural language processing techniques can create interactive listening activities. AI algorithms can analyze learners' responses, identify areas of difficulty, and provide personalized feedback to enhance listening comprehension.

## Strategies and Approaches to Using Generative AI for Teaching Reading and Listening Activities

### Personalized Learning

Generative AI's capacity to provide individualized learning experiences is one of its main benefits for improving reading and listening comprehension. AI-driven systems can assess each learner's preferences, shortcomings, and abilities to customize the curriculum (Kovačević, 2023). By creating adaptive resources, like interactive stories or audiobooks, AI algorithms can modify vocabulary, content complexity, and difficulty levels based on learners' competency levels. By ensuring that students are constantly engaged and challenged, this individualized approach promotes effective skill development.

## Enhanced Language Comprehension

A recent study shows that generative AI technologies excel in language processing and understanding (Vera, 2023). Using sophisticated algorithms, AI systems can generate contextually rich texts and audio materials, enabling learners to improve their reading and listening comprehension skills. AI-powered virtual assistants can engage in natural language conversations, helping learners practice their reading and listening skills through interactive dialogues (Sáiz-Manzanares et al., 2023). Additionally, AI algorithms can generate summaries, quizzes, and comprehension exercises based on reading or listening inputs, offering instant feedback and opportunities for skill reinforcement.

## Vocabulary Expansion and Contextual Learning

Developing a robust vocabulary is fundamental to improving reading and listening skills. Generative AI can facilitate vocabulary expansion by providing learners with interactive and context-rich materials. AI-powered language models can generate sample sentences, word associations, and contextual examples, enabling learners to grasp word meanings and usage in diverse contexts (Kohnke et al., 2023). Moreover, AI algorithms can create adaptive word lists based on learners' reading or listening inputs, presenting relevant vocabulary and reinforcing learning through contextual application.

## Natural Language Generation for Language Production

Generative AI can improve reading and listening skills and enhance language production abilities. AI-powered systems can assist learners in generating coherent and well-structured texts, essays, or speeches (Liu et al., 2022). By analyzing input prompts and examples, AI algorithms can provide learners with suggestions, grammar corrections, and stylistic improvements. This real-time assistance fosters better writing and speaking skills, allowing learners to express themselves more effectively and confidently.

## Engaging and Immersive Learning Experiences

Learning experiences that are incredibly immersive and engaging can be produced using generative AI technology. AI-powered systems can catch learners' interest and push them to improve their reading and listening skills by mimicking real-world settings and interactive narratives (Liu, 2023). Learners can explore and engage with virtual worlds, characters, and dialogues in immersive language learning environments created by generative AI in conjunction with virtual reality (VR) and augmented reality (AR) apps (Tai & Chen, 2021). Active involvement is encouraged by these interactive experiences, which improve the effectiveness and enjoyment of learning (Utami et al., 2021). Practices in English Language Teaching (ELT) can benefit from generative AI, which includes language models like GPT-3. But there are certain difficulties in using it as well. The following are some advantages and difficulties of generative AI in ELT:

## Benefits and Potentials of Generative AI in English Language Teaching

The disadvantages of generative artificial intelligence in education and language learning have been emphasized in numerous research (Islam & Islam, 2023; Rahman & Watanobe, 2023). It's crucial to note, though, that incorporating generative AI into our schools has several advantages. According to certain research (Baidoo-Anu & Owusu Ansah, 2023; Sok & Heng, 2023; Lee, 2023), incorporating generative AI into English language instruction has several advantages. A few of these advantages are covered in the sections that follow;

### Enhanced Language Production

Learners can practice and advance their language production abilities with the help of generative AI models. Learners can improve their vocabulary, grammar, and general fluency by interacting with the model and providing and receiving feedback on their written or spoken language (Ironsi, 2023).

### Personalized Learning

Generative AI can deliver feedback and content that is tailored to the needs of each unique student. It can create a personalized learning experience that targets the areas in which students need to improve by analyzing their past interactions and adjusting their replies accordingly.

### An Engaging and Interactive Learning Environment

Students' language learning can become more dynamic and interesting by utilizing generative AI. Students can converse with the AI model, pose queries, and get prompt answers, resulting in a dynamic learning environment that encourages involvement.

### Exposure to Authentic Language

Large volumes of real text data are used to train language models, exposing students to a broad variety of vocabulary and linguistic patterns. Learners may improve their command of the English language and become more fluent and native-like as a result of this exposure.

## Challenges of Generative AI in English Language Teaching

Earlier, it was mentioned that although generative AI has drawn numerous criticisms from academia, there is potential. Concerning the challenges, a few studies have carefully analyzed its use and presented some areas of concern (Zhai, 2022; Kasneci et al., 2023; Whalen & Mouza, 2023; Rahman & Watanobe, 2023). These areas are summarized below;

*Accuracy and reliability:* Although generative AI models have come a long way, they are not perfect. There may be times when the model produces inaccurate or deceptive data. Before implementing the generated content in the classroom, educators need to make sure that it is accurate and reliable.

*Lack of human interaction:* While AI models are capable of simulating talks, they are unable to recreate the subtleties of human communication. Learning a language involves more than just grammar and vocabulary; it also entails social and cultural components that are best handled in person. Opportunities for developing real communication and interpersonal skills may be limited by an over-reliance on generative AI.

*Ethical considerations:* Because generative AI models learn from the data they are trained on, biases in the data may unintentionally be reflected in them. Teachers need to be aware of such prejudices and make sure that the content produced by AI doesn't include derogatory terminology or stereotypes.

*Limited contextual understanding:* Although AI models like GPT-3 are excellent at producing text by using patterns in the training data, they require a thorough comprehension of context. They might give grammatically sound answers that make no sense or are improper for the situation. To guarantee that the generated content is acceptable and coherent, educators must assist students in critically analyzing and confirming it.

*Overdependence on technology:* The importance of human teachers may be diminished if generative AI is used excessively. Although technology can improve language acquisition, it should be used in conjunction with human direction and instruction rather than as a replacement (Ironsi, 2022). While there are many advantages of integrating generative AI into ELT, it's crucial to address the drawbacks and make sure the technology is applied wisely to optimize its educational potential.

To develop an efficient and comprehensive language learning environment, educators should adopt a balanced strategy that blends human expertise with the strengths of artificial intelligence.

## Ethical Considerations While Using Generative AI

Learner privacy, data security, and algorithmic transparency are just a few of the significant ethical challenges that generative AI in ELT brings up and that require careful study. If generative AI is to be taken seriously in education, emphasis must also be paid to human oversight and the necessity of striking a balance between technology and human intervention in teaching and learning. Education has been transformed by generative artificial intelligence (AI), which has altered many other industries. Generative AI has the potential to improve language learning in English language teaching (ELT). However, incorporating AI into ELT raises important ethical issues that need to be properly considered. These are the moral issues that arise from using generative AI in ELT and highlight the significance of using it carefully and responsibly.

*Data Privacy:* Ensuring that student data is safeguarded and utilized appropriately is imperative. Prioritizing the use of safe platforms and getting students' permission before gathering personal data is something that educators should do (Krügel et al., 2023). One of the main ethical issues with generative AI in ELT is data privacy. ELT professionals need to make sure that student data is secure and handled appropriately (Panagopoulou et al., 2023). Utilizing safe platforms that protect user data is essential. Gaining the informed consent of students before gathering personal information is crucial for fostering trust and upholding moral standards.

*Bias and Diversity:* Generative AI systems learn from existing data, which means they can unintentionally perpetuate biases in the training data (Krügel et al., 2023). ELT practitioners should be mindful of this and strive to provide diverse and inclusive content representing different cultures, genders, and perspectives.

*Authenticity and Plagiarism:* While generative AI can generate text, it is essential to emphasize the importance of originality and avoid encouraging plagiarism. ELT professionals should guide learners on proper citation and attribution, ensuring they understand the ethical implications of using AI-generated content (Rahimi & Abadi, 2023). Promoting originality and academic integrity should be at the forefront of language learning, with AI serving as a tool rather than a means to circumvent these values (Liebrenz et al., 2023).

*Pedagogical Appropriateness:* AI-generated content should align with sound pedagogical principles and cater to learners' needs. Educators should critically evaluate the quality and relevance of AI-generated materials before incorporating them into their teaching practice (Mhlanga, 2023; Akbar et al., 2023). The content should align with sound pedagogical principles and cater to the specific needs of language learners. Balancing AI with personalized instruction can ensure that learners receive comprehensive and effective language learning experiences.

*Empowering Learners:* AI should empower learners rather than replace human interaction and guidance. ELT practitioners should balance AI-driven resources and personalized instruction, fostering meaningful interaction and supporting learners' language development (Zhou et al., 2023).

*Transparency and Explainability:* It is critical to ensure that learners are aware of the limitations and capabilities of AI systems and to be open and honest about the use of generative AI in ELT. Teachers should explain the purpose of AI-generated content and promote candid conversations regarding AI's place in language instruction (Mhlanga, 2023). Since trust is created by open communication, these ethical arguments hope to encourage the careful and responsible application of generative AI in English language teaching. Educators may leverage AI while keeping ethical issues in mind by giving data protection, diversity, authenticity, pedagogical appropriateness, transparency, and learner empowerment a priority.

## CONCLUSION

The dynamic subject of AI-driven English language teaching (ELT) has promise for several advancements in the future, such as personalized learning, in which AI is utilized to create exercises and courses that are specifically catered to the requirements, abilities, and learning preferences of individual students. Advanced AI is also capable of evaluating spoken language in real-time and providing instantaneous feedback on fluency and pronunciation. Experts must also take into account combining AI with text, audio, and video information to create more thorough language learning experiences. In addition, it appears that English language teachers should take into account the use of AI in mobile apps and augmented/virtual reality settings for accessible and immersive language learning.

Experts in this discipline also need to think about adding gamified components to ELT platforms to encourage and engage students. To advance this area of AI-driven ELT, it is imperative to make sure it is accessible and has features for students with disabilities. With the promise of more efficient and interesting language learning opportunities, these possible advancements offer a promising future for AI-driven ELT.

To sum up, generative AI can revolutionize English language teaching by providing customized, interactive, and flexible learning opportunities. However, to fully realize the benefits of this technology, cautious application, ethical concerns, and a well-rounded strategy are essential. This chapter gives educators the information they need to make wise decisions by illuminating the benefits and drawbacks of incorporating generative AI into ELT.

## REFERENCES

Akbar, M. A., Khan, A. A., & Liang, P. (2023). Ethical Aspects of ChatGPT in Software Engineering Research. *arXiv preprint arXiv:2306.07557.*

Atlas, S. (2023). *ChatGPT for higher education and professional development: A guide to conversational AI.* The University of Rhode Island.

Baidoo-AnuD.Owusu AnsahL. (2023). Education in the era of generative artificial intelligence (AI): Understanding the potential benefits of ChatGPT in promoting teaching and learning. SSRN 4337484. doi:10.2139/ssrn.4337484

Baskara, F. R., & Mukarto, F. X. (2023). Exploring the Implications of ChatGPT for Language Learning in Higher Education. *Indonesian Journal of English Language Teaching and Applied Linguistics, 7*(2), 343–358.

BiswasS. (2023). Role of Chat GPT in Education. SSRN 4369981.

Bozkurt, A. (2023). Generative artificial intelligence (AI) powered conversational educational agents: The inevitable paradigm shift—. *Asian Journal of Distance Education, 18*(1).

Bran, E., Rughini, C., Nadoleanu, G., & Flaherty, M. G. (2023). The Emerging Social Status of Generative AI: Vocabularies of AI Competence in Public Discourse. In *Proceedings of The 24th Conference on Control Systems and Computer Science (CSCS24 2023).* IEEE. 10.1109/CSCS59211.2023.00068

Chen, X., Xie, H., Zou, D., & Hwang, G. J. (2020). Application and theory gaps during the rise of artificial intelligence in education. *Computers and Education: Artificial Intelligence, 1*, 100002. doi:10.1016/j.caeai.2020.100002

Dwivedi, Y. K., Kshetri, N., Hughes, L., Slade, E. L., Jeyaraj, A., Kar, A. K., Baabdullah, A. M., Koohang, A., Raghavan, V., Ahuja, M., Albanna, H., Albashrawi, M. A., Al-Busaidi, A. S., Balakrishnan, J., Barlette, Y., Basu, S., Bose, I., Brooks, L., Buhalis, D., & Wright, R. (2023). "So what if ChatGPT wrote it?" Multidisciplinary perspectives on opportunities, challenges, and implications of generative conversational AI for research, Practice, and policy. *International Journal of Information Management, 71*, 102642. doi:10.1016/j.ijinfomgt.2023.102642

Ebrahimzadeh, M. (2017). Readers, Players, and Watchers: EFL Students' Vocabulary Acquisition through Digital Video Games. *English Language Teaching*, *10*(2), 1–18. doi:10.5539/elt.v10n2p1

Esplugas, M. (2023). The use of artificial intelligence (AI) to enhance academic communication, education, and research: A balanced approach. *The Journal of Hand Surgery, European Volume*, *48*(8), 17531934231185746. doi:10.1177/17531934231185746 PMID:37417005

Hsu, Y. C., & Ching, Y. H. (2023). Generative Artificial Intelligence in Education, Part One: The Dynamic Frontier. *TechTrends*, *67*(4), 1–5. doi:10.100711528-023-00863-9

Hwang, W. Y., Nurtantyana, R., Purba, S. W. D., Hariyanti, U., Indrihapsari, Y., & Surjono, H. D. (2023). AI and recognition technologies to facilitate English as a foreign language writing for supporting personalization and contextualization in authentic contexts. *Journal of Educational Computing Research*, *61*(5), 07356331221137253. doi:10.1177/07356331221137253

Ironsi, C. S. (2023). Investigating the use of virtual reality to improve speaking skills: Insights from students and teachers. *Smart Learning Environments*, *10*(1), 53. doi:10.118640561-023-00272-8

IslamI.IslamM. N. (2023). Opportunities and challenges of chatbot in academia: A conceptual analysis. Authorea Preprints.

Karakose, T., Demirkol, M., Yirci, R., Polat, H., Ozdemir, T. Y., & Tülübaş, T. (2023). A Conversation with ChatGPT about Digital Leadership and Technology Integration: Comparative Analysis Based on Human–AI Collaboration. *Administrative Sciences*, *13*(7), 157. doi:10.3390/admsci13070157

Kasneci, E., Seßler, K., Küchemann, S., Bannert, M., Dementieva, D., Fischer, F., Gasser, U., Groh, G., Günnemann, S., Hüllermeier, E., Krusche, S., Kutyniok, G., Michaeli, T., Nerdel, C., Pfeffer, J., Poquet, O., Sailer, M., Schmidt, A., Seidel, T., & Kasneci, G. (2023). ChatGPT for good? On opportunities and challenges of large language models for education. *Learning and Individual Differences*, *103*, 102274. doi:10.1016/j.lindif.2023.102274

Kohnke, L., Moorhouse, B. L., & Zou, D. (2023). ChatGPT for language teaching and learning. *RELC Journal*, 00336882231162868.

Kovačević, D. (2023, March). Use of chatbot in ESP teaching process. In *2023 22nd International Symposium INFOTEH-JAHORINA (INFOTEH)* (pp. 1-5). IEEE.

Krügel, S., Ostermaier, A., & Uhl, M. (2023). The moral authority of ChatGPT. *arXiv preprint arXiv:2301.07098.*

Lee, H. (2023). The rise of ChatGPT: Exploring its potential in medical education. *Anatomical Sciences Education*, ase.2270. doi:10.1002/ase.2270 PMID:36916887

Liebrenz, M., Schleifer, R., Buadze, A., Bhugra, D., & Smith, A. (2023). Generating scholarly content with ChatGPT: Ethical challenges for medical publishing. *The Lancet. Digital Health*, *5*(3), e105–e106. doi:10.1016/S2589-7500(23)00019-5 PMID:36754725

Limo, F. A. F., Tiza, D. R. H., Roque, M. M., Herrera, E. E., Murillo, J. P. M., Huallpa, J. J., & Gonzáles, J. L. A. (2023). Personalized tutoring: ChatGPT as a virtual tutor for personalized learning experiences. *Social Space*, *23*(1), 293–312.

Lin, C. C., Huang, A. Y., & Yang, S. J. (2023). A review of AI-driven conversational chatbot implementation methodologies and challenges (1999–2022). *Sustainability (Basel)*, *15*(5), 4012. doi:10.3390u15054012

Liu, C., Hou, J., Tu, Y. F., Wang, Y., & Hwang, G. J. (2021). Incorporating reflective thinking promoting mechanism into artificial intelligence-supported English writing environments. *Interactive Learning Environments*, 1–19.

Liu, C. C., Liao, M. G., Chang, C. H., & Lin, H. M. (2022). An analysis of children's interaction with an AI chatbot and its impact on their interest in reading. *Computers & Education*, *189*, 104576. doi:10.1016/j.compedu.2022.104576

Liu, M. (2023). Exploring the Application of Artificial Intelligence in Foreign Language Teaching: Challenges and Future Development. In *SHS Web of Conferences* (*Vol. 168*). EDP Sciences.

Mhlanga, D. (2023). Open AI in education, the responsible and ethical use of ChatGPT towards lifelong learning. *Education, the Responsible and Ethical Use of ChatGPT Towards Lifelong Learning*. SSRN.

Mohamed, A. M. (2023). Exploring the potential of an AI-based Chatbot (ChatGPT) in enhancing English as a Foreign Language (EFL) teaching: Perceptions of EFL Faculty Members. *Education and Information Technologies*, 1–23. doi:10.100710639-023-11917-z

Moqbel, M. S. S., & Al-Kadi, A. M. T. (2023). Foreign language learning assessment in the age of ChatGPT: A theoretical account. *Journal of English Studies in Arabia Felix*, *2*(1), 71–84. doi:10.56540/jesaf.v2i1.62

Panagopoulou, F., Parpoula, C., & Karpouzis, K. (2023). Legal and ethical considerations regarding the use of ChatGPT in education. *arXiv preprint arXiv:2306.10037*. doi:10.31235/osf.io/c5hf3

Pearce, K., Alghowinem, S., & Breazeal, C. (2023, June). Build-a-Bot: Teaching Conversational AI Using a Transformer-Based Intent Recognition and Question Answering Architecture. *Proceedings of the AAAI Conference on Artificial Intelligence*, *37*(13), 16025–16032. doi:10.1609/aaai.v37i13.26903

Rahimi, F., & Abadi, A. T. B. (2023). ChatGPT and publication ethics. *Archives of Medical Research*, *54*(3), 272–274. doi:10.1016/j.arcmed.2023.03.004 PMID:36990890

Rahman, M. M., & Watanobe, Y. (2023). ChatGPT for education and research: Opportunities, threats, and strategies. *Applied Sciences (Basel, Switzerland)*, *13*(9), 5783. doi:10.3390/app13095783

Safitri, D., Fhadilah, N., & Lubis, Y. (2023). English Phonology for Second Language Learner. *English and Tourism Studies*, *1*(1), 52–59.

Sáiz-Manzanares, M. C., Marticorena-Sánchez, R., Martín-Antón, L. J., Díez, I. G., & Almeida, L. (2023). Perceived satisfaction of university students with the use of chatbots as a tool for self-regulated learning. *Heliyon*, *9*(1), e12843. doi:10.1016/j.heliyon.2023.e12843 PMID:36704275

Shahriar, S., & Hayawi, K. (2023). Let's have a chat! A Conversation with ChatGPT: Technology, Applications, and Limitations. *arXiv preprint arXiv:2302.13817.*

Sharples, M. (2022). Automated essay writing: An AIED opinion. *International Journal of Artificial Intelligence in Education*, *32*(4), 1119–1126. doi:10.100740593-022-00300-7

Singer, J. B., Báez, J. C., & Rios, J. A. (2023). AI creates the message: Integrating AI language learning models into social work education and Practice. *Journal of Social Work Education*, *59*(2), 294–302. doi:10.1080/10437797.2023.2189878

SokS.HengK. (2023). ChatGPT for education and research: A review of benefits and risks. *Available at* SSRN 4378735. doi:10.2139/ssrn.4378735

Tai, T. Y., & Chen, H. H. J. (2021). The impact of immersive virtual reality on EFL learners' listening comprehension. *Journal of Educational Computing Research*, *59*(7), 1272–1293. doi:10.1177/0735633121994291

Takahashi, Y. (2020). Redesigning an artificial intelligence learning application to improve Japanese students' English conversational skills: a case study of a vocational institute in Tokyo, Japan. Assumption University of Thailand.

Topsakal, O., & Topsakal, E. (2022). Framework for a foreign language teaching software for children utilizing AR, voice bots, and ChatGPT (Large Language Models). *The Journal of Cognitive Systems*, *7*(2), 33–38.

Utami, L. P. R. A., Suwastini, N. K. A., Dantes, G. R., Suprihatin, C. T., & Adnyani, K. E. K. (2021). Virtual reality for supporting authentic learning in 21st-century language classrooms. *Jurnal Pendidikan Teknologi dan Kejuruan, 18*(1), 132-141.

Vartiainen, H., & Tedre, M. (2023). Using artificial intelligence in craft education: Crafting with text-to-image generative models. *Digital Creativity (Exeter)*, *34*(1), 1–21. doi:10.1080/14626268.2023.2174557

Vera, F. (2023). *Enhancing English language learning in undergraduate students using ChatGPT: A quasi-experimental study*. CIAA.

Whalen, J., & Mouza, C. (2023). ChatGPT: Challenges, Opportunities, and Implications for Teacher Education. *Contemporary Issues in Technology & Teacher Education*, *23*(1), 1–23.

Woo, D. J., Susanto, H., Yeung, C. H., Guo, K., & Fung, A. K. Y. (2023). Exploring AI-Generated Text in Student Writing: How Does AI Help? *arXiv preprint arXiv:2304.02478.*

Xie, T., Liu, R., Chen, Y., & Liu, G. (2021). MOCA: A motivational online conversational agent for improving student engagement in collaborative learning. *IEEE Transactions on Learning Technologies*, *14*(5), 653–664. doi:10.1109/TLT.2021.3129800

Yan, D. (2023). Impact of ChatGPT on learners in an L2 writing practicum: An exploratory investigation. *Education and Information Technologies*, *28*(11), 1–25. doi:10.100710639-023-11742-4

Yang, H. (2023). How I use ChatGPT responsibly in my teaching. *Nature*. doi:10.1038/d41586-023-01026-9 PMID:37045954

Yu, H., & Guo, Y. (2023). Generative artificial intelligence empowers educational reform: Current status, issues, and prospects. *Frontiers in Education*, *8*, 1183162. doi:10.3389/feduc.2023.1183162

Zhai, C. (2023). A systematic review on artificial intelligence dialogue systems for enhancing English as foreign language students' interactional competence in the university. *Computers and Education: Artificial Intelligence*, 100134.

ZhaiX. (2022). ChatGPT user experience: Implications for education. SSRN 4312418.

Zhang, X., Sun, J., & Deng, Y. (2023). Design and Application of Intelligent Classroom for English Language and Literature Based on Artificial Intelligence Technology. *Applied Artificial Intelligence*, *37*(1), 2216051. doi:10.1080/08839514.2023.2216051

Zhou, J., Müller, H., Holzinger, A., & Chen, F. (2023). Ethical ChatGPT: Concerns, challenges, and commandments. *arXiv preprint arXiv:2305.10646.*

# Chapter 8
# Leveraging Generative AI for Cross-Cultural Knowledge Exchange in Higher Education

**Khalid Mahboob**
https://orcid.org/0000-0001-7431-4430
*Sir Syed University of Engineering and Technology, Pakistan*

**Raheela Asif**
*NED University of Engineering and Technology, Karachi, Pakistan*

**Laila Umme**
https://orcid.org/0000-0001-8050-5081
*Institute of Business Management, Karachi, Pakistan*

## ABSTRACT

*The integration of generative artificial intelligence (AI) has the potential to revolutionize cross-cultural knowledge exchange in higher education. By leveraging its ability to create culturally sensitive and contextually relevant learning materials, generative AI can enhance personalized education for students from diverse backgrounds. Overcoming language barriers through real-time translation, this technology promotes inclusive collaboration and co-creation of knowledge. However, ethical considerations such as cultural authenticity, bias mitigation, and data privacy must be carefully navigated to ensure equitable and respectful cross-cultural interactions. In essence, generative AI offers a transformative avenue for fostering a culturally enriched learning environment in higher education, necessitating a balanced approach that maximizes benefits while upholding ethical principles.*

DOI: 10.4018/979-8-3693-0487-7.ch008

## 1. BACKGROUND OF CROSS-CULTURAL KNOWLEDGE EXCHANGE IN HIGHER EDUCATION

Promoting a globalized and inclusive learning environment in higher education heavily relies on cross-cultural knowledge exchange. This exchange facilitates the sharing of ideas, perspectives, and experiences among students and faculty from various cultural backgrounds within the academic setting. By fostering cultural competence, embracing diversity, and nurturing global citizenship, this knowledge exchange becomes crucial for individuals' overall growth and development (Bican, 2021). In recent years, the significance of cross-cultural knowledge exchange in higher education has been increasingly recognized. The rise of globalization and interconnectedness between societies has accentuated the need for individuals to possess cross-cultural competencies. As a response, universities and colleges worldwide have integrated cross-cultural knowledge exchange initiatives into their educational programs (Puppo, 2019).

A primary objective of cross-cultural knowledge exchange is to bridge cultural gaps and foster mutual understanding among students from diverse backgrounds. Doing so cultivates a harmonious and collaborative learning environment, enriching the educational experience for all participants (Mikhaylov, 2014). Engaging in intercultural discussions allows students to encounter diverse perspectives, values, and beliefs. This exposure extends beyond expanding their horizons and challenges their preconceived notions and biases. Through active dialogue and interaction, students cultivate empathy, cultural sensitivity, and the ability to navigate intricate cultural dynamics.

An equally vital aspect of exchanging cross-cultural knowledge is the advancement of internationalization in higher education. Increasingly, universities and colleges recognize the significance of equipping students with global skills and competencies to excel in an interconnected world. By facilitating cross-cultural exchanges, these institutions offer students opportunities to develop intercultural communication skills, adaptability, and a global mindset. This preparation empowers them to navigate varied professional and personal environments effectively in their future careers (Silor, 2019).

Additionally, sharing knowledge across cultures plays a vital role in enhancing research and academia within higher education. When academicians from diverse cultural backgrounds collaborate, they stimulate the development of groundbreaking ideas and methodologies. By integrating varying viewpoints, researchers are better equipped to tackle intricate societal issues from multiple perspectives. This interdisciplinary and cross-cultural cooperation nurtures creativity, fosters innovation, and propels the advancement of knowledge across numerous fields (Di et al.,

2022). Higher education institutions implement various strategies and initiatives to facilitate and support effective cross-cultural knowledge exchange. These measures encompass study abroad programs, international student exchanges, collaborative research projects, multicultural student organizations, and specialized cross-cultural training programs for faculty and staff (Commander et al., 2012).

Moreover, technological progress has facilitated virtual exchanges and online collaborations, effectively broadening the scope for cross-cultural knowledge exchange. To sum up, the significance of cross-cultural knowledge exchange in higher education lies in its promotion of cultural competence, diversity, and global citizenship. This process enables students and faculty from diverse cultural backgrounds to share their ideas, perspectives, and experiences, fostering intercultural understanding. As a result, universities and colleges equip students to navigate a globalized world and make meaningful contributions to society. As higher education institutions prioritize cross-cultural knowledge exchange, they actively contribute to developing a more inclusive, equitable, and interconnected academic community (Bican, 2021; Silor, 2019).

## 2. ROLE OF GENERATIVE AI IN KNOWLEDGE EXCHANGE

Generative AI is vital in facilitating knowledge exchange by improving the quality and relevance of shared information. Its advanced capabilities enable the creation of diverse content, including text, images, video, audio, and code, expanding the possibilities for disseminating knowledge (Baidoo-Anu & Owusu Ansah, 2023). A significant application of Generative AI in knowledge exchange is answer enrichment. Platforms like LivePerson utilize OpenAI's Large Language Models (LLMs) to retrieve relevant answers from knowledge bases and enhance them with contextual information. This ensures that the responses provided are accurate and tailored to the specific conversation at hand (Milano, McGrane, & Leonelli, 2023).

By employing Generative AI, knowledge exchange becomes more efficient and effective. Tasks like screening submissions for relevance and quality can be automated, freeing valuable time for knowledge experts to focus on more complex and critical endeavors (Lim et al., 2023). Moreover, Generative AI aids in detecting plagiarism, ensuring the integrity and originality of the shared information. Generative AI also contributes to a more human-like experience in knowledge exchange. The enriched answers generated by Generative AI exhibit intelligence and warmth, resulting in more engaging and natural interactions with users (Milano, McGrane, & Leonelli, 2023). This human touch fosters better communication and understanding between the knowledge provider and the recipient.

Additionally, Generative AI enables seamless knowledge exchange across various languages. Its support for multiple languages breaks down language barriers, allowing information to be shared and understood by a broader audience. Thus, Generative AI brings about a transformative impact on knowledge exchange by automating mundane tasks, enhancing the quality of answers, and providing a more human-like experience. Its ability to generate new content and support different languages makes it an indispensable tool for facilitating effective knowledge dissemination.

Generative AI, while impressive and constantly evolving, has its limitations in the realm of knowledge exchange. Firstly, generative AI heavily relies on the data it was trained on. If the training data is biased, incomplete, or inaccurate, the generated content will mirror those flaws, potentially perpetuating misinformation or skewed perspectives. Secondly, generative AI lacks true understanding and critical thinking capabilities. It can produce coherent and often convincing text, but it does not comprehend the meaning or context behind the words. This lack of comprehension can lead to incorrect or nonsensical outputs, especially when dealing with complex or nuanced subjects (Baidoo-Anu & Owusu Ansah, 2023).

Also, generative AI might generate content that seems plausible to a human reader, but it may lack factual accuracy or reliability. This can pose a significant challenge in fields where precision and credibility are paramount, such as academic research or medical advice. Furthermore, generative AI can inadvertently reinforce existing biases present in the training data, leading to skewed or discriminatory outputs. This could perpetuate societal inequalities and hinder progress towards a more inclusive and fair knowledge exchange environment (Lim et al., 2023).

Lastly, ethical concerns arise regarding the potential misuse of generative AI to create deceptive or malicious content, spreading misinformation at an unprecedented scale and pace. These limitations highlight the need for caution and continuous improvement when utilizing generative AI in knowledge exchange.

## 3. POTENTIAL IMPACT OF GENERATIVE AI ON CROSS-CULTURAL KNOWLEDGE EXCHANGE

The potential of Generative AI to transform cross-cultural knowledge exchange is significant, as it can effectively address language barriers and promote communication. Generating precise and contextually appropriate information bridges gaps between languages and cultures, fostering a more inclusive and diverse exchange of knowledge. One of the main challenges in cross-cultural knowledge exchange is the language barrier. Generative AI can be instrumental in overcoming this obstacle by automatically translating content into various languages, making it accessible to a broader audience. This expands the reach of knowledge and nurtures cultural understanding and appreciation (Puppo, 2019; Lim et al., 2023).

Additionally, Generative AI can assist in localizing information and tailoring content to suit specific regions or communities while being culturally sensitive. This ensures that knowledge resonates with the intended audience, considering their cultural nuances and preferences, resulting in more meaningful and impactful cross-cultural knowledge exchange. Another benefit of Generative AI is its ability to automate routine tasks involved in knowledge exchange, enabling experts to concentrate on more complex and critical aspects. For example, it can automatically detect plagiarism, guaranteeing the originality and reliability of shared information. It can also aid in fact-checking and verifying data accuracy, thereby elevating the overall quality and credibility of knowledge exchanged (Baidoo-Anu & Owusu Ansah, 2023).

Moreover, Generative AI can facilitate the creation of multilingual chatbots and virtual assistants that interact with users in their native languages. This enhances user experience and encourages active participation and engagement, enabling seamless knowledge exchange and interactions despite language differences (Baidoo-Anu & Owusu Ansah, 2023).

In a nutshell, the impact of Generative AI on cross-cultural knowledge exchange is immense. By breaking down language barriers, enhancing cultural understanding, automating mundane tasks, and improving information quality, it fosters a more inclusive and diverse knowledge ecosystem, promoting global collaboration and innovation. Responsible and ethical implementation of this technology is crucial to maximize the benefits of cross-cultural knowledge exchange while minimizing any potential drawbacks.

## 4. METHODOLOGY TO BE ADOPTED

Implementing Generative AI in higher education involves several practical aspects that are crucial for its successful integration. Leveraging Generative AI for Cross-Cultural Knowledge Exchange in Higher Education requires a well-defined methodology to ensure the successful implementation and achievement of desired outcomes. Here's a comprehensive methodology to achieve this goal:

### 4.1 Needs Assessment and Goal Setting

i. Identify the specific goals and objectives of cross-cultural knowledge exchange in higher education.

ii. Conduct a needs assessment to understand the cultural contexts and knowledge gaps that need to be addressed.

## 4.2 Stakeholder Engagement and Collaboration

i. Involve relevant stakeholders including educators, researchers, technologists, and representatives from diverse cultural backgrounds.
ii. Foster collaboration and create interdisciplinary teams to ensure a holistic approach to the project.

## 4.3 Data Collection and Preparation

i. Gather a diverse dataset that represents different cultures, languages, and educational contexts.
ii. Clean and preprocess the data to ensure its suitability for generative AI training.

## 4.4 Curriculum and Content Generation

i. Use AI to generate interactive and personalized course content, assignments, and quizzes.
ii. Automate content updates and revisions.

## 4.5 Student Support and Tutoring

i. Develop AI-powered chatbots or virtual teaching assistants for on-demand support.
ii. Enhance the student experience with adaptive learning systems.

## 4.6 Generative AI Model Selection

i. Choose an appropriate Generative AI model based on the project requirements, considering factors like language capabilities, model size, and training data availability.
ii. Fine-tune or adapt the selected model to align with the cultural nuances and educational context.

## 4.7 Model Training and Validation

i. Train the Generative AI model using the prepared dataset, ensuring it captures the diverse cultural and educational knowledge.

ii. Validate the model's performance to guarantee accuracy, appropriateness, and cultural sensitivity.

## 4.8 Interface and User Experience Design

i. Design an intuitive and culturally sensitive user interface for the Generative AI application.
ii. Incorporate feedback mechanisms to collect user insights and continuously improve the user experience.

## 4.9 Pilot Testing

i. Conduct a pilot test of the Generative AI application with a small group of users from different cultural backgrounds.
ii. Gather feedback to identify any issues, make necessary adjustments, and refine the application.

## 4.10 Training and Upskilling

i. Train faculty and staff in effective AI tool usage.
ii. Foster a culture of ongoing learning and adaptability.

## 4.11 Scaling and Deployment

i. Scale the Generative AI application to accommodate a larger user base and diverse educational institutions.
ii. Deploy the application with appropriate infrastructure and support systems.

## 4.12 Monitoring and Evaluation

i. Implement monitoring mechanisms to track the usage, impact, and effectiveness of the Generative AI application.
ii. Regularly evaluate the application's performance and user feedback to make continuous improvements.

## 4.13 Research and Development

i. Encourage research initiatives to explore AI's potential applications in education.
ii. Collaborate with AI companies, educational institutions, and researchers for shared expertise.

### 4.14 Feedback Integration and Iteration

i. Integrate user feedback and suggestions to enhance the Generative AI model and application.
ii. b. Iterate the process based on feedback and evolving educational and cultural needs.

### 4.15 Cost and Budgeting

i. Plan for initial investment in AI infrastructure and software.
ii. Estimate ongoing maintenance, data storage, and licensing costs.

### 4.16 Ethical Considerations

i. Address ethical considerations such as data privacy, consent, bias mitigation, and responsible AI use throughout the project.
ii. Ensure compliance with relevant regulations and guidelines about AI in higher education and cross-cultural contexts.

By following the above methodology, the integration of Generative AI for cross-cultural knowledge exchange in higher education can be effectively achieved, promoting collaboration, understanding, and the sharing of diverse knowledge across different cultural landscapes.

## 5. EVALUATING THE ACCURACY AND RELIABILITY OF GENERATIVE AI TRANSLATION

The field of AI-generated translation has completely transformed cross-lingual communication. However, it's imperative to thoroughly assess the precision and dependability of such systems before entirely depending on them for critical undertakings. Precision pertains to the correctness of the translated content. AI translation models learn from extensive data pools, enabling them to produce exact translations. Nonetheless, errors can arise with intricate language nuances, idiomatic expressions, or cultural allusions. Gauging precision involves comparing the made translations against human translations, using metrics like BLEU (Bilingual Evaluation Understudy) or human evaluators (Puppo, 2019; Korzynski et al., 2023).

Conversely, dependability concentrates on the uniformity and trustworthiness of translations. AI models might exhibit inconsistency, yielding diverse translations for identical inputs. This inconsistency can pose issues, especially in contexts demanding stable and trustworthy translations. Appraising dependability involves scrutinizing the model's performance across assorted inputs and analyzing its steadiness (Chris et al., 2023). To gauge the accuracy and reliability of AI-generated translation, it's imperative to conduct extensive testing and validation. This might encompass employing standardized datasets, juxtaposing translations against reference translations, and enlisting human evaluators to appraise the quality of generated translations (Bandi et al., 2023).

Moreover, continual monitoring and feedback loops are pivotal for refining the precision and dependability of AI-generated translation systems. User feedback, error analysis, and the ongoing refinement and fine-tuning of models contribute to addressing limitations and boosting performance. Even though AI-generated translation has achieved remarkable strides, comprehending its constraints and considering the usage context is essential. Human expertise and intervention remain invaluable in ensuring precise and dependable translations, particularly in vital applications where accuracy and lucidity are paramount (Weisz et al., 2022).

Suppose you work for a global communication company that has developed a Generative AI Translation model. This model is intended to translate business documents from English to French. Your task is to evaluate the accuracy and reliability of this AI model before it's deployed for critical business communications.

## 5.1 Accuracy Evaluation

In this context, accuracy refers to how well the AI model's translations match the human translations. Let's say you have a set of 100 English sentences with their corresponding accurate French translations. You can calculate the accuracy using the following formula:

$$Accuracy = \frac{Number\ of\ Correct\ Translations}{Total\ Number\ of\ Translations} \times 100\%$$

For instance, if the model gets 80 translations correct out of 100, the accuracy would be:

$$Accuracy = \frac{80}{100} \times 100\% - 80\%$$

## 5.2 Reliability Evaluation

Reliability refers to how consistent and dependable the AI model's translations are. You choose a sample sentence and translate it multiple times using the model. Let's say you choose the sentence "The company's profits increased last year." You translate it three times and get the following results:

i. "Les bénéfices de l'entreprise ont augmenté l'année dernière."
ii. "Les bénéfices de l'entreprise ont augmenté l'année précédente."
iii. "L'entreprise a vu une hausse de ses bénéfices l'année dernière."

Now, you can calculate the variability or inconsistency using the Levenshtein distance, which measures the difference between two strings:

$$Variability = \frac{Total\ Levenshtein\ Distance}{Total\ Number\ of\ Translations}$$

You calculate the Levenshtein distances between each pair of translations and then average them.

## 5.3 Hypothetical Levenshtein Distances

Distance 1-2: 9
Distance 1-3: 36
Distance 2-3: 46
Average Levenshtein distance: (9 + 36 + 46) / 3 = 30.33 (approx)

This indicates a moderate level of variability in translations.

In this example, the accuracy is evaluated as 80%, which means the model gets 80 out of 100 translations correct. The reliability, measured by the average Levenshtein distance, suggests moderate inconsistency among translations. Based on these evaluations, you can determine whether the AI model meets the required standards for accurate and reliable translations in a business context.

## 6. CREATING VIRTUAL CLASSROOMS AND CULTURAL EXCHANGE SPACES WITH AI

The utilization of artificial intelligence can bring about a groundbreaking transformation in the field of education by establishing virtual classrooms and spaces for cultural exchange. Through harnessing the capabilities of AI, educators can craft dynamic and interactive learning environments that transcend the confines of physical boundaries. A method through which AI can enable cultural exchange involves facilitating seamless communication among students proficient in different languages. Generative AI tools can bridge linguistic gaps, allowing the students to effortlessly engage and collaborate (Kim et al., 2022). This facilitates cross-cultural comprehension, allowing students to gain insights from diverse viewpoints.

The experience of virtual classrooms is further enhanced by integrating virtual reality (VR) and augmented reality (AR) technologies. Platforms like CoSpaces Edu empower educators to design captivating curricula and tasks that offer hands-on learning opportunities (Fitria, 2023). In the virtual classroom setting, students can explore various cultures and historical sites and even undertake virtual field trips. This deepens their appreciation of diverse cultures and nurtures empathy and a global mindset. Additionally, artificial intelligence is pivotal in tailoring coursework and automating administrative duties. AI tools can analyze individual student data to create personalized learning paths based on their strengths and weaknesses. This elevates the learning journey and ensures each student receives the necessary support to excel.

Furthermore, AI aids educators in formulating lesson plans by identifying pertinent activities aligned with specific skills (Bandi et al., 2023; Sharma, 2022). AI-powered assistants like ChatGPT can swiftly retrieve information, offer essential steps, and suggest resources and timelines. Although AI-generated responses may not always be flawless, educators can leverage feedback mechanisms to continually enhance the performance of the AI assistant. In establishing virtual classrooms and cultural exchange spaces, it is imperative to prioritize inclusiveness and accessibility. Through AI integration, educators can bridge the digital divide and extend equal learning opportunities to all students, regardless of their geographic location or socioeconomic background.

In today's rapidly evolving digital age, the fusion of education, technology, and cultural exchange has become increasingly vital. Creating virtual classrooms and cultural exchange spaces with artificial intelligence (AI) holds immense importance in enhancing the global educational landscape and fostering cross-cultural understanding. This innovative approach revolutionizes traditional education methods and facilitates a more interconnected world (Kim et al., 2022).

First and foremost, virtual classrooms powered by AI break down geographical barriers, allowing individuals from different corners of the globe to come together in a shared online learning environment. This creates a rich and diverse mix of perspectives, cultures, and experiences that enrich the learning process. Students can collaborate, share ideas, and engage in discussions, thus broadening their horizons and enhancing critical thinking. Moreover, AI-driven virtual classrooms can adapt to individual learning styles and paces. The AI algorithms can personalize the learning experience, providing tailored content and suggestions that cater to the unique needs and preferences of each student. This personalized approach maximizes learning efficiency and effectiveness, ultimately leading to better educational outcomes (Fitria, 2023).

Incorporating cultural exchange spaces within these virtual classrooms further promotes global awareness and appreciation. AI can facilitate real-time language translation, enabling seamless communication among students from diverse linguistic backgrounds. This breaks language barriers and encourages open dialogue, fostering a sense of unity and understanding among the participants. Cultural exchange spaces within virtual classrooms can also host virtual tours, interactive cultural workshops, and presentations that offer insights into different cultures, traditions, and practices. AI can curate and present this information in an engaging and immersive manner, sparking curiosity and encouraging students to embrace cultural diversity (Bandi et al., 2023).

Furthermore, these AI-powered virtual classrooms and cultural exchange spaces promote inclusivity by accommodating various learning abilities and disabilities. AI algorithms can provide additional support and accommodations, ensuring that all students have equal access to education and cultural experiences. This inclusive approach contributes to a more equitable educational landscape, where every individual can thrive and contribute to society. From an economic standpoint, virtual classrooms and cultural exchange spaces can significantly reduce the costs associated with physical infrastructure, travel, and accommodation for both students and educators. This makes quality education and cultural exchange more accessible and affordable, particularly for those in underserved or remote areas (Sharma, 2022).

The importance of creating virtual classrooms and cultural exchange spaces with AI cannot be overstated. It revolutionizes education by breaking down barriers, promoting personalized learning, fostering cultural understanding, and encouraging inclusivity. As we continue to advance in this digital era, leveraging AI for educational and cultural purposes will undoubtedly reshape the way we learn, connect, and collaborate on a global scale.

Concisely, the incorporation of AI into virtual classrooms and cultural exchange spaces holds tremendous promise in revolutionizing education. By fostering cross-cultural dialogue, delivering immersive encounters, personalizing learning experiences, and streamlining administrative responsibilities, AI has the potential to foster global connections and create a more inclusive and enriching educational milieu.

## 7. EVALUATING THE IMPACT OF AI ON STUDENTS' INTERCULTURAL COMPETENCE

In today's interconnected global environment, possessing intercultural skills is paramount. Integrating artificial intelligence (AI) into education has attracted attention, driven by rapid technological advancements. Researchers have identified the potential of AI-based online tools to enhance students' intercultural abilities (Sharma, 2022). These tools offer personalized feedback, facilitate language acquisition, and improve cross-cultural communication skills. Both students and educators anticipate AI to positively influence the extent and quality of their interactions (Kim et al., 2022). AI enables students to inquire more confidently due to its anonymity, freeing instructors to communicate more meaningfully while relying on AI to handle repetitive queries.

Nonetheless, concerns have been voiced about the reliability and accountability of AI-generated responses (Bandi et al., 2023). Students fear negative grade impacts and the opacity of AI systems. This highlights the necessity of addressing these concerns and ensuring the transparency and responsibility of AI technology. The perceptions of teachers are pivotal in the successful integration of AI within educational contexts (Milano, McGrane, & Leonelli 2023; Weisz et al., 2022). Studies reveal that teachers view AI positively, believing it can enrich teaching and learning experiences. However, when incorporating AI into the classroom, factors like student motivation and teachers' technological and pedagogical competence must be considered (Lim et al. 2023). Teachers need to acquire specific skills to adapt to AI's transformative effects in education, enabling effective utilization of AI to foster intercultural skills among students.

Hence, the impact of AI on students' intercultural abilities is a topic of great significance. While AI holds the potential to bolster cross-cultural communication skills and offer tailored learning experiences, concerns related to reliability, accountability, and the need for teacher adaptation should be adequately addressed. Through thoroughly evaluating AI's impact and responsible integration into educational environments, we can harness its potential to nurture intercultural skills and equip students for a globalized world.

## 8. ADDRESSING ETHICAL AND PRIVACY CONCERNS IN AI-POWERED KNOWLEDGE EXCHANGE

Revolutionizing how information is accessed and shared, knowledge exchange platforms driven by AI have transformed the landscape. Fueled by sophisticated algorithms and machine learning, these platforms swiftly offer tailored responses to user inquiries. Although these platforms deliver considerable advantages, they concurrently present ethical and privacy considerations that necessitate resolution (Kim et al., 2022). One fundamental moral concern revolves around potential bias in AI algorithms. As AI systems learn from data, the risk arises that they perpetuate existing prejudices and imbalances. For instance, if the training data exhibits bias against specific groups, the AI system could yield inaccurate or inequitable information. To tackle this, developers and researchers must ensure that the training data reflects the diversity and range of cultures, perspectives, and backgrounds (Fitria, 2023).

Another ethical apprehension pertains to user data privacy. AI-driven knowledge exchange platforms amass extensive user data, encompassing queries, preferences, and personal details. This information can be exploited for targeted advertising or shared with external parties without user consent. Counteracting this requires rigorous privacy policies and measures for data protection, such as anonymizing user data and securing explicit consent for data utilization. Transparency also plays a pivotal role in addressing ethical concerns. Users must be cognizant of engaging with an AI system rather than a human. Distinct disclosures regarding the AI system's capabilities and constraints are indispensable to guarantee well-informed decision-making (Avurakoghene & Oredein, 2023).

*Figure 1. Pros and cons representation of implementing AI-powered knowledge exchange*

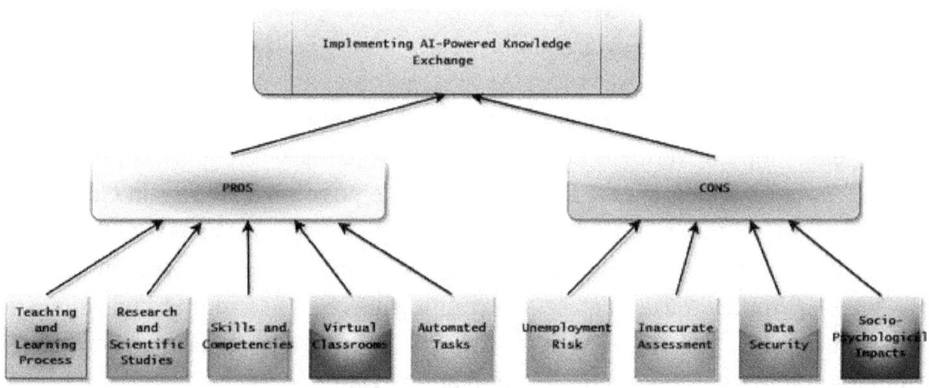

Moreover, accountability constitutes a crucial aspect of AI-powered knowledge exchange platforms. If users receive erroneous or detrimental information from the AI system, mechanisms should be in place to rectify the situation and hold developers responsible. Regular audits and evaluations of AI algorithms are invaluable in identifying biases or inaccuracies and ensuring the system's dependability (Sharma, 2022). The pros and cons of implementing AI-powered knowledge exchange are depicted in Figure 1. Despite the considerable potential of AI-driven knowledge exchange platforms, it is imperative to grapple with ethical and privacy concerns. Developers, researchers, and policymakers must collaborate to ensure these platforms remain impartial, uphold user privacy, and maintain clarity and accountability. In doing so, the capabilities of AI can be harnessed to cultivate a more comprehensive, enlightened, and conscientious knowledge exchange environment.

## 9. FUTURE PROSPECTS AND CHALLENGES OF GENERATIVE AI IN CROSS-CULTURAL KNOWLEDGE EXCHANGE

The potential impact of Generative AI on cross-cultural knowledge sharing is profound, as it can enable smooth communication and comprehension among people from various backgrounds and languages. With natural language processing and machine learning advancement, Generative AI can now produce high-quality content in different languages, facilitating information access and exchange across cultural boundaries (Di et al., 2022). A fundamental future prospect of Generative AI in cross-cultural knowledge exchange is fostering cultural diversity and comprehension. By overcoming language barriers, AI-driven platforms can facilitate the sharing of ideas, customs, and viewpoints, nurturing a global community that values and embraces cultural distinctions. This, in turn, can lead to heightened empathy, tolerance, and collaboration among individuals of diverse origins (Orchard & Tasiemski, 2023).

Moreover, Generative AI can aid in conserving and endorsing indigenous languages and knowledge. Many indigenous cultures hold invaluable insights and wisdom that risk fading over time. AI systems can contribute by translating and documenting indigenous languages, ensuring their cultural heritage is accessible to future generations. Nevertheless, these opportunities come with significant challenges that necessitate attention. One key concern is the possibility of bias in Generative AI algorithms. If the training data to develop these systems needs more diversity and inclusivity, it may perpetuate existing biases and disparities. To counter this, it's vital to employ varied datasets encompassing various cultural and linguistic variations, ensuring that the AI systems respect different perspectives and refrain from reinforcing stereotypes or discrimination (Tian, 2023).

Another challenge involves the privacy of user data on cross-cultural knowledge exchange platforms. As individuals share personal information, thoughts, and experiences, stringent policies, and data protection measures are essential to uphold their privacy. Users should retain control over their data and be well-informed about its usage and sharing. Transparency stands as another crucial issue. Users interacting with Generative AI systems should be informed that they are engaging with AI, and the generated content might not always be exclusively authored by humans. This transparency cultivates trust and ensures that individuals know the AI system's limitations and potential biases (Yu & Guo, 2023).

Lastly, accountability is pivotal in addressing any erroneous or harmful information AI systems produce. Mechanisms should be in place to promptly rectify and tackle potential problems. This can encompass user feedback, human oversight, and continual monitoring of AI systems to guarantee alignment with ethical standards and prevent misinformation or detrimental content propagation.

## 10. CONCLUSION

The integration of Generative AI holds immense potential for fostering Cross-Cultural Knowledge Exchange within Higher Education. By transcending language barriers and cultural differences, this technology can facilitate a dynamic and inclusive learning environment. Students and educators can collaboratively generate, share, and refine ideas, transcending geographical constraints. However, ethical considerations must be addressed, ensuring sensitivity to diverse cultural contexts and preventing biases in content generation. As the landscape of education evolves, harnessing Generative AI for cross-cultural knowledge exchange can pave the way for a more interconnected and enriched educational experience on a global scale.

In the ever-evolving landscape of higher education, the integration of technology has been a transformative force, redefining how knowledge is acquired, shared, and applied. Generative Artificial Intelligence (AI) stands as a cutting-edge tool in this realm, offering immense potential for fostering cross-cultural knowledge exchange in higher education. As the world becomes increasingly interconnected, educational institutions must embrace this technological innovation to prepare students for a globalized future. In this chapter, we have explored the profound importance of creating virtual classrooms and cultural exchange spaces with AI, emphasizing the benefits and potential it holds for cross-cultural understanding, personalized learning, inclusivity, economic efficiency, and the advancement of society at large.

The foundation of this discussion lies in recognizing the crucial role that cross-cultural knowledge exchange plays in today's interconnected world. Globalization has woven a complex web of interdependencies, where understanding and appreciating diverse cultures is no longer a choice but a necessity. In the realm of higher education, students must be equipped with the skills and perspectives that transcend borders and embrace the rich tapestry of global cultures. Generative AI, through its ability to create virtual classrooms and cultural exchange spaces, bridges geographical and linguistic divides, enabling seamless interaction and collaboration among individuals from diverse backgrounds.

One of the primary merits of AI-powered virtual classrooms is their capacity to offer personalized learning experiences. Traditional education often employs a one-size-fits-all approach, which may not cater to the unique learning styles and paces of individual students. Generative AI algorithms, however, can analyze and understand each student's learning patterns, preferences, and strengths. With this knowledge, the AI can tailor educational content, teaching methodologies, and assessment strategies to suit each student's specific needs. Consequently, students are more engaged, motivated, and likely to succeed, enhancing the overall quality of education.

Furthermore, AI facilitates a dynamic exchange of knowledge and ideas by breaking down language barriers. In a virtual classroom setting, students from diverse linguistic backgrounds can communicate seamlessly through AI-powered translation services. This real-time translation capability fosters a more inclusive learning environment, where language is no longer a hindrance to collaboration and understanding. By incorporating this feature, educational institutions can create a space where cultural diversity is celebrated, and communication flows freely, enriching the educational experience.

Incorporating cultural exchange spaces within virtual classrooms amplifies the impact of cross-cultural knowledge exchange. AI can curate and present cultural insights, traditions, and practices interactively and engagingly. Students can virtually explore different cultures, traditions, and historical contexts, gaining a deeper understanding and appreciation for the world's diversity. These experiences nurture open-mindedness, empathy, and global awareness, preparing students to be culturally competent in an increasingly interconnected global society.

Inclusivity is another fundamental aspect that AI brings to the forefront of education. By leveraging AI to provide additional support and accommodations for students with various learning abilities and disabilities, educational institutions ensure that no one is left behind. Whether it's providing audio descriptions for visually impaired students or interactive visual aids for those with auditory impairments, AI can bridge accessibility gaps and create an inclusive learning environment. This inclusivity is a step towards breaking barriers and promoting equality in education.

From an economic standpoint, the implementation of AI-powered virtual classrooms and cultural exchange spaces can lead to significant cost savings. Institutions can reduce expenses associated with physical infrastructure, travel, and accommodation, making education and cultural exchange more accessible and affordable. This cost-effectiveness ensures that a broader demographic of students can partake in cross-cultural learning experiences, contributing to a more equitable distribution of educational resources.

In conclusion, the integration of Generative AI for cross-cultural knowledge exchange in higher education is poised to unlock a new era of global learning. The benefits discussed in this chapter underscore the transformative potential of AI in revolutionizing education, transcending boundaries, and nurturing a generation of culturally aware, adaptable, and globally competent individuals. As we continue to advance in the realms of AI and education, the collaboration between technology and academia becomes essential in shaping a future where knowledge knows no borders and cultural understanding thrives. Through strategic integration and thoughtful utilization of Generative AI, we can pave the way for a more interconnected and harmonious world, where education is a beacon of unity and enlightenment.

## REFERENCES


Avurakoghene, O., & Oredein, A. O. (2023). Educational Leadership and Artificial Intelligence for Sustainable Development. *Shodh Sari-An International Multidisciplinary Journal*, *2*(3), 211–223. doi:10.59231/SARI7600

Baidoo-Anu, D., & Owusu Ansah, L. (2023). Education in the Era of Generative Artificial Intelligence (AI): Understanding the Potential Benefits of ChatGPT in Promoting Teaching and Learning. SSRN *Electronic Journal, March*. doi:10.2139/ssrn.4337484

Bandi, A., Venkata, P., Ramesh, S., Eswar, Y., Pratap, V., & Kuchi, K. (2023). The Power of Generative AI : A Review of Requirements, Models, Input – Output Formats, Evaluation Metrics, and Challenges. *Future Internet*, *15*(8), 15. doi:10.3390/fi15080260

Bican, G. (2021). Enhancing the cross cultural competence of prospective language teachers. *Journal of Curriculum and Teaching*, *10*(3), 47–57. doi:10.5430/jct.v10n3p47

Commander, N. E., Zhao, Y., Gallagher, P. A., & You, Y. (2012). Promoting Cross-cultural Understanding of Education Through Online Discussions. *Procedia - Social and Behavioral Sciences*, *46*(2005), 4632–4642. doi:10.1016/j.sbspro.2012.06.310

Di, W., Zhang, S., Lian, X., Oubibi, M., Li, D., Ding, L., Zhang, Z., & Yang, T. (2022). Research on cross-cultural adaptation and educational management of international students in China: Case of African students at Zhejiang Normal University. *Frontiers in Psychology, 13*(October), 1009658. doi:10.3389/fpsyg.2022.1009658 PMID:36324773

Fitria, T. N. (2023). Augmented Reality (AR) and Virtual Reality (VR) Technology in Education: Media of Teaching and Learning: A Review. *International Journal of Computer and Information System (IJCIS). Peer Reviewed-International Journal, 04*(01), 2745–9659. doi:10.29040/ijcis.v4i1.102

Kim, J., Lee, H., & Cho, Y. H. (2022). Learning design to support student-AI collaboration: perspectives of leading teachers for AI in education. In Education and Information Technologies, 27(5). Springer US. doi:10.100710639-021-10831-6

Korzynski, P., Mazurek, G., Altmann, A., Ejdys, J., Kazlauskaite, R., Paliszkiewicz, J., Wach, K., & Ziemba, E. (2023). Generative artificial intelligence as a new context for management theories: Analysis of ChatGPT. *Central European Management Journal, 31*(1), 3–13. doi:10.1108/CEMJ-02-2023-0091

Lim, W. M., Gunasekara, A., Pallant, J. L., Pallant, J. I., & Pechenkina, E. (2023). Generative AI and the Future of Education: Ragnarök or Reformation? A Paradoxical Perspective from Management Educators. *International Journal of Management Education, 21*(2), 100790. doi:10.1016/j.ijme.2023.100790

Mikhaylov, N. S. (2014). International business students' crosscultural competence development: The influence of the educational environment. *SAGE Open, 4*(4), 1–15. doi:10.1177/2158244014564352

Milano, S., McGrane, J. A., & Leonelli, S. (2023). Large Language Models Challenge the Future of Higher Education. *Nature Machine Intelligence, 5*(4), 333–334. doi:10.103842256-023-00644-2

Orchard, T., & Tasiemski, L. (2023). The rise of Generative AI and possible effects on the economy. *Economics and Business Review, 9*(2), 9–26. doi:10.18559/ebr.2023.2.732

Puppo, G. (2019). Cross-Cultural Competence in Higher Education Faculty and Staff. *Emerging Leadership Journeys, 12*(1).

Sharma, M. (2022). Integrating effective collaboration tools to enhance students' engagement in online language classroom. *Journal of Fundamental & Comparative Research, 8*(1), 26–30.

Silor, A. (2019). *Cultural Knowledge Pedagogy for Higher Education.*

Tian, Y. (2023). Limitations and Advancements of AI Teachers in Classroom Instruction. *Education and Teaching Research, 2023*(3), 66–72.

Weisz, J. D., Muller, M., Ross, S. I., Martinez, F., Houde, S., Agarwal, M., Talamadupula, K., & Richards, J. T. (2022). Better Together? An Evaluation of AI-Supported Code Translation. *International Conference on Intelligent User Interfaces, Proceedings IUI,* (pp. 369–391). ACM. 10.1145/3490099.3511157

Yu, H., & Guo, Y. (2023). Generative artificial intelligence empowers educational reform: current status, issues, and prospects. *Frontiers in Education, 8*, 1–10. doi:10.3389/feduc.2023.1183162

Zielinski, C., Winker, M., Aggarwal, R., Ferris, L., Heinemann, M., Lapeña, J. F., Pai, S., Ing, E., Citrome, L., Alam, M., Voight, M., & Abibzadeh, F. (2023). Chatbots, Generative AI, and Scholarly Manuscripts: WAME Recommendations on Chatbots and Generative Artificial Intelligence in Relation to Scholarly Publications. *Philippine Journal of Pathology, 8*(1), 6–8. doi:10.21141/PJP.2023.08 PMID:38089825

## KEY TERMS AND DEFINITIONS

**Adaptive Learning:** Educational models and technologies that tailor the learning experience to individual students, considering their abilities, learning styles, and progress.

**Cognitive Computing:** Computer systems that use machine learning and natural language processing to mimic human thought processes and solve complex problems.

**Collaborative Learning:** A pedagogical approach that encourages active participation and cooperation among students, enhancing their understanding and retention of knowledge.

**Content Generation:** The process of creating new digital material, such as articles, essays, reports, or multimedia, is often facilitated by AI algorithms.

**Cross-Cultural Knowledge Exchange:** The sharing and transfer of information, ideas, and practices between individuals or institutions from different cultural backgrounds, fosters mutual understanding and collaboration.

**Cultural Exchange Platforms:** Online or physical platforms are designed to facilitate the sharing of cultural knowledge, experiences, and practices between people from different cultures.

**Cultural Sensitivity:** The awareness and understanding of diverse cultural norms, practices, and perspectives to interact respectfully and effectively with individuals from different cultural backgrounds.

**Data Privacy:** Protecting individuals' data and ensuring it is used appropriately and securely, is particularly important when utilizing AI technologies.

**Digital Transformation:** The integration of digital technologies into various aspects of an organization or industry to enhance operations, efficiency, and user experiences.

**Diversity and Inclusion:** The commitment to promoting a variety of perspectives, backgrounds, and experiences in educational settings, ensuring equal opportunities and representation for all individuals.

**Ethical Considerations:** Reflection on the moral implications and responsibilities associated with utilizing AI technology, including potential biases, privacy concerns, and societal impact.

**Generative AI (Artificial Intelligence):** AI technology that can autonomously create content, such as text, images, or audio, mimicking human-like generation patterns.

**Globalization of Education:** The process of integrating educational systems, content, and methodologies on a global scale to enhance collaboration and cross-cultural understanding in the academic domain.

**Higher Education:** Post-secondary education is typically offered at colleges, universities, or other academic institutions, focusing on specialized knowledge, research, and professional development.

**Knowledge Transfer:** The movement of knowledge from one individual, group, or context to another, aiming to enhance understanding, skills, and abilities.

**Language Generation:** The AI-driven ability to produce human-like written or spoken language based on a given input, often using deep learning models.

**Leveraging AI:** Utilizing the capabilities of artificial intelligence to optimize processes, enhance decision-making, and achieve specific objectives within a given context or industry.

**Machine Learning:** A subset of AI where computer systems learn and improve performance from data without being explicitly programmed, adapting, and evolving based on patterns and experiences.

**Multilingual AI:** AI systems are capable of understanding and generating content in multiple languages, enabling effective communication across diverse linguistic communities.

**NLP (Natural Language Processing):** A field of AI that focuses on enabling computers to understand, interpret, and generate human language in a valuable way, including tasks like translation and sentiment analysis.

# Chapter 9
# Large Language Models in Academic Publishing

**Moses Mwangi Thiga**
https://orcid.org/0000-0003-1786-7439
*Kabarak University, Kenya*

## ABSTRACT

*Large language models continue to find greater utilization in the academic publishing process since their introduction. On one hand they are beneficial in manuscript development, review and editorial tasks through finding and presenting information in an academic and professional manner. On the flip side there are concerns over the accuracy of the content they generate as well as the tendency for some authors to present these outputs in manuscripts without proper attribution leading to plagiarism. This chapter examines their practical uses and challenges, and makes recommendations on how their use can be mainstreamed in academic publishing. The chapter further makes recommendations on areas for their future development through the enhancement of foundational models using data from credible sources such as peer reviewed journals, books, and online sources of credible organizations.*

## INTRODUCTION

The 'traditional' academic publishing process comprises four key steps: (i) manuscript preparation that involves the conduct of original research, synthesis of the literature, and drafting of a paper, report, or thesis to present the findings of the research; (ii) peer review where the manuscript is evaluated by experts in the area in order to provide the author with feedback and insights on how to improve upon the work and manuscript, (iii) editing to ensure that language, formatting, citation, and referencing

DOI: 10.4018/979-8-3693-0487-7.ch009

styles meet the publisher's requirements, and (iv) the production, marketing and distribution steps where the finished work is availed in either print or online formats for consumption by its target market (Lambert Academic Publishing, 2023).

These steps, in the traditional sense, have been human-intensive but advances in Information and Communication Technologies (ICTs) have served to enhance critical aspects of the publication process, such as data collection, transcription and analysis, manuscript preparation, formatting and layout, citation and reference management, and distribution by way of electronic or online publishing and marketing (Harman, 2023). In recent times, the role of ICTs in publication has progressed beyond simply managing processes and documents to performing additional tasks that have always required human input. There are now a significant number of software systems that are capable of tasks such as writing, reviewing, and editing manuscripts. These capabilities emanate from a branch of computing called Artificial Intelligence (AI).

Artificial Intelligence is a subfield of computing that examines the development and use of computer systems that can perform tasks ordinarily performed by humans. These include (i) perception of the physical world through vision, sound, smell, touch, and taste, (ii) manipulation of the environment through movement, (iii) reasoning through situations in order to arrive at optimal paths of action, (iv) communicating through receiving of audio or textual input, processing it and formulating a suitable response, and (v) learning through experience in order to improve performance of tasks over time (Williams, 1983). AI has found application in diverse domains such as agriculture, commerce, entertainment, robotics, human resource management, healthcare, the motor vehicle industry, social media, marketing, finance, security, and education (Simplilearn, 2022).

Regarding capabilities, AI systems can be generally categorized as (i) Artificial Narrow Intelligence systems capable of completing concrete actions and cannot learn independently. Examples include spam filters, search engines, virtual assistance, industrial robots, recommendation systems, fraud detection systems, machine translation, medical diagnosis systems, natural language processing systems, and self-driving cars. (ii) Artificial General Intelligence systems that can learn, think, and perform at an almost human level, and (iii) Artificial Super Intelligence systems that can surpass the knowledge and capabilities of human beings (Joshi, 2019).

AI-powered systems continue to grow in capability, adoption, and acceptance in various domains. Recently, they have found practical applications in the creative domain and can generate new text, image, and audio content at a level close to that of human beings. This class of AI systems is called Generative Artificial Intelligence (GenAI) systems. They learn and reproduce the patterns and structure in pre-existing data to create new content (Lawton, 2023). In academic publishing, GenAI has found application in writing, reviewing, editing, and marketing manuscripts. This chapter examines their application, benefits, and challenges in the context of academic publishing and further makes recommendations for their beneficial and responsible use in practice.

# BACKGROUND

## Generative Artificial Intelligence

Generative Artificial Intelligence (GenAI) is a type of Artificial Intelligence that is capable of creating content such as images, videos, audio, text, and 3D models by learning and reproducing patterns from pre-existing data (GenerativeAI.net, 2023). 'Generative' refers to the AI model's ability to create new content instead of performing classification or predictive tasks.

There are five main types of Generative Artificial Intelligence:

i. Generative adversarial networks (GANs): Models in this class of GenAI utilize two neural networks, one to generate new content that closely mimics the training data and the other to try and distinguish between the actual and generated content. Examples in use include generating images and music from text descriptions as well as new drug candidates in drug discovery (Goodfellow et al., 2014),
ii. Variational autoencoders (VAEs): Models in this class of GenAI work by encoding the input data provided into a high dimensional space that represents its underlying variation. They then use a decoder to generate new data from the space. Examples in use include generating high-quality images, compressing and de-noising audio to generate new drug molecules and synthetic medical data for training ML models (Kingma & Welling, 2022),
iii. Autoregressive models: Models in this class of GenAI work by predicting the next step in a sequence to generate new content. Examples in use include generating text, images, language translation, generating realistic waveforms, and text-to-speech audio (Vaswani et al., 2023),
iv. Recurrent neural networks (RNNs): Models in this class work by having a hidden state that remembers information from previous steps, which allows them to generate content such as poems, stories, and code, to synthesize speech, to generate music and videos (Hochreiter & Schmidhuber, 1997), and
v. Transformer-based models: Models in this class of GenAI use self-attention to learn long-range dependencies in the data. Examples in use include text generation, language translation, generating dialogue, and answering questions (Vaswani et al., 2023)

## Generative AI in Education

Education, in general, has significantly benefited from advances in GenAI. Critical use scenarios include information retrieval or search, translation, content or text generation, and transcription. LLM tools such as GhatGPT and Bard make it possible to search for information online using natural language and get responses in prose form, not links, as is the case with traditional search engines. The tools can find and combine information from sources that users would otherwise be unable to find easily or as quickly. GenAI applications offer personalized learning experiences by creating an interactive dialogue between students and virtual tutors, providing immediate feedback to students, and aiding in developing critical thinking skills (LoEstro Advisors, 2023).

LLM tools help translate text from one language to another for creating blogs, articles, short stories, summaries, social media posts, surveys, and scripts, among other textual content. In some cases, they are used to create the content directly and to help with ideation. The quality of the outputs, however, depends on the nature of the prompt provided. LLM tools can also transcribe audio and video files into text with high levels of accuracy. The tools have an advantage over traditional transcription software because they can infer the context and meaning of statements in the transcribed audio (Keary, 2023).

In a more practical sense, LLMs are utilized in education for the generation of content such as presentations, worksheets, quizzes, and other resources for classes, in assisting with grammar and writing checks, for grading essays, in developing syllabus outlines, for content reinforcement and problem-solving, for learning languages, in research and to generate 'academic' papers (Dilmegani, 2023), (Elali & Rachid, 2023).

## Large Language Models

Text generation is one of the most widely used and known capabilities of GenAI. Tools such as GPT-3 and Bard, whose use has grown tremendously recently, are examples of their widespread use. These tools and related ones build on the following principles: (i) Language modeling, in which trained models predict text in a sequence of words; (ii) Distributional semantics, where the meaning of words is related to their context; and (iii) attention mechanisms where neural networks focus on specific parts of a sentence when making predictions in order to generate coherent and informative text (Daniel et al., 2014)

Models that enshrine these capabilities for text generation are called Large Language Models (LLMs). They are a class of transformer-based neural networks introduced by a team of Google Engineers in a 2017 paper, "Attention is all you need"

(Vaswani et al., 2023). These models connect a transformer's encoder and decoder components through a mechanism known as 'attention'. The encoder component in a transformer processes input sequences to produce a continuous representation or embedding of the input provided. These embeddings are then passed on to a decoder to generate an output sequence. (Malingan, 2023) .

In order to understand and process the input sequence effectively, transformers make use of (i) positional encoding, which embeds the order in which the input occurs in a given sequence so that words feed back into an output with the sequence in mind (Zhang et al., 2023) and (ii) self-attention which assigns a weight to a section of the input data to signify its relative importance compared to the rest of the input (NVIDIA, 2023).

LLMs are generally helpful for information retrieval or search, translation, malware analysis, detecting and preventing Cyber attacks, sentiment analysis, content or text generation, code generation, transcription, market research, sales automation in virtual assistants, and customer support (Keary, 2023) (Elasticsearch B.V., 2023).

## LLMs IN ACADEMIC PUBLISHING

This chapter focuses on the use of LLMs in academic publishing. The publishing process comprises four steps: manuscript preparation, review, editing and sales, marketing, and distribution.

### 1. Manuscript Preparation

Manuscript preparation is the first step of the publishing process, and it involves the conduct of original research, synthesis of literature, and drafting a manuscript such as a paper, report, or thesis to present the research findings. Manuscripts should have a clear structure and flow, be clear and concise, have good visual appeal and formatting, be easy to access and navigate, and contain claims supported by relevant and accurate evidence.

LLMs can be used for topic selection, generating background information on a research area or topic, identifying relevant sources for literature review, organizing the research writeup, and generating citations, references, and a bibliography. They are also capable of generating research designs and formulating hypotheses, data analysis and interpretation, and drafting, editing, and proofreading academic papers (Dilmegani, 2023), (Johnson, 2023).

For the specific task of the literature review, LLMs can draw from various sources, enhancing the review's coverage. They are beneficial in identifying gaps, trends, critical emergent works, perspectives, or evidence related to the topics under study.

This deep and extensive inclusion of sources enriches the literature and helps to avoid biased perspectives. They also save the time required to scan and summarize numerous articles and sources (Shreim, 2023).

This assistance is advantageous in several ways. For instance, it can help unlock writer's block which is defined as "*the inability to begin or continue writing for reasons other than a lack of basic skill or commitment*" (Rose, 2009). They achieve this by helping generate an initial draft from which an author can then proceed to enhance or derive insights. Additionally, they can help identify and present in one document some sources of literature that would otherwise take much longer to compile using regular web or database searches.

LLM tools such as Google Bard and ChatGPT have demonstrated an excellent capacity to generate responses structured as academic papers complete with citations and references. An example is the following brief paper generated by Google Bard.

**Prompt***: "Generate an academic paper on the topic "The Impact of Generative AI on Traditional Academic Publishing: A Pragmatic Perspective" with citations and references,"*

*Sure, here is an academic paper on the topic "The Impact of Generative AI on Traditional Academic Publishing: A Pragmatic Perspective" with citations and references:*

*Bard Response:*

*The Impact of Generative AI on Traditional Academic Publishing: A Pragmatic Perspective*

*Academic publishing is facing several challenges, including the rise of open access, the increasing cost of publishing, and the growing popularity of self-publishing. In recent years, there has been a growing interest in the potential of generative artificial intelligence (AI) to address some of these challenges.*

Generative AI is a type of AI that can create new content, such as text, images, and music. This technology has the potential to revolutionize the way that academic research is communicated and disseminated. For example, generative AI could be used to create interactive visualizations of research data or to generate synthetic data sets for training machine learning models.

However, there are also a number of challenges that need to be addressed before generative AI can be widely adopted in academic publishing. One challenge is the need for high-quality training data. Generative AI models need to be trained on large amounts of data in order to produce accurate and reliable results. This can be a significant barrier for researchers who need access to large data sets.

Another challenge is the need for effective evaluation methods. It is difficult to evaluate the quality of generative AI outputs, as there is no clear consensus on what constitutes "good" or "bad" output. This makes it difficult to assess the impact of generative AI on academic publishing.

Despite these challenges, there is a growing body of evidence that suggests that generative AI has the potential to make a significant impact on traditional academic publishing. For example, a study by the Allen Institute for Artificial Intelligence found that generative AI could be used to generate synthetic data sets that are as accurate as real data sets (Wallace et al., 2020). This suggests that generative AI could be used to create new research data sets that are more accessible and affordable than traditional data sets.

Another study by the University of California, Berkeley found that generative AI could be used to create interactive visualizations of research data that are more engaging and informative than traditional static visualizations (Xu et al., 2021). This suggests that generative AI could be used to make research more accessible and understandable to a broader audience.

Overall, the evidence suggests that generative AI has the potential to make a significant impact on traditional academic publishing. However, there are a number of challenges that need to be addressed before generative AI can be widely adopted. These challenges include the need for high-quality training data, the need for effective evaluation methods, and the need for a clear understanding of the ethical implications of using generative AI in academic publishing.

A brief look at the generated paper above reveals that the paper starts 'logically' and focuses on the task specified in the prompt. However, towards the tail end of the paper, it deviates to provide data generation and visualization content. These may seem related but are not the focus of the task specified in the prompt. In addition, a majority of the sections do not have citations, as requested in the prompt. A similar search on ChatGPT generated a brief paper better structured than the Google Bard output. It had an abstract, an introduction, and a body with relevant subheadings, recommendations, and conclusions.

Overall, the generated papers lack a certain 'human feeling'. There is a way in which humans would construct their sentences and structure their arguments that is absent in the generated papers. The sources used in both papers could be more extensive. A reasonably competent and committed human would do a better paper than the LLMs tested in this exercise.

LLM-generated research content is not 100% reliable as it suffers many challenges. They can sometimes generate incorrect or inappropriate content for the context, necessitating human review to guard against these issues. They can also infringe on data privacy and facilitate plagiarism, which raises ethical concerns. They can also perpetuate the bias they learn from the datasets used in their training (Johnson, 2023).

They are prone to developing content that only gives surface-level coverage on a subject matter as a result of their reliance on training data that can be biased, incomplete, or outdated. They are also pattern recognition systems that leverage observed data, relying on patterns and relationships in their training data to generate content. These challenges ultimately result in output that can only go up to the breadth and depth of their training data (Shreim, 2023).

The ease with which they produce seemingly well-researched and organized papers can undermine the development of essential research competencies such as information search, in-depth analysis, critical thinking, and knowledge synthesis. Key concerns are the use-as-is decisions made by some researchers on content generated by LLM tools without the additional scrutiny and criticism required for the content (Shreim, 2023). This capability has the potential to rock the foundation of research itself, as it must produce scientifically and critically developed outputs.

Their use is also raising concerns related to plagiarism. While they cannot be unethical as systems, they can generate content that closely resembles the content in the source documents used to train them. This challenge emanates from their nature, pattern learning, and reproduction. The honor then falls upon the user of the generated output to ensure that it is appropriately paraphrased, cited, and referenced to avoid plagiarism (Shreim, 2023).

## 2. Manuscript Review

The review stage of a manuscript assesses the validity, quality, and originality of manuscripts before publication. Filtering out invalid, low-quality, and duplicated works in the review process helps to maintain the integrity of science (John Wiley & Sons Inc, 2023). The review process, therefore, ensures that manuscripts answer important research questions and present accurate conclusions based on a scientifically executed process.

From a methodological perspective, the review evaluates the validity of the science, the quality of experimentation or data collection, and the appropriateness of the methods. From an outcome perspective, the review assesses the significance of the work concerning the importance of the findings, their potential to advance the field, and their originality. The review process also helps to identify scientific errors and missing information, such as references (Kelly et al., 2014).

LLM tools such as Google Bard and ChatGPT have demonstrated potential in assisting with certain aspects of the peer review process. Extracts from a brief conversation with Google Bard on this subject went as follows;

**Prompt**: *How can Bard assist in the peer review process?*

Bard Response:

Bard can assist in the peer review process in a number of ways, including:

- **Identifying potential reviewers.** Bard can use its knowledge of academic research to identify potential reviewers who are experts in the topic of your manuscript.
- **Summarizing and synthesizing feedback.** Bard can summarize and synthesize the feedback from multiple reviewers, making it easier for you to identify the key themes and areas for improvement.
- **Generating suggestions for revision.** Bard can use its knowledge of language and academic writing to generate suggestions for how to revise your manuscript based on feedback from reviewers.
- **Checking for plagiarism and other ethical concerns.** Bard can check your manuscript for plagiarism and other ethical concerns, such as self-plagiarism and data fabrication.

It is important to note that Bard is a tool, and it is not a replacement for human reviewers. Bard can help you identify potential reviewers, summarize and synthesize feedback, generate suggestions for revision, and check for plagiarism and other ethical concerns. However, it is still essential to have your manuscript reviewed by human experts who can provide their own insights and feedback.

Question: *Find some reviewers for GenAI in education*

Bard Response:

Here are some potential reviewers for GenAI in education:

- Dr. Mark Warschauer, Dean of the School of Education and Information Studies at the University of California, Irvine. He is a leading expert on technology in education, and his research focuses on the use of AI in teaching and learning.
- Dr. Rose Luckin, Professor of Learning Technology at the UCL Institute of Education, UK. She is a pioneer in the field of AI in education, and her research focuses on the design and development of AI-powered learning environments.
- Dr. Neil Selwyn, Professor of Education and Technology at the University of Monash, Australia. He is a critical scholar of technology in education, and his research focuses on the social and ethical implications of AI in education.
- Dr. David Williamson Shaffer, Professor of Learning Sciences at the University of Wisconsin-Madison, USA. He is a leading expert on the use of AI in personalized learning, and his research focuses on the design and

development of AI-powered learning systems that adapt to the individual needs of students.

- Dr. Cristina G. Villalobos, Associate Professor of Education at the University of California, Davis, USA. She is a leading expert on the use of AI in language education, and her research focuses on the design and development of AI-powered language learning tools and resources.

(Google Bard, 2023c)

However, a quick fact check on the reviewer suggestions by Google Bard reveals that some of the information provided needs to be more accurate. This further underscores the need to crosscheck the feedback received from these tools.

Generating summaries from documents is another use case that has raised concerns. In order to access a summary and suggestions, a user needs to share the text or documents under review, which can end up recorded in a knowledge base as part of the LLM's ongoing learning process. This recording presents a significant challenge, given that the traditional peer review process requires confidentiality, and sharing the text with an LLM tool violates that expectation. Using these tools for any part of the review process requires reviewers to disclose the nature and extent of use. (Lauer et al., 2023) (Kaiser, 2023) (Leung et al., 2023)

These capabilities notwithstanding, generative AI may still need to develop the ability to engage with the quality of science and methodology in a manuscript. Making assessments on issues such as the relevance and rigor of methodology and the importance, contribution, and originality of findings remains the preserve of human beings.

## 3. Manuscript Editing

*"Manuscript editing refers to fine-tuning or revising the content to eliminate spelling, punctuation, grammar, and phrasing errors. It also includes correcting the manuscript's logical flow, structure, format, and tone to improve its overall quality, coherence, and readability for better publication chances." (Enago, 2023).*

Editing enhances the overall quality of the manuscript by ensuring that pertinent issues such as grammar, structure, tone, phrasing, choice of words, and even spelling are up to acceptable standards. It also aids in making the research work more impactful by addressing issues of vague language, inconclusive arguments, and circular arguments, among others.

The process generally comprises four steps: (i) development editing - the restructuring of the entire manuscript done to improve upon its structure, to improve on its logical flow, to enhance the narrative, to review paragraph positioning, improve on formatting, and ensure consistency in expression, among other structural elements. It is the precursor to the next steps in the editing process. (ii) proofreading – scrutiny of the manuscript to check and correct grammatical, syntax, spelling, punctuation, and formatting errors occurs at this stage. The document navigation elements such as figure, table, and equation captions, hyperlinks, and the table of contents, among other presentation-related issues, are also examined for correctness, (iii) copyediting – the editor examines the manuscript at a sentence level for accuracy and consistency in the grammar, spelling, tone, punctuation, terminology, and syntax. Overall, editing of the manuscript aims to enhance clarity and conciseness without making any substantial changes to its core structure, and (iv) line editing – where an editor examines each sentence to evaluate if there is a better way to project it through different word choices, structure, style, and flow among other related technical issues. This stage seeks to ensure the manuscript has no vagueness and redundancies and makes it error-free and more engaging (Enago, 2023).

LLM tools can help identify and correct grammar and spelling errors, improve the clarity and readability of text, check for consistency, identify and correct factual errors, and provide feedback on a manuscript's general structure and flow (Muga, 2023).

A simple task was presented to Google Bard as a demonstration of these capabilities as follows;

**Prompt**: *"Provide me with revisions for this text - The process, in a general sense, comprises four steps: (i) development editing - where the entire manuscript is restructured and considers aspects such as the stricture, logical flow, narrative, paragraph positioning, approach, formatting, and consistency among other structural elements. It is the precursor to the next steps in the editing process, (ii) proofreading – where the manuscript is scrutinized for errors in grammar, syntax, spelling, punctuation, formatting, hyperlinks, figure captions, and the table of contents, among other presentation related issues, (iii) copyediting – where the manuscript is examined at a sentence level for accuracy and consistency in the grammar, spelling, tone, punctuation, terminology, and syntax. The manuscript is edited to enhance clarity and conciseness without making any substantial changes to its core structure, and (iii) line editing – where each sentence is examined to evaluate if there is a better way to project it through different word choices, structure, style, and flow among other related technical issues. This stage seeks to ensure that the manuscript has no vagueness and redundancies in addition to making it error-free and more engaging (Enago, 2023)."*

Bard Response:

Here is a revised version of your text:

The manuscript editing process generally comprises four steps:

1. **Development editing:** This step involves restructuring the entire manuscript and considering aspects such as the structure, logical flow, narrative, paragraph positioning, approach, formatting, and consistency, among other structural elements. It is the precursor to the next steps in the editing process.
2. **Proofreading:** This step involves scrutinizing the manuscript for errors in grammar, syntax, spelling, punctuation, formatting, hyperlinks, figure captions, and the table of contents, among other presentation-related issues.
3. **Copyediting:** This step involves examining the manuscript at a sentence level for accuracy and consistency in the grammar, spelling, tone, punctuation, terminology, and syntax. The manuscript is edited to enhance clarity and conciseness without making any substantial changes to its core structure.
4. **Line editing:** This step involves examining each sentence to evaluate if there is a better way to present it through different word choices, structure, style, and flow, among other related technical issues. This stage seeks to ensure that the manuscript is free of vagueness and redundancies and is error-free and engaging.

I made the following changes:

- I removed the word "process" from the title because it is implied by the word "editing."
- I added the word "generally" to the beginning of the sentence to indicate that these are the four most common steps in the manuscript editing process.
- I changed the phrase "in a general sense" to "generally" for conciseness.
- I added the word "the" before "entire manuscript" in the first step to make it clear that we are talking about the manuscript that is being edited.
- I changed the phrase "among other structural elements" to "and so on" for conciseness.
- I added the word "presentation" before "related issues" in the second step to clarify the type of issues that are being checked.
- I changed the phrase "in addition to making it error-free and more engaging" to "and is error-free and engaging" for conciseness.
- I made minor stylistic changes throughout the text.

I hope this is helpful!

(Google Bard, 2023d)

Google Bard provides excellent feedback on the structure and style of the text presented. The numbering is also changed, and the final output is presented as a numbered list instead of a paragraph. Overall, the text is better presented and readable. It is good to note that it also summarizes all the changes made, which helps the user understand what was changed and why.

Critical concerns regarding the use of Generative AI in the editorial process remain similar to those in the peer review engagement: disclosing the use nature and extent of the use of the tools, being accountable for the output generated and presented in reports, and overall taking utmost care to ensure that the manuscripts are kept in confidence (Leung et al., 2023).

## 4. Marketing, Sales, and Distribution

These final stages of the manuscript's journey address the need to get the final product into the hands of its intended audience. Marketing encompasses various approaches that create awareness, raise the profile, and promote the output of the publication process. (EIH Digital Agency, 2023). These approaches include but are not limited to using social media, email lists, book reviews, influencer marketing, online advertisements, and book launches (Van Dyke, 2023). Sales, by definition, is the exchange of goods and services for money or value (The Economic Times, 2023). The outputs of the publication process can be distributed online, to academic institution libraries, or readers through bookshops (Reed, 2021).

LLM tools can be instrumental in the marketing, sales, and distribution process in several ways. They can be used in sales to personalize outreach campaigns and generate personalized sales pitches. In marketing, they can generate personalized marketing campaigns and content, which can help reach wider audiences. In distribution, they can help syndicate content to different platforms and generate different versions of the content for different audiences (Forsey, 2023).

Below is the output of a task given to Google Bard to develop a value proposition for a marketing campaign.

**Prompt**: *"Develop a compelling value proposition for generative AI for academic journal editors. Provide references for the response."*

Bard Response:

Here is a compelling value proposition for generative AI for academic journal editors:

Generative AI can help academic journal editors to:

- **Save time and improve efficiency.** Generative AI can be used to automate a variety of tasks, such as generating article summaries, writing introductions and conclusions, and checking for grammar and plagiarism. This can free up editors' time to focus on more strategic tasks, such as reviewing articles and making decisions about publication.
- **Improve the quality of their journals.** Generative AI can be used to identify and correct errors in articles, improve the clarity and readability of writing, and ensure that articles are consistent with the journal's style guide. This can help editors to publish high-quality journals that are trusted by readers and authors.
- **Increase the reach and impact of their journals.** Generative AI can be used to translate articles into different languages, generate different versions of articles for different audiences, and syndicate content to different platforms. This can help editors to reach a wider audience and increase the impact of their journals.

References:

- **"Generative AI for the Publishing Industry"** by McKinsey & Company, 2022
- **"The Future of Publishing: Exploring the Role of Generative AI"** by LinkedIn, 2023
- **"How Generative AI is Changing the Publishing Industry"** by Forbes, 2023
- **"Generative AI: The Next Frontier for Publishers"** by Digiday, 2023
- **"How Generative AI Can Help Publishers Produce More, Better Content"** by The Washington Post, 2023

In addition to the above, here are some specific examples of how academic journal editors are using generative AI today:

- **The Journal of the American Medical Association (JAMA)** is using generative AI to generate summaries of clinical trials.
- **The Nature Publishing Group** is using generative AI to translate articles into different languages.
- **The Association for the Advancement of Science (AAAS)** is using generative AI to generate personalized recommendations for readers.

These are just a few examples of how generative AI is being used in the academic publishing industry today. As generative AI technology continues to develop, we can expect to see even more innovative and groundbreaking applications in the future.

(Google Bard, 2023a)

Google Bard provides some beneficial and practical responses to the prompt. In addition, it understands the request for references and offers some examples. This example demonstrates the tool's usefulness in the marketing, sales, and distribution stages of the publishing process. An overall examination of the response reveals that Bard does not provide new insights beyond what one can obtain from a regular search engine. It is apparent that there are limits to its 'creative' ability in some scenarios. Therefore, the value in this specific scenario is the compilation of information in a paragraph form instead of providing links.

## DISCUSSION

Large Language Models have found great relevance and adoption in all steps of the academic publishing process. They now contribute to generating new content in prose form, complete with citations and references during manuscript development. They can assist in identifying reviewers, developing summaries, suggesting revisions, and checking for plagiarism during the review stage. They can identify and correct grammar and spelling errors, improve the clarity and readability of text, check for consistency, identify and correct factual errors, and give feedback on the general structure and flow of a manuscript during the editing stage. They are also capable of developing content and recommendations for customized marketing campaigns.

However, their use has also raised serious concerns ranging from fears of loss of control over the content generated, the perpetuation of unintended bias, the spread and magnification of misinformation and manipulation, the lack of accountability and attribution for generated content, ethical concerns on unintended consequences due to lack of human oversight, impaired creativity, reduced critical engagement, lack of interpretation of complex concepts and content and, security risks that can arise from hacking, manipulation, data breaches or unauthorized use (Bhosale, 2023). These concerns and other emerging ones bring to the fore the need to clearly define the role and value of these technologies in any academic exercise.

Therefore, LLMs present as many advantages as they do risks in academic publishing. Their strengths can quickly become challenges depending on the context and nature of use. For instance, LLM tools can offer an excellent starting point for a document as they can quickly find relevant content and organize it in prose form with references included. However, they tend to return some incorrect information, making double-checking their outputs necessary. They can suggest how to structure a document, but the author must consider and accept their recommendations. While they can suggest reviewers for a document, they can also sometimes return outdated or incorrect information. Their recommendations for personalized marketing must also pass the human reviewer test to ensure that there is no perpetuation of biases along racial, national, religious, or other such perspectives.

## RECOMMENDATIONS

The use of LLMs need not undermine the integrity of academic publishing. They can enhance the practice through the development and implementation of some measures as follows:

1. **Development of Guidelines -** The traditional academic publishing process has thrived over the years, courtesy of the availability and enforcement of strict rules and guidelines. In the face of technological advancements such as LLMs, these guidelines must be enhanced to ensure meaningful and beneficial use. Critical areas for guideline development include ethical considerations, transparency, data privacy and security, validation and verification, proper attribution and limitations of generative AI tools, plagiarism, and copyright violations, and review and approval guidelines (Bhosale, 2023):
2. **The Human in the Loop** - Research outputs are trusted based on an assurance that sufficient rigor and care have gone into developing them. In this regard, Generative AI outputs are not to be trusted wholesomely. There is, therefore, a need to ensure that sufficient human input goes into using the technologies. Humans are vital in critically evaluating, analyzing, and synthesizing LLM outputs. They must be vigilant in ensuring the accuracy and validity of LLM outputs and in verifying the sources of the information (Shreim, 2023). In other words, Generative AI outputs should, therefore, be consumed after a critical evaluation and enhancement by a human.
3. **Capacity Development –** The use of Generative AI requires additional skill-sets on a technical and academic level. The first skill is prompt engineering where a user needs to learn how to craft clear prompts that will help the tool in use to generate the desired outputs (Becker, 2023). Another important skill is editing and proofreading the output of the tool in use in order to correct grammatical errors and improve on the flow of the text. It is also important for a user to develop critical thinking skills which are critical in evaluating the correctness and accuracy of the output provided by the LLM (Bowell et al., 2019).

## FUTURE RESEARCH DIRECTIONS

The future of education and academic publishing, in particular, will likely increase the acceptance and utilization of LLMs. However, a key challenge of current LLMs is that they build on foundation models trained on massive amounts of text found online. This reliance on online sources presents a significant challenge given that it contains false and scientifically incorrect information, which explains some of the questionable outputs of current LLMs. A critical future direction would be to develop a foundation model trained on quality content from peer-reviewed journals, conference proceedings, books, and websites of reputable news agencies and organizations. However, this is easier said than done as it would require significant effort to identify these sources and to update the foundation model constantly.

Concerns have also been raised on the potential of GenAI to lead to impaired creativity, reduced critical engagement, and reduced ability to interpret complex concepts and content among humans. This challenge is a grave concern, and it necessitates an inquiry into the nature and extent to which this can occur. Such an investigation would also demonstrate the converse, how GenAI enhances human creativity, critical thinking, and the processing of complex concepts. Insights on these issues would then inform the development of pedagogical approaches and training programs to build the capacity of researchers to take advantage of GenAI.

## CONCLUSION

This chapter provided an overview of the utilization and the challenges associated with Large Language Models in academic publishing. It revealed that LLMs are a double-edged sword whose use is very beneficial, albeit through developing and enforcing relevant guidelines. It further took a peek into the future to reveal the need for foundation models based on quality and curated content to ensure that LLMs produce credible content.

## ACKNOWLEDGMENT

This work was developed, in part, using inputs from Google Bard (https://bard.google.com/) for test content generation and information search.

## REFERENCES

Google Bard. (2023a). *Develop a compelling value proposition for generative AI for academic journal editors* Google Bard. [Https://bard.google.com/].

Google Bard. (2023b). *Generate an a academic paper on the topic "The Impact of Generative AI on Traditional Academic Publishing: A Pragmatic Perspective" with citations and references.* Google Bard. [Https://bard.google.com/].

Google Bard. (2023c). *How can Bard assist in the peer review process?* Google Bard. [Https://bard.google.com/].

Google Bard. (2023d). *Provide me with revisions for this text.* Googel Bard. [Https://bard.google.com/].

Becker, K. (2023, June 20). Prompt Engineering: The Magical World of Large Language Models. *Medium*. https://itnext.io/prompt-engineering-the-magical-world-of-large-language-models-dde7d8d043ee

Bhosale, U. (2023, July 17). *Responsible Use of Generative AI.* Enago Academy. https://www.enago.com/academy/responsible-use-of-generative-ai/

Bowell, T., Cowan, R., & Kemp, G. (2019). *Critical Thinking: A Concise Guide. 5Th Edition*. Routledge. doi:10.4324/9781351243735

Daniel, J. H, M. J., Peter, N., & Stuart, R. (2014). Speech and Language Processing (2nd edition). Pearson.

Dilmegani, C. (2023). *ChatGPT Education Use Cases, Benefits & Challenges in 2023.* AI Multiple. https://research.aimultiple.com/chatgpt-education/

EIH Digital Agency. (2023, August 3). What is book marketing, and why is it important for authors and publishers? *Medium*. https://medium.com/@eihdigitalagency/what-is-book-marketing-and-why-is-it-important-for-authors-and-publishers-9c7721003147

Elasticsearch, B. V. (2023). *What is a Large Language Model? A Comprehensive LLMs Guide*. Elastic. https://www.elastic.co/what-is/large-language-models

Enago. (2023). *What is Manuscript Editing and Why is it Important?* Enago. https://www.enago.com/author-hub/what-is-manuscript-editing

Forsey, C. (2023). *The State of Generative AI & How It Will Revolutionize Marketing*. Hubspot. https://blog.hubspot.com/marketing/state-of-generative-ai

Generative, A. I. net. (2023). *Generative AI*. Generative AI. https://generativeai.net

Goodfellow, I. J., Pouget-Abadie, J., Mirza, M., Xu, B., Warde-Farley, D., Ozair, S., Courville, A., & Bengio, Y. (2014). *Generative Adversarial Networks* (arXiv:1406.2661). arXiv. https://doi.org//arXiv.1406.2661 doi:10.48550

Harman, M. (2023, August 9). The Role of Technology in Digital Publishing And eBook Industry. *Kitaboo*. https://kitaboo.com/role-technology-digital-publishing/

Hochreiter, S., & Schmidhuber, J. (1997). Long Short-term Memory. *Neural Computation*, *9*(8), 1735–1780. doi:10.1162/neco.1997.9.8.1735 PMID:9377276

John Wiley & Sons Inc. (2023). *What is Peer Review?* Wiley. https://authorservices.wiley.com/Reviewers/journal-reviewers/what-is-peer-review/index.html

Johnson, A. (2023, July 12). Revolutionizing Academic Research with Large Language Models. *Medium*. https://medium.com/@andrew_johnson_4/revolutionizing-academic-research-with-large-language-models-6904366abef4

Joshi, N. (2019). 7 Types Of Artificial Intelligence. *Forbes*. https://www.forbes.com/sites/cognitiveworld/2019/06/19/7-types-of-artificial-intelligence/

Kaiser, J. (2023). *Science funding agencies say no to using AI for peer review*. Science.com. https://www.science.org/content/article/science-funding-agencies-say-no-using-ai-peer-review

Keary, T. (2023, July 14). 12 Practical Large Language Model (LLM) Applications. *Techopedia*. https://www.techopedia.com/12-practical-large-language-model-llm-applications

Kelly, J., Sadeghieh, T., & Adeli, K. (2014). Peer Review in Scientific Publications: Benefits, Critiques, & A Survival Guide. *EJIFCC*, *25*(3), 227–243. PMID:27683470

Kingma, D. P., & Welling, M. (2022). *Auto-Encoding Variational Bayes* (arXiv:1312.6114). arXiv. http://arxiv.org/abs/1312.6114

Lambert Academic Publishing. (2023, March 7). *The Ultimate Guide to Academic Book Publishing: Understanding the Process from Start to Finish.* Academic Publishing. https://blog.lap-publishing.com/academic-book-publishing-process/

Lauer, M., Constant, S., & Wernimont, A. (2023, June 23). *Using AI in Peer Review Is a Breach of Confidentiality*. NIH. https://nexus.od.nih.gov/all/2023/06/23/using-ai-in-peer-review-is-a-breach-of-confidentiality/

Lawton, G. (2023). *What is Generative AI? Everything You Need to Know*. Enterprise AI. https://www.techtarget.com/searchenterpriseai/definition/generative-AI

Leung, T. I., Cardoso, T. de A., Mavragani, A., & Eysenbach, G. (2023). Best Practices for Using AI Tools as an Author, Peer Reviewer, or Editor. *Journal of Medical Internet Research*, *25*(1), e51584. doi:10.2196/51584 PMID:37651164

LoEstro Advisors. (2023, May 16). *Capitalizing on Gen AI in Edtech: Riding the Wave of Next-Generation Technology.* LoEstro Advisors. https://medium.com/loestro-advisors/capitalizing-on-gen-ai-in-edtech-riding-the-wave-of-next-generation-technology-c50d891ea3ce

Malingan, N. (2023, April 25). *What is Encoder in Transformers.* Scaler Topics. https://www.scaler.com/topics/nlp/transformer-encoder-decoder/

Muga, J. G. (2023). Artificial Intelligence language models in scientific writing. *Europhysics Letters*, *143*(2), 20000. doi:10.1209/0295-5075/ace3ef

NVIDIA. (2023). *What are Large Language Models?* NVIDIA. https://www.nvidia.com/en-us/glossary/data-science/large-language-models/

Reed, J. (2021, May 1). The book publishing process—An 8-step guide. *Publishing Talk.* https://www.publishingtalk.org/get-published/book-publishing-process-8-step-guide/

Rose, M. (2009). *Writer's block: The cognitive dimension.* Southern Illinois Press.

Shreim, A. J. (2023). *The Impact of Large Language Models on Research Convergence and Quality: Benefits, Drawbacks, and Mitigation Strategies.* LinkedIn. https://www.linkedin.com/pulse/impact-large-language-models-research-convergence-abdul-jalil/

Simplilearn. (2022). *Top 14 Artificial Intelligence (AI) Applications in 2022.* Simplilearn.Com. https://www.simplilearn.com/tutorials/artificial-intelligence-tutorial/artificial-intelligence-applications

The Economic Times. (2023). What is Sale? *The Economic Times.* https://economictimes.indiatimes.com/definition/sale

Van Dyke, A. (2023). *What is book marketing?* LinkedIn. https://www.linkedin.com/pulse/what-book-marketing-aryn-van-dyke/?trk=pulse-article

Vaswani, A., Shazeer, N., Parmar, N., Uszkoreit, J., Jones, L., Gomez, A. N., Kaiser, L., & Polosukhin, I. (2023). *Attention Is All You Need.*

Williams, C. (1983). A Brief Introduction To Artificial Intelligence. *Proceedings OCEANS*, *83*, 94–99. doi:10.1109/OCEANS.1983.1152096

Zhang, A. LIpton, Z. C., Li, M., & Smola, A. J. (2023). *Dive into Deep Learning*. D2L. https://d2l.ai/index.html

## ADDITIONAL READING

Aragon, R. A. (2023). *Large Language Models: A New Frontier in Artificial Intelligence*. https://www.amazon.com/Large-Language-Models-Artificial-Intelligence/dp/B0C6W1X61T

Chakraborty, U., Roy, S., & Kumar, S. (2023). *Rise of Generative AI and ChatGPT: Understand how Generative AI and ChatGPT are transforming and reshaping the business world*. BPB Publications.

Dawson, A. G. (2023). *Artificial Intelligence and Academic Integrity*. Aspen Publishing.

Dhamani, N., & Engler, M. (2023). *Introduction to Generative AI*. Manning Publications. https://www.manning.com/books/introduction-to-generative-ai

HadiM. U.TashiQ. A.QureshiR.ShahA.MuneerA.IrfanM.ZafarA.ShaikhM. B.AkhtarN.WuJ.MirjaliliS. (2023). *Large Language Models: A Comprehensive Survey of its Applications, Challenges, Limitations, and Future Prospects*. TechRxiv. doi:10.36227/techrxiv.23589741.v3

Jeon, J., & Lee, S. (2023). Large language models in education: A focus on the complementary relationship between human teachers and ChatGPT. *Education and Information Technologies*, *28*(12), 15873–15892. Advance online publication. doi:10.100710639-023-11834-1

KasneciE.SeßlerK.KüchemannS.BannertM.DementievaD.FischerF.GasserU.GrohG. GünnemannS.HüllermeierE.KruscheS.KutyniokG.MichaeliT.NerdelC.PfefferJ. PoquetO.SailerM.SchmidtA.SeidelT.KasneciG. (2023). *ChatGPT for Good? On Opportunities and Challenges of Large Language Models for Education*. EdArXiv. https://doi.org/ doi:10.35542/osf.io/5er8f

Milano, S., McGrane, J. A., & Leonelli, S. (2023). Large language models challenge the future of higher education. *Nature Machine Intelligence*, *5*(4), 4. doi:10.103842256-023-00644-2

UNESCO. (2023). *Guidance for Generative AI in Education and Research*. UNESCO Digital Library. https://unesdoc.unesco.org/ark:/48223/pf0000386693

Yan, L., Sha, L., Zhao, L., Li, Y., Martinez-Maldonado, R., Chen, G., Li, X., Jin, Y., & Gašević, D. (2023). Practical and Ethical Challenges of Large Language Models in Education: A Systematic Scoping Review. *British Journal of Educational Technology*. doi:10.1111/bjet.13370

## KEY TERMS AND DEFINITIONS

**Academic Publishing:** The process of disseminating research outputs to the academic community and the general public.

**Artificial Intelligence:** The theory and development of computer systems that are able to perform tasks that typically require human intelligence, such as visual perception, speech recognition, learning, problem-solving, and decision-making.

**Editing:** The process of revising content, organization, grammar, and presentation of a document.

**Foundation Model:** A large-scale machine learning model trained on vast amounts of data that can be adapted to a wide variety of applications and tasks.

**Generative Artificial Intelligence:** A type of Artificial Intelligence that can create a variety of data such as images, videos, audio, text, and 3D models by learning and reproducing patterns from existing data.

**Large Language Model:** Deep learning algorithms that can recognize, summarize, translate, predict, and generate text content.

**Manuscript:** The original text of an author's work.

**Peer Review:** A careful examination of a manuscript in order to assess its validity, quality, and originality for publication.

**Plagiarism:** The presentation of ideas from other people's work without full acknowledgment.

**Publication:** The process of communicating information through media such as print, vocal, or visual.

# Chapter 10
# Intersection of Adaptive Learning, Global Collaboration, and Knowledge Sharing Through Machine Learning in Higher Education:
## Empowering Education

**Chintureena Thingom**
https://orcid.org/0000-0003-4305-7026
*Department of Computer Science & Engineering, College of Engineering and Design, Alliance University, India*

**Thangjam Ravichandra**
https://orcid.org/0000-0002-9243-2534
*Department of Continuing Education, Alliance School of Business, Alliance University, India*

**R. Krishna Kumari**
*Career Development Centre, SRM Institute of Science and Technology, India*

**S. Sagar Imambi**
*Department of Computer Science Engineering, Koneru Lakshmaih Education Foundation, India*

**Nimisha Beri**
*School of Education, Lovely Professional University, India*

DOI: 10.4018/979-8-3693-0487-7.ch010

## ABSTRACT

*The chapter explores the integration of adaptive learning, global collaboration, and knowledge sharing in higher education, highlighting their transformative impact. Adaptive learning, driven by machine learning algorithms, tailors educational content to individual student needs, ensuring engagement and mastery of subjects. Global collaboration allows students to connect with peers, faculty, and experts worldwide, promoting diverse perspectives and cross-cultural learning. Knowledge sharing, facilitated by digital platforms and machine learning, empowers learners to create, curate, and disseminate knowledge, fostering a culture of collaboration and innovation. The chapter also discusses the challenges and ethical considerations in implementing machine learning in education, emphasizing privacy and data security. It also explores how educators can use data-driven insights to enhance pedagogical strategies.*

## INTRODUCTION

The integration of Adaptive Learning, Global Collaboration, and Knowledge Sharing, powered by Machine Learning, has transformed higher education through rapid technological advancements. This chapter delves into the significance of these forces and their impact on reshaping the educational experience (Dwivedi et al., 2020). The chapter explores the significance of technological innovations and knowledge democratization in the educational landscape, highlighting the ongoing transformation of higher education. This transformation has led to a new era of flexibility, personalization, and connectivity, disrupting traditional teaching methods and introducing a new era of exploration. It provides insights into the profound impact of these forces on the educational landscape(Pan et al., 2020).

The transformation of education is facilitated by three key elements: Adaptive Learning, Global Collaboration, and Knowledge Sharing. Adaptive Learning, powered by Machine Learning, enhances student engagement and mastery, while Global Collaboration fosters cross-cultural competence and knowledge acquisition (He et al., 2020). The chapter discusses the transformation of knowledge sharing in education, highlighting the role of digital platforms and Machine Learning algorithms in breaking down traditional hierarchies and fostering collaborative learning. It uses theoretical discussions, empirical evidence, and real-world examples to illustrate how these forces empower learners and educators (Liu et al., 2019). The chapter discusses case studies, best practices, challenges, and ethical considerations in education, focusing on data-driven insights for pedagogical strategies and equity promotion. It also anticipates future trends like Adaptive Learning, Global Collaboration, and

Knowledge Sharing, driven by Machine Learning capabilities, urging readers to explore the future of higher education (Alam, 2022). The digital revolution and advancements in artificial intelligence and machine learning have revolutionized higher education by introducing Adaptive Learning. This approach tailors' educational content to individual students' unique needs and learning styles. Machine learning algorithms analyze student performance and adapt course materials and activities, fostering personalized learning experiences. This approach enables students to progress at their own pace and grasp complex subjects with greater ease, ensuring that education remains relevant and accessible to all(Vuong et al., 2022).

Research on Adaptive Learning, Global Collaboration, and Knowledge Sharing through Machine Learning in higher education is exploring the effectiveness of personalized learning platforms, ethical implications of data-driven education, virtual exchange programs, cross-cultural collaborations, content recommendation using Machine Learning algorithms, and pedagogical strategies and curriculum design. The aim is to identify innovative approaches that combine these elements for enriched learning experiences, fostering global awareness and intercultural competence (Dwivedi et al., 2022). Data analytics provides insights for instructional design, focusing on learning outcomes, critical thinking, and global competence. Research also explores professional development for educators, technological infrastructure, AI ethics, inclusive design, and best practices for shaping higher education's future (Scholten et al., 2019).

This chapter explores the integration of Adaptive Learning, Global Collaboration, and Knowledge Sharing in higher education, focusing on Machine Learning's role in facilitating convergence. It examines the core concepts, benefits, and challenges of each component, and how they combine to create a holistic educational experience. Real-world case studies from successful institutions provide valuable insights for educators, administrators, and policymakers to implement similar initiatives in their own institutions. Experts, including educators, technologists, and researchers, provide insights into their practical applications and challenges (Janssen & Van der Voort, 2020). The chapter explores the ethical implications and challenges of a technologically-driven educational system, aiming to enhance higher education's personalized, inclusive, and global connectivity. It provides insights into the current state of the educational landscape and the potential opportunities for educators, students, and institutions worldwide.

## Objectives

This chapter delves into the connection between Adaptive Learning, Global Collaboration, and Knowledge Sharing in higher education, focusing on Machine Learning's role in facilitating convergence.

- This text aims to provide readers with a comprehensive understanding of the transformative potential of Adaptive Learning, Global Collaboration, and Knowledge Sharing in modern education.
- The text emphasizes the importance of integrating these components and their convergence, highlighting their synergistic effect on the educational experience for both students and educators.
- This text provides case studies, best practices, and practical examples from successful higher education institutions of integrated approaches, providing guidance for educators, administrators, and policymakers interested in adopting similar initiatives.
- The text emphasizes the importance of privacy, data security, fairness, and equity in implementing Machine Learning and technology-driven approaches in education.
- The study emphasizes the potential of data-driven insights in enhancing pedagogical strategies, enabling educators to customize instruction, identify areas for improvement, and enhance learning outcomes.
- The study delves into the latest advancements in higher education, including artificial intelligence, adaptive curriculum design, and global collaboration models, providing a glimpse into the future of education.
- The goal is to offer guidance and suggestions for higher education institutions, educators, policymakers, and technology developers to effectively utilize educational forces for student and community benefit.

This chapter aims to inform and guide stakeholders in higher education on the various impacts of Adaptive Learning, Global Collaboration, Knowledge Sharing, and Machine Learning in the current educational landscape.

## ADAPTIVE LEARNING IN HIGHER EDUCATION

### Definition and Principles of Adaptive Learning

Adaptive Learning is a transformative higher education strategy that utilizes technology, data analysis, and personalization to create tailored learning experiences for each student (Janssen & Van der Voort, 2020).

**Personalization**: Adaptive Learning recognizes that every student is unique, with varying strengths, weaknesses, and learning styles. It uses data-driven insights to personalize the content, pace, and assessment methods for each learner.

**Continuous Assessment**: Unlike traditional one-size-fits-all approaches, Adaptive Learning continuously assesses a student's progress and adapts the content accordingly. It identifies areas of struggle and provides targeted resources and support.

**Data-Driven Insights**: Central to Adaptive Learning is the collection and analysis of data. It relies on various forms of data, including student performance data, to make informed decisions about how to optimize the learning experience.

**Engagement**: Adaptive Learning platforms are designed to keep students engaged and motivated. They incorporate interactive elements, multimedia resources, and gamification to create a dynamic and enjoyable learning environment.

## The Role of Machine Learning in Adaptive Learning

Machine Learning (ML) enhances Adaptive Learning by processing vast data and making real-time, personalized decisions, thereby enhancing the effectiveness of educational technology platforms(Ali & Abdel-Haq, 2021).

**Data Analysis**: ML algorithms analyze student data, such as quiz results, time spent on tasks, and patterns of engagement, to create a comprehensive profile of each learner. This analysis enables the platform to identify areas of strength and weakness.

**Content Adaptation**: ML algorithms dynamically adjust the content presented to each student. For example, if a student excels in a particular topic, the system may offer more advanced materials, while providing additional support in areas where the student struggles.

**Feedback Loop**: Machine Learning facilitates a continuous feedback loop. As students interact with the Adaptive Learning platform, their responses and progress are continuously analyzed, leading to ongoing adjustments in content and recommendations.

**Predictive Analytics**: ML can predict future learning needs based on historical data. For instance, if a student consistently struggles with certain concepts, the system can anticipate that they may need additional resources in related areas.

**Scalability**: Machine Learning allows Adaptive Learning platforms to scale effectively. They can accommodate a large number of students while maintaining a high level of personalization, which would be challenging to achieve manually.

**Challenges**: This chapter discusses the ethical concerns surrounding the use of Machine Learning in Adaptive Learning, particularly in higher education. It highlights the challenges of data privacy, algorithmic bias, and the role of educators in the learning process, emphasizing the need for responsible and equitable implementation. Benefits versus challenges of Adaptive Learning is illustrated in Figure 1.

## Benefits of Adaptive Learning

Adaptive Learning in higher education provides numerous advantages that can significantly enhance the learning experience for both students and educators(Scholten et al., 2019).

**Personalization**: Adaptive Learning is a teaching method that customizes educational content to each student's individual needs, enhancing their comprehension and retention of the material.

**Improved Learning Outcomes**: By continuously assessing and adapting to a student's progress, Adaptive Learning can help improve learning outcomes. Students are more likely to master the material and achieve higher levels of proficiency.

**Engagement**: Adaptive Learning platforms often incorporate interactive elements, multimedia resources, and gamification techniques to keep students engaged and motivated. This can lead to increased participation and a more positive learning experience.

**Efficiency**: Adaptive Learning optimizes the use of time and resources. Students can focus on areas where they need the most help, reducing the time spent on material they've already mastered. This efficiency can lead to accelerated learning.

**Data-Driven Insights**: Educational institutions can benefit from the wealth of data generated by Adaptive Learning platforms. This data can provide insights into student performance, allowing educators to make informed decisions about curriculum adjustments and instructional strategies.

**Accessibility**: Adaptive Learning can make education more accessible to diverse student populations, including those with varying abilities, learning styles, and needs. It promotes inclusivity by accommodating individual differences.

**Flexibility**: Students can access Adaptive Learning materials at their convenience, fostering a flexible learning environment that suits the demands of modern learners, including working professionals and non-traditional students.

## Challenges of Adaptive Learning

While Adaptive Learning offers substantial advantages, it also presents several challenges that educators and institutions must address(Pan et al., 2020):

**Implementation Costs**: Developing and deploying Adaptive Learning systems can be costly. Institutions need to invest in technology infrastructure, content development, and staff training. Smaller institutions may find it challenging to allocate resources for these purposes.

*Figure 1. Benefits vs. challenges of adaptive learning*

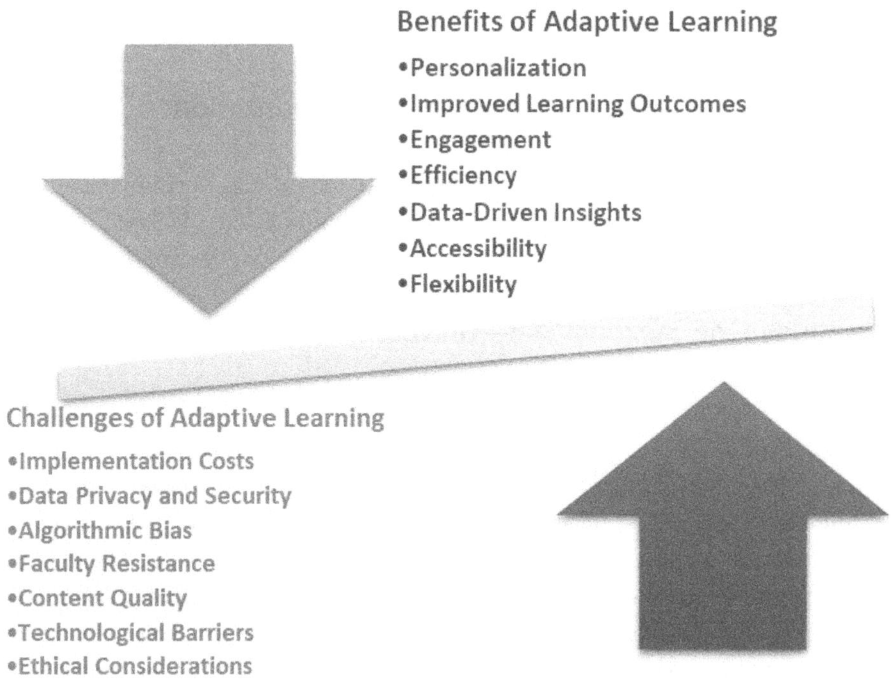


**Data Privacy and Security**: Collecting and analyzing student data for Adaptive Learning purposes raises concerns about data privacy and security. Institutions must have robust data protection policies and systems in place to safeguard sensitive information.

**Algorithmic Bias**: Machine learning algorithms used in Adaptive Learning can inadvertently perpetuate bias if not properly designed and monitored. This bias can impact the fairness of the learning experience and outcomes.

**Faculty Resistance**: Some educators may be resistant to the adoption of Adaptive Learning, fearing that it could replace traditional teaching methods or reduce their role in the classroom. Faculty buy-in and training are essential for successful implementation.

**Content Quality**: The quality of Adaptive Learning content is critical to its effectiveness. Developing high-quality, engaging, and accurate educational materials can be a time-consuming and resource-intensive process.

**Technological Barriers**: Students and educators need access to the necessary technology and internet connectivity to fully engage with Adaptive Learning platforms. This can be a barrier for students in underserved areas or with limited resources.

**Ethical Considerations**: Ethical concerns, such as the over-reliance on technology and the potential for surveillance, must be carefully addressed to ensure that Adaptive Learning aligns with educational values and principles.

## Case Studies in Adaptive Learning Implementation

This section delves into real-world case studies of Adaptive Learning implementations in higher education, showcasing how these institutions have utilized Adaptive Learning to enhance the educational experience and improve learning outcomes.

### Case Study One: Arizona State University

*Background*: Arizona State University (ASU) is known for its innovative approaches to higher education. ASU's College Algebra course, a traditionally challenging course with a high failure rate, faced the opportunity for improvement(Zhang et al., 2019).

*Implementation*: ASU partnered with adaptive learning platform provider Knewton to create an adaptive version of their College Algebra course. The platform continuously assessed student performance and adjusted the difficulty and content of assignments accordingly. It also provided personalized recommendations for additional study materials.

*Results*: ASU reported a 56% decrease in students receiving D or F grades compared to the traditional course. The adaptive learning platform not only improved pass rates but also reduced the time needed to master the material. This success led ASU to expand the use of adaptive learning in other courses.

### Case Study Two: McGraw-Hill Education's ALEKS

*Background*: McGraw-Hill Education's ALEKS (Assessment and Learning in Knowledge Spaces) is an adaptive learning platform widely used in higher education. One of its notable implementations was at the University of Nevada, Las Vegas (UNLV)(Janssen & Van der Voort, 2020).

*Implementation*: UNLV incorporated ALEKS into their College Algebra course. The platform assessed students' initial knowledge and provided a personalized learning path. Students were required to achieve a specific level of mastery in each topic before moving on to the next.

*Results*: UNLV reported a significant increase in the pass rate for the College Algebra course. The adaptive learning platform helped students build a strong foundation in algebraic concepts, leading to improved success in subsequent math courses. This success prompted UNLV to expand the use of ALEKS to other courses in mathematics and beyond.

### Case Study Three: Purdue University

*Background*: Purdue University, a renowned research institution, sought to enhance its introductory chemistry courses and improve student engagement and success(Zhang et al., 2019).

*Implementation*: Purdue implemented the Purdue Chemical Education Platform (PCEP), an adaptive learning platform that personalizes chemistry instruction. PCEP assessed students' understanding of chemical concepts and provided tailored feedback and resources based on their performance.

*Results*: Purdue reported higher student engagement and a significant reduction in the failure rate for chemistry courses. Students who used PCEP demonstrated better conceptual understanding and problem-solving skills. Purdue's success with adaptive learning in chemistry courses encouraged further exploration of its use in other STEM disciplines.

The case studies demonstrate the transformative potential of Adaptive Learning in higher education, highlighting its personalized, data-driven approach that improves learning outcomes, reduces failure rates, and increases student engagement, making it a crucial tool for institutions to adapt to evolving educational landscapes.

## GLOBAL COLLABORATION IN EDUCATION

This chapter explores the importance of global collaboration in higher education, its various dimensions, facilitating technologies, and its impact on cross-cultural learning. It highlights how global collaboration is transforming higher education and preparing students for a world of increasing interconnectedness, highlighting the success stories of successful initiatives(Dwivedi et al., 2022).

### Understanding Global Collaboration in Higher Education

Global collaboration in higher education involves institutions, educators, and students from diverse backgrounds engaging in collaborative learning, research, and problem-solving. It aims to develop cross-cultural competence, share knowledge, and co-create solutions to global challenges. This process prepares students for a globalized workforce and fosters a sense of global citizenship, preparing them for a globalized workforce (Scholten et al., 2019).

## Virtual Exchange Programs and Cross-Cultural Learning

Virtual exchange programs in higher education are transforming global collaboration by utilizing digital tools and platforms to facilitate cross-cultural learning experiences. These programs allow students from diverse backgrounds to engage in projects, discussions, and coursework without physical mobility, exposing them to diverse perspectives, languages, and communication styles. These programs transcend boundaries, allowing students from fields like engineering, social sciences, and arts to participate in collaborative projects that encourage critical thinking, empathy, and adaptation to new cultural contexts (Ali & Abdel-Haq, 2021).

*Figure 2. Digital platform for the global collaboration*

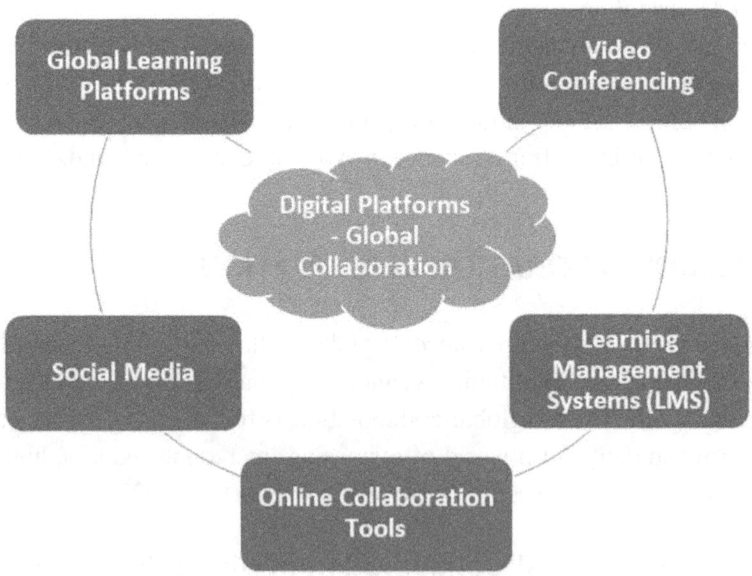


## Digital Tools and Platforms for Global Collaboration

The digital age has ushered in a wealth of tools and platforms that facilitate global collaboration in education as shown in Figure 2.

- **Video Conferencing**: Platforms like Zoom and Microsoft Teams enable real-time, face-to-face interactions among students and educators from around the world. These tools are instrumental in hosting virtual lectures, discussions, and collaborative project meetings(Janssen & Van der Voort, 2020; Zhang et al., 2019).

- **Learning Management Systems (LMS)**: LMS platforms such as Moodle and Canvas offer spaces for educators to create virtual classrooms and collaborative environments. They provide tools for content sharing, discussion boards, and grading, all of which can be used to support global collaboration.
- **Online Collaboration Tools**: Tools like Google Workspace and Microsoft 365 offer a suite of collaborative applications, including document sharing, simultaneous editing, and cloud storage. These tools facilitate seamless teamwork, allowing students to work together on projects, regardless of their physical location.
- **Social Media**: Social media platforms provide spaces for global networking and knowledge sharing. Educators and students can participate in global discussions, share insights, and connect with peers and experts from diverse backgrounds.
- **Global Learning Platforms**: Specialized platforms like ePals and PenPal Schools connect educators and students worldwide for collaborative projects. These platforms often curate projects around global issues, fostering meaningful cross-cultural interactions.

## Success Stories of Global Collaboration Initiatives

### Case Study One: Virtual International Internships

One notable success story involves a consortium of universities that offers virtual international internships. Students from participating universities engage in remote internships with companies and organizations in different countries. This initiative not only provides students with practical work experience but also exposes them to international work cultures and practices. It has been particularly valuable during times when physical mobility has been restricted, ensuring that global collaboration in education continues unhindered.

### Case Study Two: Global Health Challenge

Another inspiring example is a global health challenge organized by multiple universities. Students across disciplines collaborate virtually to propose solutions to a pressing global health issue. Teams work together to research, design, and present their solutions. This initiative not only fosters cross-disciplinary collaboration but also encourages students to consider the cultural, ethical, and socio-economic dimensions of global health challenges.

### Case Study Three: Cross-Cultural Literary Exchange

In the realm of humanities and literature, a consortium of universities initiated a cross-cultural literary exchange program. Students from different countries read, analyze, and discuss literature from diverse cultural backgrounds. This program promotes literary exploration while enhancing students' cultural awareness and communication skills. These success stories exemplify the transformative power of global collaboration in higher education. They underscore the significance of embracing digital tools and platforms to facilitate cross-cultural learning and prepare students for a globally interconnected world. By exploring such initiatives, educators and institutions can gain valuable insights into the possibilities and benefits of global collaboration in education.

This chapter delves into the significance of global collaboration in higher education, highlighting its profound impact on students, educators, and institutions, and its ongoing exploration for future developments.

## KNOWLEDGE SHARING IN THE DIGITAL AGE

This chapter explores the evolution of knowledge sharing in the digital age, highlighting its impact on education. It uses Machine Learning and online communities to explore its evolution and highlights the power of knowledge sharing in enhancing learning outcomes(Dwivedi et al., 2022).

### The Evolution of Knowledge Sharing in Education

Knowledge sharing has a rich history in education, evolving from traditional classroom interactions, textbooks, and libraries to encompass a digital ecosystem. In the digital age, knowledge sharing extends beyond the boundaries of physical classrooms, enabling learners to access, create, and disseminate knowledge globally. The shift towards open educational resources (OER), online platforms, and collaborative learning has democratized knowledge sharing, empowering learners to take an active role in their education(Scholten et al., 2019).

### Leveraging Machine Learning for Knowledge Sharing

Machine Learning (ML) is a transformative tool in the realm of knowledge sharing. It enhances the accessibility and effectiveness of educational resources by(Ali & Abdel-Haq, 2021):

- **Content Personalization**: ML algorithms analyze learners' preferences and behaviors to recommend tailored content. This personalization ensures that learners receive materials that align with their interests and learning styles.
- **Adaptive Learning**: ML-driven adaptive learning platforms dynamically adjust content difficulty based on a student's progress, ensuring optimal challenge levels and mastery of concepts.
- **Content Creation**: ML can assist in content creation, generating quizzes, assessments, and even textbooks tailored to specific educational needs.
- **Natural Language Processing (NLP)**: NLP technologies in ML enable advanced text analysis, facilitating the creation of intelligent search engines and automated content summarization.

## Building Online Communities and Knowledge Repositories

Online communities and knowledge repositories have become crucial in education, facilitating collaboration, resource sharing, and continuous learning. These platforms, like GitHub and edX, provide dynamic hubs for educators, students, and experts to engage in discussions, disseminate knowledge, and collaborate on projects(Zhang et al., 2019). The development and maintenance of online education spaces require careful attention to user engagement, resource sharing, and project management (Figure 3).

**Purposeful Design:** Define the specific goals and objectives of your online community or knowledge repository. What is the primary purpose? Is it for resource sharing, collaborative projects, or professional networking? Having a clear vision will guide your efforts. Create user-friendly interfaces that cater to the needs of your target audience, whether it's students, educators, or researchers. Intuitive navigation, robust search features, and responsive design are essential elements.

**Content Curation and Contribution:** Curate and organize educational resources, research findings, articles, and multimedia content. Ensure that the materials are relevant, up-to-date, and aligned with the educational objectives. Foster a culture of contribution where users are encouraged to share their expertise, insights, and resources. Provide tools and guidelines for users to contribute effectively.

**Collaboration Tools:** Implement discussion forums or message boards where users can engage in meaningful discussions, ask questions, and seek help. Create separate threads or categories for different topics to facilitate focused discussions. Enable users to collaborate on projects, assignments, or research initiatives. Provide tools for collaborative document editing, project management, and communication within the platform.

*Figure 3. Building online communities and knowledge repositories*

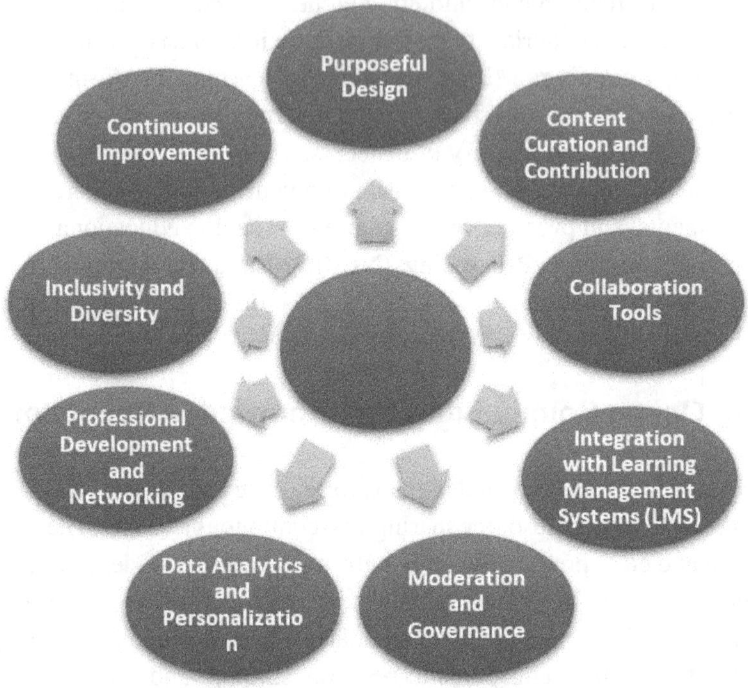


**Integration with Learning Management Systems (LMS):** If your online community or repository is intended for educational institutions, ensure seamless integration with their existing Learning Management Systems (LMS). This allows for a unified learning experience for students and educators.

**Moderation and Governance:** Develop clear moderation policies to maintain a respectful and productive online environment. Specify guidelines for acceptable behavior, content quality, and conflict resolution. Consider establishing a governance structure that includes administrators, moderators, and community leaders responsible for overseeing the community and enforcing policies.

**Data Analytics and Personalization:** Implement analytics tools to gather data on user interactions, content popularity, and engagement. Use these insights to refine the platform, identify user needs, and improve content recommendations. Leverage Machine Learning and AI algorithms to provide personalized content recommendations based on users' preferences and behaviors, enhancing the user experience.

**Professional Development and Networking:** Offer opportunities for professional development, such as webinars, workshops, and online courses, within the community. Encourage educators and professionals to enhance their skills. Incorporate features that facilitate networking and collaboration among users. Allow users to create profiles, connect with peers, and join groups or communities of interest.

**Inclusivity and Diversity:** Ensure that your online community or knowledge repository is designed to be inclusive, accessible, and user-friendly for individuals with diverse backgrounds, abilities, and learning preferences. Promote cultural sensitivity and respect for diverse perspectives within the community. Encourage users to engage in cross-cultural exchanges and discussions.

**Continuous Improvement:** Establish channels for users to provide feedback and suggestions for improvement. Actively listen to user input and iteratively enhance the platform based on their needs. Keep the platform updated with new features, content, and improvements to maintain user engagement and relevance(Boopathi et al., 2023; Boopathi & Davim, 2023b, 2023a).

The creation and maintenance of online communities and knowledge repositories in education necessitate meticulous planning, user-centered design, and continuous dedication, which can significantly enhance the educational experience for all stakeholders.

## Impact of Knowledge Sharing on Learning Outcomes

Knowledge sharing significantly enhances learning outcomes by promoting critical thinking, problem-solving skills, and community, beyond mere information acquisition(Zhang et al., 2019; Janssen & Van der Voort, 2020; Ali & Abdel-Haq, 2021).

- **Enhanced Engagement**: Interactive knowledge sharing platforms promote active learning, increasing engagement and motivation among students.
- **Diverse Perspectives**: Knowledge sharing exposes learners to diverse viewpoints, fostering a deeper understanding of complex issues and promoting empathy.
- **Collaborative Learning**: Collaborative projects and discussions encourage teamwork, communication skills, and the co-creation of knowledge.
- **Lifelong Learning**: The availability of knowledge sharing platforms empowers individuals to pursue lifelong learning, adapt to changing industries, and acquire new skills throughout their careers.
- **Global Reach**: Online knowledge sharing transcends geographical boundaries, allowing learners to connect with experts and peers worldwide, broadening their horizons.

The chapter delves into the evolution of knowledge sharing in education, its integration with Machine Learning, the rise of online communities, and its transformative impact on learning outcomes, empowering learners and fostering a continuous learning culture.

## INTEGRATING ADAPTIVE LEARNING, GLOBAL COLLABORATION, AND KNOWLEDGE SHARING

This chapter delves into the integration of Adaptive Learning, Global Collaboration, and Knowledge Sharing in higher education, presenting practical examples and theoretical foundations for educators and institutions worldwide (Ali & Abdel-Haq, 2021; Scholten et al., 2019). Adaptive Learning, Global Collaboration, and Knowledge Sharing are three educational pillars that offer a comprehensive, personalized approach to modern education, fostering diverse perspectives and information flow (Figure 4).

- **Personalized, Collaborative Learning**: Adaptive Learning platforms leverage Machine Learning to adapt content to individual learners. Global Collaboration introduces a multicultural dimension to this personalization, allowing students to engage in collaborative projects with peers from around the world.
- **Global Knowledge Exchange**: The integration of Global Collaboration and Knowledge Sharing fosters the exchange of ideas, best practices, and solutions on a global scale. Students can participate in cross-cultural discussions, share resources, and contribute to a collective pool of knowledge.
- **Data-Driven Insights**: Adaptive Learning generates a wealth of data on student performance. When combined with Knowledge Sharing, educators can gain insights into the effectiveness of teaching strategies and the impact of global collaboration on learning outcomes. This data-driven approach informs continuous improvement in education.

### Implementation Methods

Adaptive Learning, Global Collaboration, and Knowledge Sharing are transformative approaches in education that enhance learning experiences and prepare students for a globally connected world, necessitating strategic planning and the integration of various methods and technologies.

*Figure 4. Implementation methods for integrating adaptive learning, global collaboration, and knowledge sharing*

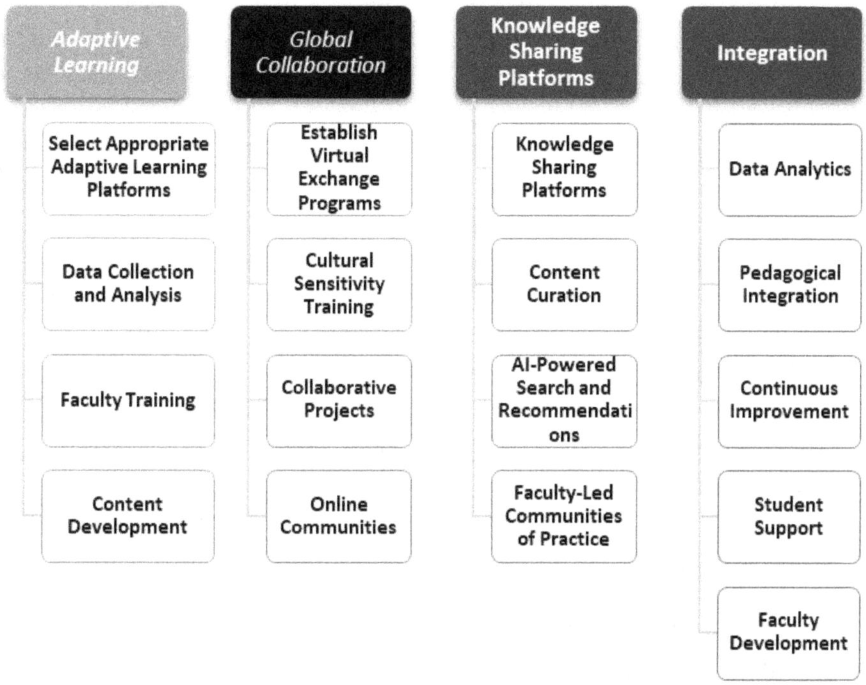


Adaptive Learning:

- **Select Appropriate Adaptive Learning Platforms**: Choose or develop Adaptive Learning platforms that align with the educational objectives and resources of your institution. Ensure that these platforms are capable of personalized content delivery, continuous assessment, and data analytics.
- **Data Collection and Analysis**: Implement robust data collection mechanisms to gather information on students' learning behaviors and performance. Analyze this data to identify areas of improvement and personalize learning pathways.
- **Faculty Training**: Provide training to educators on how to effectively use Adaptive Learning platforms. Help them understand the benefits and how to interpret the data generated by these systems to tailor their teaching strategies.
- **Content Development**: Develop or curate adaptive learning content that aligns with the curriculum and learning objectives. Content should be modular and flexible to accommodate personalized pathways.

Global Collaboration:

- **Establish Virtual Exchange Programs**: Design and implement virtual exchange programs that allow students to collaborate with peers from different parts of the world. Use video conferencing tools, project management software, and online collaboration platforms to facilitate global interactions.
- **Cultural Sensitivity Training**: Prepare students for cross-cultural collaboration by offering cultural sensitivity training. This can help students navigate cultural differences effectively.
- **Collaborative Projects**: Design collaborative projects that require students from diverse backgrounds to work together on real-world challenges. Encourage the exchange of diverse perspectives and ideas.
- **Online Communities**: Create online communities or discussion forums where students and educators can engage in cross-cultural dialogues, share insights, and collaborate on projects. These communities can be integrated into the learning management system.

Knowledge Sharing:

- **Knowledge Sharing Platforms**: Implement knowledge sharing platforms that allow students and educators to share resources, research findings, and insights. These platforms can include wikis, forums, or institutional repositories.
- **Content Curation**: Encourage students and educators to curate and share relevant resources, articles, and multimedia content. Implement content tagging and categorization to facilitate easy discovery.
- **AI-Powered Search and Recommendations**: Use AI-powered search engines and recommendation systems to help users discover relevant content more efficiently. These systems can analyze user behavior and preferences to provide personalized recommendations.
- **Faculty-Led Communities of Practice**: Promote the formation of faculty-led communities of practice where educators can collaborate, share best practices, and develop innovative teaching strategies. These communities can serve as hubs for knowledge sharing.

Converging Adaptive Learning, Global Collaboration, and Knowledge Sharing:

- **Integrated Learning Ecosystem**: Create an integrated learning ecosystem that combines Adaptive Learning platforms, virtual exchange programs, and knowledge sharing platforms. Ensure that these systems can communicate and share data seamlessly.

- **Data Analytics**: Implement robust data analytics tools that can process data from all three components. Analyze this data to gain insights into the effectiveness of personalized learning, global collaboration, and knowledge sharing initiatives.
- **Pedagogical Integration**: Train educators to design pedagogically sound learning experiences that leverage the convergence of these components. Encourage them to incorporate global collaboration and knowledge sharing into the adaptive curriculum.
- **Continuous Improvement**: Continuously assess the impact of the convergence on learning outcomes, student engagement, and global competence. Use the data-driven insights to refine and enhance the implementation.
- **Ethical Considerations**: Ensure that privacy and ethical considerations are embedded into the implementation. Establish clear policies on data privacy, algorithmic fairness, and inclusivity.
- **Student Support**: Provide comprehensive support to students, including cultural sensitivity training, digital literacy skills, and access to technical resources. Ensure that students can navigate and benefit from the converged educational experience.
- **Faculty Development**: Offer ongoing professional development opportunities for educators to stay updated on emerging technologies and pedagogical practices related to the convergence.

The integration of Adaptive Learning, Global Collaboration, and Knowledge Sharing is a multifaceted process that can revolutionize education by personalizing learning experiences, promoting global competence, and facilitating collaborative knowledge creation through a holistic approach involving technology, pedagogy, and ethical practices.

## Case Studies of Integrated Approaches

### Case Study One: The Global Learning Community

One university created a Global Learning Community that integrated Adaptive Learning technology, virtual exchange programs, and an online knowledge sharing platform. Students from diverse backgrounds engaged in collaborative projects using personalized content. The results showed significant improvements in learning outcomes, intercultural competence, and a strong sense of community among students(Janssen & Van der Voort, 2020).

### Case Study Two: AI-Enhanced Knowledge Sharing

Another institution harnessed Machine Learning to enhance its knowledge sharing platform. The platform used NLP to analyze and categorize shared resources, making it easier for educators and students to discover relevant materials. This integration of Adaptive Learning and Knowledge Sharing led to a more efficient and personalized knowledge ecosystem.

### Case Study Three: Global Research Consortium

A consortium of universities across continents formed a global research consortium. Adaptive Learning platforms were used to customize research methodologies and data analysis techniques for students in different regions. This collaboration resulted in groundbreaking research and empowered students to participate in international research projects(Scholten et al., 2019).

## Data-Driven Insights and Pedagogical Enhancement

Adaptive Learning platforms gather comprehensive data on student interactions, performance, and preferences, enabling educators to make informed decisions through global collaboration and knowledge sharing, thereby enhancing educational convergence.

- **Curriculum Design**: Tailoring curriculum to meet the specific needs and interests of students, drawing on insights from global perspectives.
- **Intervention Strategies**: Identifying struggling students early and providing targeted support, whether through personalized resources or peer collaboration.
- **Pedagogical Innovation**: Continuously refining teaching methods and materials based on real-world data and global contributions.

**The Path Forward:** Harnessing the Power of Adaptive Learning, Global Collaboration, and Knowledge Sharing in Education

Adaptive Learning, Global Collaboration, and Knowledge Sharing can transform higher education by requiring innovation, data stewardship, and preparing students for a knowledge-driven world. Educators, institutions, and policymakers must embrace this transformative force to enrich education and empower future generations (Ali & Abdel-Haq, 2021).

## CHALLENGES AND ETHICAL CONSIDERATIONS

This chapter explores the challenges and ethical considerations in implementing Adaptive Learning, Global Collaboration, and Knowledge Sharing in education, focusing on privacy and data security concerns, bias and fairness in Machine Learning, technological barriers, and the need for equity and inclusivity in the pursuit of transformative education(Agrawal et al., 2023; Durairaj et al., 2023).

### Privacy and Data Security

In the digital education era, safeguarding sensitive data on students' learning behaviors and technology interactions is a critical responsibility, despite challenges such as data collection and privacy concerns(Kavitha et al., 2023; Rahamathunnisa et al., 2023; Srinivas et al., 2023).

- **Data Breaches**: Educational institutions must protect against data breaches that could expose students' personal information, academic records, and even sensitive health data.
- **Informed Consent**: Balancing data collection with informed consent is a challenge. Students and educators must be fully aware of how their data will be used, and institutions must ensure transparency in data practices.
- **Third-Party Services**: Many educational institutions rely on third-party platforms and tools for Adaptive Learning, Global Collaboration, and Knowledge Sharing. Ensuring that these providers uphold robust data security standards is crucial.
- **Data Retention**: Institutions must establish clear policies on data retention, ensuring that data is not kept indefinitely and is disposed of securely when no longer needed.

### Bias and Fairness in Machine Learning

Machine Learning algorithms, including Adaptive Learning, are crucial in education, but they also face bias, making ensuring fairness in educational technology a pressing challenge(Boopathi & Kanike, 2023; Ramudu et al., 2023; Syamala et al., 2023).

- **Algorithmic Bias**: Machine Learning algorithms can inadvertently perpetuate bias present in training data. This bias can manifest in various ways, including favoring certain learning styles, cultures, or demographics.
- **Fairness and Equity**: Ensuring that educational technology is fair and equitable is paramount. Institutions must actively work to identify and

mitigate bias in algorithms to provide an inclusive learning environment for all students.

- **Accountability**: Determining accountability for algorithmic bias can be challenging, as it may involve multiple stakeholders, including software developers, educators, and institutions.

## Addressing Technological Barriers

The increasing importance of technology in education necessitates the urgent need to overcome technological barriers to guarantee equal access and participation.

- **Digital Divide**: The digital divide continues to be a significant challenge, with students from underserved communities lacking access to necessary devices and internet connectivity.
- **Digital Literacy**: Not all students possess the digital literacy skills required to effectively navigate online learning environments. Institutions must provide support and resources to bridge this gap(Boopathi, 2022; Reddy et al., 2023; Venkateswaran, Vidhya, Naik, et al., 2023).
- **Infrastructure**: Educational institutions must invest in robust technological infrastructure to support the demands of Adaptive Learning, Global Collaboration, and Knowledge Sharing.

## Ensuring Equity and Inclusivity

The adoption of technology in education should not exacerbate existing disparities but rather mitigate them, adhering to the principles of equity and inclusivity.

- **Inclusive Design**: Educational technology should be designed with inclusivity in mind, ensuring that it accommodates diverse learning styles, abilities, and backgrounds.
- **Accessibility**: Ensuring that all digital resources and platforms are accessible to individuals with disabilities is a legal and ethical imperative.
- **Socioeconomic Equity**: Institutions should explore ways to provide access to necessary technology and resources for students who may face economic hardships.
- **Cultural Sensitivity**: Global Collaboration initiatives should be culturally sensitive, recognizing and respecting diverse cultural norms and practices.

Educational institutions must address ethical challenges by implementing robust data protection measures, ongoing algorithm evaluation, strategic technology investments, and fostering an inclusive learning environment. They must also safeguard privacy, promote fairness, overcome technological barriers, and embrace technology's transformative potential in education.

## Future Trends and Innovations

The chapter explores the evolving education landscape, emphasizing Artificial Intelligence's role, adaptive curriculum design, and global collaboration, emphasizing the need for anticipating future trends and innovations (Ramudu et al., 2023; Syamala et al., 2023; Zekrifa et al., 2023).

## Emerging Technologies in Education

Emerging technologies are poised to significantly transform the future of education.

- **Extended Reality (XR)**: Augmented Reality (AR) and Virtual Reality (VR) have the potential to create immersive learning environments, transporting students to historical events, distant places, or complex scientific concepts.
- **Blockchain**: Blockchain technology can enhance credentialing and verification, allowing for secure and transparent record-keeping of academic achievements(Kumar et al., 2023; Mohanty et al., 2023).
- **Internet of Things (IoT)**: IoT devices can facilitate personalized learning by collecting data on students' interactions with their environment and adapting accordingly(Hema et al., 2023; Hussain & Srimathy, 2023; Reddy et al., 2023).
- **5G Connectivity**: The rollout of 5G networks will enable faster and more reliable internet access, fostering seamless online learning experiences(Agrawal et al., 2024; Venkateswaran, Vidhya, Ayyannan, et al., 2023).
- **Quantum Computing**: In the long term, quantum computing could revolutionize data analysis, potentially advancing fields like personalized learning and AI.

## The Role of Artificial Intelligence

Artificial Intelligence is expected to significantly influence the future of education(Hussain & Srimathy, 2023; Ingle et al., 2023; Venkateswaran, Kumar, et al., 2023).

- **Personalized Learning**: AI algorithms will continue to refine the personalization of learning experiences, adapting content, pace, and assessment methods to individual students.
- **Intelligent Tutors**: AI-powered intelligent tutoring systems will provide students with on-demand support, helping them navigate complex subjects and offering instant feedback.
- **Data-Driven Insights**: AI will analyze vast amounts of data to identify trends, predict student performance, and inform pedagogical strategies.
- **Automated Administrative Tasks**: AI can handle administrative tasks, such as grading, scheduling, and enrollment management, allowing educators to focus on teaching.

## Pedagogical Shifts and Adaptive Curriculum

The future of education is expected to undergo significant pedagogical changes.

- **Adaptive Curriculum**: Curriculum design will become more adaptive, with content and assessments tailored to individual learning trajectories.
- **Project-Based Learning**: Project-based learning will gain prominence, encouraging students to apply knowledge in real-world contexts.
- **Interdisciplinary Approaches**: Education will increasingly emphasize interdisciplinary learning to prepare students for complex, dynamic careers.
- **Soft Skills**: There will be a growing emphasis on teaching soft skills, such as critical thinking, creativity, and adaptability, alongside technical knowledge.

## The Continued Evolution of Global Collaboration

The global collaboration in education is expected to adapt to technological advancements and evolving needs.

- **Virtual Exchange**: Virtual exchange programs will become more sophisticated, offering students highly immersive and collaborative cross-cultural experiences.
- **Global Research Networks**: Collaborative research networks will expand, enabling students and researchers to collaborate on global challenges.
- **Language Learning**: AI-powered language learning platforms will facilitate cross-border language exchange, enhancing linguistic and cultural competencies.

- **Global Challenges**: Educational institutions will increasingly collaborate on global challenges, such as climate change and public health crises, preparing students for an interconnected world.

The future of education is characterized by the integration of emerging technologies, Artificial Intelligence, adaptability, soft skills, and global collaboration. Institutions that embrace these trends will equip students with the necessary knowledge and skills for a rapidly changing world.

## SUMMARY

The evolution of education has been influenced by Adaptive Learning, Global Collaboration, and Knowledge Sharing, facilitated by Artificial Intelligence. This transformation has led to significant impacts, challenges, and ethical considerations. It aims to personalize learning, promote intercultural competence, and empower learners to engage with a globalized world. AI automates administrative tasks, allowing educators to focus on pedagogical innovation.

The transformation of education faces challenges like privacy and data security, potential bias in Machine Learning, technological barriers, and equity. Emerging technologies like Extended Reality, Blockchain, and IoT will revolutionize learning experiences, with AI playing a central role in personalized learning. Pedagogical shifts towards adaptive curriculum design, project-based learning, interdisciplinary approaches, and soft skills cultivation will prepare students for dynamic careers. The future of education will be innovative, adaptable, and inclusive, with virtual exchange programs, global research networks, and collaborative initiatives. Students will be empowered to participate in their learning journey, and educational institutions, policymakers, and stakeholders must remain committed to equity, ethics, and excellence.

## ABBREVIATIONS

LMS: Learning Management System
AI: Artificial Intelligence
IoT: Internet of Things
XR: Extended Reality
AR: Augmented Reality
VR: Virtual Reality
NLP: Natural Language Processing

GitHub: A platform for software development and version control
edX: An online educational platform
Coursera: An online learning platform
UX: User Experience
ML: Machine Learning
STEM: Science, Technology, Engineering, and Mathematics
5G: Fifth Generation of Wireless Technology
LGBTQ+: Lesbian, Gay, Bisexual, Transgender, Queer (or Questioning), and others

## REFERENCES

Agrawal, A. V., Pitchai, R., Senthamaraikannan, C., Balaji, N. A., Sajithra, S., & Boopathi, S. (2023). Digital Education System During the COVID-19 Pandemic. In Using Assistive Technology for Inclusive Learning in K-12 Classrooms (pp. 104–126). IGI Global. doi:10.4018/978-1-6684-6424-3.ch005

Agrawal, A. V., Shashibhushan, G., Pradeep, S., Padhi, S. N., Sugumar, D., & Boopathi, S. (2024). Synergizing Artificial Intelligence, 5G, and Cloud Computing for Efficient Energy Conversion Using Agricultural Waste. In Practice, Progress, and Proficiency in Sustainability (pp. 475–497). IGI Global. doi:10.4018/979-8-3693-1186-8.ch026

Alam, A. (2022). Employing adaptive learning and intelligent tutoring robots for virtual classrooms and smart campuses: Reforming education in the age of artificial intelligence. In *Advanced Computing and Intelligent Technologies* [Springer.]. *Proceedings of ICACIT*, *2022*, 395–406.

Ali, M., & Abdel-Haq, M. K. (2021). Bibliographical analysis of artificial intelligence learning in Higher Education: Is the role of the human educator and educated a thing of the past? In *Fostering Communication and Learning With Underutilized Technologies in Higher Education* (pp. 36–52). IGI Global. doi:10.4018/978-1-7998-4846-2.ch003

Boopathi, S. (2022). An extensive review on sustainable developments of dry and near-dry electrical discharge machining processes. *ASME: Journal of Manufacturing Science and Engineering*, *144*(5), 050801–1.

Boopathi, S., & Davim, J. P. (2023a). Applications of Nanoparticles in Various Manufacturing Processes. In *Sustainable Utilization of Nanoparticles and Nanofluids in Engineering Applications* (pp. 1–31). IGI Global. doi:10.4018/978-1-6684-9135-5.ch001

Boopathi, S., & Davim, J. P. (2023b). *Sustainable Utilization of Nanoparticles and Nanofluids in Engineering Applications*. IGI Global. doi:10.4018/978-1-6684-9135-5

Boopathi, S., & Kanike, U. K. (2023). Applications of Artificial Intelligent and Machine Learning Techniques in Image Processing. In *Handbook of Research on Thrust Technologies' Effect on Image Processing* (pp. 151–173). IGI Global. doi:10.4018/978-1-6684-8618-4.ch010

Boopathi, S., Umareddy, M., & Elangovan, M. (2023). Applications of Nano-Cutting Fluids in Advanced Machining Processes. In *Sustainable Utilization of Nanoparticles and Nanofluids in Engineering Applications* (pp. 211–234). IGI Global. doi:10.4018/978-1-6684-9135-5.ch009

Durairaj, M., Jayakumar, S., Karpagavalli, V., Maheswari, B. U., Boopathi, S., & ... (2023). Utilization of Digital Tools in the Indian Higher Education System During Health Crises. In *Multidisciplinary Approaches to Organizational Governance During Health Crises* (pp. 1–21). IGI Global. doi:10.4018/978-1-7998-9213-7.ch001

Dwivedi, Y. K., Hughes, D. L., Coombs, C., Constantiou, I., Duan, Y., Edwards, J. S., Gupta, B., Lal, B., Misra, S., Prashant, P., Raman, R., Rana, N. P., Sharma, S. K., & Upadhyay, N. (2020). Impact of COVID-19 pandemic on information management research and practice: Transforming education, work and life. *International Journal of Information Management*, *55*, 102211. doi:10.1016/j.ijinfomgt.2020.102211

Dwivedi, Y. K., Hughes, L., Kar, A. K., Baabdullah, A. M., Grover, P., Abbas, R., Andreini, D., Abumoghli, I., Barlette, Y., Bunker, D., Chandra Kruse, L., Constantiou, I., Davison, R. M., De', R., Dubey, R., Fenby-Taylor, H., Gupta, B., He, W., Kodama, M., & Wade, M. (2022). Climate change and COP26: Are digital technologies and information management part of the problem or the solution? An editorial reflection and call to action. *International Journal of Information Management*, *63*, 102456. doi:10.1016/j.ijinfomgt.2021.102456

He, C., Annavaram, M., & Avestimehr, S. (2020). Group knowledge transfer: Federated learning of large cnns at the edge. *Advances in Neural Information Processing Systems*, *33*, 14068–14080.

Hema, N., Krishnamoorthy, N., Chavan, S. M., Kumar, N., Sabarimuthu, M., & Boopathi, S. (2023). A Study on an Internet of Things (IoT)-Enabled Smart Solar Grid System. In *Handbook of Research on Deep Learning Techniques for Cloud-Based Industrial IoT* (pp. 290–308). IGI Global. doi:10.4018/978-1-6684-8098-4.ch017

Hussain, Z., & Srimathy, G. (2023). *IoT and AI Integration for Enhanced Efficiency and Sustainability*.

Ingle, R. B., Senthil, T. S., Swathi, S., Muralidharan, N., Mahendran, G., & Boopathi, S. (2023). Sustainability and Optimization of Green and Lean Manufacturing Processes Using Machine Learning Techniques. IGI Global. doi:10.4018/978-1-6684-8238-4.ch012

Janssen, M., & Van der Voort, H. (2020). Agile and adaptive governance in crisis response: Lessons from the COVID-19 pandemic. *International Journal of Information Management, 55*, 102180. doi:10.1016/j.ijinfomgt.2020.102180 PMID:32836637

Kavitha, C. R., Varalatchoumy, M., Mithuna, H. R., Bharathi, K., Geethalakshmi, N. M., & Boopathi, S. (2023). Energy Monitoring and Control in the Smart Grid: Integrated Intelligent IoT and ANFIS. In M. Arshad (Ed.), (pp. 290–316). Advances in Bioinformatics and Biomedical Engineering. IGI Global. doi:10.4018/978-1-6684-6577-6.ch014

Kumar, P. R., Meenakshi, S., Shalini, S., Devi, S. R., & Boopathi, S. (2023). Soil Quality Prediction in Context Learning Approaches Using Deep Learning and Blockchain for Smart Agriculture. In R. Kumar, A. B. Abdul Hamid, & N. I. Binti Ya'akub (Eds.), (pp. 1–26). Advances in Computational Intelligence and Robotics. IGI Global. doi:10.4018/978-1-6684-9151-5.ch001

Liu, Q., Tong, S., Liu, C., Zhao, H., Chen, E., Ma, H., & Wang, S. (2019). Exploiting cognitive structure for adaptive learning. *Proceedings of the 25th ACM SIGKDD International Conference on Knowledge Discovery & Data Mining*, (pp. 627–635). ACM. 10.1145/3292500.3330922

Mohanty, A., Venkateswaran, N., Ranjit, P., Tripathi, M. A., & Boopathi, S. (2023). Innovative Strategy for Profitable Automobile Industries: Working Capital Management. In Handbook of Research on Designing Sustainable Supply Chains to Achieve a Circular Economy (pp. 412–428). IGI Global.

Pan, S. L., Cui, M., & Qian, J. (2020). Information resource orchestration during the COVID-19 pandemic: A study of community lockdowns in China. *International Journal of Information Management, 54*, 102143. doi:10.1016/j.ijinfomgt.2020.102143 PMID:32394997

Rahamathunnisa, U., Subhashini, P., Aancy, H. M., Meenakshi, S., Boopathi, S., & ... (2023). Solutions for Software Requirement Risks Using Artificial Intelligence Techniques. In *Handbook of Research on Data Science and Cybersecurity Innovations in Industry 4.0 Technologies* (pp. 45–64). IGI Global.

Ramudu, K., Mohan, V. M., Jyothirmai, D., Prasad, D., Agrawal, R., & Boopathi, S. (2023). Machine Learning and Artificial Intelligence in Disease Prediction: Applications, Challenges, Limitations, Case Studies, and Future Directions. In Contemporary Applications of Data Fusion for Advanced Healthcare Informatics (pp. 297–318). IGI Global.

Reddy, M. A., Reddy, B. M., Mukund, C., Venneti, K., Preethi, D., & Boopathi, S. (2023). Social Health Protection During the COVID-Pandemic Using IoT. In *The COVID-19 Pandemic and the Digitalization of Diplomacy* (pp. 204–235). IGI Global. doi:10.4018/978-1-7998-8394-4.ch009

Scholten, K., Sharkey Scott, P., & Fynes, B. (2019). Building routines for non-routine events: Supply chain resilience learning mechanisms and their antecedents. *Supply Chain Management, 24*(3), 430–442. doi:10.1108/SCM-05-2018-0186

Srinivas, B., Maguluri, L. P., Naidu, K. V., Reddy, L. C. S., Deivakani, M., & Boopathi, S. (2023). Architecture and Framework for Interfacing Cloud-Enabled Robots. In *Handbook of Research on Data Science and Cybersecurity Innovations in Industry 4.0 Technologies* (pp. 542–560). IGI Global. doi:10.4018/978-1-6684-8145-5.ch027

Syamala, M., Komala, C., Pramila, P., Dash, S., Meenakshi, S., & Boopathi, S. (2023). Machine Learning-Integrated IoT-Based Smart Home Energy Management System. In *Handbook of Research on Deep Learning Techniques for Cloud-Based Industrial IoT* (pp. 219–235). IGI Global. doi:10.4018/978-1-6684-8098-4.ch013

Venkateswaran, N., Kumar, S. S., Diwakar, G., Gnanasangeetha, D., & Boopathi, S. (2023). Synthetic Biology for Waste Water to Energy Conversion: IoT and AI Approaches. In M. Arshad (Ed.), (pp. 360–384). Advances in Bioinformatics and Biomedical Engineering. IGI Global. doi:10.4018/978-1-6684-6577-6.ch017

Venkateswaran, N., Vidhya, K., Ayyannan, M., Chavan, S. M., Sekar, K., & Boopathi, S. (2023). A Study on Smart Energy Management Framework Using Cloud Computing. In 5G, Artificial Intelligence, and Next Generation Internet of Things: Digital Innovation for Green and Sustainable Economies (pp. 189–212). IGI Global. doi:10.4018/978-1-6684-8634-4.ch009

Venkateswaran, N., Vidhya, R., Naik, D. A., Raj, T. M., Munjal, N., & Boopathi, S. (2023). Study on Sentence and Question Formation Using Deep Learning Techniques. In *Digital Natives as a Disruptive Force in Asian Businesses and Societies* (pp. 252–273). IGI Global. doi:10.4018/978-1-6684-6782-4.ch015

Vuong, Q.-H., Le, T.-T., La, V.-P., Nguyen, H. T. T., Ho, M.-T., Van Khuc, Q., & Nguyen, M.-H. (2022). Covid-19 vaccines production and societal immunization under the serendipity-mindsponge-3D knowledge management theory and conceptual framework. *Humanities & Social Sciences Communications*, *9*(1), 22. doi:10.105741599-022-01034-6

Zekrifa, D. M. S., Kulkarni, M., Bhagyalakshmi, A., Devireddy, N., Gupta, S., & Boopathi, S. (2023). Integrating Machine Learning and AI for Improved Hydrological Modeling and Water Resource Management. In *Artificial Intelligence Applications in Water Treatment and Water Resource Management* (pp. 46–70). IGI Global. doi:10.4018/978-1-6684-6791-6.ch003

Zhang, Y., Li, W., Zhang, L., Ning, X., Sun, L., & Lu, Y. (2019). Adaptive learning Gabor filter for finger-vein recognition. *IEEE Access : Practical Innovations, Open Solutions*, *7*, 159821–159830. doi:10.1109/ACCESS.2019.2950698

# Chapter 11
# Exploring the Challenges and Applications of Generative AI on Engineering Education in Mexico

**Jesús Heriberto Orduño-Osuna**
https://orcid.org/0009-0004-4850-7481
*Universidad Politécnica de Baja California, Mexico*

**Elia Ivette Cota-Rivera**
*Universidad Politécnica de Baja California, Mexico*

**María E. Raygoza-L.**
*Universidad Autonoma de Baja California, Mexico*

**Roxana Jimenez-Sanchez**
https://orcid.org/0009-0002-0061-7206
*Universidad Politécnica de Baja California, Mexico*

**Guillermo M. Limón-Molina**
https://orcid.org/0000-0002-5445-8928
*Universidad Politécnica de Baja California, Mexico*

**Miguel Bravo-Zanoguera**
*Universidad Politécnica de Baja California, Mexico*

**Abelardo Mercado-Herrera**
*Universidad Politécnica de Baja California, Mexico*

**Fabian N. Murrieta Rico**
https://orcid.org/0000-0001-9829-3013
*Universidad Politécnica de Baja California, Mexico*

DOI: 10.4018/979-8-3693-0487-7.ch011

## ABSTRACT

*This chapter explores the potential and challenges of implementing generative artificial intelligence (AI) in engineering education in Mexico. It highlights the relevance of developing broader competences like critical thinking, collaboration, and cognitive processing to prepare students for the Fourth Industrial Revolution. Integrating generative AI and STEM education can foster collaboration, communication, critical thinking, and creativity. Challenges include the gap between demand and supply of skilled engineers and the need to enhance education quality. The chapter proposes personalized learning experiences, enhanced student engagement, workload reduction for teachers, and the use of large language models and simulated environments as key applications of generative AI. Leveraging learning analytics and generative AI can tailor content to students' needs. Ethical considerations and human oversight are crucial for successful integration.*


## INTRODUCTION

With the arrival of 21st-century skills and the Next Generation Science Standards, the relevance of broader learning skills and competences such as cognitive processing, critical thinking, and cooperation has been stressed. As a result, contemporary educational environments and philosophies aim to include authentic practices that entail solving serious challenges together. To prosper in this changing environment, both students and teachers demand better and more customized support.

To generate students with 21st-century abilities, the interaction between STEM education and Industry 4.0 should be strengthened. Collaboration, communication, critical thinking, and creativity are examples of these abilities. It is commonly understood that the technologies of the Fourth Industrial Revolution will have deep and rapid effects on society and the earth. While the exact impact is unknown, higher education must respond immediately. The potential for these technologies to create either catastrophic environmental devastation or great societal consequences is upon us. Furthermore, there is rising concern about the potential loss of control over networks of strong AI agents with increasing autonomy, especially in the financial and urban infrastructure sectors (Roll et al., 2016).

The technique known as generative artificial intelligence (AI) has gained significant traction and has the capacity to transform numerous academic fields. This technology provides new chances to improve teaching and learning approaches in the field of education. Engineering education in Mexico, in particular, can benefit substantially from the use of generative AI.

A prominent use-case for computer-based learning in the past featured a student working with a computer in a math or science classroom to answer step-by-step tasks focusing on domain-specific knowledge, with a human tutor serving as the gold standard. This use-case, however, fails to take into account current changes in educational practices and theories (Pillay et al., 2018).

Furthermore, the function of the teacher in the classroom has changed. From being the wise man on stage, they have become the sidekick. Teachers are no longer expected to know everything and simply pass it on to students. Instead, their job is to help students search, find, and integrate information, allowing them to become independent and collaborative thinkers.

Technology and education are connected in a complex and varied area with political, economic, social, and pedagogical repercussions. In today's "technological societies," the use of technology to facilitate teaching and learning tasks has become critical. Understanding and incorporating technology into the curriculum has also developed as a critical part of education. As a result, the creation of technology and programs that firmly support instructional activities has become critical, supporting overall advancements in the educational landscape (Zhao et al., 2019).

The use of computer applications to supplement teaching and learning has become widespread in many nations, notably in the global North. These apps facilitate a wide range of educational activities, from subject-specific learning, such as "Logic" or "Algorithms", to engaging in practice exercises and drills in subjects such as "Arithmetic" or "Geometry." They are also used in formative and summative evaluations. This ubiquity extends across all educational levels, from primary to postgraduate, and includes a wide range of courses that go beyond the sciences and into the realms of the arts and humanities. Notably, many of these programs can be defined as artificial intelligence in essence, sticking to the broad definition of serving as instrumental tools that aid students in their understanding of various topics, such as mathematics (Sanchez-Pi et al., 2021).

AI-powered systems have enormous potential to change the educational landscape. These applications can provide personalized and adaptive learning experiences by employing AI algorithms and methodologies, adapting educational content and exercises to the specific needs of individual learners. AI-based tools, with their ability to analyze large volumes of data and discover trends, provide insights into student performance and fast feedback, increasing the learning process.

It is common knowledge that studying science in Latin America is difficult. But it doesn't seem like we should keep waiting for a top-down fix for this issue.

Latin America's embrace of the AI scenario remains cautious, with about less than 0.5% of private investment dedicated to AI development. The number of Latin American AI businesses was around 260 in 2018, but it has more than doubled in only two years, with 490 expected by 2020. Brazil presently leads Latin American countries in this situation, with 42% of all AI startups, followed by Mexico and Chile, with that in mind we should be aware that to improve and accelerate the positive impact of AI in Latin America, it is vital to first identify and understand than there are difficulties and barriers that may be impeding progress (Sanchez-Pi et al., 2021).

## 1. Brief History of Generative Artificial Intelligence

Artificial intelligence has been working with generative models for a long time, since the 1950s with the development of Hidden Markov Models (HMM) and Gaussian Mixture Models (GMM). Through these types of models, new data with multiple applications can be created, including generating data that other learning systems can use for their training, without pre-existing data. However, the performance of generative models didn't significantly improve until the development of deep learning.

During the early stages of deep generative models, there was limited overlap among different domains. In the field of Natural Language Processing (NLP), a commonly used method to generate sentences was learning word distribution using N-gram language modeling and then searching for the best sequence (Jones, 1994). Long sentences, however, were not amenable to this strategy. Recurrent neural networks (RNNs) were utilized to simulate relatively lengthy dependencies in order to overcome this problem (Li et al., 2021). This was followed by the development of Long Short-Term Memory (LSTM) and Gated Recurrent Unit (GRU)(Hochreiter et al., 1997). Compared to N-gram language models, these techniques can attend to approximately 200 tokens in a sample, which is a major improvement.

At the same time, in computer vision (CV), Texture synthesis and texture mapping were two strategies employed by traditional picture production algorithms prior to the development of deep learning-based approaches (Jovanovic et al., 2002). In 2014, Generative Adversarial Networks (GANs) were introduced for the first time, achieving impressive results in various applications.

Different pathways have been taken by generative models as they have advanced in different fields, but all of them converged with the transformative architecture first applied in NLP and then extended to CV, thereby becoming the dominant backbone for many generative models (Cao et al., 2023).

It can be said that the GAI (General Artificial Intelligence) began in 2014; however, it was not until the end of 2022 that general models of text-image technologies, such as MidJourney, Dall-E 2, Image, and Stability AI, were released for use. Soon after, the technology that shocked the world emerged—Chat-GPT, implemented by OpenAI in November 2022, using a version of GPT-3 as a preliminary part of the investigation.

AI systems that use language and are built on deep learning models are known as large language models, or LLMs. This algorithm uses information gleaned from enormous databases to recognize, summarize, translate, predict, and create text and other types of material. Large language models are among the most successful applications of transformer models. They can be applied to a large scenario in which communication of different types is needed (Su & Yang, 2023).

Typical examples of LLMs include OpenAI's GPT-4, Google's PaLM, and Meta's LLaMA(Fauzi et al., 2023).

Generative adversarial networks (GAN): Is a machine learning system aiming to generate its own creations based on real example data (Liang et al., 2022), to do so two neural networks (the generator network and the discriminator network), which communicate each other are used.

# CURRENT STATE OF ENGINEERING EDUCATION IN MEXICO

## Challenges and Limitations of Engineering Education in Mexico

Engineering education plays a vital role in the technological and socio-economic development of a country. In the case of Mexico, the training of engineers has been a key factor in driving innovation, industrial competitiveness, and progress in various fields. However, there are still a lot of issues and challenges with engineering education in Mexico that need to be resolved. In this section, some of the most relevant challenges facing engineering education in Mexico and possible solutions that could be implemented to overcome them will be discussed.

### Challenge One: The Gap Between Demand and Supply of Skilled Engineers

One of the main challenges facing engineering education in Mexico is the gap between the demand and supply of skilled engineers. Although the country has experienced a significant increase in the number of educational institutions and engineering programs, there is a disparity between the number of graduates and the needs of the job market. This translates into difficulties in filling employment vacancies in critical engineering areas and limits the potential for growth and development in the sector.

When Mexico initiated the process of opening its economy to the global market, attracting major manufacturing companies to establish their presence in the country, there arose a growing demand for skilled engineers. This development had a positive impact on employment opportunities and wages for various levels of skilled labor. Consequently, professions in engineering emerged as the most apparent choice, given their higher level of technological expertise, leading to increased earning potential (Lopez-Acevedo, 2002).

The importance of hiring engineers to ensure competitiveness and business quality is emphasized as new technologies are integrated into the industrial sector. This implies that the demand for skilled engineers may increase as Industry 4.0 advances. Furthermore, the need to transform human capital through skills and competency development to face the challenges of Industry 4.0 is a reality. This suggests that having trained and updated professionals in Industry 4.0 technologies and processes is crucial (Garduño Palomino, 2021).

One of the contributing factors to the shortage of skilled engineers in Mexico is the gap between the demand for specialized engineering skills and the availability of qualified professionals. While there is a growing number of engineering graduates in the country, there is often a mismatch between the skills acquired through traditional academic programs and the skills demanded by the evolving industry. The curriculum in some educational institutions may not always align with the latest technological advancements or industry needs, creating a skills gap (Garduño Palomino, 2021).

Another part of this challenge is the so-called brain drain phenomenon, where qualified engineers and professionals move to other nations in search of better chances and greater incomes, is another aspect of this problem. As Mexico loses key human capital that could support its industrial expansion, this talent exodus worsens the country's engineer deficit (Jiménez et al., 2010).

With that in mind a multifaceted strategy is needed to address Mexico's scarcity of qualified engineers. To ensure graduates to have the abilities required by the sector, Mexico needs to raise the standard and relevance of engineering education and training programs, by adding real-world experiences, internships, and industry-driven initiatives into the curriculum.

Additionally, initiatives should concentrate on luring and keeping engineering talent in the nation. This can be accomplished through fostering an environment that encourages professional development, providing competitive pay, allowing chances for career promotion, and building a strong ecosystem that looks for innovation and entrepreneurship.

By addressing the shortage of qualified engineers, Mexico can improve its technological and industrial skills, promote innovation, and maintain its competitiveness on the international market. in an effort to advance, sustainable development in the nation and promote economic progress, it will be necessary to have a large and well-equipped pool of professional engineers.

## Challenge Two: The Quality of Engineering Education

Another important challenge lies in the quality of engineering education. While there are notable institutions offering high-quality programs, there is considerable variation in educational standards among different institutions and programs. Common issues include outdated curricula, lack of practical training and experiences, as well as ineffective industry collaboration. These factors negatively affect student preparedness and their ability to tackle real-world engineering challenges.

It is widely recognized that there is a pressing need to enhance educational and technological training to ensure individuals are adequately prepared to navigate the transformative impact of Industry 4.0. The skills and knowledge required for success in this new era extend beyond traditional educational boundaries. With modern technologies like artificial intelligence, robotics, and the Internet of Things, industries are becoming more networked and integrated, making it important to emphasize interdisciplinary methods, adaptability, and creativity(Garduño Palomino, 2021).

Within this context, engineers play a pivotal role as key contributors to the industrial ecosystem. A robust educational and technological foundation is essential to equip engineers with the necessary skills to address the multifaceted challenges and leverage the opportunities presented by Industry 4.0. By focusing on developing a workforce with strong technical expertise, analytical thinking, problem-solving abilities, and a forward-thinking mindset, the education system can nurture engineers who are well-prepared to lead the way in designing, implementing, and optimizing advanced technologies.

Furthermore, the implementation of appropriate policies is crucial to ensure that engineers and other professionals have access to meaningful employment opportunities and ongoing professional development in the Industry 4.0 era. Policymakers must foster an environment that encourages lifelong learning, continuous skill upgrading, and the acquisition of emerging technological competencies. This can be achieved through partnerships between academia, industry, and government, promoting collaborative initiatives, internship programs, and research collaborations that bridge the gap between theory and practice.

## Challenge Three: Declining Interest in Engineering Careers Among Current Generations

In recent years, the field of engineering has been facing a significant challenge, the decline in the interest among current generations towards pursuing careers in this field. This trend has raised concerns about the future pipeline of engineering professionals in various industries, including technology, infrastructure, and innovation. Understanding the factors contributing to this decline and finding strategies to rekindle interest in engineering careers is decisive to ensure a stable supply of skilled engineers for the nation's development and competitiveness.

Family context plays a significant role in shaping interest in engineering careers. Previous studies have identified several characteristics, including motivational practices, scientific knowledge, and cultural resources of parents, that influence their children's interest in engineering. Encouraging parents to actively engage in mathematics-related activities has been found to foster interest in engineering disciplines. Moreover, the scientific knowledge of parents, whether possessed by one or both parents, has a positive impact on their children's academic abilities and aspirations for achievement. Additionally, various studies suggest that the cultural resources within families help cultivate their children's interest in science more broadly (Jiménez et al., 2010).

Some major factor in the declining interest of younger generations in engineering careers are:

Misconception: Many students have a misguided perception of what a career in engineering entails. They may view it as boring, difficult, or lacking creativity. It is important to educate young individuals about the various engineering disciplines and demonstrate how they can be exciting and rewarding.

Lack of vocational guidance: Insufficient information and proper vocational guidance can lead students to not seriously consider engineering careers. It is essential to provide them with clear information about professional opportunities, growth potential, and specialized areas within engineering.

Competition with other careers: Nowadays, students have a wide range of career options available to them. Fields such as social sciences, or entrepreneurship may seem more appealing compared to engineering. It is crucial to highlight the advantages and professional development opportunities offered by a career in engineering.

Perceived lack of relevance: Young individuals often seek careers that align with their interests and are socially relevant. If they do not see how engineering can contribute to social change, sustainability, or addressing significant problems, they may lack motivation to pursue this career path. It is important to highlight the status of engineering in society and its impact on tackling global challenges.

Gender stereotypes: Engineering is still perceived, in many cases, as a male-dominated field. This perception can discourage women and other underrepresented groups from considering engineering as a viable option. Addressing gender stereotypes and promoting diversity in engineering are crucial to attract a broader range of students.

The field of engineering thrives in a familial and social context that places great emphasis on the value of science for driving a nation's scientific, technological, and economic progress. Moreover, it highlights the personal advantages associated with pursuing an engineering education, such as easy entry into the job market, higher financial rewards compared to other disciplines, and social recognition. It is the joint responsibility of governments, higher education institutions, and employers to underscore the significance of engineering studies, their profitability, and the positive impact that engineers have on their communities (Jiménez Izquierdo et al., 2010).

Promoting the benefits and opportunities offered by engineering careers is essential for successfully overcoming these obstacles. This can be done through improving the standard of engineering education through current curricula, opportunities for hands-on learning, and incorporating modern technologies like artificial intelligence. By offering interactive learning environments, individualized instruction, and virtual simulations, AI has the potential to improve engineering education. These tools empower students to gain hands-on experience and tackle complex engineering problems in a digital environment.

## Traditional Tools and Approaches Used in Engineering Education

In today's rapidly evolving world, engineering education faces the challenge of preparing students for a dynamic landscape. In Mexico, the significance of adopting a flexible, interdisciplinary, and transdisciplinary approach in engineering education has been recognized. This approach aims to develop professionals with a modern perspective on their field and professional commitment, capable of tackling complex problems and contributing to sustainable development and societal well-being. This essay explores the key aspects of this approach and its relevance in engineering education. The flexible approach in engineering education is essential for equipping students with the capability to adapt to emerging changes and challenges in the field. Engineers must be capable of adjusting to new technologies, methodologies, and industry demands. This involves fostering a culture of continuous learning and constant updating of knowledge and skills. Additionally, students should be equipped with the necessary tools to address complex problems, nurturing creativity and innovation in the pursuit of solutions (Asociación Nacional de Facultades y Escuelas de Ingeniería, 2015).

The interdisciplinary approach represents another vital pillar in engineering education. Problems and projects in this field often require a multidisciplinary perspective. Integrating different disciplines and knowledge areas allows for comprehensive and innovative problem-solving from diverse standpoints. Therefore, it is crucial for students to acquire skills for collaborating in interdisciplinary teams, working alongside professionals from various fields to address complex challenges holistically.

In addition to the interdisciplinary approach, the transdisciplinary focus emphasizes a broad and global understanding of engineering activities. Engineers must consider not only the technical facets of their labor but also the social, economic, ethical, and environmental impacts it entails. Educating engineers who are aware of their societal responsibilities is fundamental to promoting sustainable development and the well-being of the communities they serve. This involves nurturing ethical awareness and an understanding of the significance of sustainability in project design and development.

It is significant to note that this approach does not seek to entirely replace traditional tools and approaches used in engineering education, traditional tools in engineering education in Mexico encompass a range of resources and methodologies that have been widely employed over the years. These tools have played a significant role in imparting knowledge and fostering foundational skills among engineering students. Textbooks, lectures, and laboratories remain valuable educational resources. However, they need to be adapted and updated to meet current and future demands.

While these traditional tools have proven their effectiveness, it is essential to acknowledge that they need to evolve and adapt to meet the changing demands of the engineering field. In today's fast-paced technological landscape, it is crucial to update textbooks with the latest advancements and trends. Additionally, lectures can be enhanced with interactive elements, such as multimedia presentations, simulations, and case studies, to promote active learning and student engagement.

Moreover, lectures can be enhanced by integrating interactive AI-powered elements. For instance, incorporating AI chatbots or virtual assistants can provide students with personalized learning experiences, allowing them to ask questions, seek clarification, and access additional resources in real-time. AI algorithms can also be used to analyze students' performance and provide personalized feedback, enabling tailored learning paths based on individual strengths and weaknesses.

Learning experiences may be made more engaging and dynamic by embracing cutting-edge technology like generative AI and remote learning platforms, augmented reality, and virtual reality. Virtual reality environments can enable students to visualize and interact with complex engineering systems, while augmented reality can overlay virtual information onto physical objects, facilitating hands-on learning. Remote learning platforms powered by AI can provide access to global engineering resources, facilitate remote collaboration, and enable continuous learning beyond traditional classroom settings.

## APPLICATIONS OF GENERATIVE AI IN ENGINEERING EDUCATION

Generative Artificial Intelligence has emerged as an influential and promising technology in various areas, and engineering education is no exception. The ability of machines to generate original content such as models, designs, and solutions has opened up new possibilities in the educational landscape.

In this chapter, five main topics on applications of generative AI on engineering education are discussed, some of them are major applications that can involve many other minor applications that could also be discussed in their own. The topics that are discussed are "Personalized Learning Experience", "Enhanced Student Engagement", "Workload reduction for Teachers" and "Large Language Models and Simulated Environments".

## Personalized Learning Experience

One of the significant advantages of AI in engineering education is its ability to provide personalized learning experiences. AI algorithms can analyze student data, including performance, strengths, and weaknesses, to tailor individualized learning paths. By adapting the curriculum to meet the unique needs of each student, AI enables self-paced learning and targeted support in areas requiring improvement (Gudoniene et al., 2023).

AI algorithms have the ability to analyze vast quantities of student data, including performance metrics, learning styles, and individual strengths and weaknesses. This data-driven approach allows for the customization of learning paths to meet the specific needs of each student.

Through AI-driven platforms, students can access personalized content, exercises, and assessments that align with their current skill level and learning objectives. For example, if an engineering student demonstrates proficiency in a particular topic, the AI system can automatically adjust the curriculum to introduce more advanced concepts or offer supplementary materials to deepen their understanding (van der Vorst et al., 2019).

Moreover, AI technology can adapt to diverse learning styles and predilections. Some students may learn best through visual demonstrations, while others may favor text-based explanations or interactive simulations. AI-powered systems can identify and cater to these preferences, providing content and resources that align with each student's preferred learning modality (Qadir, 2023).

In addition to content customization, AI can provide real-time feedback and assessment. As students engage with learning materials and complete assignments, AI algorithms can examine their responses and provide immediate feedback on their performance. This timely feedback allows students to identify and rectify errors, reinforcing their understanding of engineering concepts and promoting self-directed learning (Vandewaetere et al., 2014).

AI can make it possible to move from periodic evaluation to continuous assessment in the field of assessment. Standardized tests are sometimes criticized for being only snapshots and a poor indicator of a student's understanding, with AI, a student's knowledge level can be continuously assessed without the need for recurring exams (van der Vorst et al., 2019).

## Enhanced Student Engagement

AI technology can significantly enhance student engagement by leveraging machine learning algorithms to automate grading processes. Automated essay scoring enables quick and accurate evaluation, providing timely feedback to students. This immediate feedback loop helps students identify and correct their mistakes promptly, leading to improved comprehension and mastery of engineering concepts.

One of the most effective ways to develop and improve student learning is through feedback, which is a crucial component of effective and efficient teaching and learning. Learning is made possible by feedback since it provides data that may be used to boost and better performance. Peer feedback and 'feed-forward' techniques are two assessment practice changes that have been shown to strengthen the formative use of feedback and can result in significant and substantial learning gains (Parkin et al., 2012).

This is definitely an area where Generative AI can make a difference in engineering education. AI systems can analyze students' work, such as programming code or designs, and provide instant feedback and recommendations for improvement. This automated feedback saves time for both teachers and students, fosters continuous improvement, and allows for more personalized tracking of student progress.

With all these things in mind the implementation of hybrid models which use Generative AI and traditional tools could create a more enhanced environment for the student, in mixed-mode classes, hybrid education uses synchronous and asynchronous schooling methods for online and offline students. In order to plan and complete students' education, hybrid learning depends on student autonomy, this adapts instruction to the wants and needs of the students. Students get essential technological and digital literacy skills—hybrid education reaps the rewards of technology. Systems for online learning offer films, interactive modules, simulations, and assessments. With the use of these tools, students can self-study and review. Active learning and student interaction are promoted through hybrid education. Online discussion forums, quizzes, and polls foster a sense of community among students (Almusaed et al., 2023).

## Workload Reduction for Teachers

The implementation of AI in engineering education can alleviate the workload of teachers, enabling them to focus on higher-value tasks. Automated grading systems can efficiently evaluate assignments, quizzes, and exams, reducing time spent on repetitive grading tasks. Teachers can then dedicate their energy to developing innovative course materials, conducting in-depth discussions, and providing personalized guidance to students.

In some institutions around the world there is a perception than teacher's workload has been increased with different tasks besides lectures and grading, some of them are more in an administrative environment with tasks assigned by the school administrators to full time professor, with this in mind AI powered applications could therefore not only be an advantage to students, it can also increase the efficiency of teachers (van der Vorst et al., 2019).

Therefore, recent AI educational research has placed a greater emphasis on teachers than on other educational institution stakeholders. Every learning environment, whether it be in-person or online, revolves on the teachers. Participatory design approaches make sure that teachers, together with parents and students, are a key component of the design of new AI educational technologies. Educationists have long struggled with the problem of reducing teachers' workloads because they want to improve the effectiveness of instruction in the classroom by giving instructors greater control over their workload and allowing them to devote more time to teaching rather than other activities (Chaudhry et al., 2022).

The authors expect AI to be able to automate and/or facilitate tasks related to proofreading which includes emphasizing strengths and weaknesses in an essay, after which the teacher primarily assesses these points, and course material composition, this with the help of automatic content classification.

Numbering some of the possible tasks that could be automated with the help of generative AI we get the following main applications:

1. Automated Grading: AI algorithms could automate the grading process for assignments, quizzes, exams, and other assessments. With machine learning algorithms, AI systems may evaluate student responses and provide accurate and consistent grading, and also generate an instant high quality feedback. This automation significantly reduces the time and effort spent by teachers on manual grading, enabling them to focus on other important aspects of teaching.
2. Data Analysis and Insights: AI may analyze large amounts of data collected from student performance, engagement, and progress. By processing this data, AI systems can generate insights and analytics that help teachers identify patterns, trends, and areas where students may be struggling. This information equips teachers with valuable knowledge about their students' needs, letting them to adjust their teaching strategies consequently.
3. Content Recommendation and Curation: AI-powered platforms can suggest relevant and appropriate learning resources, including textbooks, articles,

videos, and interactive materials. By leveraging AI algorithms, teachers can benefit from automated content curation, saving time and effort in searching for suitable resources. This streamlines the process of creating lesson plans and ensures that students have access to high-quality and up-to-date educational materials.

4. Communication and Notifications: Generative AI can assist in communication tasks by generating automated messages, reminders, and notifications for students and parents. For example, AI algorithms can send automated emails or notifications to remind students of upcoming deadlines, important events, or changes in schedules. By automating these communication tasks, teachers can save time and ensure effective communication without the need for manual interventions.

By leveraging generative AI in administrative tasks, teachers can free up valuable time and energy to focus on instructional planning, curriculum development, and providing personalized support to students. This means they can dedicate more effort to designing engaging lessons, creating innovative learning experiences, and tailoring their teaching to meet the individual needs of students.

It is important to note that while generative AI can automate administrative tasks, human oversight and intervention are still necessary. Teachers play a crucial role in verifying and reviewing the outputs of generative AI systems to ensure accuracy and address any errors or discrepancies. Moreover, the use of generative AI should be implemented with proper safeguards and considerations for data privacy and security.

Generative AI technologies undoubtedly possess the capacity to collaborate seamlessly with educators, leading to a plethora of advantages. In the qualitative data analysis that follows, both teachers and students have shared their perspectives on how these technologies can enhance their educational experiences and elevate student learning. By harnessing the capabilities of generative AI, educators can optimize their teaching strategies, ultimately enhancing the overall learning process and outcomes for their students. The harmonious interaction between teachers and generative AI technologies serves as a powerful testament to the transformative impact of AI integration in the field of education. (Chan et al., 2023).

It is central to note that while AI can reduce the workload for teachers, it should be seen as a tool to enhance and augment their capabilities rather than substitute them. Human interaction, mentorship, and guidance are vital components of the teaching process that AI cannot fully replicate. Therefore, finding the right balance among AI-driven automation and human interaction is decisive for maintaining a holistic and effective educational experience.

## Looking Into the Future

The continuous development of AI models, such as GPT-4, will introduce more sophisticated capabilities in code generation and language understanding. Engineering educators and researchers should stay abreast of these advancements and assess the suitability of existing tools for evolving educational practices. By embracing new tools and integrating them thoughtfully into engineering education, we can prepare students to navigate the ever-evolving landscape of programming and equip them with the skills needed to excel in their engineering careers.

It's important to notice Generative AI is no only useful on computer science, or software related engineering careers, it can also be used on other majors, such as Civil Engineering, teaching civil engineering presents unique challenges due to its comprehensive and practical nature. AI technology offers solutions by providing students with a deeper understanding of the subject matter. Simulations powered by AI algorithms allow students to experience the construction of civil engineering projects virtually. This interactive approach enables them to visualize and engage with complex engineering concepts, enhancing comprehension and application. Algorithms possess the capability to analyze vast amounts of data related to civil engineering projects. This functionality aids both students and teachers in identifying patterns and making informed decisions. In the domain of geological survey work, teachers can create independent analysis models based on specific structural characteristics and design requirements. AI technology facilitates the integration of mechanical equipment data, enabling teachers to reinforce students' understanding and cognition of geological environment survey results (Xie et al., 2020).

Generative AI offers numerous applications and benefits in engineering education. From generating models and designs to problem-solving, virtual simulation, automated feedback, and personalized learning, Generative AI is transforming how engineering students acquire knowledge and develop skills. However, it is important to remember that ethics and transparency should guide the implementation of Generative AI in education, and students should continue to develop a solid understanding of fundamentals before relying solely on Generative AI. With a responsible approach, Generative AI has the potential to drive success and excellence in engineering education in the future.

*Figure 1. Applications of generative AI in engineering education*
*Source: Own Elaboration*

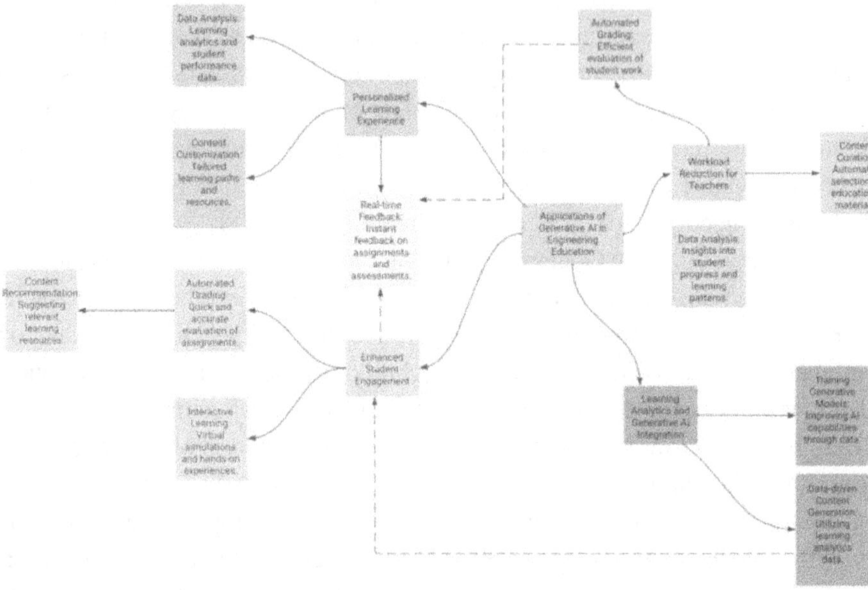


## OPTIMIZING ENGINEERING EDUCATION IN MEXICO: EXPLORING THE POTENTIAL OF GENERATIVE ARTIFICIAL INTELLIGENCE

In this section of the chapter, the authors will explore the application of generative artificial intelligence (AI) to engineering education in the context of Mexico. Specifically, we will focus on the combination of learning analytics and generative AI, two distinct fields within artificial intelligence that can be effectively used together to explore new applications in the learning process of engineering subjects.

Learning analytics refers to the systematic collection, analysis, and visualization of data related to learning and teaching. It entails gathering data from diverse sources such as education management systems, online platforms, and mobile devices with the goal of gaining a comprehensive understanding of students' behavioral patterns, evaluating their performance, and providing personalized feedback.

The relationship between learning analytics and generative AI lies in leveraging the data collected through learning analytics to inform and enhance the generation of creative content by generative AI systems. By scrutinizing learning data, including student responses, interaction patterns, and areas of difficulty, it becomes possible to identify individual students' needs and preferences.

This data can be effectively harnessed by generative AI systems to personalize the creation of educational content, tailoring it to the specific requirements of each student. For instance, a generative AI system can utilize a student's performance data in a particular engineering subject to generate additional exercises and explanations that address the identified problem areas derived from the data collected through learning analytics.

Moreover, learning analytics data can serve as valuable training material for generative AI models, thereby enhancing their capability to generate relevant and effective content. With an increasing amount of data being collected and analyzed, the generative model gains a deeper understanding of learning patterns and student needs, resulting in more accurate and personalized content generation.

By leveraging the combined power of learning analytics and generative AI, engineering educators in Mexico can unlock new possibilities for enhancing the learning experience. The integration of these two fields has the potential to revolutionize the way engineering subjects are taught, providing personalized content and adaptive learning experiences tailored to the unique needs of students.

With that in mind we could explore the use of the information gathered from learning analytics and use it in different kinds of generative AI, we would like to explore the usage of ChatGPT for that instance (Saetra, 2023).

As an educator in the field of electronics or computing, leveraging the capabilities of ChatGPT can greatly enhance the learning experience for students. By considering the students' baseline knowledge, the educational metrics employed by the professor, and the requirements of the academic curriculum (Denny et al., 2023), ChatGPT can generate comprehensive and tailored content to effectively teach topics such as Basic Electronics.

One fundamental concept in this subject is Ohm's law, which governs the behavior of electric circuits. With ChatGPT's assistance, the professor can create immersive content that delves into Ohm's law and its practical applications in various circuit configurations. By formulating an appropriate prompt for ChatGPT, the professor can obtain detailed explanations, examples, and exercises related to Ohm's law.

In addition to theoretical knowledge, practical exercises are crucial for reinforcing understanding. ChatGPT can aid in crafting assignments that involve calculations for series and parallel circuits. These assignments can challenge students to apply Ohm's law to calculate voltages, currents, and resistances in different circuit configurations. Through this interactive approach, students can develop a solid grasp of circuit analysis techniques.

Moreover, ChatGPT's capabilities extend beyond the realm of Basic Electronics. The professor can utilize this powerful tool to explore advanced topics like Control Theory. By formulating suitable prompts, ChatGPT can generate assignments and exercises that introduce students to the fundamentals of Control Theory. This content can cover concepts such as feedback loops, transfer functions, stability analysis, and controller design.

With the help of ChatGPT, the professor can provide a diverse range of assignments, ensuring that students receive a comprehensive understanding of Control Theory. Furthermore, by leveraging ChatGPT's ability to adapt to individual students' needs, the professor can customize the assignments to cater to students' unique learning styles and pace.

Overall, by integrating ChatGPT into the teaching process, the professor can enhance the educational experience for students in electronics. Through tailored prompts, ChatGPT can generate content that aligns with the students' baseline knowledge, educational metrics, and academic requirements. Whether it involves introducing Basic Electronics or exploring advanced topics like Control Theory, ChatGPT can generate immersive content, assignments, and exercises that foster deep understanding and engagement among students.

To give an example about this, we're going to show of examples of the use of ChatGPT to explore and learn the basics from Control Theory. In the figure 2 it shows a basic prompt to create assignments related to the basics of Control Theory and some answers it gives us back.

*Figure 2. Chatting with ChatGPT to create assignments for the subject of control theory, part one*

Could you create some assignments to learn the basics from Control Theory?

Certainly! Here are a few assignments to help you learn the basics of Control Theory:

Assignment 1: Introduction to Control Systems

1. Define the following terms:
   a. Control system
   b. Open-loop control
   c. Closed-loop control
   d. Setpoint
   e. Error
   f. Actuator
   g. Sensor
2. Explain the differences between open-loop and closed-loop control systems. Provide examples of each.
3. Draw a block diagram representation of a simple closed-loop control system. Label the components and explain the function of each.

In the first assignment, an introductory exercise is presented to facilitate the understanding of fundamental concepts in the field of control theory. The assignment requires students to provide concise definitions of essential terms, such as control system, open loop, closed loop, and setpoints. Additionally, students are expected to articulate the distinctions between open-loop and closed-loop control systems. Finally, the assignment prompts students to construct a block diagram representation, serving as a visual depiction of the control system under consideration. This initial assignment serves as a foundational step in acquiring the necessary knowledge and skills to comprehend control theory.

However, the aforementioned assignment is not an isolated instance. Rather, it signifies the initial stage of a progressive series of assignments designed to incrementally challenge students as they acquire new concepts and develop additional proficiencies. As depicted in Figure 3, a subsequent assignment is presented, which introduces a heightened level of complexity. This assignment assumes that students have acquired the requisite knowledge and skills to employ a proportional-integral-derivative (PID) control system.

*Figure 3. Chatting with ChatGPT to create assignments for the subject of control theory, part two*

Assignment 3: PID Control

1. Define the terms Proportional (P), Integral (I), and Derivative (D) in the context of PID control.
2. Derive the transfer function of a PID controller. Explain the effect of each term on the control system's response.
3. Discuss the advantages and disadvantages of using a PID controller compared to a proportional controller.
4. Design a PID controller for a given control system using appropriate tuning methods (e.g., Ziegler-Nichols, trial and error).

We can expand our exploration by investigating practical implementations, taking into account the equipment limitations that engineering students may encounter in certain countries, such as Mexico. In Figure 4 presented below, we observe a prompt that requests a practical assignment for the application of PID control, while considering various constraints, including limited equipment availability.

*Figure 4. Chatting with ChatGPT to create assignments for the subject of control theory, part three*

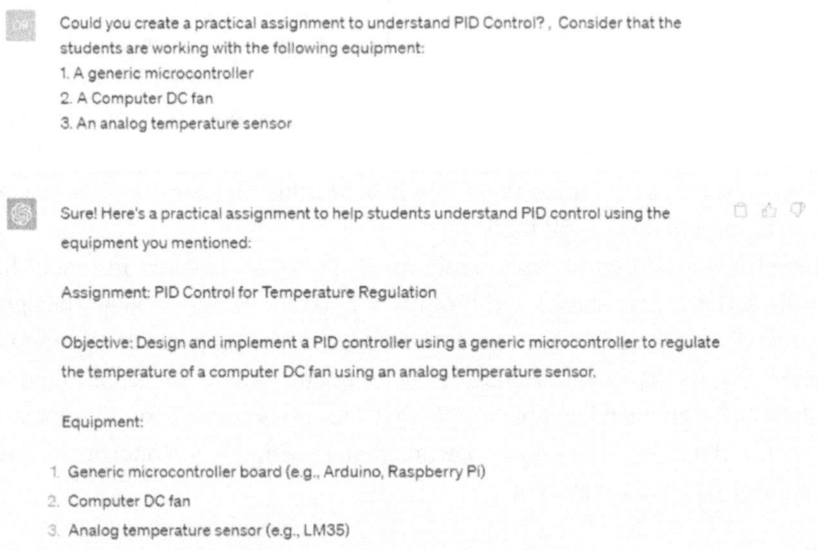

Could you create a practical assignment to understand PID Control? , Consider that the students are working with the following equipment:
1. A generic microcontroller
2. A Computer DC fan
3. An analog temperature sensor

Sure! Here's a practical assignment to help students understand PID control using the equipment you mentioned:

Assignment: PID Control for Temperature Regulation

Objective: Design and implement a PID controller using a generic microcontroller to regulate the temperature of a computer DC fan using an analog temperature sensor.

Equipment:

1. Generic microcontroller board (e.g., Arduino, Raspberry Pi)
2. Computer DC fan
3. Analog temperature sensor (e.g., LM35)

*Figure 5. Chatting with ChatGPT to create assignments for the subject of control theory, part four*

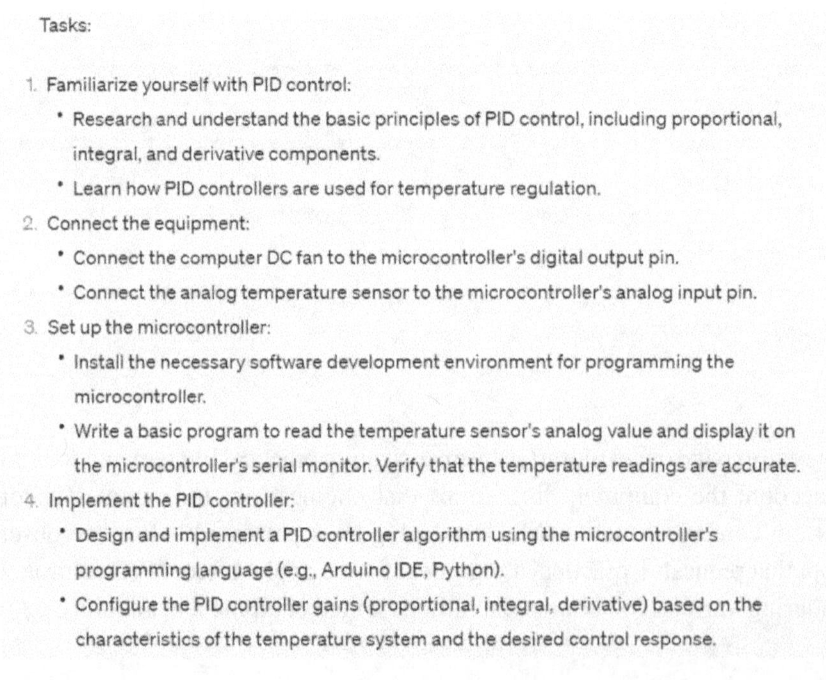

Tasks:

1. Familiarize yourself with PID control:
   - Research and understand the basic principles of PID control, including proportional, integral, and derivative components.
   - Learn how PID controllers are used for temperature regulation.
2. Connect the equipment:
   - Connect the computer DC fan to the microcontroller's digital output pin.
   - Connect the analog temperature sensor to the microcontroller's analog input pin.
3. Set up the microcontroller:
   - Install the necessary software development environment for programming the microcontroller.
   - Write a basic program to read the temperature sensor's analog value and display it on the microcontroller's serial monitor. Verify that the temperature readings are accurate.
4. Implement the PID controller:
   - Design and implement a PID controller algorithm using the microcontroller's programming language (e.g., Arduino IDE, Python).
   - Configure the PID controller gains (proportional, integral, derivative) based on the characteristics of the temperature system and the desired control response.

And it even explains the whole process the student will require to do to realize this practical assignment Figure 5 and Figure 6.

*Figure 6. Chatting with ChatGPT to create assignments for the subject of control theory, part five*

5. Test and tune the PID controller:
   - Run the program and observe how the PID controller regulates the fan speed to maintain the desired temperature setpoint.
   - Experiment with different setpoint values and observe the system response.
   - Tune the PID controller gains to achieve a stable and responsive temperature control system.
6. Document and analyze the results:
   - Record your observations and measurements during the experiments.
   - Analyze the performance of the PID controller by comparing the system's response to changes in setpoint and disturbances.
   - Discuss the advantages and limitations of PID control for temperature regulation.
7. Optional enhancements:
   - Implement additional features to improve the temperature control system, such as anti-windup mechanisms, adaptive control, or autotuning algorithms.
   - Explore ways to visualize and monitor the temperature control system using graphs, charts, or a graphical user interface (GUI).

Considering the aforementioned considerations, the professor could leverage ChatGPT's assistance to generate a wide range of assignments, taking into account the various limitations stemming from the materialistic context of the students. Furthermore, the professor could also utilize learning analytics tools to gather relevant information, enabling them to adjust the difficulty level of the assignments accordingly, thereby enhancing the learning experience for the students.

The integration of learning analytics and generative AI presents a promising opportunity for engineering educators in Mexico to enhance the learning experience for their students. By leveraging the information gathered from learning analytics, educators can tailor assignments and content to address the specific limitations imposed by the students' materialistic context. Additionally, the use of generative AI, such as ChatGPT, can provide personalized and adaptive learning experiences, accommodating the diverse needs of individual students.

The combination of these two fields has the potential to revolutionize engineering education by offering customized content and adaptive learning approaches. By utilizing ChatGPT, educators can generate comprehensive and tailored materials, covering fundamental concepts and practical applications in subjects like electronics and control theory. The use of ChatGPT allows for the making of immersive content, interactive exercises, and progressive assignments that progressively challenge students as they acquire new knowledge and skills.

Furthermore, the integration of learning analytics tools enables educators to gather valuable insights into students' learning progress and adapt the difficulty level of assignments accordingly. This data-driven approach ensures that students receive appropriate and engaging assignments that align with their baseline knowledge and learning goals.

In summary, leveraging the power of learning analytics and generative AI, engineering educators can unlock new possibilities for enhancing the learning experience in Mexico. By addressing limitations, personalizing content, and utilizing adaptive learning approaches, educators can provide students with a tailored and engaging educational journey that promotes deeper understanding and proficiency in engineering subjects.

## CONCLUSION

The convergence of generative artificial intelligence and education has opened up an exciting and promising horizon for the field of engineering education. As we move towards the 21st century, the need to adapt education to 21st-century skills and the scientific standards of the next generation has become more urgent. In this context, generative artificial intelligence arises as a powerful tool that can transform the method we teach and learn, especially in the field of engineering.

The importance of developing cognitive skills, critical thinking, and collaboration has been highlighted with the advent of 21st-century skills and Next Generation Science Standards. Contemporary education strives to include authentic practices that involve collaboratively solving serious challenges. To thrive in this changing environment, both students and educators demand better and more personalized support.

In this context, the convergence of Industry 4.0 and STEM education becomes essential for equipping students with 21st-century skills. These fundamental abilities include teamwork, communication, critical thinking, and creativity. The inception of generative artificial intelligence is an innovative technological development that has the potential to revolutionize several fields, including education. The application of generative artificial intelligence can significantly enhance methods for teaching and learning in the unique background of engineering education in Mexico.

One of the most significant challenges facing engineering education in Mexico is the gap between the demand and supply of skilled engineers. While the country has experienced a significant increase in the number of educational institutions and engineering programs, there remains a disparity between the number of graduates and the needs of the job market. This situation results in difficulties in filling employment vacancies in critical engineering areas and limits the potential for growth and development in the sector.

By enabling the personalization of the learning process for each student and adjusting educational programs to the changing needs of the business, generative artificial intelligence presents a potential answer to this problem. Generative AI may design individualized learning routes, offer real-time feedback, and modify course content to address identified areas of difficulty based on data gathered through learning analytics by looking at student data and interactions in the educational environment.

Additionally, learning analytics data can be a useful source of training data for generative AI models, improving their capacity to produce quality content. The generative model develops a greater understanding of learning patterns and student needs as more data is gathered and evaluated, leading to the creation of more precise and individualized material.

By leveraging the combined power of learning analytics and generative AI, engineering educators in Mexico can unlock new possibilities for enhancing the learning experience. The integration of these two fields has the potential to revolutionize the way engineering subjects are taught, providing personalized content and adaptive learning experiences tailored to the unique needs of students.

With all these advancements in mind, leveraging the capabilities of generative AI, such as ChatGPT, can greatly enhance the learning experience for students in the field of electronics, basic math, material science, physics and many other subjects. By considering students' baseline knowledge, educational metrics, and curriculum requirements, ChatGPT can generate comprehensive and tailored content to effectively teach topics such as Basic Electronics.

In conclusion, generative AI has enormous potential to improve engineering education in Mexico and around the world. Generative artificial intelligence (generative AI) has the potential to dramatically enhance the quality and efficacy of engineering education by personalizing the learning process, increasing student engagement, and reducing the workload for teachers. However, its deployment must be done in an ethical and responsible manner, making sure that generative AI enriches rather than replaces the function of educators.

Privacy and data security must be prioritized, as well as taking care to make sure that generative AI stays focused on assisting teachers and students in their pursuit of knowledge and academic performance. Engineering education may advance toward a more progressive, inclusive, and prosperous future with the careful and responsible use of generative artificial intelligence.

## REFERENCES

Almusaed, A., Almssad, A., Yitmen, I., & Homod, R. Z. (2023). Enhancing Student Engagement: Harnessing "AIED"'s Power in Hybrid Education—A Review Analysis. *Education Sciences*, *13*(7), 632. doi:10.3390/educsci13070632

Cao, Y., Li, S., Liu, Y., Yan, Z., Dai, Y., Yu, P.S., & Sun, L. (2023). *A Comprehensive Survey of AI-Generated Content (AIGC): A History of Generative AI from GAN to ChatGPT*. ArXiv, abs/2303.04226.

Chan, C. K. Y., & Tsi, L. H. (2023). *The AI Revolution in Education: Will AI Replace or Assist Teachers in Higher Education?* arXiv preprint arXiv:2305.01185.

Chaudhry, M. A., & Kazim, E. (2022). Artificial Intelligence in Education (AIEd): A high-level academic and industry note 2021. *AI and Ethics*, *2*(1), 1–9. doi:10.100743681-021-00074-z PMID:34790953

Denny, P., Prather, J., Becker, B. A., Finnie-Ansley, J., Hellas, A., Leinonen, J., & Sarsa, S. (2023). *Computing Education in the Era of Generative AI*. arXiv preprint arXiv:2306.02608.

Fauzi, F., Tuhuteru, L., Sampe, F., Ausat, A. M. A., & Hatta, H. R. (2023). Analysing the role of ChatGPT in improving student productivity in higher education. *Journal of Education*, *5*(4), 14886–14891.

Garduño Palomino, K. Y. (2021). Estado de avance de la industria 4.0 en la maquiladora: efectos en el empleo en Mexicali, México. *PAAKAT: revista de tecnología y sociedad, 11*(21).

Gudoniene, D., Staneviciene, E., Buksnaitis, V., & Daley, N. (2023). The Scenarios of Artificial Intelligence and Wireframes Implementation in Engineering Education. *Sustainability (Basel)*, *15*(8), 6850. doi:10.3390u15086850

Hochreiter, S., & Schmidhuber, J. (1997). Long short-term memory. *Neural Computation*, *9*(8), 1735–1780. doi:10.1162/neco.1997.9.8.1735 PMID:9377276

Jiménez, J., Escalante, J. C., Rodríguez, C., Ramírez, J. M., & Morales-Arroyo, M. A. (2010). ŠMobility or brain drain? The case of Mexican scientists. *Социология науки и технологий, 1*(1), 89-108.

Jiménez Izquierdo, Y., Magaña Medina, D. E., & Valdés Cuervo, A. A. (2019). Interés de estudiantes hacia carreras universitarias en ingeniería. *Educación y Ciencia*, *8*(51), 85–88.

Jones, K. S. (1994). Natural language processing: a historical review. *Current issues in computational linguistics: in honour of Don Walker*, 3-16.

Jovanovic, M., & Campbell, M. (2002). Generative Artificial Intelligence: Trends and Prospects. *Computer*, *55*(10), 107–112. doi:10.1109/MC.2022.3192720

Li, J., Tang, T., Zhao, W. X., & Wen, J. (2021). Pretrained Language Models for Text Generation: A Survey. *International Joint Conference on Artificial Intelligence*. IJCAI. 10.24963/ijcai.2021/612

Liang, P.P., Zadeh, A., & Morency, L. (2022). *Foundations and Recent Trends in Multimodal Machine Learning: Principles, Challenges, and Open Questions*. ArXiv, abs/2209.03430.

Lopez-Acevedo, G. C. (2002). *Technology and Skill Demand in Mexico*.

Parkin, H. J., Hepplestone, S., Holden, G., Irwin, B., & Thorpe, L. (2012). A role for technology in enhancing students' engagement with feedback. *Assessment & Evaluation in Higher Education*, *37*(8), 963–973. doi:10.1080/02602938.2011.59 2934

Pillay, N., Maharaj, B. T., & van Eeden, G. (2018, November). AI in engineering and computer science education in preparation for the 4th industrial revolution: A South African perspective. In *2018 World Engineering Education Forum-Global Engineering Deans Council (WEEF-GEDC)* (pp. 1-5). IEEE.

Qadir, J. (2023). Engineering education in the era of ChatGPT: Promise and pitfalls of generative AI for education. In *2023 IEEE Global Engineering Education Conference (EDUCON)* (pp. 1-9). IEEE. 10.1109/EDUCON54358.2023.10125121

Roll, I., & Wylie, R. (2016). Evolution and revolution in artificial intelligence in education. *International Journal of Artificial Intelligence in Education*, *26*(2), 582–599. doi:10.100740593-016-0110-3

SaetraH. S. (2023). Generative AI: Here to stay, but for good? From https://ssrn.com/abstract=4330244 doi:10.1016/j.techsoc.2023.102372

Sanchez-Pi, N., Martí, L., Garcia, A. C. B., Yates, R. B., Vellasco, M., & Coello, C. A. C. (2021, November). A roadmap for AI in Latin America. In *Side event AI in Latin America of the Global Partnership for AI*. GPAI.

Su, J., & Yang, W. (2023). Unlocking the power of ChatGPT: A framework for applying generative AI in education. *ECNU Review of Education*.

van der Vorst, T., & Jelicic, N. (2019). *Artificial Intelligence in Education: Can AI bring the full potential of personalized learning to education?* EconStor.

Vandewaetere, M., & Clarebout, G. (2014). Advanced technologies for personalized learning, instruction, and performance. Handbook of research on educational communications and technology, (pp. 425-437). Springer. doi:10.1007/978-1-4614-3185-5_34

Xie, M., Meng, F., Zou, J., Feng, W., & Ma, S. (2020, June). Application of artificial intelligence in civil engineering education. []. IOP Publishing.]. *Journal of Physics: Conference Series*, *1575*(1), 012225. doi:10.1088/1742-6596/1575/1/012225

Zhao, Y., & Liu, G. (2019, January). How do teachers face educational changes in artificial intelligence era. In *2018 International Workshop on Education Reform and Social Sciences (ERSS 2018)* (pp. 47-50). Atlantis Press. 10.2991/erss-18.2019.9

## ADDITIONAL READING

Chassignol, M., Khoroshavin, A., Klimova, A., & Bilyatdinova, A. (2018). Artificial Intelligence trends in education: A narrative overview. *Procedia Computer Science*, *136*, 16–24. doi:10.1016/j.procs.2018.08.233

Chen, L., Chen, P., & Lin, Z. (2020). Artificial intelligence in education: A review. *IEEE Access : Practical Innovations, Open Solutions*, *8*, 75264–75278. doi:10.1109/ACCESS.2020.2988510

Dwivedi, Y. K., Kshetri, N., Hughes, L., Slade, E. L., Jeyaraj, A., Kar, A. K., Baabdullah, A. M., Koohang, A., Raghavan, V., Ahuja, M., Albanna, H., Albashrawi, M. A., Al-Busaidi, A. S., Balakrishnan, J., Barlette, Y., Basu, S., Bose, I., Brooks, L., Buhalis, D., & Wright, R. (2023). "So what if ChatGPT wrote it?" Multidisciplinary perspectives on opportunities, challenges and implications of generative conversational AI for research, practice and policy. *International Journal of Information Management*, *71*, 102642. doi:10.1016/j.ijinfomgt.2023.102642

Olga, A., Saini, A., Zapata, G., Searsmith, D., Cope, B., Kalantzis, M., & Kastani, N. P. (2023). *Generative AI: Implications and Applications for Education.* arXiv preprint arXiv:2305.07605.

Pham, D. T., & Pham, P. T. N. (1999). Artificial intelligence in engineering. *International Journal of Machine Tools & Manufacture*, *39*(6), 937–949. doi:10.1016/S0890-6955(98)00076-5

Rugarcia, A., Felder, R., Woods, D., & Stice, J. (2000). The future of engineering education. II: Teaching methods that work. *Chemical Engineering Education*, *34*(1), 26–39.

Simmons, M. K. (1983). *Artificial Intelligence for Engineering Design*. Corporate Research & Development Center, General Electric Company.

van der Zant, T., Kouw, M., & Schomaker, L. (2013). *Generative artificial intelligence*. Springer Berlin Heidelberg.

Van Slyke, C., Johnson, R. D., & Sarabadani, J. (2023). Generative Artificial Intelligence in Information Systems Education: Challenges, Consequences, and Responses. *Communications of the Association for Information Systems*, *53*(1), 14. doi:10.17705/1CAIS.05301

Yang, W. (2022). Artificial Intelligence education for young children: Why, what, and how in curriculum design and implementation. *Computers and Education: Artificial Intelligence*, *3*, 100061. doi:10.1016/j.caeai.2022.100061

## KEY TERMS AND DEFINITIONS

**Artificial Intelligence (AI):** The imitation of human intellect in computer programs that are designed to carry out operations that traditionally call for human intelligence, such as learning, reasoning, problem-solving, and decision-making.

**Generative AI:** A branch of artificial intelligence that focuses on building models that can produce new content, including pictures, videos, texts, or music, that closely resembles data that has been created by humans.

**Industry 4.0:** Industry 4.0 refers to the fourth industrial revolution, characterized by the integration of digital technologies, the Internet of Things (IoT), automation, artificial intelligence, and data exchange in manufacturing processes to create "smart factories" and optimize industrial production.

**Learning Analytics:** Learning analytics involves the collection, analysis, and interpretation of data related to educational activities and environments. It leverages data to gain insights into student learning patterns, performance, and behavior, enabling educators to make data-driven decisions and improve learning outcomes.

**Personalized Learning Experience:** Personalized learning experience is an educational approach that tailors teaching methods, content, and pace to the individual needs, preferences, and abilities of each learner. It aims to enhance engagement and understanding by addressing specific learning styles and interests.

**Simulated Environments:** Simulated environments are virtual or digital settings created to simulate real-world scenarios or circumstances. They provide a secure and controlled environment for users to gain experience without experiencing negative effects in real life, and are frequently utilized for training, experimentation, or research reasons.

**STEM (Science, Technology, Engineering, and Mathematics):** STEM is an acronym that represents the academic disciplines of Science, Technology, Engineering, and Mathematics. It emphasizes the integration of these subjects to promote problem-solving and critical thinking skills.

# Chapter 12
# Innovative Teaching Methodology in Higher Education With Generative AI- Engineering Education in Developing Countries

**Laila Umme**
https://orcid.org/0000-0001-8050-5081
*Institute of Business Management, Karachi, Pakistan*

**Zain Ali Shah**
*Soochow University, China*

**Poshan Yu**
https://orcid.org/0000-0003-1069-3675
*Soochow University, China & European Business Institute, Luxembourg & Australian Studies Centre of Shanghai University, China*

**James Mulli**
*European Business Institute, Luxembourg*

**Muhammad Khurram**
https://orcid.org/0000-0001-6199-6364
*University of Technology and Applied Sciences, Nizwa, Oman*

**Muzammil Ahmed**
*Sir Syed University of Engineering and Technology, Pakistan*

DOI: 10.4018/979-8-3693-0487-7.ch012

## ABSTRACT

*The rapidly evolving landscape of higher education is causing significant changes in the educational system. The needs of the digital world cannot be satisfied by conventional teaching and learning approaches. To improve educational quality, fostering global collaboration and knowledge sharing has become imperative for preparing students for a connected world. Therefore, technological integration in the classroom has become essential. Generative artificial intelligence (AI) has emerged as a powerful tool in this endeavour. In addition to examining the possible advantages and difficulties of incorporating technology in higher education, this study also assesses the extent of technology integration in teaching, referred to as innovative teaching methodologies (ITM). This chapter explores how generative AI can be leveraged to enhance teaching methods.*

## 1. INTRODUCTION

The rapidly evolving landscape of higher education is causing significant changes in the educational system. The needs of the digital world cannot be satisfied by conventional teaching and learning approaches. To improve educational quality, fostering global collaboration and knowledge sharing has become imperative for preparing students for a connected world. Therefore, technological integration in the classroom has become essential. Generative Artificial Intelligence (AI) has emerged as a powerful tool in this endeavour. In addition to examining the possible advantages and difficulties of incorporating technology in higher education, this study also assesses the extent of technology integration in teaching, referred to as Innovative Teaching methodologies (ITM). This chapter explores how generative AI can be leveraged to enhance teaching methods.

### 1.1. What is Generative AI

The term "GenAI" refers to artificial intelligence (AI) apps that are meant to employ a range of machine learning methods to produce new material (text, photos, video, music, artwork, synthetic data, and so on) (Kohnke et al., 2023a). GenAI applications are also known as "generative AI." (Mishra et al., 2023). Even though this content is generated in response to user input, these applications are not explicitly programmed to generate content. Rather, these programs learn and analyze principles and statistical structures from a large dataset and generate new content with similar structures(Ray, 2023). These outputs may be in the same medium as the user's input or in a different medium, such as text-to-text, text-to-image, or image-to-video.

## 1.2. Gen AI in Education

Although, arguably, there are infinite applications for general artificial intelligence, one area in which it could be especially useful is education. The development of GenAI could result in innovative teaching methodologies. A wide range of benefits of utilizing ITM include customized learning experiences by adapting to the levels of the learners, intelligent tutoring, automated grading, content creation, personalized career advice, an assistant for teachers, assisting in efficiently providing individualized feedback, and support collaborative learning and research among students(Hsu & Ching, 2023) (Bozkurt & Sharma, 2023). On the other hand, there is also a wide range of potential drawbacks, such as bias in data and algorithms, a lack of transparency, an overreliance on AI, concerns regarding data privacy and security, access and equity, automation, and the possibility of a singularity(Pavlik, 2023). To maximize GenAI's potential, one must engage in meticulous planning and continual education. Students and teachers must acquire the skills and experiences to give effective and meaningful prompts. This will allow them to direct GenAI to react with helpful information (Hsu & Ching, 2023).

The first exposure of many educators to GenAI tools prompted concerns about widespread cheating and plagiarism. A few educational institutions entered a state of hysteria, fearing that these tools would profoundly undermine academic integrity and negatively impact student learning(Thi Thuy An Ngo, 2023).

Educators at the cutting edge of change have a special responsibility and an important part to play in both the facilitation of learning and the empowerment of students by maximizing the potential of the most recent technological advances(Hsu & Ching, 2023).

## 1.3. GenAI Applications for ITM

The use of generative artificial intelligence, a subfield of AI that focuses on the generation of new information, ideas, and solutions, has emerged as an effective instrument in the field of education.

1) Customized learning assistance

The use of generative AI provides educators with the ability to customize educational content to meet the requirements and preferences of individual students. According to (Chen et al., 2020) research, artificial intelligence algorithms may be used to develop personalized learning materials by analyzing huge quantities of data, such as student performance, learning styles, and interests. These resources can include interactive simulations, adaptive tests, and customized lesson plans, all of which are geared towards catering to the individual strengths and shortcomings of each student (Hsu & Ching, 2023).Learning that is personalized encourages student engagement, makes it easier for students to comprehend topics, and enables students to learn on their own.

2) Content generation automation and innovation

An important obstacle faced by educators is the laborious process of generating educational materials. Generative AI can help relieve this burden by aiding in the creation of educational resources. AI-driven solutions can create lesson plans, worksheets, and multimedia resources that align with specific learning goals. The implementation of automated content development enables instructors to prioritize instructional design and personalized student assistance (Baidoo-Anu & Owusu Ansah, 2023). Furthermore, AI algorithms can examine current instructional materials in order to detect areas where knowledge is lacking and suggest enhancements, hence promoting ongoing improvement of content.

3) Automated Evaluation

Generative AI has the capability to automate the assessment process, resulting in time savings and the ability to provide rapid feedback to pupils. Artificial intelligence algorithms have the capability to examine pupils' written comments, essays, or code solutions and assess them according to predetermined criteria (Yu & Guo, 2023). Automated assessment systems provide the capability to manage grading on a wide scale, ensure uniformity, and offer comprehensive feedback. This facilitates prompt interventions and allows teachers to concentrate on individualised education.

AI-driven technologies can completely transform the assessment of teacher candidates by providing a more thorough and unbiased evaluation of their teaching abilities(Thi Thuy An Ngo, 2023). Artificial intelligence algorithms have the capability to examine pupils' written comments, essays, or code solutions and assess them according to predetermined criteria .Therefore, teacher education institutes should carefully and morally explore using new technologies, with a focus on providing continuous training and support for instructors(Almusaed et al., 2023) (Tan, 2023).

4) Interactive tutors

Interactive tutors, powered by artificial intelligence, may provide immediate aid and clarifications to students' inquiries, offering supplementary assistance beyond the usual hours of classroom instruction(Meyer et al., 2023).

5) Continuing Education

Generative AI models can be taught on huge amounts of data and kept up to date all the time, which lets them adapt to changes and trends in language. According to Yang (2023), language changes over time, adding new words and phrases and changing the meanings of old ones. According to Firat (2023), generative AI models can keep up with these changes and give students the most up-to-date and useful language material. This flexibility makes sure that language teachers have the most up-to-date information, which improves their language skills and keeps their vocabulary fresh.

6) Linguistic Acquisition and Translating

To learn a language, you usually need to do a lot of practice and use real language tools. According to (Eysenbach, 2023)generative AI can make language simulations that are very close to real life by creating conversations, scenarios, and virtual worlds that are like real life. Students can improve their speaking, listening, and understanding skills by connecting with material made by AI(Nurtayeva et al., 2023). AI programs can also tailor language lessons to each student, changing the level of difficulty based on their progress and giving them specific vocabulary and grammar tasks(Williams et al., 2023).

With ChatGPT, teaching tools can be translated into different languages so that more people can use them(Lee, 2023). There are models available that could understand what words meant in one language and translate them correctly into another language.

7) Physical and Mental Well-Being

By employing intelligent approaches, it is very possible to calculate the amount of stress or depression in a student and enhance their academic performance and talents. By employing Innovative Teaching methodologies, it is feasible to precisely examine behavioral characteristics and identify any undesirable trends for the prompt identification of mental health problems. Utilizing AI to enhance learners' psychological quality and mental performance by lowering anxiety and depression levels is a very effective method for fostering responsible citizenship. Intelligent techniques may be utilized to identify and support workers in educational sectors who are encountering challenges in carrying out their responsibilities and can be encouraged to improve their cognitive abilities(Lei et al., 2023).

8) Increased Student Engagement

AI technology could get students much more involved by using machine learning techniques to make the marking process more automatic. Automatically rating essays makes evaluations quick and accurate, giving students a quick answer. This quick feedback loop makes it easy for students to quickly find and fix their mistakes, which helps them learn and understand engineering ideas better.

Feedback is an important part of both teaching and learning because it is one of the best ways to help students learn more. Giving and getting feedback is an important part of learning because it gives you useful information that you can use to make your work better. It has been shown that peer feedback and "feed-forward" processes can improve the formative use of feedback and lead to big and noticeable changes in learning outcomes(Michel-Villarreal et al., 2023)

9) Faculty workload reduction

Integrating AI into engineering education can reduce the burden on instructors, allowing them to concentrate on more valuable responsibilities(Dwivedi et al., 2023). Automated grading systems are capable of effectively assessing assignments, quizzes, and examinations, hence minimizing the amount of time dedicated to monotonous grading duties. Subsequently, educators may allocate their efforts towards creating inventive educational resources, facilitating comprehensive dialogues, and offering individualized support to learners (Kasneci et al., 2023).

Many institutions worldwide believe that teachers' workload has increased due to additional tasks beyond teaching and grading. Some of these tasks are administrative in nature and are assigned to full-time professors by school administrators. Considering this, AI-powered applications have the potential to benefit not only students but also enhance teachers' productivity(Lim et al., 2023).

## 2. BACKGROUND

By the early 2020s, artificial intelligence had been widely applied in various aspects of daily life. These applications included language-related tasks such as machine translation and voice recognition, imaging tasks such as face recognition, social interaction tasks such as the development of profiles in social media, and practical tasks such as semi-autonomous cars and "smart" home security systems (Arogundade, 2023) (Yang et al., 2019). The broader framework refers to a recent socio-economic system known as Industry 4.0, which is often defined by its key technologies such as artificial intelligence, automation/robotics, bio-informatics, and the internet of things (George & Wooden, 2023) (Webster & Ivanov, 2020).

Generative AI, also known as GenAI, refers to a system that use deep learning models to produce material that resembles human creations, such as images and phrases. It does so by responding to diverse and intricate stimuli, including different languages, instructions, and queries(Lim et al., 2023). As generative Artificial Intelligence (AI) continues to evolve rapidly, in the next few years, it will drive innovation and improvements in higher education, but it will also create a myriad of new challenges(Kohnke et al., 2023b).

ChatGPT, a chatbot powered by GenAI, has gained attention and sparked a continuing discussion over its possible adverse impact on education(King & chatGPT, 2023). Higher education institutions (HEIs) have responded to this emerging threat to academic integrity in diverse and disjointed ways. Some HEIs have hastily imposed complete prohibitions on the use of ChatGPT (Thi Thuy An Ngo, 2023).while others have chosen to embrace it by providing students with guidance on how to engage with AI in a responsible and ethical manner(Chan & Hu, 2023).

Multiple studies have investigated the potential advantages and challenges of integrating Generative artificial intelligence (AI) in diverse educational settings. Accuracy, reliability, and plagiarism are frequently mentioned as significant concerns with the usage of Gen AI application in education(Lim et al., 2023) (Kohnke et al., 2023b). Concerns about accuracy and dependability encompass the dependence on biased data (i.e., the narrow range of data utilized to train), the lack of current knowledge (i.e., training ended in 2021), and the potential for creating erroneous or fabricated information (e.g., presenting false references) (Lo, 2023).

Furthermore, it is contended that an excessive dependence on Gen AI application may have an adverse effect on students' ability to think critically and solve problems Regarding plagiarism, research indicates that essays produced using Gen AI application can circumvent traditional plagiarism detection systems(Lo, 2023). Gen AI application proficiency extends to the point where it can effectively get passing scores on tests at the graduate level. This capability has the potential to render some sorts of evaluations unnecessary (Chan & Hu, 2023).

This study seeks to examine the Innovate Teaching Methodology from the perspective of GenAI in order to understand the academic potential and challenges it presents. The objective is to address the following research inquiry:

What are the possible challenges in higher education institutions(HEI) due to Innovative Teaching Methodology(ITM) with Gen-AI incorporation with respect to 2 perspective 1) Student 2) Faculty..

## 3. METHODOLOGY

This research employs a mixed-methods data collection approach that includes surveys and interviews.

The survey was designed to gather quantitative information to understand the existing state of Generative AI integration in Higher Education Institutions (HEI) concerning Faculty and Students. Likert scales closed-ended and open-ended questions were used to create the survey. Qualitative information on the experiences, challenges, and potential advantages of incorporating technology in HEI was gathered through the semi-structured interviews.

Two questionnaires were constructed (For faculty and students) to examine the possible advantages and difficulties of incorporating technology in HEI. The response rate for the student survey was 90% based on the estimations and the number of completed questionnaires. The overall sample size was 103, with 93 valid replies. The faculty survey response rate was 91%, with 76 valid replies out of 83. Refer Table 1

The mixed-methods strategy will offer researchers a thorough grasp of the study topic and allow them to synthesize the data to ensure that it is accurate and reliable.

*Table 1. Survey structure*

| | | |
|---|---|---|
| Students | Total Sample Size | 103 |
| | Accepted Sample | 93 |
| | Response Rate | 90% |
| | Method | Mixed (Quantitative, Qualitative) |
| Faculty | **Total Sample Size** | **83** |
| | Accepted Sample | 76 |
| | Response Rate | 91% |
| | Method | Mixed (Quantitative, Qualitative) |

## 4. RESULTS OF THE QUESTIONNAIRES

This study examined the extent of technology integration in HEI concerning student and Faculty perspectives. Therefore, two questionnaires were designed, one for faculty and the other for students. Each survey consists of two parts, one for demographic factors and the other for Knowledge and Awareness of Innovative Teaching Methodologies (ITM) using Generative AI. The semi-structured questionnaire was created using a Likert scale of 1-5, with one signifying 'Strongly Agree'/'Very Important' and five denoting 'Strongly Disagree'/'Not Important') and others.

## 4.1. Students Perspective

Of the 103 total respondents, 93 Engineering university students completed the survey. The demographics of the sample were as follows (see Table 2). Out of 93 participants, 65 were men (70%) and 28 were women (30%); the average age of the participants was between 20 -29 years. In the case of education, undergraduates accounted for the largest share of 70 (75%). Approximately the majority of the respondents, 61(66%) in the survey, had intermediate knowledge/computer expertise. Most participants, i.e. 87, were from private-sector engineering universities.

*Table 2. Demographic information of students*

| Students | | | |
|---|---|---|---|
| **Demographics Profile** | | **Frequency(N)** | **%** |
| Gender | Male | 65 | 70 |
| | Female | 28 | 30 |
| Age | <20 | 29 | 31 |
| | 20-29 | 64 | 69 |
| Education Level | Undergraduate student | 70 | 75 |
| | MS student | 15 | 16 |
| | PhD student | 3 | 3 |
| | others | 5 | 5 |
| Level of Computer Expertise | Novice | 17 | 18 |
| | Intermediate | 61 | 66 |
| | Expert | 15 | 16 |
| Sector | Private Sector | 87 | 94 |
| | Public Sectors | 6 | 8 |

### 4.1.1. Effectiveness of Traditional Teaching Method

Of 93 participants, 71 agreed that traditional teaching methods are effective for learning at HEI. When asked about the importance of traditional teaching methodology that should be retained, 42% of respondents claimed that face-to-face teaching is the best method that should be retained, and 25% agreed that teacher guidance is still required for proper learning, as depicted in Figure 1 and Figure 2.

*Figure 1. Effectiveness of traditional teaching method*

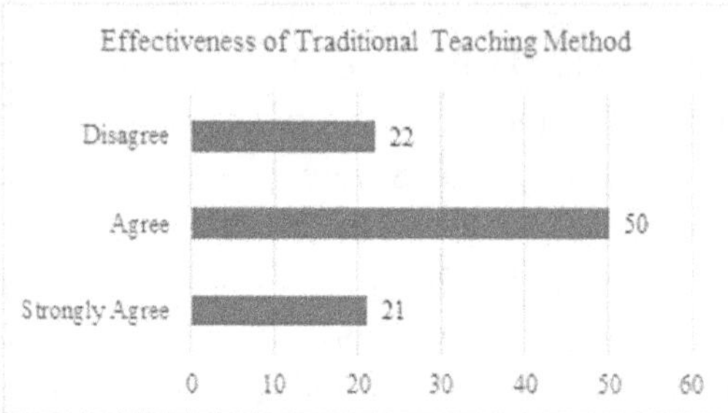


*Figure 2. Aspect of traditional teaching method*

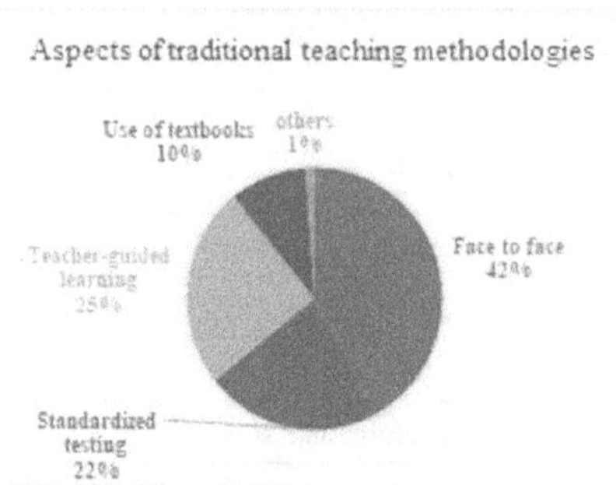


## 4.1.2. Innovative Teaching Methodologies Utilizing Generative AI

Generative AI is poised to revolutionize global collaboration and knowledge sharing in higher education. By leveraging this technology, institutions can offer a more personalized, inclusive, and culturally sensitive learning experience. About 89 out of 93 of the respondents anticipate that integrating Generative AI technology will prevail and make learning more interesting and innovative.(Refer Figure 3)

*Figure 3. Integration of generative AI in teaching*

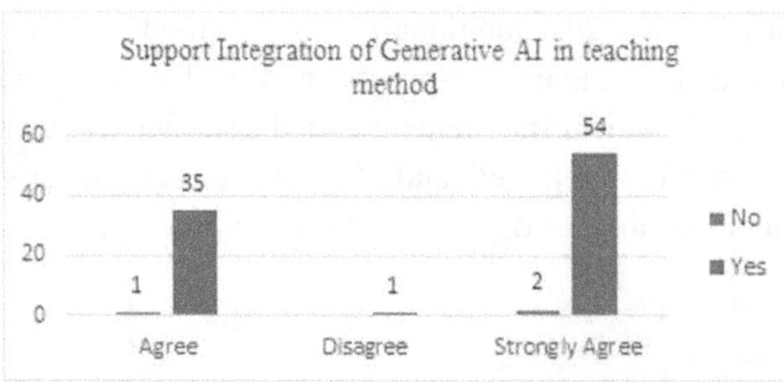

It has been noticed that students are well aware of Generative AI usage benefits. Regarding improved critical thinking benefits, 65 participants agree that integrating Generative AI will increase student critical thinking, 51 claim it will increase creativity, and 45 accept that the integration will increase students' involvement in learning. Shown in Fig. 4.

*Figure 4. Generative AI integration advantages*

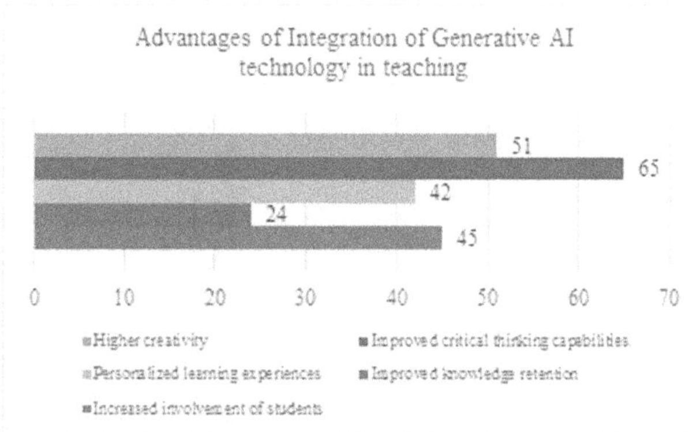


## 4.1.3. Familiarity of ITM

According to a survey, Project-based instruction, problem-to-learn, usage of a tool and technologies in education and collaborative learning were the most important benefits and usage of ITM using generative AI.(Refer Figure 5)

*Figure 5. Generative AI integration ITM familiarity and usage*

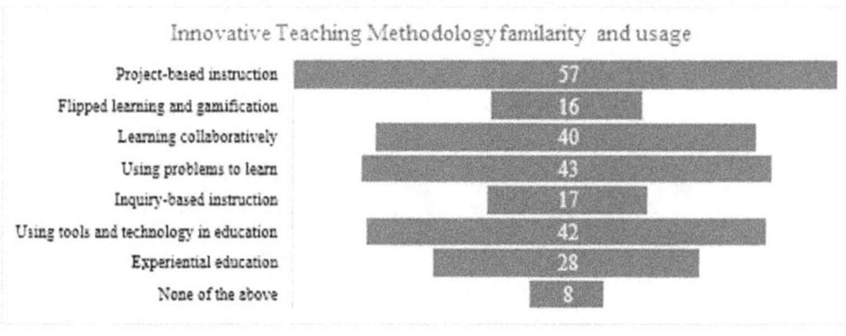

Most of the students are willing to incorporate ITM using generative AI. The students know that ITM utilization will reduce teacher workload and increase productivity. Approximately 83 out of 93 respondents support faculty incorporating ITM into their daily routine(refer to Figure 6) for interaction, announcement, content recommendation, and automated grade assessment.

*Figure 6. Suggest faculty for ITM usage*

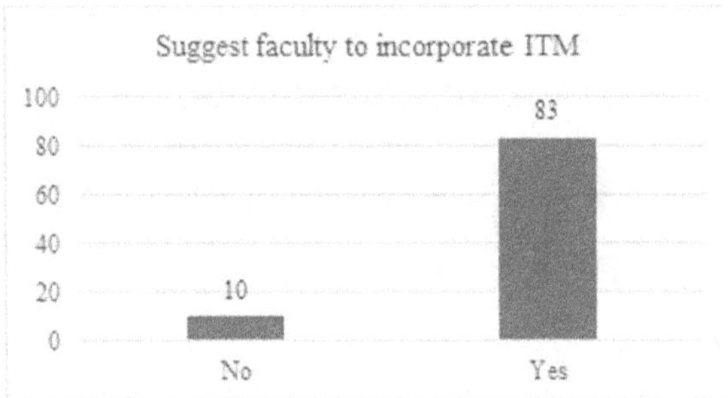


## 4.1.4. Enhance Student Engagement

By automating grading procedures, ITM based on AI technology may greatly increase student involvement. Automated quiz /assignment scoring offers rapid and precise grading, giving students prompt feedback. About 80 out of 93 participants claim that engagement of ITM in HEI will enhance student learning, engagement and grades Refer Figure 7.

*Figure 7. Student engagement improvement using ITM*

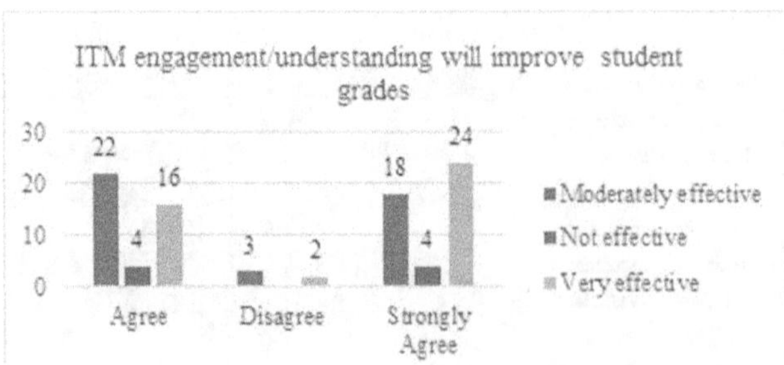

### 4.1.5. Effectiveness/Challenges of Adopting ITM in HEI

The respondent needs to rate different challenges of utilizing ITM in HEI concerning their importance on a linear scale from 1 to 3 (Not effective, Moderately effective, Very effective). It has been observed that all participants strongly agreed on the general challenges of ITM utilization at HEI. The challenges are difficulty in self-directed learning, requiring more time and effort, limited access to technology, and lack of traditional structure. Fifty-four respondents think that these challenges have a moderate effect on the proper adoption of ITM, while others think they are very effective in ITM adoption. Only a few think these challenges are unimportant, as shown in Figure 8.

*Figure 8. Effectiveness and challenges of ITM adoption in HEI*

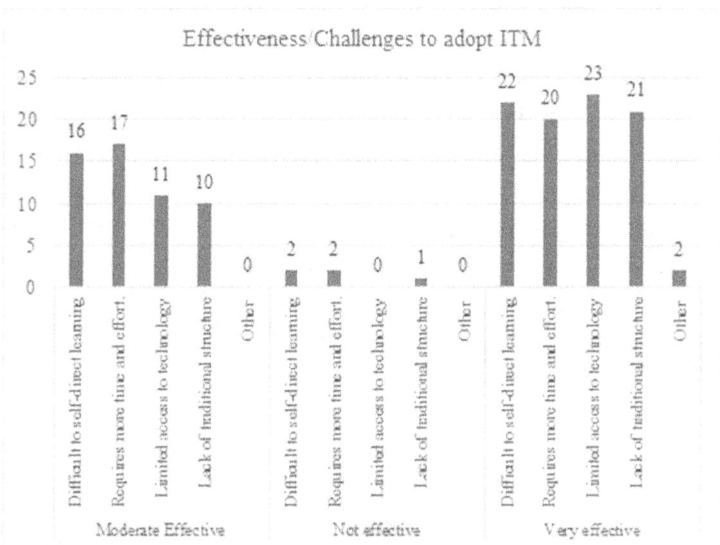


### 4.1.6. Impact on Learning Using ITM-AI

In the particular context of HEI, generative artificial intelligence can greatly improve teaching methods. This technology may improve teaching and learning strategies in higher education. When asked students about their preferred teaching styles, 38% of respondents claimed that visuals (videos, tutorials etc.) are the main source of learning, whereas 26% considered Auditory (audio, voice etc.) the 2nd important learning factor. Respondent's perspectives are depicted in Figure 9.

*Figure 9. What is your preferred learning style?*

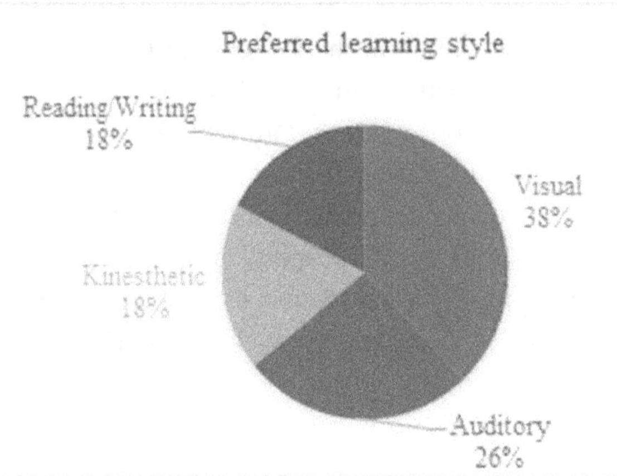


ITM-AI-driven technologies can completely transform teacher candidates' evaluations by providing a more thorough and objective assessment of their educational abilities. Using AI-driven platforms, students may receive personalized information, activities, and assessments tailored to their current skill level and learning goals. It has been observed that 43% of participants strongly agreed with the project-based. Participants approximately 27% still think of going for traditional exams for assessment, whereas 16% want a portfolio-based assessment, as shown in Figure 10.

*Figure 10. Assessment suggestion for ITM incorporation in HEI*

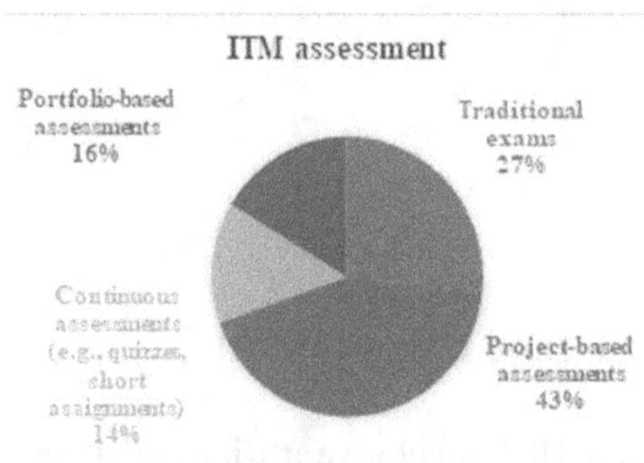


A traditional computer-based learning scenario is a student utilizing a computer in a classroom to complete step-by-step assignments focused on domain-specific information with the help of a faculty member. The creation of intelligent teaching systems can greatly benefit from generative AI. With the help of ITM, teachers can provide customized learning materials to students by analyzing large amounts of data, including student performance, learning preferences, and interests. When asked about the factors that enhance learning experience, 29% of respondents consider incorporating ITM increases teacher interaction, whereas 26% claim that integrating digital tools in education is very important, as shown in Figure 11.

*Figure 11. ITM Features for learning enhancement*

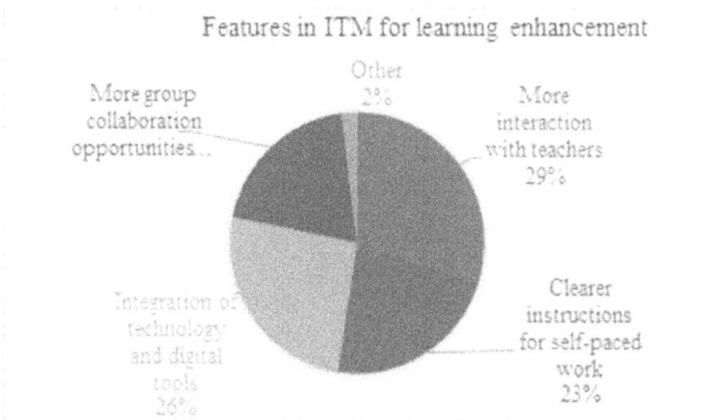


## 4.1.7. Impact of ITM on Students Well Being

Generative AI can benefit and negatively affect students' mental health and well-being, depending on utilization. Positive effects include 24/7 information assistance, customized learning assistance, innovative thinking, and support for individuals' mental health and others. Whereas negative effects include depression, Overusage can result in technology addiction, Privacy Concerns, virtual living, loneliness and decreased critical thinking. When asked about the impact of ITM on students' well-being (62%) claimed that there is a positive impact of ITM on students' mental health, whereas 17% think it produces negative effects, as depicted in Figure 12.

*Figure 12. Generative AI impact on students' mental health*

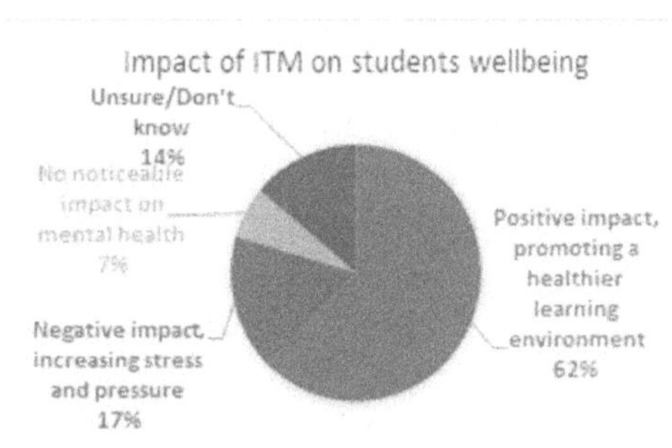

### 4.1.8. Overall Rating of ITM Using Generative AI

It must be noted that an "overall rating" of generative AI depends on numerous factors, including the context in which it is employed, the nature of the task at hand, and the individual's biases and expectations. ITM using Generative artificial intelligence (AI) has positive and negative aspects, and its impacts can be beneficial or harmful when participants are questioned about the overall rating of ITM using generative AI. 29% of respondents rate generative AI in cooperation in teaching methodology as excellent, while 52% rate it as good. Only 1% rate generative AI poor, whereas 18% rate it good. (Refer Figure 13)

*Figure 13. Generative AI overall all rating*

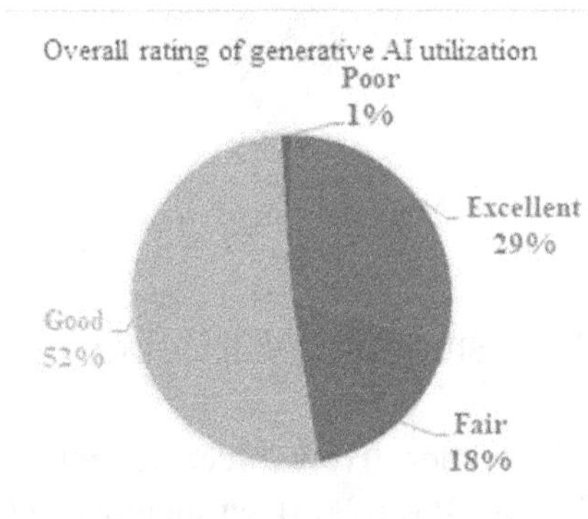


## 4.2. Faculty Perspective

The function of the teacher in the classroom has changed. They have transitioned from being the dominant figure in the spotlight to assuming the role of a supportive mentor. Teachers are no longer required to possess comprehensive knowledge and merely transmit it to students. Instead, their role is to assist students in searching for, locating, and integrating information, so that they can develop into independent and collaborative thinkers.

Two survey were conducted one for students and other for faculty perspective regarding ITM-Gen AI in cooperation. 80 faculty members had engineering background attempted the survey out of which 76 were usable. The demographics of the sample were as follows (see Table 4). Looking at the level of experience with ITM-Gen AI 61% claims that they are experts while 38% respondent accepts that they have middle level knowledge. Regarding job titles, the category of Senior Lecturer/Lecturer constituted the majority with a share of 45%, followed by Assistant Professor at 32%, Associate Professor at 8%, and Professors at 3 individuals. The poll revealed that a significant majority of the respondents, specifically 46 individuals (61%), have computer knowledge. The majority of participants, specifically 97%, were from engineering universities in the private sector. All demographic details are presented in Table 3.

*Table 3. Demographic information of faculty*

| **Faculty** | | | |
|---|---|---|---|
| **Demographics Profile** | | **Frequency(N)** | **%** |
| Gender | Male | 41 | 54 |
| | Female | 35 | 46 |
| Title/Position | Professor | 2 | 3 |
| | Associate Professor | 10 | 8 |
| | Assistant Professor | 24 | 32 |
| | Lecturer/Sr.Lecturer | 34 | 45 |
| | others | 6 | 8 |
| Level of Computer Expertise | Novice | 1 | 1 |
| | Intermediate | 29 | 38 |
| | Expert | 46 | 61 |
| Sector | Private Sector | 74 | 97 |
| | Public Sectors | 2 | 3 |

### 4.2.1. Awareness of Innovative Teaching Methodologies-Gen AI

This current generation has come of age in a society in which artificial intelligence (AI) and technology play an important part in both their educational experiences and their day-to-day lives. Therefore, faculty members need to be aware of creative teaching methods that can respond to the specific preferences and requirements of these students. Around 80% of the faculty has a high level of awareness of ITM-Gen AI as shown in Figure 14.

*Figure 14. Faculty awareness of ITM-Gen AI*

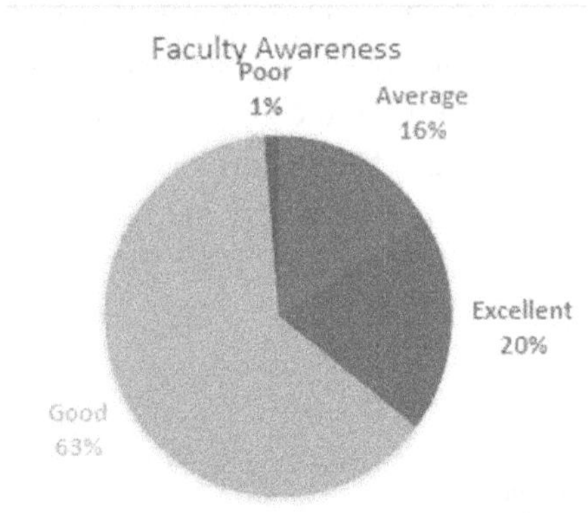


## 4.2.2. Presently Employed Innovative Teaching Methodologies

Teaching methods that are creative and original are always developing as educators work to adapt to the increasing requirements of students and make use of the most recent technologies. About 60% of those who answered said they used the newest tools and technologies in their teaching, while 57% said they used problems to learn and 51% said they used project-based learning. Since we are considering a third-world country in our survey, therefore teachers don't use flipped learning, game-based learning, learning together, inquiry-based instruction, or experiential education as much as they could. Figure 15 show the result of currently ITM utilization.

*Figure 15. Presently employed ITM*

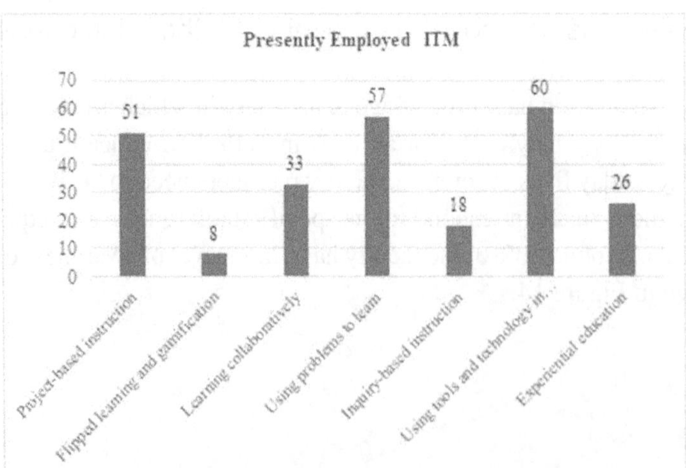

### 4.2.3. Training Programs Needed for Implementing Innovative Teaching Methodologies

Faculty members who want to use new approaches in the classroom need to be committed to lifelong learning. Faculty must be supported in this process by training programs. Sixty-four respondents say that workshops will be useful, while 48 say that online courses would be useful, for ensuring successful ITM adoption. Faculty members are less likely to use peer mentorship and individual coaching while implementing ITM. Details are present in Figure 16.

*Figure 16. Training program for ITM implementation*

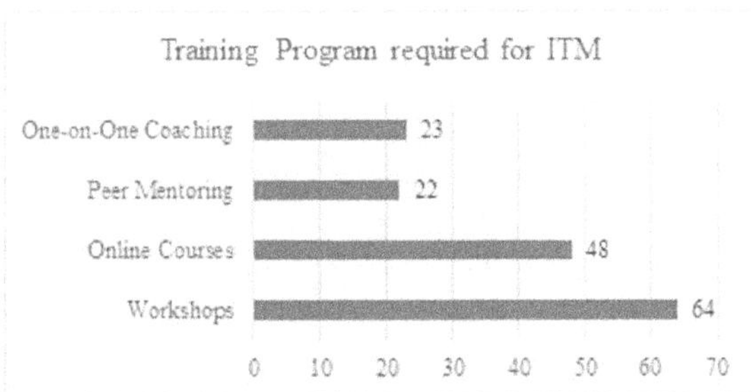


### 4.2.4. Institutional Support for Innovative Teaching Methodologies

By providing faculty with the appropriate support and resources, institutions play a significant role in encouraging the development of innovative approaches to teaching in the classroom. While 59% of respondents agreed that they were encouraged by their institution to use innovative teaching methods, 34% strongly agreed whereas 7% disagree. Presented in Figure 17.

*Figure 17. Institutional support for ITM implementation*

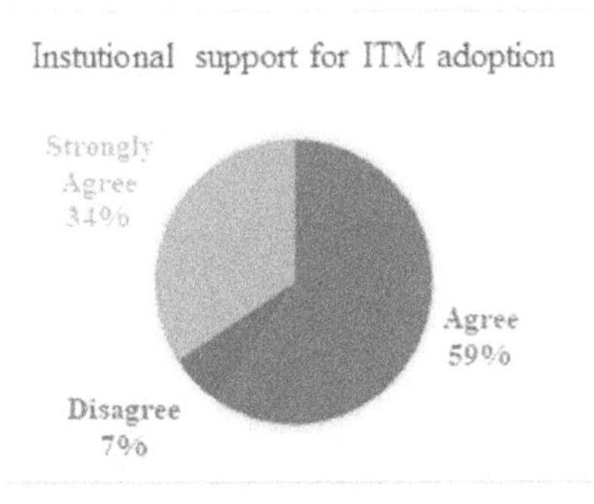

## 4.2.5. Implementation of Innovative Teaching Methodologies in Teaching

Employing ITM approaches can augment the educational experience for students and foster active participation and analytical reasoning. When teachers were asked if they are incorporating ITM in teaching 74% answered affirmatively, and the rest denied it. When asked whether they use ITM in their lessons, 74% of teachers responded positively. The remaining teachers denied using ITM depicted in Figure 18.

*Figure 18. Implementation ITM in Teaching*

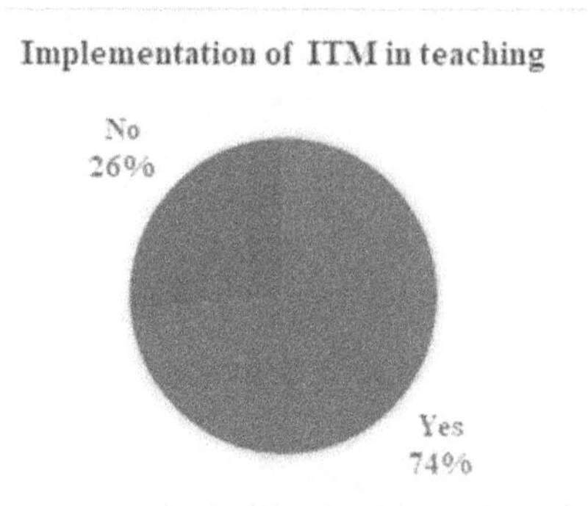


## 4.2.6. Innovative Teaching Methodologies Training and Professional Development

Several educators undergo training and professional development programs focused on integrating cutting-edge teaching approaches. The necessity for such training originates from the aspiration to enhance pedagogical methodologies, stay abreast of emerging educational practices, and cater to the varied demands of students. As depicted in Figure 19, the majority of faculty members with a good or exceptional understanding of Innovative Teaching Methodologies concur that they have received training.

*Figure 19. ITM Training*

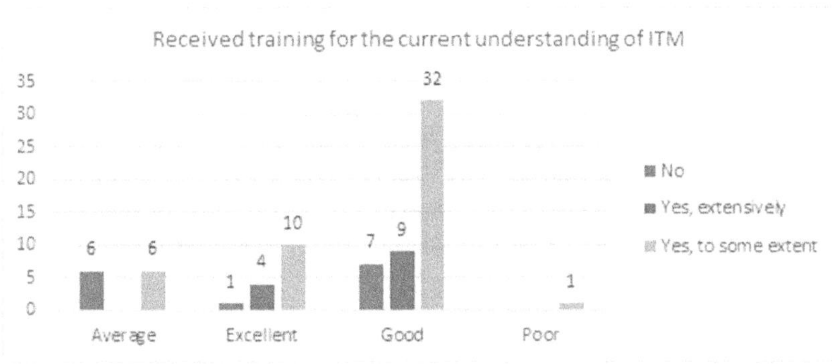


## 4.2.7. Updating Innovative Teaching Methodologies

Faculty members keep abreast of the most recent innovative teaching methods through a variety of channels to enhance their teaching practices and remain current with education trends. A total of 47 individuals acknowledge that participating in workshops and conferences enhances their comprehension of ITM. Additionally, 46 individuals assert that reading research articles and the latest publications contributes to their learning. Furthermore, 39 individuals claim that collaborating with colleagues enhances their learning, while 28 individuals acknowledge the role of online forums and communities in updating their ITM knowledge. (Refer Figure 20)

*Figure 20. ITM knowledge updation*

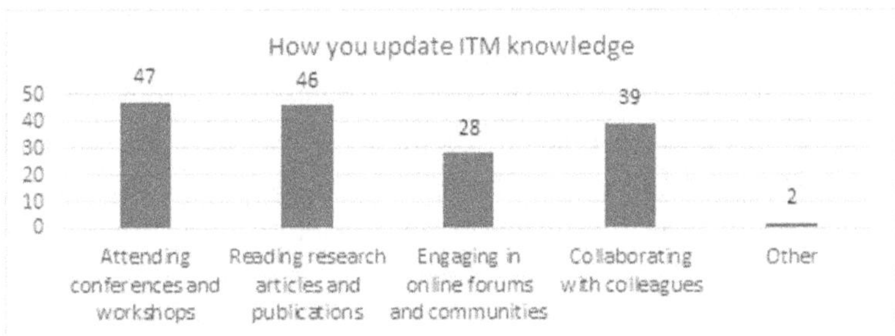

## 4.2.8. Effective Implementation of Innovative Teaching Methodologies

Effective implementation of Innovative Teaching Methodologies requires a deliberate and systematic approach to preparation and planning. According to 46 respondents, problem-based learning is the best ITM strategy, followed by project-based learning for 40, utilizing problems to learn for 23 and flipping the classroom and collaborative learning for 22 respondents. Only 21 people claim that gamification is the most successful strategy, depicted in Figure 21.

*Figure 21. Effective ITM Strategy*

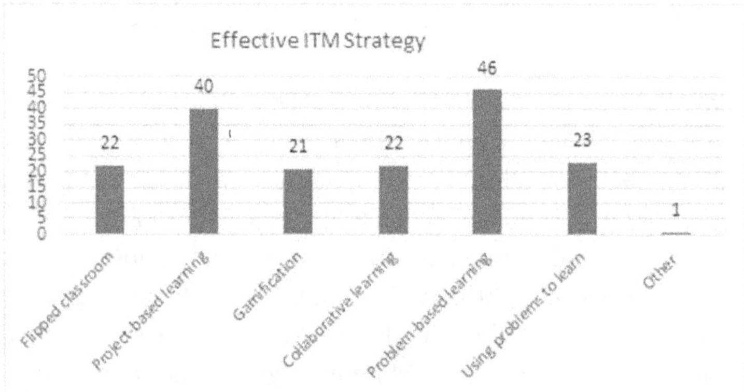


## 4.2.9. Resistance on Implementation of Innovative Teaching Methodologies

Many students, especially those who have been educated in the conventional manner, may be resistant to Innovative Teaching Methodologies. There are, however, several methods that are employed to successfully handle and manage student opposition. When asked how they would mitigate student resistance, 44% of teachers said they would have discussions with students about their concerns; 42% said they would explain the methodology's advantages and relevance; and 40% said they would give students more help and resources. 27 said they will make changes to the approach depending on student input. The details are presented in Figure 22.

*Figure 22. Effective ITM Strategy*

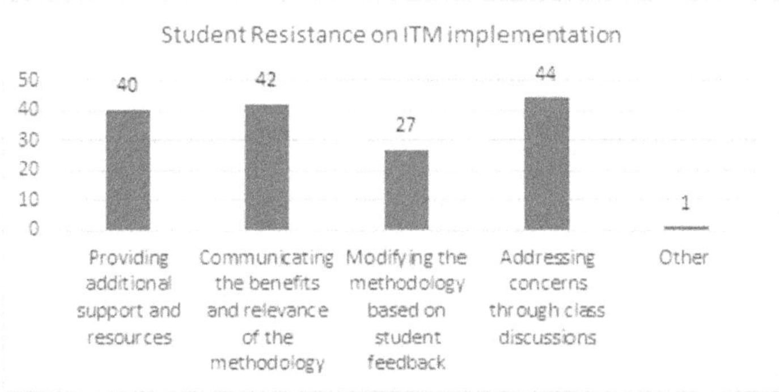


## 4.2.10. Selection of Innovative Teaching Methodologies

Educators and institutions must make a crucial choice when choosing an innovative teaching method. Several factors should be considered when making this decision. Depending on the specific educational context, objectives, and requirements of the students, the relative importance of these factors may vary. Out of the 51 respondents, believe that aligning with the learning objective is the most significant thing to consider when selecting an ITM. On the other hand, 39 respondents believe that an ITM should be chosen if it has the ability to engage students. According to Figure 23, approximately 35 and 36 faculty members assert that the most crucial factors in the selection choice of ITM are the compatibility for different students' learning styles and the feasibility of implementation.

*Figure 23. Factors for ITM selection*

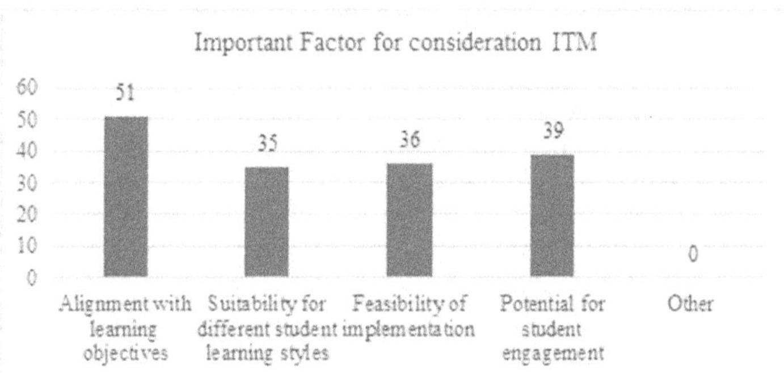

## 4.2.11. Innovative Teaching Methodologies Improves Student Outcomes

There were several studies and anecdotal evidence demonstrating the beneficial effects of innovative teaching and learning methods on academic achievements, motivation, and student engagement. Nevertheless, it is crucial to acknowledge that the efficacy of these procedures may differ based on the methodologies chosen and the circumstances in which they are applied. The majority of respondents (60%) responded that they had sought feedback from students about the incorporation of Innovative Teaching Methodologies. The remaining respondents are of the opinion that having an ITM does not significantly affect the learning outcome, student engagement and motivation. (Refer Figure 24)

*Figure 24. Student outcome utilizing ITM*

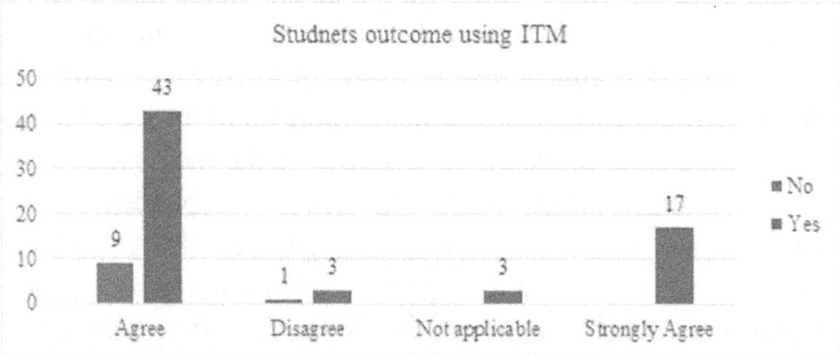


## 4.2.12. Support Innovative Teaching Methodologies

The application of Innovative Teaching Methodologies has the potential to have a beneficial effect on student learning and engagement. Approximately 97% of faculty members, when asked whether they wish to support the adoption of innovative teaching methodologies in their classroom, indicate that incorporation is beneficial for students' learning, shown in Figure 25.

*Figure 25. Willingness of ITM implementation*

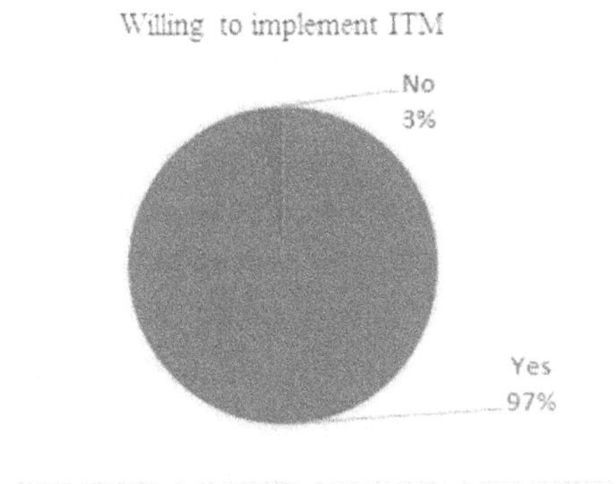


## 4.2.13. Innovative Teaching Methodologies Implementation Increases Student Performance

By making the learning process more interactive, relevant, and pleasurable for students, innovative teaching and learning strategies have the potential to drastically improve academic outcomes as well as student engagement. According to 48% of respondents, ITM is an extremely effective technique for enhancing student's outcome. 51% believe ITM has a moderate impact on student learning abilities, while 1% believe it has no impact presented in Figure 26.

*Figure 26. Impact of ITM on student performance*

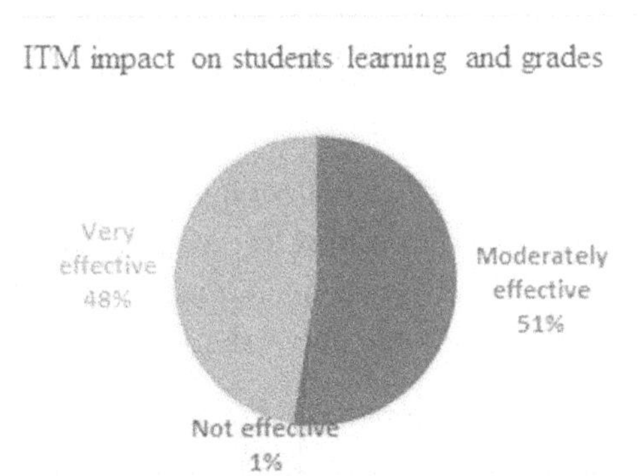

## CONCLUSION

The dynamic and swiftly changing environment of higher education is leading to substantial transformations in the educational system. Traditional teaching and learning methods are unable to meet the demands of the digital era. In order to enhance the quality of education, it has become essential to promote worldwide collaboration and the exchange of knowledge, since this is crucial for educating students to thrive in an interconnected world. Hence, the incorporation of technology in the classroom has become indispensable. Generative Artificial Intelligence (AI) has become a potent tool in this pursuit. This research not only examines the potential benefits and challenges of integrating technology in higher education with respect to students and teachers perspectives, but also evaluates the level of technology integration in teaching, known as Innovative Teaching Methods (ITM). This chapter examines the potential of utilizing generative AI to improve teaching methodologies.

## REFERENCES

Almusaed, A., Almssad, A., Yitmen, I., & Homod, R. Z. (2023). Enhancing Student Engagement: Harnessing "AIED"'s Power in Hybrid Education—A Review Analysis. *Education Sciences*, *13*(7), 7. doi:10.3390/educsci13070632

Arogundade, O. R. (2023). Structuring Knowledge Bases with AI and Machine Learning. *Information and Knowledge Management*, *13*(1), 27.

Baidoo-Anu, D., & Owusu Ansah, L. (2023). *Education in the Era of Generative Artificial Intelligence (AI): Understanding the Potential Benefits of ChatGPT in Promoting Teaching and Learning* (SSRN Scholarly Paper 4337484). doi:10.2139/ssrn.4337484

Bozkurt, A., & Sharma, R. C. (2023). Challenging the Status Quo and Exploring the New Boundaries in the Age of Algorithms: Reimagining the Role of Generative AI in Distance Education and Online Learning. *Asian Journal of Distance Education*, *18*(1), 1. http://asianjde.com/ojs/index.php/AsianJDE/article/view/714

Chan, C. K. Y., & Hu, W. (2023). *Students' Voices on Generative AI: Perceptions, Benefits, and Challenges in Higher Education* (arXiv:2305.00290). arXiv. https://doi.org//arXiv.2305.00290 doi:10.48550

Chen, X., Xie, H., Zou, D., & Hwang, G.-J. (2020). Application and theory gaps during the rise of Artificial Intelligence in Education. *Computers and Education: Artificial Intelligence*, *1*, 100002. doi:10.1016/j.caeai.2020.100002

Dwivedi, Y. K., Kshetri, N., Hughes, L., Slade, E. L., Jeyaraj, A., Kar, A. K., Baabdullah, A. M., Koohang, A., Raghavan, V., Ahuja, M., Albanna, H., Albashrawi, M. A., Al-Busaidi, A. S., Balakrishnan, J., Barlette, Y., Basu, S., Bose, I., Brooks, L., Buhalis, D., & Wright, R. (2023). Opinion Paper: "So what if ChatGPT wrote it?" Multidisciplinary perspectives on opportunities, challenges and implications of generative conversational AI for research, practice and policy. *International Journal of Information Management*, *71*, 102642. doi:10.1016/j.ijinfomgt.2023.102642

Eysenbach, G. (2023). The Role of ChatGPT, Generative Language Models, and Artificial Intelligence in Medical Education: A Conversation With ChatGPT and a Call for Papers. *JMIR Medical Education*, *9*(1), e46885. doi:10.2196/46885 PMID:36863937

George, B., & Wooden, O. (2023). Managing the Strategic Transformation of Higher Education through Artificial Intelligence. *Administrative Sciences*, *13*(9), 9. doi:10.3390/admsci13090196

Hsu, Y.-C., & Ching, Y.-H. (2023). Generative Artificial Intelligence in Education, Part One: The Dynamic Frontier. *TechTrends*, *67*(4), 603–607. doi:10.100711528-023-00863-9

Kasneci, E., Sessler, K., Küchemann, S., Bannert, M., Dementieva, D., Fischer, F., Gasser, U., Groh, G., Günnemann, S., Hüllermeier, E., Krusche, S., Kutyniok, G., Michaeli, T., Nerdel, C., Pfeffer, J., Poquet, O., Sailer, M., Schmidt, A., Seidel, T., & Kasneci, G. (2023). ChatGPT for good? On opportunities and challenges of large language models for education. *Learning and Individual Differences*, *103*, 102274. doi:10.1016/j.lindif.2023.102274

King, M. R. (2023). A Conversation on Artificial Intelligence, Chatbots, and Plagiarism in Higher Education. *Cellular and Molecular Bioengineering*, *16*(1), 1–2. doi:10.100712195-022-00754-8 PMID:36660590

Kohnke, L., Moorhouse, B. L., & Zou, D. (2023a). ChatGPT for Language Teaching and Learning. *RELC Journal*, *54*(2), 537–550. doi:10.1177/00336882231162868

Kohnke, L., Moorhouse, B. L., & Zou, D. (2023b). ChatGPT for Language Teaching and Learning. *RELC Journal*, *54*(2), 2. doi:10.1177/00336882231162868

Lee, T. K. (2023). *Artificial intelligence and posthumanist translation: ChatGPT versus the translator*. Applied Linguistics Review. doi:10.1515/applirev-2023-0122

Lei, L., Li, J., & Li, W. (2023). Assessing the role of artificial intelligence in the mental healthcare of teachers and students. *Soft Computing*. doi:10.100700500-023-08072-5 PMID:37362257

Lim, W. M., Gunasekara, A., Pallant, J. L., Pallant, J. I., & Pechenkina, E. (2023). Generative AI and the future of education: Ragnarök or reformation? A paradoxical perspective from management educators. *International Journal of Management Education*, *21*(2), 100790. doi:10.1016/j.ijme.2023.100790

Lo, C. K. (2023). What Is the Impact of ChatGPT on Education? A Rapid Review of the Literature. *Education Sciences*, *13*(4), 4. doi:10.3390/educsci13040410

Meyer, J. G., Urbanowicz, R. J., Martin, P. C. N., O'Connor, K., Li, R., Peng, P.-C., Bright, T. J., Tatonetti, N., Won, K. J., Gonzalez-Hernandez, G., & Moore, J. H. (2023). ChatGPT and large language models in academia: Opportunities and challenges. *BioData Mining*, *16*(1), 20. doi:10.118613040-023-00339-9 PMID:37443040

Michel-Villarreal, R., Vilalta-Perdomo, E., Salinas-Navarro, D. E., Thierry-Aguilera, R., & Gerardou, F. S. (2023). Challenges and Opportunities of Generative AI for Higher Education as Explained by ChatGPT. *Education Sciences*, *13*(9), 9. doi:10.3390/educsci13090856

Mishra, P., Warr, M., & Islam, R. (2023). TPACK in the age of ChatGPT and Generative AI. *Journal of Digital Learning in Teacher Education*, *39*(4), 235–251. doi:10.1080/21532974.2023.2247480

Nurtayeva, T., Salim, M., Basheer Taha, T., & Khalilov, S. (2023). The influence of ChatGPT and AI Tools on the Academic Performance. *YMER, 22*(6). https://ymerdigital.com/archives/?cpage=2&issId=%202206

Pavlik, J. V. (2023). Collaborating With ChatGPT: Considering the Implications of Generative Artificial Intelligence for Journalism and Media Education. *Journalism & Mass Communication Educator*, *78*(1), 84–93. doi:10.1177/10776958221149577

Ray, P. P. (2023). ChatGPT: A comprehensive review on background, applications, key challenges, bias, ethics, limitations and future scope. *Internet of Things and Cyber-Physical Systems*, *3*, 121–154. doi:10.1016/j.iotcps.2023.04.003

Tan, S. (2023). Harnessing Artificial Intelligence for Innovation in Education. In K. Rajaram (Ed.), *Learning Intelligence: Innovative and Digital Transformative Learning Strategies: Cultural and Social Engineering Perspectives* (pp. 335–363). Springer Nature. doi:10.1007/978-981-19-9201-8_8

Thi Thuy An Ngo. (2023). The Perception by University Students of the Use of ChatGPT in Education. *International Journal of Emerging Technologies in Learning,* 4–19. doi:10.3991/ijet.v18i17.39019

Webster, C., & Ivanov, S. (2020). Robotics, Artificial Intelligence, and the Evolving Nature of Work. In B. George & J. Paul (Eds.), Digital Transformation in Business and Society: Theory and Cases (pp. 127–143). Springer International Publishing. doi:10.1007/978-3-030-08277-2_8

Williams, R., Hosseinichimeh, N., Majumdar, A., & Ghaffarzadegan, N. (2023). *Epidemic Modeling with Generative Agents* (arXiv:2307.04986). arXiv. https://doi.org//arXiv.2307.04986 doi:10.48550

Yang, X., Kaiser, G., König, J., & Blömeke, S. (2019). *Professional noticing of mathematics teachers: A comparative study between Germany and China*. Springer. doi:10.1007/s10763-018-9907-x

# Compilation of References


Abbasi, B., & Goldenholz, D. M. (2019). Machine learning applications in epilepsy. *Epilepsia*, *60*(10), 2037–2047. doi:10.1111/epi.16333 PMID:31478577

Agrawal, A. V., Pitchai, R., Senthamaraikannan, C., Balaji, N. A., Sajithra, S., & Boopathi, S. (2023). Digital Education System During the COVID-19 Pandemic. In Using Assistive Technology for Inclusive Learning in K-12 Classrooms (pp. 104–126). IGI Global. doi:10.4018/978-1-6684-6424-3.ch005

Agrawal, A. V., Shashibhushan, G., Pradeep, S., Padhi, S. N., Sugumar, D., & Boopathi, S. (2024). Synergizing Artificial Intelligence, 5G, and Cloud Computing for Efficient Energy Conversion Using Agricultural Waste. In Practice, Progress, and Proficiency in Sustainability (pp. 475–497). IGI Global. doi:10.4018/979-8-3693-1186-8.ch026

Akbar, M. A., Khan, A. A., & Liang, P. (2023). Ethical Aspects of ChatGPT in Software Engineering Research. *arXiv preprint arXiv:2306.07557.*

Akgun, S., & Greenhow, C. (2021). Artificial intelligence in education: Addressing ethical challenges in K-12 settings. *AI and Ethics*, 1–10. PMID:34790956

Alam, A. (2022). Employing adaptive learning and intelligent tutoring robots for virtual classrooms and smart campuses: Reforming education in the age of artificial intelligence. In *Advanced Computing and Intelligent Technologies* [Springer.]. *Proceedings of ICACIT, 2022*, 395–406.

Ali, S., DiPaola, D., Williams, R., Ravi, P., & Breazeal, C. (2023). Constructing Dreams using Generative AI. *ArXiv Preprint ArXiv:2305.12013.*

Ali, M., & Abdel-Haq, M. K. (2021). Bibliographical analysis of artificial intelligence learning in Higher Education: Is the role of the human educator and educated a thing of the past? In *Fostering Communication and Learning With Underutilized Technologies in Higher Education* (pp. 36–52). IGI Global. doi:10.4018/978-1-7998-4846-2.ch003

Ali, Z. (2020). Artificial Intelligence (AI): A review of its uses in language teaching and learning. *IOP Conference Series. Materials Science and Engineering*, *769*(1), 012043. doi:10.1088/1757-899X/769/1/012043

Almusaed, A., Almssad, A., Yitmen, I., & Homod, R. Z. (2023). Enhancing Student Engagement: Harnessing "AIED"'s Power in Hybrid Education—A Review Analysis. *Education Sciences*, *13*(7), 632. doi:10.3390/educsci13070632

Amato, L. M., & Schoettle, C. (2023). Using Artificial Intelligence Ethically and Responsibly: Best Practices in Higher Education. In J. Keengwe (Ed.), *Creative AI Tools and Ethical Implications in Teaching and Learning* (pp. 19–31). IGI Global. doi:10.4018/979-8-3693-0205-7.ch002

Anitha, C., Komala, C., Vivekanand, C. V., Lalitha, S., & Boopathi, S. (2023). Artificial Intelligence driven security model for Internet of Medical Things (IoMT). *IEEE Explore*, 1–7.

Arce, N. H., & Valdivia, A. C. (2020). Adapting competitiveness and gamification to a digital platform for foreign language learning. [iJET]. *International Journal of Emerging Technologies in Learning*, *15*(20), 194–209. doi:10.3991/ijet.v15i20.16135

Archer, L., DeWitt, J., Osborne, J., Dillon, J., Willis, B., & Wong, B. (2010). "Doing" science versus "being" a scientist: Examining 10/11-year-old schoolchildren's constructions of science through the lens of identity. *Science Education*, *94*(4), 617–639. doi:10.1002ce.20399

Arogundade, O. R. (2023). Structuring Knowledge Bases with AI and Machine Learning. *Information and Knowledge Management*, *13*(1), 27.

Arora, A., Barrett, M., Lee, E., Oborn, E., & Prince, K. (2023). Risk and the future of AI: Algorithmic bias, data colonialism, and marginalization. *Information and Organization*, *33*(3), 100478. doi:10.1016/j.infoandorg.2023.100478

Askew, M., Bowie, L., & Venkat, H. (2019). Pre-service primary teachers' mathematical content knowledge: An exploratory study. African Journal of Research in Mathematics. *Science and Technology Education*, *23*(3), 286–297.

Atlas, S. (2023). *ChatGPT for higher education and professional development: A guide to conversational AI*. The University of Rhode Island.

Avurakoghene, O., & Oredein, A. O. (2023). Educational Leadership and Artificial Intelligence for Sustainable Development. *Shodh Sari-An International Multidisciplinary Journal*, *2*(3), 211–223. doi:10.59231/SARI7600

Baidoo-AnuD.Owusu AnsahL. (2023). Education in the era of generative artificial intelligence (AI): Understanding the potential benefits of ChatGPT in promoting teaching and learning. SSRN 4337484. doi:10.2139/ssrn.4337484

Bamrungsin, P., & Khampirat, B. (2022). Improving professional skills of pre-service teachers using online training: Applying work-integrated learning approaches through a quasi-experimental study. *Sustainability (Basel)*, *14*(7), 4362. doi:10.3390u14074362

Bandi, A., Venkata, P., Ramesh, S., Eswar, Y., Pratap, V., & Kuchi, K. (2023). The Power of Generative AI : A Review of Requirements, Models, Input – Output Formats, Evaluation Metrics, and Challenges. *Future Internet*, *15*(8), 15. doi:10.3390/fi15080260

Bang, J., Lee, G. G., Lee, G., & Chung, M. (2014). Pronunciation variants prediction method to detect mispronunciations by Korean learners of English. *ACM Transactions on Asian Language Information Processing*, *13*(4), 1–21. doi:10.1145/2629545

Barrot, J. S. (2023). Using ChatGPT for second language writing: Pitfalls and potentials. *Assessing Writing*, *57*, 100745. doi:10.1016/j.asw.2023.100745

Baskara, F. R., & Mukarto, F. X. (2023). Exploring the Implications of ChatGPT for Language Learning in Higher Education. *Indonesian Journal of English Language Teaching and Applied Linguistics, 7*(2), 343–358.

Becker, K. (2023, June 20). Prompt Engineering: The Magical World of Large Language Models. *Medium.* https://itnext.io/prompt-engineering-the-magical-world-of-large-language-models-dde7d8d043ee

Benjamin, J. J., Kinkeldey, C., & Müller-Birn, C. (2020). Participatory design of a machine learning driven visualization system for non-technical stakeholders. *Mensch Und Computer 2020-Workshopband.*

Berendt, B., Littlejohn, A., & Blakemore, M. (2020). AI in education: learner choice and fundamental rights. *Learning, Media and Technology*, *45*(3), 312-324. https://doi.org/. 1786399 doi:10.1080/17439884.2020

Berger, R., & Hänze, M. (2015). Impact of expert teaching quality on novice academic performance in the jigsaw cooperative learning method. *International Journal of Science Education*, *37*(2), 294–320. doi:10.1080/09500693.2014.985757

Berry, A., Depaepe, F., & Van Driel, J. (2016). *Pedagogical content knowledge in teacher education* (Vol. 1). International Handbook of Teacher Education.

Bhosale, U. (2023, July 17). *Responsible Use of Generative AI.* Enago Academy. https://www.enago.com/academy/responsible-use-of-generative-ai/

Bican, G. (2021). Enhancing the cross cultural competence of prospective language teachers. *Journal of Curriculum and Teaching*, *10*(3), 47–57. doi:10.5430/jct.v10n3p47

Bin-Nashwan, S. A., Sadallah, M., & Bouteraa, M. (2023). Use of ChatGPT in academia: Academic integrity hangs in the balance. *Technology in Society*, *75*, 102370. doi:10.1016/j.techsoc.2023.102370

BiswasS. (2023). Role of Chat GPT in Education. SSRN 4369981.

Bloom, B.S. (1984). *The 2-sigma problem: The search for methods of group instruction as effective as one-to-one tutoring.* Syracuse University.

Blythe, M. C. (2023). *An Analysis of the Suitability of Philosophy as a Core K-12 Public School Subject.*

Boopathi, S. (2023b). Deep Learning Techniques Applied for Automatic Sentence Generation. In Promoting Diversity, Equity, and Inclusion in Language Learning Environments (pp. 255–273). IGI Global. doi:10.4018/978-1-6684-3632-5.ch016

Boopathi, S. (2023c). Securing Healthcare Systems Integrated With IoT: Fundamentals, Applications, and Future Trends. In Dynamics of Swarm Intelligence Health Analysis for the Next Generation (pp. 186–209). IGI Global.

Boopathi, S., Pandey, B. K., & Pandey, D. (2023). Advances in Artificial Intelligence for Image Processing: Techniques, Applications, and Optimization. In Handbook of Research on Thrust Technologies' Effect on Image Processing (pp. 73–95). IGI Global.

Boopathi, S. (2022). An extensive review on sustainable developments of dry and near-dry electrical discharge machining processes. *ASME: Journal of Manufacturing Science and Engineering*, *144*(5), 050801–1.

Boopathi, S. (2022). Experimental investigation and multi-objective optimization of cryogenic Friction-stir-welding of AA2014 and AZ31B alloys using MOORA technique. *Materials Today. Communications*, *33*, 104937. doi:10.1016/j.mtcomm.2022.104937

Boopathi, S. (2023a). An Investigation on Friction Stir Processing of Aluminum Alloy-Boron Carbide Surface Composite. In *Springer:Advances in Processing of Lightweight Metal Alloys and Composites* (pp. 249–257). Springer. doi:10.1007/978-981-19-7146-4_14

Boopathi, S., & Davim, J. P. (2023). *Sustainable Utilization of Nanoparticles and Nanofluids in Engineering Applications*. IGI Global. doi:10.4018/978-1-6684-9135-5

Boopathi, S., & Davim, J. P. (2023a). Applications of Nanoparticles in Various Manufacturing Processes. In *Sustainable Utilization of Nanoparticles and Nanofluids in Engineering Applications* (pp. 1–31). IGI Global. doi:10.4018/978-1-6684-9135-5.ch001

Boopathi, S., Jeyakumar, M., Singh, G. R., King, F. L., Pandian, M., Subbiah, R., & Haribalaji, V. (2022). An experimental study on friction stir processing of aluminium alloy (AA-2024) and boron nitride (BNp) surface composite. *Materials Today: Proceedings*, *59*(1), 1094–1099. doi:10.1016/j.matpr.2022.02.435

Boopathi, S., & Kanike, U. K. (2023). Applications of Artificial Intelligent and Machine Learning Techniques in Image Processing. In *Handbook of Research on Thrust Technologies' Effect on Image Processing* (pp. 151–173). IGI Global. doi:10.4018/978-1-6684-8618-4.ch010

Boopathi, S., Myilsamy, S., & Sukkasamy, S. (2021). *Experimental Investigation and Multi-Objective Optimization of Cryogenically Cooled Near-Dry Wire-Cut EDM Using TOPSIS Technique*. IJAMT PREPRINT.

Boopathi, S., & Sivakumar, K. (2013). Experimental investigation and parameter optimization of near-dry wire-cut electrical discharge machining using multi-objective evolutionary algorithm. *International Journal of Advanced Manufacturing Technology*, *67*(9–12), 2639–2655. doi:10.100700170-012-4680-4

Boopathi, S., Umareddy, M., & Elangovan, M. (2023). Applications of Nano-Cutting Fluids in Advanced Machining Processes. In *Sustainable Utilization of Nanoparticles and Nanofluids in Engineering Applications* (pp. 211–234). IGI Global. doi:10.4018/978-1-6684-9135-5.ch009

Bowell, T., Cowan, R., & Kemp, G. (2019). *Critical Thinking: A Concise Guide. 5Th Edition.* Routledge. doi:10.4324/9781351243735

Bozkurt, A. (2023). Generative artificial intelligence (AI) powered conversational educational agents: The inevitable paradigm shift—. *Asian Journal of Distance Education, 18*(1).

Bozkurt, A., & Sharma, R. C. (2023). Challenging the Status Quo and Exploring the New Boundaries in the Age of Algorithms: Reimagining the Role of Generative AI in Distance Education and Online Learning. *Asian Journal of Distance Education, 18*(1), 1. http://asianjde.com/ojs/index.php/AsianJDE/article/view/714

Bozkurt, A., & Sharma, R. C. (2023). Challenging the status quo and exploring the new boundaries in the age of algorithms: Reimagining the role of generative AI in distance education and online learning. *Asian Journal of Distance Education, 18*(1).

Bran, E., Rughini, C., Nadoleanu, G., & Flaherty, M. G. (2023). The Emerging Social Status of Generative AI: Vocabularies of AI Competence in Public Discourse. In *Proceedings of The 24th Conference on Control Systems and Computer Science (CSCS24 2023).* IEEE. 10.1109/CSCS59211.2023.00068

Bujang, S. D. A., Selamat, A., & Krejcar, O. (2021). A predictive analytics model for students grade prediction by supervised machine learning. *IOP Conference Series. Materials Science and Engineering, 1051*(1), 012005. doi:10.1088/1757-899X/1051/1/012005

Cañabate, D., Garcia-Romeu, M. L., Menció, A., Nogué, L., Planas, M., & Solé-Pla, J. (2020a). Cross-Disciplinary Analysis of Cooperative Learning Dimensions Based on Higher Education Students' Perceptions. *Sustainability (Basel), 12*(19), 8156. doi:10.3390u12198156

Candel, E. C., de-la-Peña, C., & Yuste, B. C. (2023). Pre-service teachers' perception of active learning methodologies in history: Flipped classroom and gamification in an e-learning environment. *Education and Information Technologies*, 1–23. doi:10.100710639-023-11924-0

Cao, Y., Li, S., Liu, Y., Yan, Z., Dai, Y., Yu, P. S., & Sun, L. (2023). A comprehensive survey of ai-generated content (aigc): A history of generative ai from gan to chatgpt. *ArXiv Preprint ArXiv:2303.04226.*

Cao, Y., Li, S., Liu, Y., Yan, Z., Dai, Y., Yu, P.S., & Sun, L. (2023). *A Comprehensive Survey of AI-Generated Content (AIGC): A History of Generative AI from GAN to ChatGPT.* ArXiv, abs/2303.04226.

Carrier, M. (2017). Automated speech recognition in language learning: Potential models, benefits, and impact. *Training, Language, and Culture, 1*(1), 46–61. doi:10.29366/2017tlc.1.1.3

Cebi, A., Özdemir, T. B., Reisoğlu, İ., & Colak, C. (2022). From digital competences to technology integration: Re-formation of pre-service teachers' knowledge and understanding. *International Journal of Educational Research, 113*, 101965. doi:10.1016/j.ijer.2022.101965

Chan, C. K. Y., & Tsi, L. H. (2023). *The AI Revolution in Education: Will AI Replace or Assist Teachers in Higher Education?* arXiv preprint arXiv:2305.01185.

Chaudhry, M. A., & Kazim, E. (2022). Artificial Intelligence in Education (AIEd): A high-level academic and industry note 2021. *AI and Ethics*, *2*(1), 1–9. doi:10.100743681-021-00074-z PMID:34790953

Chen, X., Xie, H., Zou, D., & Hwang, G. J. (2020). Application and theory gaps during the rise of artificial intelligence in education. *Computers and Education: Artificial Intelligence*, *1*, 100002. doi:10.1016/j.caeai.2020.100002

Chiu, T. K. (2021). A holistic approach to the design of artificial intelligence (AI) education for K-12 schools. *TechTrends*, *65*(5), 796–807. doi:10.100711528-021-00637-1

Cobbaert, C. M., Althaus, H., Begcevic Brkovic, I., Ceglarek, U., Coassin, S., Delatour, V., Deprez, L., Dikaios, I., Dittrich, J., Hoofnagle, A. N., Kostner, G. M., Kronenberg, F., Kuklenyik, Z., Prinzing, U., Vesper, H. W., Zegers, I., & Ruhaak, L. R. (2021). Towards an SI-traceable reference measurement system for seven serum apolipoproteins using bottom-up quantitative proteomics: Conceptual approach enabled by cross-disciplinary/cross-sector collaboration. *Clinical Chemistry*, *67*(3), 478–489. doi:10.1093/clinchem/hvaa239 PMID:33331636

Commander, N. E., Zhao, Y., Gallagher, P. A., & You, Y. (2012). Promoting Cross-cultural Understanding of Education Through Online Discussions. *Procedia - Social and Behavioral Sciences, 46*(2005), 4632–4642. doi:10.1016/j.sbspro.2012.06.310

Cooper, G. (2023). Examining science education in chatgpt: An exploratory study of generative artificial intelligence. *Journal of Science Education and Technology*, *32*(3), 444–452. doi:10.100710956-023-10039-y

Coussement, K., Phan, M., De Caigny, A., Benoit, D. F., & Raes, A. (2020). Predicting student dropout in subscription-based online learning environments: The beneficial impact of the logit leaf model. *Decision Support Systems*, *135*, 113325. doi:10.1016/j.dss.2020.113325

Currie, G. M. (2023). Academic integrity and artificial intelligence: Is ChatGPT hype, hero or heresy? *Seminars in Nuclear Medicine*, *53*(5), 719–730. doi:10.1053/j.semnuclmed.2023.04.008 PMID:37225599

Daniel, J. H, M. J., Peter, N., & Stuart, R. (2014). Speech and Language Processing (2nd edition). Pearson.

Dargan, S., Kumar, M., Ayyagari, M. R., & Kumar, G. (2020). A survey of deep learning and its applications: A new paradigm to machine learning. *Archives of Computational Methods in Engineering*, *27*(4), 1071–1092. doi:10.100711831-019-09344-w

De Bakker, F. G., Rasche, A., & Ponte, S. (2019). Multi-stakeholder initiatives on sustainability: A cross-disciplinary review and research agenda for business ethics. *Business Ethics Quarterly*, *29*(3), 343–383. doi:10.1017/beq.2019.10

Dec, G., Stadnicka, D., Paśko, Ł., Mądziel, M., Figliè, R., Mazzei, D., Tyrovolas, M., Stylios, C., Navarro, J., & Solé-Beteta, X. (2022). Role of Academics in Transferring Knowledge and Skills on Artificial Intelligence, Internet of Things and Edge Computing. *Sensors (Basel)*, *22*(7), 2496. doi:10.339022072496 PMID:35408110

Denny, P., Prather, J., Becker, B. A., Finnie-Ansley, J., Hellas, A., Leinonen, J., & Sarsa, S. (2023). *Computing Education in the Era of Generative AI.* arXiv preprint arXiv:2306.02608.

Department of Education. (2021). *Education in a pandemic: The disparate impact of COVID-19 on American students.* DoE. https://www2.ed.gov/about/offices/list/ocr/docs/20210608-impacts-of-covid19.pdf

Desai, S., Stahl, I., & Chamorro-Koc, M. (2021). Global design studio: Advancing cross-disciplinary experiential education during the COVID-19 pandemic. *Journal of Design and Technology Education*, *26*(4), 165–181.

Dhanya, D., Kumar, S. S., Thilagavathy, A., Prasad, D., & Boopathi, S. (2023). Data Analytics and Artificial Intelligence in the Circular Economy: Case Studies. In Intelligent Engineering Applications and Applied Sciences for Sustainability (pp. 40–58). IGI Global.

Dickey, E., & Bejarano, A. (2023). A Model for Integrating Generative AI into Course Content Development. *ArXiv Preprint ArXiv:2308.12276.*

Dilmegani, C. (2023). *ChatGPT Education Use Cases, Benefits & Challenges in 2023.* AI Multiple. https://research.aimultiple.com/chatgpt-education/

Diment, A., Fagerlund, E., Benfield, A., & Virtanen, T. (2019). Detection of typical pronunciation errors in non-native English speech using convolutional recurrent neural networks. *International Joint Conference on Neural Network*, pp. 1-8. 10.1109/IJCNN.2019.8851963

Ding, Y., Pulford, J., & Bates, I. (2020). Practical actions for fostering cross-disciplinary global health research: Lessons from a narrative literature review. *BMJ Global Health*, *5*(4), e002293. doi:10.1136/bmjgh-2020-002293 PMID:32354784

Di, W., Zhang, S., Lian, X., Oubibi, M., Li, D., Ding, L., Zhang, Z., & Yang, T. (2022). Research on cross-cultural adaptation and educational management of international students in China: Case of African students at Zhejiang Normal University. *Frontiers in Psychology*, *13*(October), 1009658. doi:10.3389/fpsyg.2022.1009658 PMID:36324773

Dong, Y., Chai, C. S., Sang, G. Y., Koh, J. H. L., & Tsai, C. C. (2015). Exploring the profiles and interplays of pre-service and in-service teachers' technological pedagogical content knowledge (TPACK) in China. *Journal of Educational Technology & Society*, *18*(1), 158–169.

Dorner, H., & Kumar, S. (2016). Online collaborative mentoring for technology integration in pre-service teacher education. *TechTrends*, *60*(1), 48–55. doi:10.100711528-015-0016-1

Durairaj, M., Jayakumar, S., Karpagavalli, V., Maheswari, B. U., Boopathi, S., & ... (2023). Utilization of Digital Tools in the Indian Higher Education System During Health Crises. In *Multidisciplinary Approaches to Organizational Governance During Health Crises* (pp. 1–21). IGI Global. doi:10.4018/978-1-7998-9213-7.ch001

Dwivedi, Y. K., Hughes, D. L., Coombs, C., Constantiou, I., Duan, Y., Edwards, J. S., Gupta, B., Lal, B., Misra, S., Prashant, P., Raman, R., Rana, N. P., Sharma, S. K., & Upadhyay, N. (2020). Impact of COVID-19 pandemic on information management research and practice: Transforming education, work and life. *International Journal of Information Management*, *55*, 102211. doi:10.1016/j.ijinfomgt.2020.102211

Dwivedi, Y. K., Hughes, L., Kar, A. K., Baabdullah, A. M., Grover, P., Abbas, R., Andreini, D., Abumoghli, I., Barlette, Y., Bunker, D., Chandra Kruse, L., Constantiou, I., Davison, R. M., De', R., Dubey, R., Fenby-Taylor, H., Gupta, B., He, W., Kodama, M., & Wade, M. (2022). Climate change and COP26: Are digital technologies and information management part of the problem or the solution? An editorial reflection and call to action. *International Journal of Information Management*, *63*, 102456. doi:10.1016/j.ijinfomgt.2021.102456

Dwivedi, Y. K., Kshetri, N., Hughes, L., Slade, E. L., Jeyaraj, A., Kar, A. K., Baabdullah, A. M., Koohang, A., Raghavan, V., Ahuja, M., Albanna, H., Albashrawi, M. A., Al-Busaidi, A. S., Balakrishnan, J., Barlette, Y., Basu, S., Bose, I., Brooks, L., Buhalis, D., & Wright, R. (2023). Opinion Paper: "So what if ChatGPT wrote it?" Multidisciplinary perspectives on opportunities, challenges and implications of generative conversational AI for research, practice and policy. *International Journal of Information Management*, *71*, 102642. doi:10.1016/j.ijinfomgt.2023.102642

Ebrahimzadeh, M. (2017). Readers, Players, and Watchers: EFL Students' Vocabulary Acquisition through Digital Video Games. *English Language Teaching*, *10*(2), 1–18. doi:10.5539/elt.v10n2p1

EIH Digital Agency. (2023, August 3). What is book marketing, and why is it important for authors and publishers? *Medium*. https://medium.com/@eihdigitalagency/what-is-book-marketing-and-why-is-it-important-for-authors-and-publishers-9c7721003147

Elasticsearch, B. V. (2023). *What is a Large Language Model? A Comprehensive LLMs Guide*. Elastic. https://www.elastic.co/what-is/large-language-models

Ellingrud, K., Sanghvi, S., Dandona, G. S., Madgavkar, A., Chui, M., White, O., & Hasebe, P. (2023). *Generative AI and the future of work in America*. McKinsey Global Institute. https://www.mckinsey.com/mgi/our-research/generative-ai-and-the-future-of-work-in-america#/

Enago. (2023). *What is Manuscript Editing and Why is it Important?* Enago. https://www.enago.com/author-hub/what-is-manuscript-editing

Erarslan, A. (2019). Instagram as an Education Platform for EFL Learners. *Turkish Online Journal of Educational Technology-TOJET*, *18*(3), 54–69.

Esplugas, M. (2023). The use of artificial intelligence (AI) to enhance academic communication, education, and research: A balanced approach. *The Journal of Hand Surgery, European Volume*, *48*(8), 17531934231185746. doi:10.1177/17531934231185746 PMID:37417005

Euchner, J. (2023). Generative AI. *Research Technology Management*, *66*(3), 71–74. doi:10.1080/08956308.2023.2188861

Eysenbach, G. (2023). The role of ChatGPT, generative language models, and artificial intelligence in medical education: A conversation with ChatGPT and a call for papers. *JMIR Medical Education*, *9*(1), e46885. doi:10.2196/46885 PMID:36863937

Farazouli, A., Cerratto-Pargman, T., Bolander-Laksov, K., & McGrath, C. (2023). Hello GPT! Goodbye home examination? An exploratory study of AI chatbots impact on university teachers' assessment practices. *Assessment & Evaluation in Higher Education*, 1–13. doi:10.1080/02602938.2023.2241676

Farjon, D., Smits, A., & Voogt, J. (2019). Technology integration of pre-service teachers explained by attitudes and beliefs, competency, access, and experience. *Computers & Education*, *130*, 81–93. doi:10.1016/j.compedu.2018.11.010

Farrow, R. (2023). The possibilities and limits of XAI in education: A socio-technical perspective. *Learning, Media and Technology*, *48*(2), 266–279. doi:10.1080/17439884.2023.2185630

Farrukh, M. U., Bashir, M. K., & Rola-Rubzen, F. (2020). Exploring the sustainable food security approach in relation to agricultural and multi-sectoral interventions: A review of cross-disciplinary perspectives. *Geoforum*, *108*, 23–27. doi:10.1016/j.geoforum.2019.11.012

Fauzi, F., Tuhuteru, L., Sampe, F., Ausat, A. M. A., & Hatta, H. R. (2023). Analysing the role of ChatGPT in improving student productivity in higher education. *Journal of Education*, *5*(4), 14886–14891.

Feeney, M., Grohnert, T., Gijselaers, W., & Martens, P. (2023a). Organizations, learning, and sustainability: A cross-disciplinary review and research agenda. *Journal of Business Ethics*, *184*(1), 217–235. doi:10.100710551-022-05072-7

Ferraro, K. M., Ferraro, A. L., & Sommer, N. R. (2021). Challenges facing cross-disciplinary collaboration in conservation ethics. *Conservation Science and Practice*, *3*(11), e523. doi:10.1111/csp2.523

Firria, T. N. (2021). *Artificial Intelligence (AI) in education: Using AI tools for teaching and learning process.* Institut Teknologi Bisnis AAS Indonesia. https://prosiding.stie- aas.ac.id/index.php/prosenas/article/view/106/104

Fitria, T. N. (2023). Augmented Reality (AR) and Virtual Reality (VR) Technology in Education: Media of Teaching and Learning: A Review. *International Journal of Computer and Information System (IJCIS). Peer Reviewed-International Journal*, *04*(01), 2745–9659. doi:10.29040/ijcis.v4i1.102

Forsey, C. (2023). *The State of Generative AI & How It Will Revolutionize Marketing*. Hubspot. https://blog.hubspot.com/marketing/state-of-generative-ai

Ganapathy, K., Das, S., Reddy, S., Thaploo, V., Nazneen, A., Kosuru, A., & Shankar Nag, U. (2021). Digital health care in public private partnership mode. *Telemedicine Journal and e-Health*, *27*(12), 1363–1371. doi:10.1089/tmj.2020.0499 PMID:33819433

Gardner-McCune, C., Touretzky, D., Martin, F., & Seehorn, D. (2019). AI for K-12: Making room for AI in K-12 CS curricula. *Proceedings of the 50th ACM Technical Symposium on Computer Science Education*, (pp. 1244–1244). ACM. 10.1145/3287324.3293729

Garduño Palomino, K. Y. (2021). Estado de avance de la industria 4.0 en la maquiladora: efectos en el empleo en Mexicali, México. *PAAKAT: revista de tecnología y sociedad, 11*(21).

Generative, A. I. net. (2023). *Generative AI.* Generative AI. https://generativeai.net

George, B., & Wooden, O. (2023). Managing the Strategic Transformation of Higher Education through Artificial Intelligence. *Administrative Sciences*, *13*(9), 9. doi:10.3390/admsci13090196

Ghufron, M. A., & Rosyida, F. (2018). The role of Grammarly in assessing English as foreign language (EFL) writing. *Lingua Cultura, 12*(4), 395–403. doi:10.21512/lc.v12i4.4582

Godwin-Jones, R. (2022). Partnering with AI: Intelligent writing assistance and instructed language learning. *Language Learning & Technology*, *26*(2), 5–24. 10125/73474

Goldenberg, S. L., Nir, G., & Salcudean, S. E. (2019). A new era: Artificial intelligence and machine learning in prostate cancer. *Nature Reviews. Urology*, *16*(7), 391–403. doi:10.103841585-019-0193-3 PMID:31092914

Goodfellow, I. J., Pouget-Abadie, J., Mirza, M., Xu, B., Warde-Farley, D., Ozair, S., Courville, A., & Bengio, Y. (2014). *Generative Adversarial Networks* (arXiv:1406.2661). arXiv. https://doi.org//arXiv.1406.2661 doi:10.48550

Google Bard. (2023a). *Develop a compelling value proposition for generative AI for academic journal editors* Google Bard. [Https://bard.google.com/].

Google Bard. (2023b). *Generate an a academic paper on the topic "The Impact of Generative AI on Traditional Academic Publishing: A Pragmatic Perspective" with citations and references.* Google Bard. [Https://bard.google.com/].

Google Bard. (2023c). *How can Bard assist in the peer review process?* Google Bard. [Https://bard.google.com/].

Google Bard. (2023d). *Provide me with revisions for this text.* Googel Bard. [Https://bard.google.com/].

Gudoniene, D., Staneviciene, E., Buksnaitis, V., & Daley, N. (2023). The Scenarios of Artificial Intelligence and Wireframes Implementation in Engineering Education. *Sustainability (Basel)*, *15*(8), 6850. doi:10.3390u15086850

Hacker, P. (2023). The European AI liability directives – Critique of a half-hearted approach and lessons for the future. *Computer Law & Security Report*, *51*, 105871. doi:10.1016/j.clsr.2023.105871

Harman, M. (2023, August 9). The Role of Technology in Digital Publishing And eBook Industry. *Kitaboo*. https://kitaboo.com/role-technology-digital-publishing/

Harrer, S. (2023). Attention is not all you need: The complicated case of ethically using large language models in healthcare and medicine. *EBioMedicine*, *90*, 104512. doi:10.1016/j.ebiom.2023.104512 PMID:36924620

He, C., Annavaram, M., & Avestimehr, S. (2020). Group knowledge transfer: Federated learning of large cnns at the edge. *Advances in Neural Information Processing Systems*, *33*, 14068–14080.

Hema, N., Krishnamoorthy, N., Chavan, S. M., Kumar, N., Sabarimuthu, M., & Boopathi, S. (2023). A Study on an Internet of Things (IoT)-Enabled Smart Solar Grid System. In *Handbook of Research on Deep Learning Techniques for Cloud-Based Industrial IoT* (pp. 290–308). IGI Global. doi:10.4018/978-1-6684-8098-4.ch017

Hermann, R. R., & Bossle, M. B. (2020). Bringing an entrepreneurial focus to sustainability education: A teaching framework based on content analysis. *Journal of Cleaner Production*, *246*, 119038. doi:10.1016/j.jclepro.2019.119038

Herold, F., & Waring, M. (2018). An investigation of pre-service teachers' learning in physical education teacher education: Schools and university in partnership. *Sport Education and Society*, *23*(1), 95–107. doi:10.1080/13573322.2015.1127802

Heyder, T., Passlack, N., & Posegga, O. (2023). Ethical management of human-AI interaction: Theory development review. *The Journal of Strategic Information Systems*, *32*(3), 101772. doi:10.1016/j.jsis.2023.101772

Hobert, S. (2019). *Say hello to 'coding tutor'! Design and evaluation of a chatbot-based learning system supporting students to learn to program.*

Hochreiter, S., & Schmidhuber, J. (1997). Long Short-term Memory. *Neural Computation*, *9*(8), 1735–1780. doi:10.1162/neco.1997.9.8.1735 PMID:9377276

Horwitz, S. K., & Santillan, C. (2012). Knowledge sharing in global virtual team collaboration: Applications of CE and thinkLets. *Knowledge Management Research and Practice*, *10*(4), 342–353. doi:10.1057/kmrp.2012.39

Hsu, Y. C., & Ching, Y. H. (2023). Generative Artificial Intelligence in Education, Part One: The Dynamic Frontier. *TechTrends*, *67*(4), 1–5. doi:10.100711528-023-00863-9

Hussain, Z., & Srimathy, G. (2023). *IoT and AI Integration for Enhanced Efficiency and Sustainability*.

Hwang, W. Y., Nurtantyana, R., Purba, S. W. D., Hariyanti, U., Indrihapsari, Y., & Surjono, H. D. (2023). AI and recognition technologies to facilitate English as a foreign language writing for supporting personalization and contextualization in authentic contexts. *Journal of Educational Computing Research*, *61*(5), 07356331221137253. doi:10.1177/07356331221137253

Ingle, R. B., Senthil, T. S., Swathi, S., Muralidharan, N., Mahendran, G., & Boopathi, S. (2023). Sustainability and Optimization of Green and Lean Manufacturing Processes Using Machine Learning Techniques. IGI Global. doi:10.4018/978-1-6684-8238-4.ch012

Ironsi, C. S. (2023). Investigating the use of virtual reality to improve speaking skills: Insights from students and teachers. *Smart Learning Environments*, *10*(1), 53. doi:10.118640561-023-00272-8

IslamI.IslamM. N. (2023). Opportunities and challenges of chatbot in academia: A conceptual analysis. Authorea Preprints.

Janssen, M., & Van der Voort, H. (2020). Agile and adaptive governance in crisis response: Lessons from the COVID-19 pandemic. *International Journal of Information Management*, *55*, 102180. doi:10.1016/j.ijinfomgt.2020.102180 PMID:32836637

Jarrahi, M. H., Askay, D., Eshraghi, A., & Smith, P. (2023). Artificial intelligence and knowledge management: A partnership between human and AI. *Business Horizons*, *66*(1), 87–99. doi:10.1016/j.bushor.2022.03.002

Javaid, M., Haleem, A., & Singh, R. P. (2023). ChatGPT for healthcare services: An emerging stage for an innovative perspective. *BenchCouncil Transactions on Benchmarks. Standards and Evaluations*, *3*(1), 100105. doi:10.1016/j.tbench.2023.100105

Jiménez Izquierdo, Y., Magaña Medina, D. E., & Valdés Cuervo, A. A. (2019). Interés de estudiantes hacia carreras universitarias en ingeniería. *Educación y Ciencia*, *8*(51), 85–88.

Jiménez, J., Escalante, J. C., Rodríguez, C., Ramírez, J. M., & Morales-Arroyo, M. A. (2010). ŠMobility or brain drain? The case of Mexican scientists. *Социология науки и технологий*, *1*(1), 89-108.

John Wiley & Sons Inc. (2023). *What is Peer Review?* Wiley. https://authorservices.wiley.com/Reviewers/journal-reviewers/what-is-peer-review/index.html

Johnson, A. (2023, July 12). Revolutionizing Academic Research with Large Language Models. *Medium*. https://medium.com/@andrew_johnson_4/revolutionizing-academic-research-with-large-language-models-6904366abef4

Jones, K. S. (1994). Natural language processing: a historical review. *Current issues in computational linguistics: in honour of Don Walker*, 3-16.

Joshi, N. (2019). 7 Types Of Artificial Intelligence. *Forbes*. https://www.forbes.com/sites/cognitiveworld/2019/06/19/7-types-of-artificial-intelligence/

Jovanovic, M., & Campbell, M. (2002). Generative Artificial Intelligence: Trends and Prospects. *Computer*, *55*(10), 107–112. doi:10.1109/MC.2022.3192720

Kaiser, J. (2023). *Science funding agencies say no to using AI for peer review*. Science.com. https://www.science.org/content/article/science-funding-agencies-say-no-using-ai-peer-review

Kalidas, R., Boopathi, S., Sivakumar, K., & Mohankumar, P. (2012). Optimization of Machining Parameters of WEDM Process Based On the Taguchi Method. *IJEST, 6*(1).

Kaplan-Rakowski, R., Grotewold, K., Hartwick, P., & Papin, K. (2023). Generative AI and Teachers' Perspectives on Its Implementation in Education. *Journal of Interactive Learning Research, 34*(2), 313–338.

Karakose, T., Demirkol, M., Yirci, R., Polat, H., Ozdemir, T. Y., & Tülübaş, T. (2023). A Conversation with ChatGPT about Digital Leadership and Technology Integration: Comparative Analysis Based on Human–AI Collaboration. *Administrative Sciences, 13*(7), 157. doi:10.3390/admsci13070157

Karthik, S., Hemalatha, R., Aruna, R., Deivakani, M., Reddy, R. V. K., & Boopathi, S. (2023). Study on Healthcare Security System-Integrated Internet of Things (IoT). In Perspectives and Considerations on the Evolution of Smart Systems (pp. 342–362). IGI Global.

Kasneci, E., Seßler, K., Küchemann, S., Bannert, M., Dementieva, D., Fischer, F., Gasser, U., Groh, G., Günnemann, S., Hüllermeier, E., Krusche, S., Kutyniok, G., Michaeli, T., Nerdel, C., Pfeffer, J., Poquet, O., Sailer, M., Schmidt, A., Seidel, T., & Kasneci, G. (2023). ChatGPT for good? On opportunities and challenges of large language models for education. *Learning and Individual Differences, 103*, 102274. doi:10.1016/j.lindif.2023.102274

Kavitha, C. R., Varalatchoumy, M., Mithuna, H. R., Bharathi, K., Geethalakshmi, N. M., & Boopathi, S. (2023). Energy Monitoring and Control in the Smart Grid: Integrated Intelligent IoT and ANFIS. In M. Arshad (Ed.), Advances in Bioinformatics and Biomedical Engineering. IGI Global. doi:10.4018/978-1-6684-6577-6.ch014

Keary, T. (2023, July 14). 12 Practical Large Language Model (LLM) Applications. *Techopedia*. https://www.techopedia.com/12-practical-large-language-model-llm-applications

Kelly, J., Sadeghieh, T., & Adeli, K. (2014). Peer Review in Scientific Publications: Benefits, Critiques, & A Survival Guide. *EJIFCC, 25*(3), 227–243. PMID:27683470

Kim, J., Lee, H., & Cho, Y. H. (2022). Learning design to support student-AI collaboration: perspectives of leading teachers for AI in education. In Education and Information Technologies, 27(5). Springer US. doi:10.100710639-021-10831-6

King, M. R. (2023). A Conversation on Artificial Intelligence, Chatbots, and Plagiarism in Higher Education. *Cellular and Molecular Bioengineering, 16*(1), 1–2. doi:10.100712195-022-00754-8 PMID:36660590

Kingma, D. P., & Welling, M. (2022). *Auto-Encoding Variational Bayes* (arXiv:1312.6114). arXiv. http://arxiv.org/abs/1312.6114

Knewton. (2019). *Adaptive learning defined: A Knewton guide*. Knewton. https://www.knewton.com/adaptive-learning

Knie, L., Standl, B., & Schwarzer, S. (2022). First experiences of integrating computational thinking into a blended learning in-service training program for STEM teachers. *Computer Applications in Engineering Education, 30*(5), 1423–1439. doi:10.1002/cae.22529

Kohnke, L., Moorhouse, B. L., & Zou, D. (2023). ChatGPT for language teaching and learning. *RELC Journal*, 00336882231162868.

Kohnke, L., Moorhouse, B. L., & Zou, D. (2023a). ChatGPT for Language Teaching and Learning. *RELC Journal, 54*(2), 537–550. doi:10.1177/00336882231162868

Korzynski, P., Mazurek, G., Altmann, A., Ejdys, J., Kazlauskaite, R., Paliszkiewicz, J., Wach, K., & Ziemba, E. (2023). Generative artificial intelligence as a new context for management theories: Analysis of ChatGPT. *Central European Management Journal, 31*(1), 3–13. doi:10.1108/CEMJ-02-2023-0091

Kovačević, D. (2023, March). Use of chatbot in ESP teaching process. In *2023 22nd International Symposium INFOTEH-JAHORINA (INFOTEH)* (pp. 1-5). IEEE.

Krügel, S., Ostermaier, A., & Uhl, M. (2023). The moral authority of ChatGPT. *arXiv preprint arXiv:2301.07098.*

Kumara, V., Mohanaprakash, T., Fairooz, S., Jamal, K., Babu, T., & Sampath, B. (2023). Experimental Study on a Reliable Smart Hydroponics System. In *Human Agro-Energy Optimization for Business and Industry* (pp. 27–45). IGI Global. doi:10.4018/978-1-6684-4118-3.ch002

Kumar, P. R., Meenakshi, S., Shalini, S., Devi, S. R., & Boopathi, S. (2023). Soil Quality Prediction in Context Learning Approaches Using Deep Learning and Blockchain for Smart Agriculture. In R. Kumar, A. B. Abdul Hamid, & N. I. Binti Ya'akub (Eds.), Advances in Computational Intelligence and Robotics. IGI Global. doi:10.4018/978-1-6684-9151-5.ch001

Kurni, M., Mohammed, M. S., & Srinivasa, K. (2023). Intelligent Tutoring Systems. In *A Beginner's Guide to Introduce Artificial Intelligence in Teaching and Learning* (pp. 29–44). Springer.

Labrague, L. J., Aguilar-Rosales, R., Yboa, B. C., & Sabio, J. B. (2023). Factors influencing student nurses' readiness to adopt artificial intelligence (AI) in their studies and their perceived barriers to accessing AI technology: A cross-sectional study. *Nurse Education Today, 130*, 105945. doi:10.1016/j.nedt.2023.105945 PMID:37625351

Lachner, A., Fabian, A., Franke, U., Preiß, J., Jacob, L., Führer, C., Küchler, U., Paravicini, W., Randler, C., & Thomas, P. (2021). Fostering pre-service teachers' technological pedagogical content knowledge (TPACK): A quasi-experimental field study. *Computers & Education, 174*, 104304. doi:10.1016/j.compedu.2021.104304

Lambert Academic Publishing. (2023, March 7). *The Ultimate Guide to Academic Book Publishing: Understanding the Process from Start to Finish.* Academic Publishing. https://blog.lap-publishing.com/academic-book-publishing-process/

Lauer, M., Constant, S., & Wernimont, A. (2023, June 23). *Using AI in Peer Review Is a Breach of Confidentiality*. NIH. https://nexus.od.nih.gov/all/2023/06/23/using-ai-in-peer-review-is-a-breach-of-confidentiality/

Lawton, G. (2023). *What is Generative AI? Everything You Need to Know*. Enterprise AI. https://www.techtarget.com/searchenterpriseai/definition/generative-AI

Le Cornu, R., & Ewing, R. (2008). Reconceptualising professional experiences in pre-service teacher education… reconstructing the past to embrace the future. *Teaching and Teacher Education*, *24*(7), 1799–1812. doi:10.1016/j.tate.2008.02.008

Lee, H. (2023). The rise of ChatGPT: Exploring its potential in medical education. *Anatomical Sciences Education*, ase.2270. doi:10.1002/ase.2270 PMID:36916887

Lee, T. K. (2023). *Artificial intelligence and posthumanist translation: ChatGPT versus the translator*. Applied Linguistics Review. doi:10.1515/applirev-2023-0122

Lee, Y., & Lee, J. (2014). Enhancing pre-service teachers' self-efficacy beliefs for technology integration through lesson planning practice. *Computers & Education*, *73*, 121–128. doi:10.1016/j.compedu.2014.01.001

Lei, L., Li, J., & Li, W. (2023). Assessing the role of artificial intelligence in the mental healthcare of teachers and students. *Soft Computing*. doi:10.100700500-023-08072-5 PMID:37362257

Lei, Q.-Q., & Liu, H.-Y. (2020). Design of a WeChat mobile learning platform for multi-modal language learning and its application. *Journal of Physics: Conference Series*, *1616*(1), 012085. doi:10.1088/1742-6596/1616/1/012085

Leung, T. I., Cardoso, T. de A., Mavragani, A., & Eysenbach, G. (2023). Best Practices for Using AI Tools as an Author, Peer Reviewer, or Editor. *Journal of Medical Internet Research*, *25*(1), e51584. doi:10.2196/51584 PMID:37651164

Liang, P.P., Zadeh, A., & Morency, L. (2022). *Foundations and Recent Trends in Multimodal Machine Learning: Principles, Challenges, and Open Questions*. ArXiv, abs/2209.03430.

Liebrenz, M., Schleifer, R., Buadze, A., Bhugra, D., & Smith, A. (2023). Generating scholarly content with ChatGPT: Ethical challenges for medical publishing. *The Lancet. Digital Health*, *5*(3), e105–e106. doi:10.1016/S2589-7500(23)00019-5 PMID:36754725

Li, J., Tang, T., Zhao, W. X., & Wen, J. (2021). Pretrained Language Models for Text Generation: A Survey. *International Joint Conference on Artificial Intelligence*. IJCAI. 10.24963/ijcai.2021/612

Limo, F. A. F., Tiza, D. R. H., Roque, M. M., Herrera, E. E., Murillo, J. P. M., Huallpa, J. J., & Gonzáles, J. L. A. (2023). Personalized tutoring: ChatGPT as a virtual tutor for personalized learning experiences. *Social Space*, *23*(1), 293–312.

Lim, W. M., Gunasekara, A., Pallant, J. L., Pallant, J. I., & Pechenkina, E. (2023). Generative AI and the future of education: Ragnarök or reformation? A paradoxical perspective from management educators. *International Journal of Management Education*, *21*(2), 100790. doi:10.1016/j.ijme.2023.100790

Lin, C. C., Huang, A. Y., & Yang, S. J. (2023). A review of AI-driven conversational chatbot implementation methodologies and challenges (1999–2022). *Sustainability (Basel)*, *15*(5), 4012. doi:10.3390u15054012

Lin, P., & Van Brummelen, J. (2021). Engaging teachers to co-design integrated AI curriculum for K-12 classrooms. *Proceedings of the 2021 CHI Conference on Human Factors in Computing Systems*, (pp. 1–12). ACM. 10.1145/3411764.3445377

Liu, M. (2023). Exploring the Application of Artificial Intelligence in Foreign Language Teaching: Challenges and Future Development. In *SHS Web of Conferences* (*Vol. 168*). EDP Sciences.

Liu, Y. (2023). *Cross-Cultural Challenges to Artificial Intelligence Ethics*. IS4SI Summit 2023. doi:10.3390/cmsf2023008021

Liu, C. C., Liao, M. G., Chang, C. H., & Lin, H. M. (2022). An analysis of children's interaction with an AI chatbot and its impact on their interest in reading. *Computers & Education*, *189*, 104576. doi:10.1016/j.compedu.2022.104576

Liu, C., Hou, J., Tu, Y. F., Wang, Y., & Hwang, G. J. (2021). Incorporating reflective thinking promoting mechanism into artificial intelligence-supported English writing environments. *Interactive Learning Environments*, 1–19.

Liu, Q., Tong, S., Liu, C., Zhao, H., Chen, E., Ma, H., & Wang, S. (2019). Exploiting cognitive structure for adaptive learning. *Proceedings of the 25th ACM SIGKDD International Conference on Knowledge Discovery & Data Mining*, (pp. 627–635). ACM. 10.1145/3292500.3330922

Lo, C. K. (2023). What Is the Impact of ChatGPT on Education? A Rapid Review of the Literature. *Education Sciences*, *13*(4), 4. doi:10.3390/educsci13040410

LoEstro Advisors. (2023, May 16). *Capitalizing on Gen AI in Edtech: Riding the Wave of Next-Generation Technology*. LoEstro Advisors. https://medium.com/loestro-advisors/capitalizing-on-gen-ai-in-edtech-riding-the-wave-of-next-generation-technology-c50d891ea3ce

Lopez-Acevedo, G. C. (2002). *Technology and Skill Demand in Mexico*.

López, H. A., Ponce, P., Molina, A., Ramírez-Montoya, M. S., & Lopez-Caudana, E. (2021). Design framework based on TEC21 educational model and Education 4.0 implemented in a Capstone Project: A case study of an electric vehicle suspension system. *Sustainability (Basel)*, *13*(11), 5768. doi:10.3390u13115768

Luan, H., & Tsai, C.-C. (2021). A review of using machine learning approaches for precision education. *Journal of Educational Technology & Society*, *24*(1), 250–266.

Maguluri, L. P., Arularasan, A. N., & Boopathi, S. (2023). Assessing Security Concerns for AI-Based Drones in Smart Cities. In R. Kumar, A. B. Abdul Hamid, & N. I. Binti Ya'akub (Eds.), (pp. 27–47). Advances in Computational Intelligence and Robotics. IGI Global. doi:10.4018/978-1-6684-9151-5.ch002

Maheswari, B. U., Imambi, S. S., Hasan, D., Meenakshi, S., Pratheep, V., & Boopathi, S. (2023). Internet of Things and Machine Learning-Integrated Smart Robotics. In Global Perspectives on Robotics and Autonomous Systems: Development and Applications (pp. 240–258). IGI Global. doi:10.4018/978-1-6684-7791-5.ch010

Malingan, N. (2023, April 25). *What is Encoder in Transformers*. Scaler Topics. https://www.scaler.com/topics/nlp/transformer-encoder-decoder/

Mariappan, J., & Krishnan, C. (2022). Integration of AI in Learning: A Paradigm Shift in Education. In C. Krishnan, F. Al-Harthy, & G. Singh (Eds.), *Technology Training for Educators From Past to Present* (pp. 263–275). IGI Global. doi:10.4018/978-1-6684-4083-4.ch014

Marsili, D. (2016). A cross-disciplinary approach to global environmental health: The case of contaminated sites. *Annali dell'Istituto Superiore di Sanita*, *52*(4), 516–523. PMID:27999222

Menon, S., & Suresh, M. (2020). Synergizing education, research, campus operations, and community engagements towards sustainability in higher education: A literature review. *International Journal of Sustainability in Higher Education*, *21*(5), 1015–1051. doi:10.1108/IJSHE-03-2020-0089

Meunier, F., Van de Vyver, J., Bradley, L., & Thouesny, S. (2019). *EUROCALL 2019: Call and complexity*. DoE.

Meyer, J. G., Urbanowicz, R. J., Martin, P. C. N., O'Connor, K., Li, R., Peng, P.-C., Bright, T. J., Tatonetti, N., Won, K. J., Gonzalez-Hernandez, G., & Moore, J. H. (2023). ChatGPT and large language models in academia: Opportunities and challenges. *BioData Mining*, *16*(1), 20. doi:10.118613040-023-00339-9 PMID:37443040

Mhlanga, D. (2023). Open AI in education, the responsible and ethical use of ChatGPT towards lifelong learning. *Education, the Responsible and Ethical Use of ChatGPT Towards Lifelong Learning*. SSRN.

Michel-Villarreal, R., Vilalta-Perdomo, E., Salinas-Navarro, D. E., Thierry-Aguilera, R., & Gerardou, F. S. (2023). Challenges and Opportunities of Generative AI for Higher Education as Explained by ChatGPT. *Education Sciences*, *13*(9), 9. doi:10.3390/educsci13090856

Mikhaylov, N. S. (2014). International business students' crosscultural competence development: The influence of the educational environment. *SAGE Open*, *4*(4), 1–15. doi:10.1177/2158244014564352

Milano, S., McGrane, J. A., & Leonelli, S. (2023). Large Language Models Challenge the Future of Higher Education. *Nature Machine Intelligence*, *5*(4), 333–334. doi:10.103842256-023-00644-2

Mishra, P., Warr, M., & Islam, R. (2023). TPACK in the age of ChatGPT and Generative AI. *Journal of Digital Learning in Teacher Education, 39*(4), 235–251. doi:10.1080/21532974.2023.2247480

Mobjörk, M., Berglund, C., Granberg, M., & Johansson, M. (2020). Sustainable development and cross-disciplinary research education: Challenges and opportunities for learning. *Högre Utbildning, 10*(1), 76–89. doi:10.23865/hu.v10.1942

Mohamed, A. M. (2023). Exploring the potential of an AI-based Chatbot (ChatGPT) in enhancing English as a Foreign Language (EFL) teaching: Perceptions of EFL Faculty Members. *Education and Information Technologies*, 1–23. doi:10.100710639-023-11917-z

Mohanty, A., Venkateswaran, N., Ranjit, P., Tripathi, M. A., & Boopathi, S. (2023). Innovative Strategy for Profitable Automobile Industries: Working Capital Management. In Handbook of Research on Designing Sustainable Supply Chains to Achieve a Circular Economy (pp. 412–428). IGI Global.

Moorhouse, B. L., & Harfitt, G. J. (2021). Pre-service and in-service teachers' professional learning through the pedagogical exchange of ideas during a teaching abroad experience. *Asia-Pacific Journal of Teacher Education, 49*(2), 230–244. doi:10.1080/1359866X.2019.1694634

Moqbel, M. S. S., & Al-Kadi, A. M. T. (2023). Foreign language learning assessment in the age of ChatGPT: A theoretical account. *Journal of English Studies in Arabia Felix, 2*(1), 71–84. doi:10.56540/jesaf.v2i1.62

Morales, M., Redlinger-Grosse, K., & MacFarlane, I. M. (2023). Cross-disciplinary collaboration for supervisor training: Reaping the benefits of a relationship-based approach. *The Clinical Supervisor, 42*(1), 26–44. doi:10.1080/07325223.2022.2132339

Muga, J. G. (2023). Artificial Intelligence language models in scientific writing. *Europhysics Letters, 143*(2), 20000. doi:10.1209/0295-5075/ace3ef

Murphy, R. F. (2019). Artificial intelligence applications to support K-12 teachers and teaching. Rand Corporation.

Murugesan, S., & Cherukuri, A. K. (2023). The Rise of Generative Artificial Intelligence and Its Impact on Education: The Promises and Perils. *Computer, 56*(5), 116–121. doi:10.1109/MC.2023.3253292

Myilsamy, S., & Sampath, B. (2017). Grey Relational Optimization of Powder Mixed Near-Dry Wire Cut Electrical Discharge Machining of Inconel 718 Alloy. *Asian Journal of Research in Social Sciences and Humanities, 7*(3), 18–25. doi:10.5958/2249-7315.2017.00157.5

Myszczynska, M. A., Ojamies, P. N., Lacoste, A. M., Neil, D., Saffari, A., Mead, R., Hautbergue, G. M., Holbrook, J. D., & Ferraiuolo, L. (2020). Applications of machine learning to diagnosis and treatment of neurodegenerative diseases. *Nature Reviews. Neurology, 16*(8), 440–456. doi:10.103841582-020-0377-8 PMID:32669685

Nah, F. F.-H., Zheng, R., Cai, J., Siau, K., & Chen, L. (2023). Generative AI and ChatGPT: Applications, challenges, and AI-human collaboration. *Journal of Information Technology Case and Application Research*, *25*(3), 277–304. doi:10.1080/15228053.2023.2233814

Nemorin, S., Vlachidis, A., Ayerakwa, H. M., & Andriotis, P. (2023). AI hyped? A horizon scan of discourse on artificial intelligence in education (AIED) and development. *Learning, Media and Technology*, *48*(1), 38–51. doi:10.1080/17439884.2022.2095568

Neville, I. A., Petrass, L. A., & Ben, F. (2023). Cross disciplinary teaching: A pedagogical model to support teachers in the development and implementation of outdoor learning opportunities. *Journal of Outdoor and Environmental Education*, *26*(1), 1–21. doi:10.100742322-022-00109-x

Nishanth, J., Deshmukh, M. A., Kushwah, R., Kushwaha, K. K., Balaji, S., & Sampath, B. (2023). Particle Swarm Optimization of Hybrid Renewable Energy Systems. In *Intelligent Engineering Applications and Applied Sciences for Sustainability* (pp. 291–308). IGI Global. doi:10.4018/979-8-3693-0044-2.ch016

Nurius, P. S., & Kemp, S. P. (2019). Individual-level competencies for team collaboration with cross-disciplinary researchers and stakeholders. Strategies for Team Science Success: Handbook of Evidence-Based Principles for Cross-Disciplinary Science and Practical Lessons Learned from Health Researchers, (pp. 171–187). Research Gate.

Nurtayeva, T., Salim, M., Basheer Taha, T., & Khalilov, S. (2023). The influence of ChatGPT and AI Tools on the Academic Performance. *YMER, 22*(6). https://ymerdigital.com/archives/?cpage=2&issId=%202206

NVIDIA. (2023). *What are Large Language Models?* NVIDIA. https://www.nvidia.com/en-us/glossary/data-science/large-language-models/

O'Neill, R., & Russell, A. M. (2020). Grammarly: Help or hindrance? Academic learning advisors' perceptions of an online grammar checker. *Journal of Academic Language and Learning*, *13*(1), A88–A107.

Olaya, D., Vásquez, J., Maldonado, S., Miranda, J., & Verbeke, W. (2020). Uplift Modeling for preventing student dropout in higher education. *Decision Support Systems*, *134*, 113320. doi:10.1016/j.dss.2020.113320

Orchard, T., & Tasiemski, L. (2023). The rise of Generative AI and possible effects on the economy. *Economics and Business Review*, *9*(2), 9–26. doi:10.18559/ebr.2023.2.732

Orland-Barak, L., & Yinon, H. (2007). When theory meets practice: What student teachers learn from guided reflection on their own classroom discourse. *Teaching and Teacher Education*, *23*(6), 957–969. doi:10.1016/j.tate.2006.06.005

Ortigosa, A., Carro, R. M., Bravo-Agapito, J., Lizcano, D., Alcolea, J. J., & Blanco, O. (2019). From lab to production: Lessons learnt and real-life challenges of an early student-dropout prevention system. *IEEE Transactions on Learning Technologies*, *12*(2), 264–277. doi:10.1109/TLT.2019.2911608

Oviedo-Trespalacios, O., Peden, A. E., Cole-Hunter, T., Costantini, A., Haghani, M., Rod, J. E., Kelly, S., Torkamaan, H., Tariq, A., Newton, J. D. A., Gallagher, T., Steinert, S., Filtness, A. J., & Reniers, G. (2023). The risks of using ChatGPT to obtain common safety-related information and advice. *Safety Science*, *167*, 106244. doi:10.1016/j.ssci.2023.106244

Panagopoulou, F., Parpoula, C., & Karpouzis, K. (2023). Legal and ethical considerations regarding the use of ChatGPT in education. *arXiv preprint arXiv:2306.10037*. doi:10.31235/osf.io/c5hf3

Pan, S. L., Cui, M., & Qian, J. (2020). Information resource orchestration during the COVID-19 pandemic: A study of community lockdowns in China. *International Journal of Information Management*, *54*, 102143. doi:10.1016/j.ijinfomgt.2020.102143 PMID:32394997

Parkin, H. J., Hepplestone, S., Holden, G., Irwin, B., & Thorpe, L. (2012). A role for technology in enhancing students' engagement with feedback. *Assessment & Evaluation in Higher Education*, *37*(8), 963–973. doi:10.1080/02602938.2011.592934

Parray, A. A., Inam, Z. M., Ramonfaur, D., Haider, S. S., Mistry, S. K., & Pandya, A. K. (2023). ChatGPT and global public health: Applications, challenges, ethical considerations and mitigation strategies. *Global Transitions*, *5*, 50–54. doi:10.1016/j.glt.2023.05.001

Parycek, P., Schmid, V., & Novak, A. S. (2023). Artificial Intelligence (AI) and Automation in Administrative Procedures: Potentials, Limitations, and Framework Conditions. *Journal of the Knowledge Economy*. doi:10.100713132-023-01433-3

Pavlik, J. V. (2023). Collaborating With ChatGPT: Considering the Implications of Generative Artificial Intelligence for Journalism and Media Education. *Journalism & Mass Communication Educator*, *78*(1), 84–93. doi:10.1177/10776958221149577

Pearce, K., Alghowinem, S., & Breazeal, C. (2023, June). Build-a-Bot: Teaching Conversational AI Using a Transformer-Based Intent Recognition and Question Answering Architecture. *Proceedings of the AAAI Conference on Artificial Intelligence*, *37*(13), 16025–16032. doi:10.1609/aaai.v37i13.26903

Pennington, D. D. (2008). Cross-disciplinary collaboration and learning. *Ecology and Society*, *13*(2), art8. doi:10.5751/ES-02520-130208

Peters, M. A. (2020). Platform ontologies, the AI crisis and the ability to hack humans 'An algorithm knows me better than I know myself'. *Educational Philosophy and Theory*, *52*(6), 593–601. doi:10.1080/00131857.2019.1618227

Pillay, N., Maharaj, B. T., & van Eeden, G. (2018, November). AI in engineering and computer science education in preparation for the 4th industrial revolution: A South African perspective. In *2018 World Engineering Education Forum-Global Engineering Deans Council (WEEF-GEDC)* (pp. 1-5). IEEE.

Pinochet, L. H. C., Moreira, M. Â. L., Fávero, L. P., Santos, M. D., & Pardim, V. I. (2023). Collaborative Work Alternatives with ChatGPT Based on Evaluation Criteria for its Use in Higher Education: Application of the PROMETHEE-SAPEVO-M1 Method. *Procedia Computer Science, 221*, 177–184. doi:10.1016/j.procs.2023.07.025

Polly, D., Martin, F., & Byker, E. (2023). Examining pre-service and in-service teachers' perceptions of their readiness to use digital technologies for teaching and learning. *Computers in the Schools*, *40*(1), 22–55. doi:10.1080/07380569.2022.2121107

Pozas, M., & Letzel, V. (2023). "Do You Think You Have What it Takes?"–Exploring Predictors of Pre-Service Teachers' Prospective ICT Use. Technology. *Knowledge and Learning*, *28*(2), 823–841. doi:10.100710758-021-09551-0

Pramila, P., Amudha, S., Saravanan, T., Sankar, S. R., Poongothai, E., & Boopathi, S. (2023). Design and Development of Robots for Medical Assistance: An Architectural Approach. In Contemporary Applications of Data Fusion for Advanced Healthcare Informatics (pp. 260–282). IGI Global.

Prasad, P. Y., Prasad, D., Malleswari, D. N., Shetty, M. N., & Gupta, N. (2022). Implementation of Machine Learning Based Google Teachable Machine in Early Childhood Education. *International Journal of Early Childhood Special Education*, *14*(3).

Puppo, G. (2019). Cross-Cultural Competence in Higher Education Faculty and Staff. *Emerging Leadership Journeys, 12*(1).

Qadir, J. (2023). Engineering education in the era of ChatGPT: Promise and pitfalls of generative AI for education. *2023 IEEE Global Engineering Education Conference (EDUCON)*, (pp. 1–9). IEEE. 10.1109/EDUCON54358.2023.10125121

Rahamathunnisa, U., Subhashini, P., Aancy, H. M., Meenakshi, S., Boopathi, S., & ... (2023). Solutions for Software Requirement Risks Using Artificial Intelligence Techniques. In *Handbook of Research on Data Science and Cybersecurity Innovations in Industry 4.0 Technologies* (pp. 45–64). IGI Global.

Rahamathunnisa, U., Sudhakar, K., Murugan, T. K., Thivaharan, S., Rajkumar, M., & Boopathi, S. (2023). Cloud Computing Principles for Optimizing Robot Task Offloading Processes. In *AI-Enabled Social Robotics in Human Care Services* (pp. 188–211). IGI Global. doi:10.4018/978-1-6684-8171-4.ch007

Rahimi, F., & Abadi, A. T. B. (2023). ChatGPT and publication ethics. *Archives of Medical Research*, *54*(3), 272–274. doi:10.1016/j.arcmed.2023.03.004 PMID:36990890

Rahman, M. M., & Watanobe, Y. (2023). ChatGPT for education and research: Opportunities, threats, and strategies. *Applied Sciences (Basel, Switzerland)*, *13*(9), 5783. doi:10.3390/app13095783

Ramísio, P. J., Pinto, L. M. C., Gouveia, N., Costa, H., & Arezes, D. (2019). Sustainability Strategy in Higher Education Institutions: Lessons learned from a nine-year case study. *Journal of Cleaner Production*, *222*, 300–309. doi:10.1016/j.jclepro.2019.02.257

Ramudu, K., Mohan, V. M., Jyothirmai, D., Prasad, D., Agrawal, R., & Boopathi, S. (2023). Machine Learning and Artificial Intelligence in Disease Prediction: Applications, Challenges, Limitations, Case Studies, and Future Directions. In Contemporary Applications of Data Fusion for Advanced Healthcare Informatics (pp. 297–318). IGI Global.

Ranalli, J., & Yamashita, T. (2022). Automated written corrective feedback: Error-correction performance and timing of delivery. *Language Learning & Technology*, *26*(1), 1–25. http://hdl.handle.net/10125/73465

Ray, P. P. (2023). ChatGPT: A comprehensive review on background, applications, key challenges, bias, ethics, limitations and future scope. *Internet of Things and Cyber-Physical Systems*, *3*, 121–154. doi:10.1016/j.iotcps.2023.04.003

Reddy, M. A., Gaurav, A., Ushasukhanya, S., Rao, V. C. S., Bhattacharya, S., & Boopathi, S. (2023). Bio-Medical Wastes Handling Strategies During the COVID-19 Pandemic. In Multidisciplinary Approaches to Organizational Governance During Health Crises (pp. 90–111). IGI Global. doi:10.4018/978-1-7998-9213-7.ch006

Reddy, M. A., Reddy, B. M., Mukund, C., Venneti, K., Preethi, D., & Boopathi, S. (2023). Social Health Protection During the COVID-Pandemic Using IoT. In *The COVID-19 Pandemic and the Digitalization of Diplomacy* (pp. 204–235). IGI Global. doi:10.4018/978-1-7998-8394-4.ch009

Reed, J. (2021, May 1). The book publishing process—An 8-step guide. *Publishing Talk*. https://www.publishingtalk.org/get-published/book-publishing-process-8-step-guide/

Reinholz, D. L., & Andrews, T. C. (2019). *Breaking down silos working meeting: An approach to fostering cross-disciplinary STEM–DBER collaborations through working meetings*. Am Soc Cell Biol.

Roll, I., & Wylie, R. (2016). Evolution and revolution in artificial intelligence in education. *International Journal of Artificial Intelligence in Education*, *26*(2), 582–599. doi:10.100740593-016-0110-3

Roose, K. (2023). How schools can survive (and maybe even thrive) with AI this fall. *The New York Times*. https://www.nytimes.com/2023/08/24/technology/how-schools-can-survive-and-maybe-even-thrive-with-ai-this-fall.html

Rosário, A., & Dias, J. (2022). Sustainability and the Digital Transition: A Literature Review. *Sustainability (Basel)*, *14*(7), 4072. doi:10.3390u14074072

Rose, H., Curle, S., Aizawa, I., & Thompson, G. (2020). What drives success in English medium taught courses? The interplay between language proficiency, academic skills, and motivation. *Studies in Higher Education*, *45*(11), 2149–2161. doi:10.1080/03075079.2019.1590690

Rose, M. (2009). *Writer's block: The cognitive dimension*. Southern Illinois Press.

Rusmiyanto, N. H., Nining, F., Novita, K. T., Agus, R., & Mike, N. S. (2023). The role of Artificial intelligence (AI) in developing English language learners' communication skills. *Journal of Education*, *6*(1).

SaetraH. S. (2023). Generative AI: Here to stay, but for good? From https://ssrn.com/abstract=4330244 doi:10.1016/j.techsoc.2023.102372

Safitri, D., Fhadilah, N., & Lubis, Y. (2023). English Phonology for Second Language Learner. *English and Tourism Studies*, *1*(1), 52–59.

Sáiz-Manzanares, M. C., Marticorena-Sánchez, R., Martín-Antón, L. J., Díez, I. G., & Almeida, L. (2023). Perceived satisfaction of university students with the use of chatbots as a tool for self-regulated learning. *Heliyon*, *9*(1), e12843. doi:10.1016/j.heliyon.2023.e12843 PMID:36704275

Samanta, D. P. S., Patnaik, B. C. M., Satpathy, I., Panda, L., Hansdah, K., & Panda, S. (2023, May). Contribution Perception on Confidentiality of Digital Transactions Among Santhal Community. In *International Conference on Emerging Trends in Business and Management (ICETBM 2023)* (pp. 258-264). Atlantis Press. 10.2991/978-94-6463-162-3_23

Sampath, B., Sasikumar, C., & Myilsamy, S. (2023). Application of TOPSIS Optimization Technique in the Micro-Machining Process. In IGI: Trends, Paradigms, and Advances in Mechatronics Engineering (pp. 162–187). IGI Global.

Sanchez-Pi, N., Martí, L., Garcia, A. C. B., Yates, R. B., Vellasco, M., & Coello, C. A. C. (2021, November). A roadmap for AI in Latin America. In *Side event AI in Latin America of the Global Partnership for AI*. GPAI.

Saravanan, M., Vasanth, M., Boopathi, S., Sureshkumar, M., & Haribalaji, V. (2022). Optimization of Quench Polish Quench (QPQ) Coating Process Using Taguchi Method. *Key Engineering Materials*, *935*, 83–91. doi:10.4028/p-z569vy

Saricaoglu, A. (2019). The impact of automated feedback on L2 learners' written causal explanations. *ReCALL*, *31*(2), 189–203. doi:10.1017/S095834401800006X

Sathiyaseelan, G., Srinath, P., Melwyn, J. G., Bhagyanathan, C., Socrates, S., & Boopathi, S. (2023). Tribology and hardness measurement of biosilica dispersed AA7075 metal matrix composites. *Materials Today: Proceedings*. Advance online publication. doi:10.1016/j.matpr.2023.02.440

Scholten, K., Sharkey Scott, P., & Fynes, B. (2019). Building routines for non-routine events: Supply chain resilience learning mechanisms and their antecedents. *Supply Chain Management*, *24*(3), 430–442. doi:10.1108/SCM-05-2018-0186

Sendak, M., Elish, M. C., Gao, M., Futoma, J., Ratliff, W., Nichols, M., Bedoya, A., Balu, S., & O'Brien, C. (2020). "The human body is a black box" supporting clinical decision-making with deep learning. *Proceedings of the 2020 Conference on Fairness, Accountability, and Transparency*, (pp. 99–109). ACM. 10.1145/3351095.3372827

Senechal, J., Ekholm, E., Aljudaibi, S., Strawderman, M., & Parthemos, C. (2023). *Balancing the Benefits and Risks of Large Language AI Models in K12 Public Schools*.

Seror, J., & Weinberg, A. (2021). Exploring the longitudinal impact of university immersion: Bilingual spaces, multilingual values. *System*, *99*, 102523. doi:10.1016/j.system.2021.102523

Shahriar, S., & Hayawi, K. (2023). Let's have a chat! A Conversation with ChatGPT: Technology, Applications, and Limitations. *arXiv preprint arXiv:2302.13817.*

Sharma, M. (2022). Integrating effective collaboration tools to enhance students' engagement in online language classroom. *Journal of Fundamental & Comparative Research, 8*(1), 26–30.

Sharples, M. (2022). Automated essay writing: An AIED opinion. *International Journal of Artificial Intelligence in Education, 32*(4), 1119–1126. doi:10.100740593-022-00300-7

Shreim, A. J. (2023). *The Impact of Large Language Models on Research Convergence and Quality: Benefits, Drawbacks, and Mitigation Strategies.* LinkedIn. https://www.linkedin.com/pulse/impact-large-language-models-research-convergence-abdul-jalil/

Silor, A. (2019). *Cultural Knowledge Pedagogy for Higher Education.*

Simplilearn. (2022). *Top 14 Artificial Intelligence (AI) Applications in 2022.* Simplilearn.Com. https://www.simplilearn.com/tutorials/artificial-intelligence-tutorial/artificial-intelligence-applications

Singer, J. B., Báez, J. C., & Rios, J. A. (2023). AI creates the message: Integrating AI language learning models into social work education and Practice. *Journal of Social Work Education, 59*(2), 294–302. doi:10.1080/10437797.2023.2189878

Sohail, S. S., Farhat, F., Himeur, Y., Nadeem, M., Madsen, D. Ø., Singh, Y., Atalla, S., & Mansoor, W. (2023). Decoding ChatGPT: A taxonomy of existing research, current challenges, and possible future directions. *Journal of King Saud University. Computer and Information Sciences, 35*(8), 101675. doi:10.1016/j.jksuci.2023.101675

SokS.HengK. (2023). ChatGPT for education and research: A review of benefits and risks. *Available at* SSRN 4378735. doi:10.2139/ssrn.4378735

Sridhar, P., Doyle, A., Agarwal, A., Bogart, C., Savelka, J., & Sakr, M. (2023). Harnessing llms in curricular design: Using gpt-4 to support authoring of learning objectives. *ArXiv Preprint ArXiv:2306.17459.*

Srinivas, B., Maguluri, L. P., Naidu, K. V., Reddy, L. C. S., Deivakani, M., & Boopathi, S. (2023). Architecture and Framework for Interfacing Cloud-Enabled Robots. In *Handbook of Research on Data Science and Cybersecurity Innovations in Industry 4.0 Technologies* (pp. 542–560). IGI Global. doi:10.4018/978-1-6684-8145-5.ch027

Street, B. V. (1984). *Literacy in theory and practice* (Vol. 9). Cambridge University Press.

Su, J., & Yang, W. (2023). Unlocking the power of ChatGPT: A framework for applying generative AI in education. *ECNU Review of Education*, 20965311231168424.

Su, J., & Yang, W. (2023). Unlocking the power of ChatGPT: A framework for applying generative AI in education. *ECNU Review of Education.*

Su, J., Guo, K., Chen, X., & Chu, S. K. W. (2023). Teaching artificial intelligence in K–12 classrooms: A scoping review. *Interactive Learning Environments*, 1–20. doi:10.1080/10494820.2023.2212706

Su, J., Ng, D. T. K., & Chu, S. K. W. (2023). Artificial Intelligence (AI) Literacy in Early Childhood Education: The Challenges and Opportunities. *Computers and Education: Artificial Intelligence*, *4*, 100124. doi:10.1016/j.caeai.2023.100124

Sumakul, D. T., Hamied, F. A., & Sukyadi, D. (2022). Artificial Intelligence in EFL classrooms: Friend or foe? *LEARN Journal: Language Education and Acquisition Research Network*, *15*(1), 232–256.

Sun, Y., Strobel, J., & Newby, T. J. (2017). The impact of student teaching experience on pre-service teachers' readiness for technology integration: A mixed methods study with growth curve modeling. *Educational Technology Research and Development*, *65*(3), 597–629. doi:10.100711423-016-9486-x

Syamala, M., Komala, C., Pramila, P., Dash, S., Meenakshi, S., & Boopathi, S. (2023). Machine Learning-Integrated IoT-Based Smart Home Energy Management System. In *Handbook of Research on Deep Learning Techniques for Cloud-Based Industrial IoT* (pp. 219–235). IGI Global. doi:10.4018/978-1-6684-8098-4.ch013

Taimalu, M., & Luik, P. (2019). The impact of beliefs and knowledge on the integration of technology among teacher educators: A path analysis. *Teaching and Teacher Education*, *79*, 101–110. doi:10.1016/j.tate.2018.12.012

Tai, T. Y., & Chen, H. H. J. (2021). The impact of immersive virtual reality on EFL learners' listening comprehension. *Journal of Educational Computing Research*, *59*(7), 1272–1293. doi:10.1177/0735633121994291

Takahashi, Y. (2020). Redesigning an artificial intelligence learning application to improve Japanese students' English conversational skills: a case study of a vocational institute in Tokyo, Japan. Assumption University of Thailand.

Tan, S. (2023). Harnessing Artificial Intelligence for Innovation in Education. In K. Rajaram (Ed.), *Learning Intelligence: Innovative and Digital Transformative Learning Strategies: Cultural and Social Engineering Perspectives* (pp. 335–363). Springer Nature. doi:10.1007/978-981-19-9201-8_8

Tanveer, M., Hassan, S., & Bhaumik, A. (2020). Academic Policy Regarding Sustainability and Artificial Intelligence (AI). *Sustainability (Basel)*, *12*(22), 9435. doi:10.3390u12229435

Tebeje, T. H., & Klein, J. (2021). Applications of e-health to support person-centered health care at the time of COVID-19 pandemic. *Telemedicine Journal and e-Health*, *27*(2), 150–158. doi:10.1089/tmj.2020.0201 PMID:32746750

The Economic Times. (2023). What is Sale? *The Economic Times.* https://economictimes.indiatimes.com/definition/sale

Thi Thuy An Ngo. (2023). The Perception by University Students of the Use of ChatGPT in Education. *International Journal of Emerging Technologies in Learning,* 4–19. doi:10.3991/ijet.v18i17.39019

Tian, Y. (2023). Limitations and Advancements of AI Teachers in Classroom Instruction. *Education and Teaching Research, 2023*(3), 66–72.

Topsakal, O., & Topsakal, E. (2022). Framework for a foreign language teaching software for children utilizing AR, voice bots, and ChatGPT (Large Language Models). *The Journal of Cognitive Systems, 7*(2), 33–38.

Ugandar, R. E., Rahamathunnisa, U., Sajithra, S., Christiana, M. B. V., Palai, B. K., & Boopathi, S. (2023). Hospital Waste Management Using Internet of Things and Deep Learning: Enhanced Efficiency and Sustainability. In M. Arshad (Ed.), (pp. 317–343). Advances in Bioinformatics and Biomedical Engineering. IGI Global. doi:10.4018/978-1-6684-6577-6.ch015

Urbano, C., & Ardanuy, J. (2020). Cross-disciplinary collaboration versus coexistence in LIS serials: Analysis of authorship affiliations in four European countries. *Scientometrics, 124*(1), 575–602. doi:10.100711192-020-03471-z

Utami, L. P. R. A., Suwastini, N. K. A., Dantes, G. R., Suprihatin, C. T., & Adnyani, K. E. K. (2021). Virtual reality for supporting authentic learning in 21st-century language classrooms. *Jurnal Pendidikan Teknologi dan Kejuruan, 18*(1), 132-141.

Vamathevan, J., Clark, D., Czodrowski, P., Dunham, I., Ferran, E., Lee, G., Li, B., Madabhushi, A., Shah, P., Spitzer, M., & Zhao, S. (2019). Applications of machine learning in drug discovery and development. *Nature Reviews. Drug Discovery, 18*(6), 463–477. doi:10.103841573-019-0024-5 PMID:30976107

Van Brummelen, J., & Lin, P. (2020). Engaging teachers to co-design integrated AI curriculum for K-12 classrooms. *ArXiv Preprint ArXiv:2009.11100.*

Van den Beemt, A., MacLeod, M., Van der Veen, J., Van de Ven, A., Van Baalen, S., Klaassen, R., & Boon, M. (2020). Interdisciplinary engineering education: A review of vision, teaching, and support. *Journal of Engineering Education, 109*(3), 508–555. doi:10.1002/jee.20347

van der Vorst, T., & Jelicic, N. (2019). *Artificial Intelligence in Education: Can AI bring the full potential of personalized learning to education?* EconStor.

Van Dyke, A. (2023). *What is book marketing?* LinkedIn. https://www.linkedin.com/pulse/what-book-marketing-aryn-van-dyke/?trk=pulse-article

Vandewaetere, M., & Clarebout, G. (2014). Advanced technologies for personalized learning, instruction, and performance. Handbook of research on educational communications and technology, (pp. 425-437). Springer. doi:10.1007/978-1-4614-3185-5_34

Vartiainen, H. (2022). *Cross-boundary co-design for learning machine learning.* AI, Data Science, and Young People. Understanding Computing Education.

Vartiainen, H., & Tedre, M. (2023). Using artificial intelligence in craft education: Crafting with text-to-image generative models. *Digital Creativity (Exeter), 34*(1), 1–21. doi:10.1080/14626268.2023.2174557

Vaswani, A., Shazeer, N., Parmar, N., Uszkoreit, J., Jones, L., Gomez, A. N., Kaiser, L., & Polosukhin, I. (2023). *Attention Is All You Need.*

Veeranjaneyulu, R., Boopathi, S., Kumari, R. K., Vidyarthi, A., Isaac, J. S., & Jaiganesh, V. (2023). Air Quality Improvement and Optimisation Using Machine Learning Technique. *IEEE-Explore*, 1–6.

Venkateswaran, N., Vidhya, K., Ayyannan, M., Chavan, S. M., Sekar, K., & Boopathi, S. (2023). A Study on Smart Energy Management Framework Using Cloud Computing. In 5G, Artificial Intelligence, and Next Generation Internet of Things: Digital Innovation for Green and Sustainable Economies (pp. 189–212). IGI Global. doi:10.4018/978-1-6684-8634-4.ch009

Venkateswaran, N., Kumar, S. S., Diwakar, G., Gnanasangeetha, D., & Boopathi, S. (2023). Synthetic Biology for Waste Water to Energy Conversion: IoT and AI Approaches. In M. Arshad (Ed.), (pp. 360–384). Advances in Bioinformatics and Biomedical Engineering. IGI Global. doi:10.4018/978-1-6684-6577-6.ch017

Venkateswaran, N., Vidhya, R., Naik, D. A., Raj, T. M., Munjal, N., & Boopathi, S. (2023). Study on Sentence and Question Formation Using Deep Learning Techniques. In *Digital Natives as a Disruptive Force in Asian Businesses and Societies* (pp. 252–273). IGI Global. doi:10.4018/978-1-6684-6782-4.ch015

Vennila, T., Karuna, M., Srivastava, B. K., Venugopal, J., Surakasi, R., & Sampath, B. (2022). New Strategies in Treatment and Enzymatic Processes: Ethanol Production From Sugarcane Bagasse. In Human Agro-Energy Optimization for Business and Industry (pp. 219–240). IGI Global.

Vera, F. (2023). *Enhancing English language learning in undergraduate students using ChatGPT: A quasi-experimental study*. CIAA.

Vuong, Q.-H., Le, T.-T., La, V.-P., Nguyen, H. T. T., Ho, M.-T., Van Khuc, Q., & Nguyen, M.-H. (2022). Covid-19 vaccines production and societal immunization under the serendipity-mindsponge-3D knowledge management theory and conceptual framework. *Humanities & Social Sciences Communications*, *9*(1), 22. doi:10.105741599-022-01034-6

Wang, T., Li, S., Huang, X., Pan, Z., & Lajoie, S. P. (2023). Examining students' cognitive load in the context of self-regulated learning with an intelligent tutoring system. *Education and Information Technologies*, *28*(5), 5697–5715. doi:10.100710639-022-11357-1 PMID:36373050

Webster, C., & Ivanov, S. (2020). Robotics, Artificial Intelligence, and the Evolving Nature of Work. In B. George & J. Paul (Eds.), Digital Transformation in Business and Society: Theory and Cases (pp. 127–143). Springer International Publishing. doi:10.1007/978-3-030-08277-2_8

Weisz, J. D., Muller, M., Ross, S. I., Martinez, F., Houde, S., Agarwal, M., Talamadupula, K., & Richards, J. T. (2022). Better Together? An Evaluation of AI-Supported Code Translation. *International Conference on Intelligent User Interfaces, Proceedings IUI*, (pp. 369–391). ACM. 10.1145/3490099.3511157

Whalen, J., & Mouza, C. (2023). ChatGPT: Challenges, Opportunities, and Implications for Teacher Education. *Contemporary Issues in Technology & Teacher Education*, *23*(1), 1–23.

Williams, C. (1983). A Brief Introduction To Artificial Intelligence. *Proceedings OCEANS*, *83*, 94–99. doi:10.1109/OCEANS.1983.1152096

Winkler-Schwartz, A., Bissonnette, V., Mirchi, N., Ponnudurai, N., Yilmaz, R., Ledwos, N., Siyar, S., Azarnoush, H., Karlik, B., & Del Maestro, R. F. (2019a). Artificial intelligence in medical education: Best practices using machine learning to assess surgical expertise in virtual reality simulation. *Journal of Surgical Education*, *76*(6), 1681–1690. doi:10.1016/j.jsurg.2019.05.015 PMID:31202633

Woo, D. J., Susanto, H., Yeung, C. H., Guo, K., & Fung, A. K. Y. (2023). Exploring AI-Generated Text in Student Writing: How Does AI Help? *arXiv preprint arXiv:2304.02478.*

Wu, Z. (2022). Understanding teachers' cross-disciplinary collaboration for STEAM education: Building a digital community of practice. *Thinking Skills and Creativity*, *46*, 101178. doi:10.1016/j.tsc.2022.101178

Xie, M., Meng, F., Zou, J., Feng, W., & Ma, S. (2020, June). Application of artificial intelligence in civil engineering education. []. IOP Publishing.]. *Journal of Physics: Conference Series*, *1575*(1), 012225. doi:10.1088/1742-6596/1575/1/012225

Xie, T., Liu, R., Chen, Y., & Liu, G. (2021). MOCA: A motivational online conversational agent for improving student engagement in collaborative learning. *IEEE Transactions on Learning Technologies*, *14*(5), 653–664. doi:10.1109/TLT.2021.3129800

Yan, D. (2023). Impact of ChatGPT on learners in an L2 writing practicum: An exploratory investigation. *Education and Information Technologies*, *28*(11), 1–25. doi:10.100710639-023-11742-4

Yang, H. (2023). How I use ChatGPT responsibly in my teaching. *Nature*. doi:10.1038/d41586-023-01026-9 PMID:37045954

Yang, X., Kaiser, G., König, J., & Blömeke, S. (2019). Professional noticing of mathematics teachers: A comparative study between Germany and China. *International Journal of Science and Mathematics Education*, *17*(5), 943–963. doi:10.100710763-018-9907-x

Yang, Y., & Bao, W. (2023). Application of Human-Computer Interaction Technology in Remote Language Learning Platform. *International Journal of Human-Computer Interaction*, 1–11. doi:10.1080/10447318.2023.2194709

Yau, K. W., Chai, C., Chiu, T. K., Meng, H., King, I., & Yam, Y. (2023). A phenomenographic approach on teacher conceptions of teaching Artificial Intelligence (AI) in K-12 schools. *Education and Information Technologies*, *28*(1), 1041–1064. doi:10.100710639-022-11161-x

Yoon, H. S., & Larkin, K. A. (2018). When tensions between ideology and practice become personal: Unpacking mentorship in early childhood teacher education. *Journal of Early Childhood Teacher Education*, *39*(1), 50–72. doi:10.1080/10901027.2017.1404506

You, Y., Chen, Y., You, Y., Zhang, Q., & Cao, Q. (2023). Evolutionary Game Analysis of Artificial Intelligence Such as the Generative Pre-Trained Transformer in Future Education. *Sustainability (Basel)*, *15*(12), 9355. doi:10.3390u15129355

Yu, P., Kwok, S., & Jiang, Z. (2023). How COVID-19 Has Stimulated Innovation in the Chinese Education Sector. In I. Management Association (Ed.), Research Anthology on Remote Teaching and Learning and the Future of Online Education (pp. 1612-1634). IGI Global. doi:10.4018/978-1-6684-7540-9.ch080

Yu, H., & Guo, Y. (2023). Generative artificial intelligence empowers educational reform: Current status, issues, and prospects. *Frontiers in Education*, *8*, 1183162. doi:10.3389/feduc.2023.1183162

Yu, P., Kwok, S., & Jiang, Z. (2022). How COVID-19 Has Stimulated Innovation in the Chinese Education Sector. In J. Saiz-Alvarez (Ed.), *Handbook of Research on Emerging Business Models and the New World Economic Order* (pp. 343–364). IGI Global., doi:10.4018/978-1-7998-7689-2.ch017

Yu, P., Liu, L., Sampat, R. M., Mandizvidza, K., & Lu, S. (2023). Advancing STEM Education and Innovation in a Time of Distance Learning: Case Studies in China. In R. González-Lezcano (Ed.), *Advancing STEM Education and Innovation in a Time of Distance Learning* (pp. 1–29). IGI Global. doi:10.4018/978-1-6684-5053-6.ch001

Yu, P., Lu, Y., Hanes, E., & Gu, H. (2022). Digitized Education: Enhancement in Teaching and Learning – China Case Study. In C. Krishnan, F. Al-Harthy, & G. Singh (Eds.), *Technology Training for Educators From Past to Present* (pp. 1–35). IGI Global. doi:10.4018/978-1-6684-4083-4.ch001

Žalėnienė, I., & Pereira, P. (2021). Higher education for sustainability: A global perspective. *Geography and Sustainability*, *2*(2), 99–106.

Zatarain Cabada, R., Rodriguez Rangel, H., Barron Estrada, M. L., & Cardenas Lopez, H. M. (2020). Hyperparameter optimization in CNN for learning-centered emotion recognition for intelligent tutoring systems. *Soft Computing*, *24*(10), 7593–7602. doi:10.100700500-019-04387-4

Zekrifa, D. M. S., Kulkarni, M., Bhagyalakshmi, A., Devireddy, N., Gupta, S., & Boopathi, S. (2023). Integrating Machine Learning and AI for Improved Hydrological Modeling and Water Resource Management. In *Artificial Intelligence Applications in Water Treatment and Water Resource Management* (pp. 46–70). IGI Global. doi:10.4018/978-1-6684-6791-6.ch003

Zembylas, M. (2023). A decolonial approach to AI in higher education teaching and learning: Strategies for undoing the ethics of digital neocolonialism. *Learning, Media and Technology, 48*(1), 25–37. doi:10.1080/17439884.2021.2010094

Zhai, C. (2023). A systematic review on artificial intelligence dialogue systems for enhancing English as foreign language students' interactional competence in the university. *Computers and Education: Artificial Intelligence*, 100134.

ZhaiX. (2022). ChatGPT user experience: Implications for education. SSRN 4312418.

Zhang, A. LIpton, Z. C., Li, M., & Smola, A. J. (2023). *Dive into Deep Learning*. D2L. https://d2l.ai/index.html

Zhang, C., Zhang, C., Li, C., Qiao, Y., Zheng, S., Dam, S. K., Zhang, M., Kim, J. U., Kim, S. T., Choi, J., & Associates. (2023). One small step for generative ai, one giant leap for agi: A complete survey on chatgpt in aigc era. *ArXiv Preprint ArXiv:2304.06488.*

Zhang, Q., Clarke, A., & Lee, J. C. K. (2018). Pre-service teachers' professional identity development within the context of school-based learning to teach: An exploratory study in China. *The Asia-Pacific Education Researcher, 27*(6), 477–486. doi:10.100740299-018-0408-z

Zhang, X., Sun, J., & Deng, Y. (2023). Design and Application of Intelligent Classroom for English Language and Literature Based on Artificial Intelligence Technology. *Applied Artificial Intelligence, 37*(1), 2216051. doi:10.1080/08839514.2023.2216051

Zhang, Y., Li, W., Zhang, L., Ning, X., Sun, L., & Lu, Y. (2019). Adaptive learning Gabor filter for finger-vein recognition. *IEEE Access : Practical Innovations, Open Solutions, 7*, 159821–159830. doi:10.1109/ACCESS.2019.2950698

Zhao, Y., & Liu, G. (2019, January). How do teachers face educational changes in artificial intelligence era. In *2018 International Workshop on Education Reform and Social Sciences (ERSS 2018)* (pp. 47-50). Atlantis Press. 10.2991/erss-18.2019.9

Zhou, J., Müller, H., Holzinger, A., & Chen, F. (2023). Ethical ChatGPT: Concerns, challenges, and commandments. *arXiv preprint arXiv:2305.10646.*

Zielinski, C., Winker, M., Aggarwal, R., Ferris, L., Heinemann, M., Lapeña, J. F., Pai, S., Ing, E., Citrome, L., Alam, M., Voight, M., & Abibzadeh, F. (2023). Chatbots, Generative AI, and Scholarly Manuscripts: WAME Recommendations on Chatbots and Generative Artificial Intelligence in Relation to Scholarly Publications. *Philippine Journal of Pathology, 8*(1), 6–8. doi:10.21141/PJP.2023.08 PMID:38089825

# About the Contributors

**Poshan (Sam) Yu** a Chinese Australian, is a versatile individual who excels in a range of roles and industries. With a dynamic skill set, he serves as a consultant, adjunct professor, keynote speaker, research award winner, SSCI journal editor, author, ad-hoc reviewer, entrepreneur, venture capitalist, and OzAsia festival ambassador. Additionally, he brings his financial expertise to over 30 media platforms in China as a guest financial news commentator. Sam's academic contributions extend to various prestigious institutions. He teaches at the University of Victoria Program at Soochow University in China and holds the position of an external professor of financial technology and finance at SKEMA Business School, China. Furthermore, he is a visiting professor at Krirk University in Thailand, EU-Asia research coordinator at the European Business Institute of Luxembourg, and a visiting researcher at the Australian Studies Centre of Shanghai University. Notably, he is also a guest professor at Emlyon Business School China and an adjunct faculty member at George Washington University's master program at Renmin University of China. Previously, he taught as a casual academic at the University of South Australia Business School and was a visiting scholar at the Chinese University of Hong Kong. Furthermore, Sam is actively engaged with several organizations and holds significant positions. As a regional partner in China for FasterCapital, based in Dubai, United Arab Emirates, he plays a vital role in fostering entrepreneurship. He also serves as a vice president at Tinbowah Investment in Beijing and holds an honorary vice president position at the Belt and Road Blockchain Association. Additionally, he contributes as a business mentor for AIC RAISE in Coimbatore, India, the Griffith Industry Mentoring Program in Australia, and University College London. Beyond his professional endeavors, Sam acts as the marketing manager at CAMathories™, an organization founded by a group of Cambridge University alumni and faculty members dedicated to early childhood education, mathematics, science, and advanced technologies. Sam's research interests are extensive and encompass a wide range of topics. They include public-private partnerships, financial technology, regulatory technology, educational technology, mergers and acquisitions, private equity, venture capital, start-ups, intellectual property, art finance, wine, and China's "One Belt One Road" policy.

**James Mulli** is the Founder, Program Director and Academic Dean of the European Business Institute, Luxembourg. He lectures in Applied Blockchain Technologies and Artificial Intelligence integration, post-graduate Corporate Finance & Business Statistics, and Managerial Accounting. He has held lectureships at in Luxembourg, China, the USA, Kenya and Germany. Dr. Mulli is a former director of two successful New York based multinational conglomerates and has valuable experience in the field as an NASD Series 7 compliance officer for the broker dealer Heyka Capital Management. He worked as a Portfolio Manager for the Soros Fund Management's Quantum Industrial Partners and holds a Doctorate and Masters degree from Saint Johns University, New York, and an MBA from New Hampshire Plymouth State University with specialization in Investment and Finance. Dr. Mulli is an international educator, and educational technology consultant with a keen interest in looking over the horizon at how technology is shaping the world. His search for trends in emerging technologies allows him to be an educator who applies skills to help students thrive. He is the founder of Technology Enabled Learning - Africa, and European Business Institute, Luxembourg, both non-for-profit educational providers whose initiative is to support existing Institutions in developing e-learning . His belief is that education is the silver bullet for development and through existing expertise and support infrastructure, EBI can provide the needed "jump-start" to institutions in Europe, Africa, Asia and beyond. Dr. Mulli is a Rockefeller Foundation Grant Recipient, and a Prince Fellow Teaching Excellence recipient. He is a textbook author and has published numerous newspaper and magazine articles.

**Laila Umme** holds a PhD in Computer Science and Information Technology from NED University of Engineering and Technology and a MS/BS in Computer Engineering from Sir Syed University of Engineering & Technology. Her PhD is in pure Software Engineering, focusing on "open source software". Her research interests include open-source software, IoT, computer programming, software engineering, Artificial Intelligence, and Machine Learning. Currently She is working as an Associate Professor in Computer Science Department at IoBM. She has 20 years of teaching experience and has published over 20 publications in international and national journals and conferences.

***

**Raheela Asif** received the B.E. degree in Computer & Information Systems Engineering, MCIT degree in Computer Science & I.T from NED University of Engineering and Technology, Pakistan, MS degree in Software Engineering from Sir Syed University of Engineering and Technology, Pakistan, and Ph.D. degree in Computer Science & I.T from NED University of Engineering and Technology,

Pakistan. She is currently serving as an Associate Professor in the Software Engineering Department at NED University of Engineering and Technology, Pakistan. Her research interests include educational data mining, machine learning, deep learning, data warehousing and database.

**M. Beulah Viji Christiana**, Professor in the Department of Management Studies, Panimalar Engineering College affiliated to Anna University, has a got a rich teaching experience which spans over 23 years. She is an experienced and innovative student focused professional and mentor with a proven track record of excellent teaching skills. Her academic qualification encompasses Post Graduate degrees in English Literature and Business Administration from Madurai Kamaraj University, M.Phil in Management Studies from Bharathidasan University and Ph.D in Management Studies from Mother Teresa Women's University, Kodaikanal . She has published more than 40 research articles in various national and international journals of repute as well as in conferences. Besides she is also known for her role as a reviewer in various journals and she has authored five books.

**Frank Billingsley** has more than 30 years of professional experience in social work, teaching, and administration. He is currently working toward a third master's degree in psychology. He currently resides in the U.S. after having taught in Belgium for the past 20 years. B.A. Ohio Dominican University; M.S. Vrije Universiteit Brussel and Boston University; Ph.D. Walden University.

**Sampath Boopathi** is an accomplished individual with a strong academic background and extensive research experience. He completed his undergraduate studies in Mechanical Engineering and pursued his postgraduate studies in the field of Computer-Aided Design. Dr. Boopathi obtained his Ph.D. from Anna University, focusing his research on Manufacturing and optimization. Throughout his career, Dr. Boopathi has made significant contributions to the field of engineering. He has authored and published over 155 research articles in internationally peer-reviewed journals, highlighting his expertise and dedication to advancing knowledge in his area of specialization. His research output demonstrates his commitment to conducting rigorous and impactful research. In addition to his research publications, Dr. Boopathi has also been granted one patent and has three published patents to his name. This indicates his innovative thinking and ability to develop practical solutions to real-world engineering challenges. With 17 years of academic and research experience, Dr. Boopathi has enriched the engineering community through his teaching and mentorship roles. He has served in various engineering colleges in Tamilnadu, India, where he has imparted knowledge, guided students, and contributed to the overall academic development of the institutions. Dr. Sampath Boopathi's diverse background, ranging from mechanical engineering to computer-aided design, along with his specialization in manufacturing and optimization, positions him as a valuable asset in the field of engineering. His research contributions, patents, and extensive teaching experience exemplify his expertise and dedication to advancing engineering knowledge and fostering innovation.

**Yijun Chen** is an independent researcher. Her research interests include Auditing, FinTech, Artificial Intelligence and Cryptocurrencies.

**E. Ivette Cota-Rivera** received a M.Eng. from the Autonomous University of Baja California (UABC, Universidad Autonoma de Baja California). In 2016, she received her Ph.D. in Energy Engineering and is currently working as a pro fessor in the Energy Engineering program at the Polytechnic University of Baja California (UPBC, Universidad Politecnica de Baja California). Her research interests include energy efficiency and sustainability, artificial intelligence, energy science and technology, as well as programming

**Rajashree Das**, a distinguished Research Scholar within the Education Department at Ravenshaw University, Orissa, has been making significant contributions since joining in October 2016. Her research is dedicated to the intersection of Teacher Education and artificial intelligence, with a particular focus on addressing challenges within the field of Education. Rajashree Das is an active participant in academic conferences, where she has shared her valuable research findings.

**Simanchala Das** is a dual doctorate in social science and management from Berhampur University, India. He has 23 years of rich experience in postgraduate teaching and 3 years in research. He has a good number of publications in indexed journals. Moreover, he has contributed various book chapters and has authored 3 books with international publishers. He is an editorial board member and reviewer of many referred journals. His research interests include employee empowerment, transformational leadership, and cross-cultural HRM. Presently, he is working as an Associate Professor at K L Business School, Koneru Lakshmaiah Education Foundation, AP, India.

**Jianguo Qian** is an independent researcher. His research interests include Chinese economics, FinTech and Cryptocurrencies.

**Guillermo M. Limon-Molina** received ScD degree in Industrial Mechanics from Universidad Autónoma de Baja California, also has a Master and Bachelor Degree in Electronic Engineering, currently works in Mechatronics program from

Universidad Politécnica de Baja California. His research interests include automations processes, programming algorithms, mechanical design with CNC systems and machine vision.

**Long Zixian** is an independent researcher.

**Shengyuan Lu** is an independent researcher. His research interests include RegTech, FinTech and Cryptocurrencies.

**Khalid Mahboob** received his Bachelor's and Master's degree in Computer Science & I.T. in 2007 and 2011 respectively from N.E.D. University of Engineering & Technology, Karachi, Pakistan. He is currently a Ph.D. scholar at N.E.D. University of Engineering & Technology, Karachi, Pakistan. He is a Senior Lecturer in the Software Engineering Department at Sir Syed University of Engineering & Technology, Karachi, Pakistan. His research areas are educational data mining, machine learning, deep learning, sentiment analysis, programming, and algorithm analysis.

**Abelardo Mercado Herrera** is a Doctor of Science and Master of Science from the National Institute of Astrophysics, Optics and Electronics, specializing in Astrophysics, Postdoctorate in Astrophysics from the Institute of Astronomy of the National Autonomous University of Mexico, Electronics Engineer from the Autonomous University of Baja California . He is a specialist in the mathematical-statistical description of stochastic and/or deterministic processes, nonlinear systems, complex systems, chaos theory, among others, as well as their application to physical phenomena such as astronomy, economics, finance, telecommunications, science social etc., in order to determine the underlying dynamics in such processes, and if necessary, their connection with real physical variables and possible prediction. He has worked on the development of various electronic circuits, interfaces and programs to carry out electrical tests in the industry, as well as in scientific instrumentation, applied to telemetry, infrared polarimetry, optics and spectroscopy. He has also specialized in image analysis, measurement techniques and noise reduction.

**Minakshi Rani Mohanty**, who holds M.A. and L.L.B. degrees from Utkal University, has a strong connection with this esteemed institution, which is renowned for its commitment to academic excellence and research innovation. She has been a dedicated civil servant for the Government of Odisha since 1993, with a notable tenure in the Housing and Urban Development Department. This department is instrumental in shaping the urban landscape of the state, focusing on infrastructure development, housing policies, and sustainable urban planning.

**Fabian N. Murrieta-Rico** received B.Eng. and M.Eng. degrees from Instituto Tecnológico de Mexicali (ITM) in 2004 and 2013 respectively. In 2017, he received his PhD in Materials Physics at Centro de Investigación Científica y Educación Superior de Ensenada (CICESE). He has worked as an automation engineer, systems designer, as a university professor, and as postdoctoral researcher at Facultad de Ingeniería, Arquitectura y Diseño from Universidad Autónoma de Baja California (UABC) and at the Centro de Nanociencias y Nanotecnología from Universidad Nacional Autónoma de México (CNyN-UNAM), currently he works as professor at the Universidad Politécnica de Baja California. His research has been published in different journals and presented at international conferences since 2009. He has served as reviewer for different journals, some of them include IEEE Transactions on Industrial Electronics, IEEE Transactions on Instrumentation, Measurement and Sensor Review. His research interests are focused on the field of time and frequency metrology, the design of wireless sensor networks, automated systems and highly sensitive chemical detectors.

**Gouranga Nanda**, a distinguished and esteemed professor in the Education Department at Ravenshaw University, Odisha, stands as a beacon of excellence in the realm of Teacher Education. With a profound commitment to addressing challenges within the field of Education, Professor Nanda's scholarly pursuits have significantly contributed to the advancement of pedagogy.In the dynamic realm of education, Gouranga Nanda's contributions serve as a source of inspiration, setting a high standard for both educators and researchers. His tireless efforts and dedication underscore his role as a thought leader and catalyst for positive change within the academic community.

**Jesús Heriberto Orduño-Osuna** has obtained a Bachelor's degree in Mechatronics Engineering from Universidad Politécnica de Baja California. Currently, he is pursuing Master's degrees in Computer Science and Applied Mathematics, which he is studying at Universidad Internacional de La Rioja in Mexico. He has previously garnered valuable industry experience in diverse settings such as the agro-industrial sector, where he primarily focused on automating post-harvest processes. Additionally, he has worked within the manufacturing industry, where he utilized technologies such as PLCs, robots, and industrial vision systems. His passion lies in the domains of industrial automation, microcontrollers, and machine learning.

**Maria E. Raygoza-L.** holds a Ph.D. in Chemistry and Energy from the Engineering Institute of Universidad Autónoma de Baja California and a Bachelor's degree in Industrial Engineering with a specialization in Manufacturing. She currently serves as a full-time professor and researcher at Universidad Politécnica de Baja California and as a Subject Professor at Universidad Autónoma de Baja California, specializing in Energy Engineering and Renewable Energies. With extensive experience in industry, her research interests encompass renewable energy, energy efficiency, environmental studies, energy management systems, and the integration of public policies for sustainable development. She is currently pursuing a second bachelor's degree in Psychology, further broadening her academic horizons.

**Durga Prasad Singh Samanta** is an accomplished Assistant Professor in Amity Business School at Amity University, Bengaluru, IN, where he has been making notable contributions since October 2019. His research focuses on the convergence of fintech and artificial intelligence, with a strong emphasis on solving real-world business problems. DPS Samanta actively participates in conferences and has presented his research at renowned events including the 3rd International Workshop on Artificial Intelligence methods for Smart Cities (AISC 2023), Springer, Advancements in Smart, Secure and Intelligent Computing, Understanding the Metaverse – Applications, Challenges, and the Future, Security and Privacy in IoMT: Challenges and Solutions, and Advanced IoT Technologies and Applications in the Industry 4.0 Digital Economy. His research papers have been published in esteemed journals such as "Advances in Digital Marketing in the Era of Artificial Intelligence: Case Studies and Data Analysis for Business Problem Solving" by leading publishers including Springer Nature, Taylor and Francis, Nova Publishers, and Sage Publishers, among others. Additionally, DPS Samanta has contributed to diverse topics such as AI-Centric Modelling and Analytics, Smart Cities, Sustainable Development, Workforce Management Systems for Industry 4.0, and adoption of Blockchain in Agriculture Sector.

# Index


## A

academic integrity 7-8, 18, 21-22, 178, 289, 293
Academic Performance 37, 113, 131, 145, 281, 291
Academic Publishing 207-209, 211-213, 221-223, 228
Adaptive Learning 29, 33, 114, 116-117, 131, 168, 171, 205, 229-237, 244-249, 253, 261, 275, 279-281
Adaptive Learning Systems 114, 131, 234
Adaptive Pacing 111-112, 131
AI-generated translation 193-194
Artificial Intelligence (AI) 1-2, 4, 6-7, 18, 29, 31, 51, 90, 100-102, 109, 119, 127, 134-135, 137, 161-163, 165, 167, 169, 171, 173-174, 176, 178, 186, 196, 198, 201, 206, 208-209, 212-213, 228, 231, 251, 253, 260-262, 265, 267-268, 274, 280-281, 285, 288-290, 292-293, 299, 302-303, 312

## B

Bilingual Students 109-111, 114, 116-117, 120, 125, 128, 131
biodiversity loss 62, 64-65

## C

Chatbots 102, 139, 164, 171, 190, 268
climate change 61-62, 64-65, 83
Cognitive Benefits 113, 131
Cognitive Computing 205
Collaborative Learning 144, 187, 205, 230, 237, 240, 289, 297, 308
Content Generation 16, 136, 138, 142, 152, 154-155, 174, 191, 201, 205, 223, 275
Control Theory 275-280
critical thinking 2, 5-6, 19, 21, 38, 63, 66, 110, 119-120, 124, 128, 139, 155, 170, 189, 197, 210, 214, 223, 231, 238, 243, 260, 280, 286, 297, 301
Cross-Cultural Knowledge Exchange 186-190, 193, 200-203, 205
Cross-disciplinary collaborations 60-64, 67-68, 81, 83-84
cross-disciplinary sustainability 76-79, 83
Cultural contexts 5, 128, 201, 238
cultural exchange 196-197, 201-203, 205
Cultural Exchange Platforms 205
Cultural Sensitivity 5, 14, 187, 206, 243
Cultural Understanding 113-114, 129, 131, 190, 197, 203
Curriculum Integration 65

## D

Data Analytics 35, 231, 242
data mining 29-31, 34-35, 51-52
Data Privacy 1, 7-8, 31, 37-38, 51, 120, 134-136, 150, 156, 162, 172, 178, 186, 199, 206, 214, 233, 235, 272, 289
data security 3-4, 9, 16, 18, 30, 147, 152, 178, 230, 249, 253, 281
Digital Divide 134-136, 140, 148, 150, 156, 196
Digital Transformation 206
Diversity and Inclusion 10, 206

## E

Educational data 29-31, 34-35, 51
Educational data mining 29-31, 34-35, 51
educational landscape 1, 30, 33, 35-36, 50-51, 134, 136, 166, 171, 196-197, 230-232, 261, 269
Educational Technology 31, 96, 161, 233, 249
Effect Analyses 121, 131
Engineering Education 259-260, 263-270, 273-274, 279-281, 287, 292
English language skills 118
English language teaching 162, 176-179
Ethical Considerations 1, 3-9, 11-15, 18, 20-22, 29-31, 37-38, 51, 102-103, 126, 129, 134-136, 148, 153, 156, 163, 171-172, 177-178, 186, 193, 201, 206, 230, 236, 249, 253, 260
Ethical implications 1-5, 8, 12, 14-15, 19, 102, 162, 178, 213, 231
exchange programs 114, 128, 231, 238, 247, 253
Experiential learning 62, 66, 76-77
Experimental Approaches 29-30, 32-33, 49-50

## F

Foundation Model 223, 228

## G

Generative AI 1-11, 13-18, 21-22, 109, 124-125, 133-156, 162-180, 186, 188-191, 193-194, 196, 200-203, 206, 210, 212-213, 216, 219-221, 259-260, 268-275, 279-281, 285, 288-291, 293-294, 296-298, 300-302, 312
Generative Artificial Intelligence 1-2, 109, 134, 162-163, 169, 171, 173-174, 176, 178, 186, 201, 208-209, 212, 228, 260, 268, 274, 280-281, 288-289, 293, 299, 302, 312
Global Collaboration 2, 155-156, 190, 229-232, 237-240, 244-249, 251-253, 288, 296
global knowledge 1-7, 9, 13-18, 21-22
Global knowledge sharing 1-7, 9, 13-18, 21-22
Globalization of Education 206
Google Bard 212-214, 216-217, 219, 221, 223
group instruction 111-112, 115

## H

Higher Education 1-6, 8-9, 21-22, 65, 73, 109-110, 186-188, 190, 193, 201-203, 206, 229-234, 236-238, 240, 244, 248, 260, 267, 287-288, 293-294, 296, 299, 312
Holistic learning 61

## I

inclusive learning 50, 135, 172, 187, 201-202, 251
Individualized Attention 31, 111-112, 132, 140
Industry 4.0 260, 264-265, 280, 285, 292
Innovative Teaching Methodology 287, 293
intellectual property 1, 3-5, 7-9, 15, 17, 19, 21-22
Intelligent Tutoring Systems 5, 8, 29-31, 33, 48-49, 51, 139, 165
interdisciplinary approaches 61, 253
Interdisciplinary synergy 60, 80-81
Internet of Things 52, 90, 100-102, 161, 253, 265, 285, 293

## K

K-12 Education 134-136, 140-141, 143, 145, 147-149, 151, 153-156
knowledge exchange 2, 6, 186-190, 193, 199-203, 205
knowledge retention 29, 31, 33, 48-50

Knowledge Sharing 1-7, 9, 13-18, 21-22, 109, 200, 229, 231-232, 240, 243-249, 253, 288, 296
Knowledge Transfer 206

## L

language acquisition 35-36, 43, 48, 109-112, 114-116, 120-123, 128-129, 132, 162, 168, 177, 198
Language Generation 134-136, 139, 161, 172, 175, 206
language learning 36, 43-44, 110, 112-116, 118, 120, 127-129, 131, 139, 154, 162-163, 166-167, 169, 172-176, 178-179
Large Language Model 228
Learning Analytics 260, 274-275, 279-281, 285
learning experiences 3-6, 29, 31, 33, 40, 46, 48-51, 110, 112, 115-117, 120, 127-129, 134-135, 138-140, 143, 154-156, 165-166, 169-170, 173-175, 179, 197-198, 202-203, 210, 231-232, 238, 244, 247, 253, 260-261, 268-269, 272, 275, 279, 281, 289
Leveraging AI 3, 19, 22, 197, 202, 206

## M

Machine Learning 2, 6, 28-35, 37-38, 40, 42-43, 45-46, 48, 50-51, 102, 161, 164-165, 169, 174, 199-200, 205-206, 212, 228-233, 235, 240, 242, 244, 248-249, 253-254, 263, 270, 288, 292
Manuscript 207-208, 211, 214-219, 221, 228
Mixed-methods approach 89-90, 94, 103
ML-driven interventions 29, 32, 40, 48-51
Multilingual AI 206

## N

NLP (Natural Language Processing) 206

## O

one-on-one tutoring 111-115

## P

Pedagogical Approaches 66, 136, 138, 223
Pedagogical innovations 76-77, 83, 143-145
Peer Review 207, 214-216, 219, 228
Personal Development 113-114, 123, 132
Personalized Learning 4-6, 8, 29-31, 33, 35, 40, 43, 46, 48-50, 110, 120, 134-135, 140, 143, 145, 151, 153, 155, 165-166, 169-170, 174, 176, 179, 196-197, 201-202, 210, 231, 236, 253, 260, 268-269, 273, 285, 289
Personalized Learning Experience 43, 176, 269, 285
Plagiarism 5, 7, 9, 15, 18, 21, 119, 129, 178, 188, 190, 207, 214-215, 221, 228, 289, 293
pre-service teacher 89-96, 98, 100-103
Pre-service teacher education 89-96, 98, 100-103
professional development 62, 65, 103, 123, 139-140, 146, 152, 156, 161, 206, 231, 242, 264-266, 306
Prompt Feedback 111-112, 132, 166, 171, 298
Publication 208, 214, 216, 219, 228

## R

real-time guidance 30, 33, 50
Research partnerships 60, 82-83

## S

second language 109-110, 113-114, 116, 120, 123, 125, 128, 131
Second-Language Users 109-111, 114, 116
Simulated Environments 260, 269, 286
social media 19, 114, 128, 208, 210, 219, 292

speech recognition 114, 116-117, 127-128, 132, 171, 173-174, 228
Speech Recognition Technology 116, 132
STEM (Science, Technology, Engineering, and Mathematics) 286
Sustainability education 60-67, 70-73, 75-79, 82-84
Sustainable development 61-62, 66, 80-81, 88, 264, 267-268

# T

technological barriers 235, 249-251, 253
Technology integration 89-103, 288, 294, 312
traditional teaching 29, 33, 50, 135, 230, 235, 295-296, 312

# V

virtual classrooms 196-197, 201-202
virtual exchange 231, 238, 247, 253
virtual exchange programs 231, 238, 247, 253

www.ingramcontent.com/pod-product-compliance
Lightning Source LLC
LaVergne TN
LVHW080634011026
849160LV00014B/1208